Housing in the United Kingdom

Brian Lund

Housing in the United Kingdom

Whose Crisis?

Brian Lund
Manchester Metropolitan University
Manchester, UK

ISBN 978-3-030-04127-4   ISBN 978-3-030-04128-1   (eBook)
https://doi.org/10.1007/978-3-030-04128-1

Library of Congress Control Number: 2019930831

Cover image: © NurPhoto/Getty Images

This Palgrave Macmillan imprint is published by the registered company Springer Nature Switzerland AG
The registered company address is: Gewerbestrasse 11, 6330 Cham, Switzerland

Preface

Crisis narratives saturate the UK housing literature with 'generation rent' usually touted as the major symptom and boosting housing supply the favoured remedy. Yet, this so-called crisis is not problematic for everyone which partially explains why it exists. There have been gains for established owner-occupiers, private landlords, landowners, banks, building companies and the 'exchange professionals' operating the system. Indeed, the state has benefited from rising house prices with revenues from Land Duty Stamp Tax increasing from £4.9 billion in 2003/2004 to £11.7 billion in 2016/2017. Moreover, the victims of the deteriorating housing situation are not only the younger 'jilted generation'. There are different crises detectable through analysis of variables such as class, gender, age, ethnicity and place. This book attempts to explore the nature and scope of these housing crises.

Chapter 1 sets out media, academic and political narratives on the current housing problem and outlines its impact according to age, class, gender, ethnicity and location. Chapter 2 explores the 'slow-burning fuses'—deeply rooted in socio-economic cleavages—that have ignited into the present crises. Chapter 3 examines pathways into and through homeownership and offers a more detailed assessment of the disparities in access to decent homes. Chapter 4 scrutinises housing crises according to their spatial dimensions: globalisation; variations in housing conditions in the four 'home nations' and regional, district and neighbourhood differences in England.

In the UK housing output is determined by interactions between local and central government that regulate the housing market so Chapter 5 explores the technical and political dimensions of the central/local relations involved in determining housing requirements. Chapter 6 is concerned with the existing stock condition and its use—a neglected issue. It examines empty homes, non-decent houses, fuel efficiency, under-occupancy, etc., and explores ways that stock condition and use can be improved. Chapter 7 scrutinises contemporary constraints on housing supply and the numerous suggestions on how such barriers might be overcome. The final chapter argues that the housing crises have been framed through political party use of the voting system and that they have now spread too far to be contained by concentrating on the median voter in marginal constituencies.

Unfortunately, exploring housing outcomes according to factors such as age, ethnicity, class, gender and place is bedevilled by a data shortage on these variables—a testimony to the power relationships involved in housing distribution. None the less, responsibility for any errors and misinterpretations remains mine.

Manchester, UK   Brian Lund
December 2018

Acknowledgements

Thanks are due to a number of people who have contributed to the publication of this book. I am greatly indebted to the staff of Palgrave Macmillan and the anonymous referees for their help. My more personal gratitude is to Sukey, Rachel, Daniel, Carly, Bethany, Max and Dan for their support and encouragement.

Contents

List of Figures

List of Tables

1

The Housing Crisis

The media, think tanks, political debate and academia are replete with 'housing crisis' accounts. Press headlines proclaim 'UK facing its biggest housing shortfall on record' (*Independent* 2018) and 'The Tories are failing to fix Britain's housing crisis' (Sun 2018). 'Think tanks' declare that a 'Capitalist revolution in housebuilding is necessary' (Adam Smith Institute 2018) and analyse issues such as 'How the broken land market drives our housing crisis' (New Economics Foundation 2018) and 'The future fiscal cost of 'Generation Rent'' (Resolution Foundation 2018). Academics offer 'Radical Solutions to the UK Housing Crisis' (Bowie 2017) and Dorling (2014) has proclaimed a 'Great Housing Disaster'. An examination of housing crisis references by MPs revealed a nine-fold increase between 2006 and 2015 (Hudson 2015). Prime Minister, Theresa May, backed the crisis account declaring 'Our broken housing market is one of the greatest barriers to progress in Britain today' (May 2017).

Fatalism has accompanied these narratives. Pundits claim that housing is now the 'classic wicked problem'; deeply entrenched, complex and

© The Author(s) 2019
B. Lund, *Housing in the United Kingdom*,
https://doi.org/10.1007/978-3-030-04128-1_1

unpredictable (Taylor 2015). Resignation to events seems to have permeated the top civil service. Appearing before the Select Committee on Public Accounts, the Permanent Secretary to the Ministry of Housing, Communities and Local Government (MHCLG), when asked if she agreed that housing crisis will ever be resolved, replied:

> It will continue as it has done for decades. I agree, and that will show itself primarily in affordability and, in some places, in homelessness. I am simply being honest with you. (Dawes 2017)

Politicians stress that the housing problem is deeply embedded. Sajid Javid, when Secretary of State for Housing, Communities and Local Government, said 'for decades the pace of house building has been sluggish at best' (Javid 2017a) and Chancellor of the Exchequer, Phillip Hammond, asserting 'there is no magic bullet' to rectify the housing problem (Hammond, quoted in *Daily Mail* 2017).

Crisis stories usually spotlight the post-2004 homeownership decline as the emergency hallmark with boosting new house construction the favoured remedy. Yet, the current crisis has deep-seated roots, located in long-established cleavages in UK society based on class, age, gender, ethnicity and place. There are diverse housing crises and overcoming them requires more than a step change in housing supply.

Until 2016, the electorate seems to have accepted the 'wicked problem' story, tolerating high prices, lower space standards, exorbitant rents, declining homeownership and homelessness, as if resigned to the idea that there was no alternative to the inevitable outcomes generated by market forces. Crisis victims must wait patiently until the market solved the problem. However, as the housing situation deteriorated, its generational dimension became more pronounced and the class, gender, ethnicity and place cleavages embedded in the crisis intensified. The 2016 European Union referendum and the 2017 General Election demonstrated a changing public mood. In Greek, crisis—κρίσις—means both a 'turning point' and a 'judgement'. The electorate delivered a verdict on Conservative Party housing policies: the housing crisis had become a political crisis.

Homeownership

The press focuses on homeownership decline as the main housing crisis dimension. The *Daily Mirror* (2016) stated that the 'UK housing crisis was now a "national emergency" as number of homeowners plummets to a 30-year low' and the *Daily Mail* (2018) announced 'The end of the home-owning dream'. The homeownership rate in England fell from 68.7% in 2004 to 65.2% in 2010. This trend persuaded post-2010 Conservative-led governments to introduce measures to try to stimulate owner-occupation such as Help to Buy loans, a 3% extra Land Stamp Duty Tax levy on second homes and a reduction in tax concessions for private landlords. Nonetheless, the owner-occupier proportion in England continued to decline, reaching 62.6% in 2016/2017 (MHCLG 2018a).

In a new attempt to boost owner-occupation, Teresa May's government exempted homes costing less than £300,000 from Land Stamp Duty Tax (LSDT) if bought by first-time buyers, thereby giving them a further advantage over private landlords in the housing market. This measure, combined with the long-term impact of earlier initiatives, may increase the homeowner rate but, as Corlett and Judge (2017, p. 6) claim: 'Even in a best-case scenario millennials will not achieve the same homeownership levels the baby boomers enjoy'. Indeed, some commentators allege that homeownership is now a 'fetish' or a 'cult' (Posen 2013). It is an idealistic aspiration and 'generation rent' must be satisfied with renting. The *Guardian* (2016) announced 'Home ownership is unrealistic' and Sean O'Grady (2016), writing in the *Independent*, declared, 'Newsflash, young people: owning your own home isn't a human right — your sense of entitlement won't solve this'. In the *New Statesman*, Julia Rampen (2016) said 'The property-owning democracy is dead, so build one for renters instead'.

The overall owner-occupation figure masks marked changes in homeownership rates according to age, with owner-occupation increasing in retired households but falling amongst working households (see Fig. 1.1).

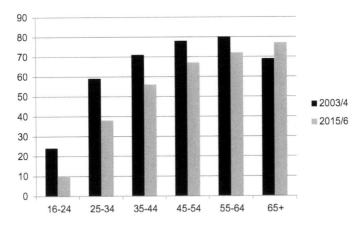

Fig. 1.1 Homeowner proportion by age: England 2003/2004 and 2015/2016 (*Sources* Department for Communities and Local Government [DCLG] [2017a]; Office for National Statistics [ONS] [2003])

One reason for the homeownership decline amongst younger people has been the increase in house prices relative to incomes. Cribb et al. (2018a) plotted the average UK house price and the average net income growth for those aged 25–34, revealing that between 1995/1996 and 2015/2016 net income grew by 21% whereas house prices increased by 156%. They state:

> …in 2015–16 almost 90% of 25-to 34-year-olds faced average regional house prices of at least four times their income, compared with less than half twenty years earlier. At the same time, 38% faced a house-price-to-income ratio of over 10, compared with just 9% twenty years ago. (Cribb et al. 2018a, p. 1)

The house price hike pushed mortgage payments as a proportion of first-time buyers' mean take-home pay from 19.0% in 1996 to 33% in 2017, ranging from 20.5% in the North to 64.9% in London (Nationwide 2018), despite the reductions in mortgage interest rates after 2009. Raising a deposit became a significant homeownership barrier. In response to 2000s credit boom, alleged to be responsible for the post-2008 recession, the deposit necessary to become a homeowner increased. In 2006, the average first-time buyer deposit across the UK was £15,168, but, in 2017, it was £33,899. In London, the average deposit needed by new entrants to the owner-occupation market increased from £26,701 in 2006 to £106,357 in 2017 (Shaw 2017). According to research by Hamptons International Estate Agent, a single first-time buyer in London needed to save for 17 years to find 15% deposit and 10.5 years in England and Wales (Jones 2018). Wood and Clarke (2018, p. 3) state:

> Hypothetically, it would currently take a 27-30 year old first time buyer around 18 years to save for a deposit if they relied solely on savings from their own disposable income. This is up from 3 years two decades ago.

To improve annual affordability 60% of first-time buyers now opt for mortgages lasting more than 25 years with the per cent of new mortgages lasting 30 years increasing from 12.6% in 2006 to 36.2% in 2016 and the proportion with terms 35 year plus jumping from 3.8 to 16.5% (Resolution Foundation 2018).

'Rabbit Hutches'

Less space is being obtained for higher prices. As Williams (2009, p. 1) states 'the general currency for housing statistics, planning practice and house sales is the number of bedrooms'. Although, in England, bedroom numbers and the house proportion relative to flats in new-build homes has increased since 2009/2010, the dwellings built post-2005 consist of 44% flats and 54% with two or less bedrooms compared to 18% flats and 37% with two or less bedrooms for dwellings built before 2005 (Wilson et al. 2018). UK figures on housing space price per square metre are sparse but new UK houses are expensive 'rabbit hutches' compared to their continental equivalents. In 2014 the average size UK new home size was 87 m² compared to 109.2 (Germany); 137 (Denmark); 112.8 (France); 96 (Austria) and 82.2 (Portugal) (Jones 2017). €200,000 bought 119 m² in Spain, 94 m² in Belgium, 97 m² in Germany and 39 m² in the UK (Deloitte 2016).

A rough and ready calculation of new house size in relationship to occupancy placed UK houses at the 12th lowest in a 16 country list, above only Hong Kong, Russia, Italy and China (Shrinkthatfootprint 2018). Central guidance on space standards—introduced in 2015 and officially known as the 'nationally described space standard'—gives local authorities the option to set minimum sizes for new homes. Although 37 m^2 is now the minimum legal standard in London for a new-build one person flat, under the 'permitted development' system, developers who convert offices into homes do not have to meet minimum floor area standards and the smallest studio flats in a London office block conversion were a 'dog kennel' 16 m^2 (*Guardian* 2017a).

Many family houses have been converted into flats. Considering all dwellings—existing and new—Williams (2009) comments:

> In terms of *dwelling size*, the UK has the 5th smallest homes in Europe, 87 m^2..... However, it has the 4th (joint) highest number of rooms (4.7). Hence, the UK has, on average, the third smallest average room sizes (18.5 m^2).... If one compares UK house sizes with countries such as the USA (average dwelling size 215 m^2) and Australia (average dwelling size 227.6 m^2) an even more contrasting picture emerges. (Williams 2009, p. 3, emphasis original)

For the majority of working-age households in England, floor space per person has been flat or has fallen since the mid-1990s and, for private renters in London, space per person declined by a quarter between 1996 and 2012 (Belfield et al. 2015). Tunstall (2015), having examined housing space distribution over time, concluded that housing space inequality declined from the 1920s to the 1980s but then increased, and, by 2011, space inequality was back to 1950s levels. By 2014 the average family home had shrunk by two square metres since 2004 and it was estimated that 150,000 children had seen their bedrooms partitioned in an attempt to create extra bedrooms (Liverpool Victoria Insurance 2014).

The English Housing Survey measures overcrowding by the 'bedroom standard' but its low sample size, leading to overcrowding figures being presented as three year moving averages and its 54.4% response rate raises questions on whether the survey includes 'difficult to reach' households. Nevertheless, the figures reveal that the per cent households deemed overcrowded in England increased from 2.3 in 2000/2001 to 3 in 2016/2017 (note that the 'bedroom standard' relates to number of rooms *not* overall space per person). The per cent of households overcrowded in the private landlord sector increased from 3.5 to 5.1 and, in the social sector, from 5.1 to 6.6 (MHCLG 2018a).

Homelessness

The homeless 'headline' figures—acceptances as homeless by local authorities and households in temporary accommodation—are generated through the operations of the 1977 Housing (Homeless Persons) Act as amended by 1985, 1996, 2002, and 2017 legislation. The statistics reflect how local authorities, influenced by government guidance, apply the law. Homelessness acceptances and households in temporary accommodation increased rapidly in the 2000s and New Labour introduced a prevention strategy involving 'housing options' interviews prior to the formal homeless acceptance process. The result was a rapid decline in homelessness acceptances in England from 135,590 in 2003 to 41,780 in 2009 (Stephens et al. 2018). The coalition government intensified the prevention strategy but, in 2018, 79,880 households containing 123,130 children were living in temporary accommodation (MHCLG 2018b). According to the official count—almost certainly a significant undercount—in 2017 there were 4751 rough sleepers on a given night—up 15% on 2016 and more than double the 2010 figure (MHCLG 2018b). Although public and media attitudes to homelessness are dominated by the 'individualism' model—'people see the causes of large-scale social problems such as poverty, crime and homelessness through a lens that looks at individual characters and situations' (Crisis 2018, p. 62)—social economic factors permeate homelessness outcomes. Shelter (2018) has revealed that 55% of families living in temporary accommodation were working and Fitzpatrick (2017) states:

Our research indicates that a mixed-ethnicity lone mother who was poor as a child, renting at age 26, who has experienced unemployment, has a predicted probability of homelessness of 71.2% by age 30. Contrast this with a white male university graduate from a relatively affluent background in the rural south of England, living with his parents at age 26, where it is a mere 0.6% by the same age, and you'll see that we aren't all equally vulnerable to homelessness.

Economic Determinism

Economic determinism underpins these housing crisis symptoms and the tepid policy responses to them. 'Globalisation'—allegedly beyond political control by national governments—is often viewed as the controlling variable. Aubrey (2016, p. 1), for example, states:

> Over the last 40 years, these regions (with high Brexit votes) have experienced a dramatic pace of change, driven largely by globalisation. These changes have disrupted people's work patterns and livelihoods, sometimes generating a catastrophic fall in hope for the future…. Wage growth has been muted, but the cost of housing has continued to rise.

The globalisation thesis is linked to neoliberalism, a doctrine that views competition as the crucial dimension in economic relationships. Buying and selling rewards merit and penalises inefficiency and markets—the driving force of economic progress—will be destroyed by state intervention. Economic fundamentalism also permeates Marxist political economy. Contemporary Marxist political economy takes its cue from Engels' claim that working class exploitation occurs when the capitalist purloins all the value created by workers in the production process, thereby making social reform via consumption initiatives futile in a capitalist economy. Social reform measures merely displace housing problems to different places (Engels 1872). Globalisation and capitalism are interlinked in Marxist working class exploitation accounts with, at best, social reform resulting only in a more 'humane' capitalism, controlling the worst outcomes but prolonging *housing* shortages (DeFazio 2014).

But Is There a Housing Crisis?

Oxford Dictionaries (2017a) defines a crisis as 'an unsustainable situation with immediate action required, a turning point, when a new policy paradigm is necessary'. Do the increase in house prices, the decline in new house construction and the fall in homeownership constitute such a crisis? There are dissenting voices.

House Prices and Consumer Spending

One dimension to housing crisis denial is the assertion that enlarged housing wealth promotes economic growth because an asset gaining in value encourages homeowners to consume, taking equity from their properties to spend on consumer goods. Indeed, an article in the *Financial Times* (Leahy 2018) recommended boosting the housing market to help the UK's ailing retail sector. The house price inflation promotes economic expansion theory has been supported by empirical evidence. Aizenman et al. (2016), having examined 19 countries from 1975 to 2013, found that house price hikes are positively associated with economic growth. However, of course, the association may not be causal and there is an argument that house price increases impede long-term growth by directing investment away from manufacturing.

The Politics of Housing Wealth

Then there is the political dimension to homeownership wealth. Many newspapers promote house price rises as desirable with Munro (2018, p. 1085) detecting 'the powerful influence of industry insiders in creating the discourse of the housing market news, and how price rises are positioned as both beneficial and the "natural order"'. The *Daily Express* is particularly enthusiastic, running headlines such as 'Prices Up By £10,000' (*Daily Express* 2017) and 'Giant rebound in house prices sees biggest rise in six months' (*Daily Express* 2018). Indeed, the owner-occupied electorate reacts badly to reductions in their housing wealth. Historically, house prices have supplied negative or positive backdrops to election campaigns. Thatcher won in 1987 when house prices were rising rapidly. Area variations in house price adjustments helped Major win in 1992 (Dorling et al. 1999) and New Labour prevailed in the 1997 General Election against a backdrop of house price decline under the Conservatives. New Labour won in 2001 and 2005 when prices were rising but lost in 2010 following a price slump. In the 2017 General Election, the Conservative Party enhanced its lead over Labour amongst outright owners, the most likely beneficiaries from rising house prices.

Renting: Not Such a Bad Thing?

Another housing crisis denial relates to homeownership decline. In 2009 John Healey, Labour's Housing Minister, noting the fall in owner-occupation, said 'I'm not sure that's such a bad thing', adding:

> So we need new choices in tenure.... That means increasing the diversity of tenures, it means allowing people to move more easily between tenures and it means putting them on a more equal footing with home ownership, as they are in other European countries. (Healey, quoted in the *Independent* 2009)

Germany, with a substantial private rented sector at about 58% of the housing stock, has become a model for an efficient housing market. It is argued that this long-term, plentiful private rented housing supply, with modest state intervention in controlling rents, not only enhances labour mobility but prevents a Gadarene rush into the owner-occupied market and generates a political majority in favour of stable house prices (Eichler 2016). Until recently, Germany has been very successful in controlling house price volatility with prices stable in the 2000s before accelerating post-2010 to reach an 8% increase in 2017 (Global Property Guide 2018).

A Supply Dearth?

Some housing crisis narratives accept that house price inflation is a problem but attribute the price hikes to credit availability, not to supply deficiency. For example, the Bow Group of Conservatives MPs claimed: 'Building more houses, despite being the solution most widely touted, is not the answer to the UK housing crisis … building more houses will not have a downward effect on prices' (Valentine 2015, p. 4). A similar position is taken by Spiers (2018), former Chief Executive of the Campaign to Protect Rural England (CPRE), who adds the social housing dearth to the housing crisis causation mix.

Oxford Economics (2016) explored the reasons for the rise in house prices from 1996 to 2006, claiming 'Rising earnings and falling interest rates, rather than insufficient supply, drove the boom in house prices between 1996 and 2006' (Oxford Economics 2016, p. 8). Mulheirn's detailed examination of the issue (Mulheirn 2018) discovered no evidence that supply limitations had influenced overall housing affordability (even in London) and reached the conclusion:

> Rather than one housing crisis caused by 'decades of undersupply', then, we in fact face two distinct housing crises: deteriorating affordability for some due to adverse trends in their incomes, and high prices caused by financial conditions. (Mulheirn 2018, p. 13)

Ryan-Collins (2018) attributed the lion's share of the blame for rising house prices to financial institution infatuation with property as an investment vehicle. In supporting his case he points to the 'debt shift' in the 1990s, when the financial institutions moved their lending away from investment in production to domestic and commercial real estate purchase. Certainly pumping money into real estate has been a significant contributor to house price inflation but, in the 1930s, credit availability helped to stimulate production. This did not happen in the UK from the 2000s indicating that supply constraints have had a major role in escalating house prices. For example, in 2005/2006, new housing construction was 3.1 per 1000 population in the UK, 13.2 in Ireland, 14 in Spain and 6.8 in the United States (Alderman 2010; Delft University of Technology 2011). Alistair Darling (2011, p. 114), New Labour's Chancellor during the 'global financial crisis', said: 'Ironically, the spectacular failure of successive British governments to deliver increased housebuilding proved to be a blessing for the housing market, which did not fall anywhere near as much as people feared'.

Whose Crisis?

Despite 'status quo' justifications, the term 'housing crisis' can be applied legitimately to the UK, but not as usually portrayed in the media and by the government with their focus on generation rent's problems and enhanced supply as the solution. Although the decline in owner-occupation amongst younger people is a major problem, the housing crisis is not only a generational issue. Class, gender, ethnicity and place factors permeate homeownership access and the crisis is reflected in other dimensions, notably rent levels and problems related to housing standards, tenure security, income distribution and social housing stigma. The new housing dearth is an important issue—supply side deniers underplay the ways that lack of homes influences household formation (see Chapter 5)—but, as Gallent (2016) states, 'building new homes is just one part of a bigger puzzle. The housing crisis and its drivers need to be seen in a broader economic context'.

Privatisation and Commodification

Privatisation and reliance on market forces were at the heart of Thatcher's housing policy and were embraced by Major and Blair (Jenkins 2006). Post-1979, housing became subject to extensive 'recommodification' that is, treated as a consumer good to be distributed through markets. The Right to Buy (RTB) resulted in a large proportion of council houses being sold to private landlords renting at market rents, housing associations were reframed as commercial organisations increasingly imitating the private landlord sector and the mortgage market was opened up to competition thereby undermining building society mutuality, albeit that much of this mutuality was a myth (Barnes 1984). According to some commentators, housing financialisation—'the increasing dominance of financial actors, markets, practices, measurements and narratives' (Aalbers 2016)—produced a new capitalist crisis (see Chapter 2). Bellamy and Magdoff (2009), claimed that, in mature capitalism, financial bubbles had become the principal means to promote growth but these inevitably burst, bringing the basic economic problems back to the surface. The systems only recourse—yet more fizz in the housing market—eventually produced another bust, in what had become a brutal cycle. The 2008 crisis was precipitated by capital's capacity to generate vast surpluses by keeping wages low, but, to continue its advance capitalism required the working class to consume. Housing financialisation created new and increasingly intricate opportunities for consumption via debt accumulation with the eventual inability of the working class to pay this debt producing the US financial crisis that permeated the global economy. In responding to the UK 2008 crisis New Labour increased state spending with bank bailouts contributing a large expenditure share. The coalition government's initial determination to reduce state debt plus workers' willingness to accept wage restraint in return for job retention produced austerity.

Despite the coalition's governments attempt to boost prices to kick-start the housing market and stimulate new build, in Theresa May's expression, 'our housing market is broken' (May 2017, p. 5). But for whom is the market broken? The housing crisis is manifest not only in high house prices, a low-level new house construction relative to assessed need and the decline in homeownership but in more deep-seated issues such as affordability, housing standards, homelessness, the 'quiet enjoyment' of a home, income/wealth distribution and state expenditure. The housing crisis is a distributional as well as a supply issue. Mulheirn (2017) records how the housing crisis has been accompanied by changes in income distribution—notably young people's incomes have fallen compared to other age groupings—more renters being subject to market rents and public spending cuts making housing less affordable to millions of households. Hence, crisis resolution is not a matter of 'fixing our broken housing market' (DCLG 2017b) because even a functioning housing market—whatever that means—will not solve the problems or rectify the deep-seated social injustices enhanced through 'financialisation' and 'privatisation'.

Social Justice

Political philosophy has rarely permeated the housing studies literature but, in recent years, there have been calls for more normative analyses of housing processes and outcomes (Taylor 2018; Fitzpatrick and

Watts 2018). Social justice is the key concept applied to such analyses but the term is subject to different interpretations. One version is that 'everyone is entitled, as a right of citizenship, to be able to meet their basic needs for income, shelter and other necessities....' (see Commission on Social Justice 1994, p. 17). 'Shelter' has been interpreted as 'everyone should have access to decent, affordable housing' (Somerville 2018) and there have been attempts to establish this definition as a basic human right to be applied nationally and internationally (see Preece 2018; Farha 2014).

There are problems in defining 'decent' and 'affordable' on both a national and international basis but the major obstacle to establishing rights to housing has been the dominance of the neoliberal notion of social justice: every action between human beings should be a market transaction, conducted in competition with other human beings and the outcomes of such market interactions are legitimate. Indeed Conservative governments have reacted angrily to UN accusations that they have breached human rights (*Guardian* 2014; *Telegraph* 2018).

Establishing basic human rights to housing would improve the outcomes of the dominant social order but, for some, more fundamental change, related to the justice involved in the resource acquisition structures, is necessary.

John Rawls

Unjust structural inequalities have been explored by a number of political philosopher's. In *A Theory of Justice* (1971), John Rawls derives his justice principles from a thought experiment whereby, behind a 'veil of ignorance', participants in a debate on constructing the basic principles for a future society know nothing about their abilities; position in society; gender, race; nationality or individual partialities. Rawls argues that such participants will agree to join a society in which:

> First: each person is to have an equal right to the most extensive basic liberty compatible with a similar liberty for others and

Second: Social and economic inequalities are to be arranged so that:
(a) they are to be of the greatest benefit to the least-advantaged members of society, consistent with the just savings principle (b) offices and positions must be open to everyone under conditions of fair equality of opportunity. (Rawls 1971, p. 302)

The discussants in the nature of just society—behind a 'veil of ignorance'—will protect themselves from the worst possible outcome by adopting the 'maximin' principle ensuring that, should they be the least advantaged in society, they will not suffer extreme hardship. Thus, on Rawls' justice notion, inequalities are permissible only if they improve the well-being of the least advantaged in society. Thus, for example, if a skilful farmer can produce more from land than a less competent farmer, the skilful farmer is entitled to more than an equal land share provided that some of the extra production is channelled to the least productive cultivator so that this his/her material position is better than it would have been with an equal land distribution.

Applied to the housing domain, Rawls' justice principles would mean eradicating all inequalities in housing distribution provided it could not be demonstrated that such elimination would destroy production incentives and that some of the extra output generated by inequality improved the position of the least advantaged. Employing these principles generates a number of questions. If homelessness is the worst possible outcome on the 'maximin' outcome why is it allowed to persist? Since landowners do not create land, why should they benefit from ownership? How luxurious does a house need to be and how many houses are necessary to promote entrepreneurial initiatives? Some commentators maintain that most current housing investment is unproductive (Murray 2010). In the past, capital spending on houses for the working class was defended as a productivity measure: it enhanced physical efficiency and hence the economic yield from the working class (Chadwick 1842; Rowntree 1901) but today, housing is primarily consumption good. Extra housing may lead to enhanced feelings of individual well-being but it is not an investment that will increase productivity in the sense of generating additional future output. Indeed, to the extent that housing is a 'positional' good (Hirsch 1977)—boosting status by conspicuous consumption—housing outlays destroy the 'real' investment necessary to enhance productivity.

Justice as Historical

Rawls' theory has been criticised because he regards the social product as a collective cake to be distributed according to fair principles whereas the cake has been produced through specific individual inputs. In *Anarchy, State and Utopia*—regarded by some as the definitive defence of market outcomes (Joseph and Sumption 1979)—Robert Nozick (1981) argues that justice is historical: current distributional justice depends on how it came about. If, considered historically, wealth and income have arisen from fair procedures—creating an object, barter between free agents or as a gift—the current distribution is just and any enforced change by the state violates individual liberty. Wealth that has been accumulated via fair procedures can be used by wealth owners as they want. Should the wealthy want to consume large homes or own several houses then these are legitimate choices. However, Nozick makes radical qualifications to his theory. Wealth acquired by unjust procedures, that is, not by free exchange and effort, must be subject to current rectification mechanisms. In the housing domain, land acquisition is crucial and Nozick struggles to justify current land distribution. He adopts a formulation of John Locke's proviso, set out in his *Second Treatise on Government* (1690), which holds that 'a process normally giving rise to a permanent bequeathable property right in a previously un-owned thing will not do so if the position of others no longer at liberty to use the thing is thereby worsened' (quoted in Nozick 1981, p. 178). Nozick claims that appropriating land is legitimate if 'enough and as good' is left behind for others to use (Nozick 1981, p. 175), begging the question, 'enough and as good for what?' However, Nozick demands rectification if land (and other resources) have not been acquired by effort and legitimate exchange. Even a cursory glance at the historical processes through which land and other resources have been acquired in the UK reveals how land was initially obtained by force and not via

Nozick's fair procedures. For example, the Duke of Westminster's £9 billion fortune, inherited when he was 27, can be traced back to his family obtaining land from William the Conqueror as a reward for helping to subjugate England by force (British History Online 2017). Under Nozick's theory that justice is historical, large-scale past injustice rectification is necessary. Thus, two celebrated 'liberal' philosophers—in the sense of having a primary emphasis on individual freedom—starting from different perspectives, have concluded that the current housing distribution is unjust.

Marxist Theory

In Marxist theory, although injustice occurs in the production process when capitalists purloin the value created by workers, this inequality is compounded via 'realisation', that is, worker exploitation arising from the worker's inability to afford to buy a house with cash thereby making it necessary to rent or take out a mortgage. Rent and mortgage is purloined over long time periods. The worker:

> ...must not only pay the interests on the building costs, but must also cover repairs and the average sum of bad debts, unpaid rents, as well as the occasional periods when the house is untenanted, and finally pay off in annual sums the building capital which has been invested in a house which is perishable and which in time becomes uninhabitable and worthless. Secondly, *it is forgotten that the rent must also pay interest on the increased value of the land upon which the building is erected...* (Engels 1872, p. 22)

This is a fundamental critique of an economic order based on market capitalism raising questions such as whether rigged'—not 'broken'—is a more appropriate term to apply to the housing market with the principal fixers being the state (with a fiscal interest in higher house prices); established owner-occupiers especially those protected by green belts; private landlords, landowners, 'exchange professionals' and property developers (Edwards 2016; Teixeira-Mendes 2017).

Housing Crises

The UK housing crisis is a social justice issue: multidimensional and reflected through factors such as age, class, gender, ethnicity, location and tenure. In the rest of this chapter, the overall impact of these variables will be examined with Chapters 3 and 4 exploring the complex interactions within and between these variables.

Age

In reporting the housing crisis, media attention has focused on the age dimension featuring headlines on 'generation rent' and 'the jilted generation'. Generational divisions are imprecise and UK classifications are often based on taxonomies from the United States. Five categories are often identified: 'Greatest generation' (born 1911–1925); 'Silent generation' (born 1926–1945); 'Baby boomers' (born 1946–1965); 'Generation X' (born 1966–1980) and the 'Millennials' (born 1981–2000) (Gardiner 2016). Some taxonomies label those people born before 1945 as the 'Forgotten Generation', with those born in the 1980s and 1990s called 'Generation Y' and 'Millennials' referring to those born post-2000. The fortunes of generations 'X' and 'Y' are often contrasted with the 'baby boomers' that, according to some commentators, 'have appropriated most of the wealth and taken their children's future' (Willetts 2011). 'Forgotten' is an apt term for those born before 1939 because the 65 + 'old age' classification, often used in academic and government publications, conceals large variations in housing conditions and housing wealth as people progress through old age, not least by residence in nursing and care homes.

Age divisions in housing outcomes are not self-contained. Following the example set by the landed aristocracy, many wealth holders want to pass wealth within their families with housing wealth accumulated in the past cascading through the generations via conduits affected by social class and other variables. Thus, examining wealth distribution—the accumulated *family* wealth across generations—based on class, has policy implications. For example, when the 2017 Conservative Party manifesto proposed that all social care costs for both partners, including residential and domestic care, should be charged to the 'family home' and other family assets, leaving £100,000 to be inherited, it would have made little impact on people with high family wealth and no impact on people with homes and assets worth less than a £100,000. However, with the cost of spending your final years in a care home, averaging between £92,000 and £65,000 per person depending on location (*Telegraph* 2017)—this does not include domestic care or higher nursing home costs—would have large effect on people with modest wealth. The *Telegraph* (2017) estimated that average residential care costs for one person (disregarding domestic care costs and higher nursing home fees) would take 18% of average house prices in London but 48% in Yorkshire. In 2017 there were 430,720 property millionaires in London, 4103 in Yorkshire and Humberside (Zoopla 2018). Under the Conservative proposals, with both partners requiring residential care, housing wealth would down to the £100,000 maximum in most areas outside London and the South East. The unspecified cap on social care costs, made during election campaign, would have probably compounded the wealth impact. The ways that *family* wealth cascades through the generations are considered in Chapter 3.

Class

The class dimension to housing wealth in old age reflects the social stratification permeating the housing crisis. In recent years class had a low profile in political and academic discourse. In the 1970s and early 1980s there was a reasonable data supply linking class to housing outcomes but, by the 2000s, class as a variable in housing outcome analysis had almost disappeared. Indeed, Charlesworth (2000, p. 14) stated 'Within the contemporary university, it is seen as a sign of backwardness to have any concern about class and one is met with a mixture of disbelief, ridicule and derision'. Allen (2008) has asserted that, in its preoccupation with consumption and postmodern debates related to urban gentrification, sociological research has neglected working class experiences.

New Labour downplayed class focusing on 'social exclusion'—an idea including the 'underclass'—and highlighted other inequality dimensions such as gender and ethnicity. Its 2010 Equality Act listed nine protected characteristics to which the legislation applied: age; disability; gender reassignment; marriage and civil partnership; race; religion or belief; sex and sexual orientation. Class was not included, although Part 1 of the Act stated:

> An authority to which this section applies must, when making decisions of a strategic nature about how to exercise its functions, have due regard to the desirability of exercising them in a way that is designed to reduce the inequalities of outcome which result from socio-economic disadvantage.

'Socio-economic disadvantage' may incorporate class but can be interpreted as 'social exclusion', an idea that elevates 'social' capital—the value of the social networks people can draw on that may accrue from living in a neighbourhood—and 'human capital'—the skills, knowledge, and experience possessed by an individual—to the relative neglect of economic capital. The coalition government axed the socio-economic disadvantage duty.

Marx claimed that there were two main classes, a bourgeoisie owning the means of production and a proletariat without capital. Through owning the means of production, capitalists are able to exploit the working class by purloining all the surplus value it produced by workers. Renwick (2017) has recorded how, influenced by concerns about differential fertility rates and 'degeneration', the Registrar General's Office developed a ranked group hierarchy with a manual/non manual dimension running through the classification but with divisions within these groups. This class taxonomy was absorbed into social research with the classifications varying over time but basically consisting of a population division based on occupation. The upper middle class (higher managerial, administrative or professional) was in Grade A. The middle class (intermediate managerial, administrative, professional) were assigned to Grade B. C1 was the lower middle class (supervisory, clerical, and junior managerial, administrative, professional). The working class was split into skilled manual workers (C2) with semi-skilled and unskilled manual workers, labelled D. Grade E consisted of casual workers and those depending on state welfare for their incomes. Academic and state information on social class was based on this classification.

In recent years, some sociologists have put forward a class representation downgrading economic capital as only one of three dimensions in class formation, the others being 'social' and 'cultural' capital with 'social' referring to contacts and connections allowing people to draw on their social networks and 'cultural' such as the ability to engage in artistic and intellectual circles plus the credentials institutionalised through educational success (Bourdieu 1984; Savage et al. 2015). Demoting the class economic dimension has contributed to a current statistical dearth on how economic class—with occupation the principal class identifier (National Centre for Social Research 2016)—affects housing outcomes with income often having to be used as a proxy for class. Such class indifference has proved unfortunate for power holders as the 2016 European Referendum and 2017 General Election voting patterns revealed (see Chapter 8). The sparse contemporary information on housing/class relationships reveals stark and growing contrasts between social classes in housing outcomes. As examples, Shelter's examination of housing conditions on affordability, quality, tenure stability, neighbourhood and space found sharp class divisions on all the dimensions under scrutiny (Shelter 2016a, b). Green (2017) demonstrated that, in 2001, compared with young people with parents in semi-skilled and unskilled jobs, those with parents in professional and associate professional employment were 1.5 times more likely to own a home. By 2013, young people whose parents had professional jobs were 2.39 times more likely to own a home as those whose parents were in semi or unskilled work. Help from the 'bank of Mum and Dad'—now the UK's ninth most important mortgage financier—has contributed to this class divide.

Gender

In the past, women had few opportunities to obtain a secure income other than to acquire a male partner. Fortunately, these dark days have gone, but gender divisions in housing outcomes remain. Women's lower earnings—the median gender pay gap was 9.1% in 2017 (*Guardian* 2017b)—influence access to homeownership but becoming a home-owner now depends on two incomes with implications for women's 'double shift' work/domestic duties. Reliance on two incomes is man-ifest in the housing circumstances of single-parent families—91% headed by women—with only 11.7% of never-married single parents living in the owner-occupied sector, 48.5% living in social housing and 39.9% in the private landlord sector (see Chapter 3). Old age also reveals the salience of a partner. By the age of 78 the male/female ratio is 82/100 but, by 90+, it is 40/100. Reduced resources—with limited income and wealth from past gender differences in pay, pension entitle-ments and domestic duties—undermines the ability of older women to enjoy good housing conditions (see Chapter 3).

Ethnicity

The term 'ethnicity' refers to 'the fact or state of belonging to a social group that has a common national or cultural tradition' (Oxford Dictionaries 2017b). The term Black and Minority Ethnic, shortened to BME, is often used to describe ethnic minorities. 'Ethnicity' is a diverse, self-ascribed characteristic hence any ethnic classification is likely to be misleading. Moreover, official classifications, by combining groups with different ethnicities, can over-simplify. For example, the cate-gory 'Black', used in the English Housing Survey, includes people with African-Caribbean ethnicity and people with origins in over 50 coun-tries including Ghana, Nigeria, Somalia, Angola and Zaire.

Comparing housing outcomes according to ethnicity is complicated by length of UK residence. 88% of EU born residents and 80% of non-EU born residents arriving between 2014 and 2016 (mainly ethnic minorities) rented privately (ONS 2017). The migrant tenure pattern tends to become closer to the UK born population as residence in the country increases. Of those entering the UK between 1991 and 2000 from non-EU countries, 49% are homeowners, 23% private renters and 28% social renters. 59% of people who came to the UK from EU countries between 1991 and 2000 are homeowners, 28% were private renters and 12% social housing tenants (ONS 2017).

Unfortunately, there is little representative data on ethnic minority housing pathways (born inside or outside the UK) as they move within the housing system. Such data would allow a more nuanced approach to the structural disadvantage experienced by ethnic minorities via discrimination in its individual, institutional and structural forms (Ginsburg 1992). Location impacts on housing opportunities. Minorities—defined as those other than white English/Welsh/Scottish/Northern Irish/British—constitute 58% of the population of London, where housing stress is high, compared to 7% in the North East and a UK average of 19.7% (ONS 2012). Nonetheless, the Resolution Foundation (2017, p. 15) concluded 'Very significant differences in typical incomes and employment between ethnicities remain, though there has been some relative narrowing of these gaps'. Theresa May's government has focused on the ethnic inequality dimension, sponsoring a website containing statistics on the housing circumstances of ethnic minorities (Gov.uk 2017). It has also shown an interest in the gender pay gap (Cabinet Office 2017) but not in the social class dimension of inequality.

Location

The phrase 'location, location, location' has been attributed to a British real estate tycoon, Lord Harold Samuel, who declared that three things sell a house 'location, location, location'. It became the title of a popular TV programme first shown in 2000. Samuels' adage is manifest in the diverse UK housing markets. In March 2018, average regional prices varied from £471,944 in London to £124, 381 in the North East (HM Land Registry 2018). A BBC investigation revealed that, after allowing for general inflation, 58% of the wards in England and Wales had house prices lower than in 2007. The North East contained the highest proportion of wards with houses that had declined in value (95%) but only the East of England, the South East and London contained wards with houses that had increased in value with the largest ward increases (99%)

in London. The BBC stated that in North Ormesby, Middlesbrough, 'In 2017, the average house pri e there was £36,000. At £2.9 m, an average home in the most exper   JK ward—Knightsbridge and Belgravia—costs the same as 80 hc   North Ormesby' (BBC News 2017).

The place factor   d to variables such as access to transport, cultural and en   t opportunities, good school proximity, area reputations, safety,   vironmental quality and, most important of all, employment opportunities, not just a job but a reasonably paid job. When housing costs are taken into account, a working-age adult in poverty is now more likely to be in a working family than a non-working (Joseph Rowntree Foundation 2018). UK employment distribution since 2007 has been uneven with, for example, the North East losing 19% of its public sector employment between 2007 and 2015 but gaining only 8% in private sector employment. The North West lost 14% in public sector workers gaining 8% private sector jobs. In contrast, London lost only 4% of its public sector employment but jobs in the private sector increased by 16% (Sheffield Political Economy Research Institute 2016). Many employment gains have been in low paid work with the 1.8 million zero-hours contracts concentrated in the more deprived regions (Statista 2018).

In England, median weekly household incomes varied from £544 in the South East, £536 in London to £447 in the North East (McGuiness 2018). The gaps between London and the South East and other UK regions in Regional Gross Value Added (RGVA)—the value generated by any unit engaged in the production of goods and services—have been increasing. In 2016, the London RGVA was £46,482, in the South East £28,613, but only £19,218 in the North East (Harari and Ward 2018).

It can be argued that the lower housing costs in some districts reduce household outgoings and thereby improves individual welfare prompting movement away from high-cost areas. If this were the case, migration away from high housing cost areas to low housing cost areas could be anticipated. Some movement is detectable—house prices are a factor in an exodus from London with the number of people between the ages of 30 and 39 leaving the capital rising 68% between 2012 and 2016 to 34,540 (*City A.M.* 2017)—but as McCann (2017, pp. 86–87) observes:

...this is not what we typically observe ... the after-tax wage-income on which such calculations would be made depends heavily on employment expectations, house price growth expectations and also equity gain via capital repayments on nominal housing mortgage values.

Analysis of housing and economic growth has focused on London in comparison to other regions but there are other UK housing 'hotspots'. Since 2007 there have been large house price increases in Cambridge, Oxford and Bristol and prices in Portsmouth, Southampton Bournemouth and Cardiff have increased significantly. Prices in Liverpool, Glasgow, Birmingham and Manchester are stirring and tipped for future house price growth. In contrast, Aberdeen—strongly influenced by oil prices—has experienced a large house price reduction (*Financial Times* 2017). There is marked house prices disparity *within* local government boundaries and these differences are increasing (see Chapter 4).

Scotland, Wales and Northern Ireland

Before the devolution initiatives in the late 1990s housing outcomes were different in England, Scotland, Wales and Northern Ireland, varying according to politics involved in the governance of each 'home nation' and different levels of de facto autonomy. However, since devolution, policy inputs have become increasingly dissimilar and this is beginning to be reflected in housing outcomes. These changes are examined in Chapter 4.

Tenure

Age, class, ethnicity, gender and place dimensions in housing inequality are partially manifest through tenure. Tenure refers to the legal rights and obligations involved in occupying a dwelling. In the UK it is conventional to distinguish four tenure types: owner-occupation; renting from a private landlord; renting from a local authority and renting from a housing association albeit that between and within these types there is extensive 'tenure blur' (Rugg and Rhodes 2018). Moreover, the legal rights and obligations involved in occupying a home are very complicated and differ between the 'home nations'. The land on which a house has been built can be occupied leasehold or freehold with, in leasehold occupation, the land and the buildings on it reverting back to the freeholder when the lease ends and the leaseholder requiring the freeholder's permission to make changes in the activities taking place on the land. Even freeholders may be subject to conditions on land use if they have been incorporated in the house deeds. It has been estimated that there are 2.8 million flats and 1.2 million houses occupied as leasehold (Birch 2017). Commonhold is another legal occupation form usually involving flats with separate ownership but with common areas managed by a commonhold association whose members are the unit owners.

Occupying a home owned by a local authority or housing association can also be subject to a range of terms conditions such as introductory tenancies—also known as probationary tenancies—with eviction a straightforward process. In the private landlord sector, houses can be let as an assured shorthold tenancy, with repossession obtained after six months provided two months notice is given or as an assured tenancy, with the tenant having the right to remain in the property unless the landlord can prove to a court that he/she has legal grounds for repossession. Unsurprisingly, 81% private landlord lets are assured shortholds (Rugg and Rhodes 2018). Tenancies taken out before January 31, 1989 are subject to different conditions with the tenant or landlord entitled to ask a rent assessment committee to determine a 'fair' rent (see Chapter 3). There are now less than 60,000 homes rented at a 'fair' rent—but the differences in the rents charged are stark with, for example, the average fair rent in Oldham in 2017 less than half the market rent (Valuation Office Agency 2018).

Tenure has been made more complicated via changing social constructions of its meaning. Since the middle 1990s local authority and housing association properties have been conjoined under the banner 'social' housing, with, for some, its associations with 'welfare' and 'dependency'. In the past, the homeowner/renter divide tended to reflect social class divisions. From the middle 1960s this association diminished but the class/tenure cleavage is now being reaffirmed (see Chapters 3 and 8). Tenure is also influenced by ~~gender and ethnicity~~ and tenure can trap households in a housing pathway. Walker (2016, p. 128, emphasis in original) summarised this impact in stating:

> A renter effectively pays not once but three times: first in rent, second as an unpaid caretaker of an inflating asset and third with the freedoms they forfeit. With the silent passing of every standing order, their roles, their status — their *class* becomes more and more entrenched, and the possibility of escape reduced.

More households in work are living in the private landlord sector and claiming HB—now know as Local Housing Allowance (LHA) for private tenants—with the proportion of private renters in employment claiming HB increasing from 19% in 2009 to 37% in 2017 (Shelter 2017). For most households owner-occupation is cheaper, both in the long and short term, than renting. There are other disadvantages to renting with security and the 'quiet enjoyment' of a home lower than for homeownership (see Chapter 3).

First-time buyers compete in the same housing market as private landlords—the cheaper homes in the lower house price quartile—and, as private landlords have become established property owners, their accumulated wealth and 'business' tax concessions has enabled them to outbid first-time buyers. Moreover, more landlords can pay cash for their house purchases thereby cutting out chains in the transaction process. A study by the Intermediary Mortgage Lenders Association (2014) revealed that only 420,000 of the additional 1,310,000 properties in the private rented sector between 2007 and 2012 were financed by buy-to-let loans. Some landlords are moving upmarket by buying family homes thereby increasing the pressure on couples wanting to buy a larger house when their children are born. In 2016/2017, the percentage of median/large terraced houses owned by private landlords was the same as the owner-occupied proportion and private landlords possessed about half the proportion of semi-detached houses as homeowners (MHCLG 2018c). According to the *Financial Times* (2018) flats and maisonettes have fallen out of favour amongst buy-to-let investors with flat sales down by 10% in 2017 compared to a 1.6% fall in detached and semi-detached homes.

The ONS (2018) found that the proportion of households owning second homes and buy-to-lets had increased from 7 to 9% between 2012 and 2016. The average size of private landlord property portfolios is accelerating with the tendency most marked in the North East, Yorkshire and London (Shaw 2017). In 2010, 78% of private landlords owned only one rented property but by 2016 this had dropped to 62% (Scanlon and Whitehead 2016) and it has been estimated that 38% of all the private landlord dwellings are now owned by landlords with five or more properties (Scanlon and Whitehead 2016). Private landlord growth limits the supply of homes for homeownership. When Chancellor of the Exchequer, George Osborne declared 'Frankly, people buying a home to let should not be squeezing out families who can't afford a home to buy' (Osborne 2015).

Conclusion

The issues spotlighted by the media in their housing 'crisis' narratives—house price increases, the homeownership eclipse and the dearth in new house construction—underplay more fundamental disadvantage divisions. These embedded socio-economic cleavages have meant housing has been the engine of growing inequality and:

> Many UK residents are spending half their salaries on housing rents or mortgages but are inadequately and insecurely housed. These expenditures could be securing decent housing for all but instead are mainly pumping up the asset values and incomes of land and property owners, incumbent owner-occupiers and the professionals linked to the process. (Edwards 2016, p. 1)

Homeownership decline is a major problem but not only because it marks 'the death of a dream' (Homeowners Alliance 2012). The growth in private renting that has accompanied the homeownership fall has repercussions for future housing outlays, both by households and state.

The long-term replacement and upgrading of older homes, with, in many cases, their poor energy efficiency standards, has been sluggish and there has been extensive house conversions producing lower space levels. Although there has been significant private landlord investment in upgrading older homes, the public sector austerity agenda has reduced state capital expenditure on improvement to the detriment of lower-income households. Recent changes in general wealth and income inequalities plus poverty incidence have been strongly influenced by changes in housing costs (see Chapter 3). Having examined the impact of housing costs on low-income households with children Cribb et al. (2018a, p. 36) concluded:

> Between 2002–03 and 2016–17, real mean housing costs among households with children in the bottom 20% of the AHC income distribution rose by 47% (from £67 to £98), compared with an increase of 11% (from £58 to £64) among children in the middle income quintile. Changes in housing costs not covered by housing benefit have also been much higher for low-income children than for middle-income children.

The Joseph Rowntree Foundation (2018, p. 4) noted that:

> The growing crisis in the UK's housing market has created especially stark problems for low-income families with children. Housing costs have grown much faster for these families than for those who are better off. This has been driven by rising costs for renters and the rapid increase in the number of families renting privately due to a lack of social rented housing and the high costs of buying a home.

Although many commentators identify the 'housing crisis' as starting in the early 2000s, it has deep-seated roots. Indeed, the term 'crisis' or its surrogates occurs frequently from the middle nineteenth century. Commenting on the latest crisis narratives, Fields and Hodkinson (2018, p. 1, emphasis original) state:

> Although the language of crisis evokes the sudden suspension of the *normal* functioning of a system … over the past decade *the housing crisis* has

become a motif for a seemingly enduring state of affairs in which rising evictions, overcrowding, unaffordability, substandard conditions, homelessness, and displacement have become the norm. The international housing crisis is thus *a feature, not a bug*, less an emergency than a consistent aspect of a capitalist political economy....

Even after years of sustained housebuilding, Berry's 1974 book declared *Housing: the Great British Failure* (Berry 1974) and, in 1981, Peter Malpass' edited volume carried the title *The Housing Crisis* (Malpass 1986). It appears that a housing crisis, like the poor, we will always have with us but, in the past progress has been expected. Slow burning fuses are now igniting into a crisis without hope that may eventually prove terminal for the politicians responsible.

References

Aalbers, M. B. (2016). *The Financialization of Housing: A Political Economy Approach*. Abingdon: Routledge.

Adam Smith Institute. (2018). *A Capitalist Revolution in House Building Is Necessary*. London: Adam Smith Institute. https://www.adamsmith.org/news/time-for-a-capitalist-revolution-in-housebuilding.

Aizenman, J., Jinjarak, Y., & Zheng, H. (2016). *House Valuations and Economic Growth: Some International Evidence*. Vox Portal. https://voxeu.org/article/housing-cycles-real-estate-valuations-and-economic-growth.

Alderman, D. (2010). *United States Housing*. Washington, DC: Department of Agriculture. https://www.fs.fed.us/nrs/pubs/rn/rn_nrs195.pdf.

Allen, C. (2008). *Housing Market Renewal and Social Class*. London: Routledge.

Aubrey, T. (2016). *The Explosive Concoction of Globalisation and the Rising Cost of Housing*. London: Centre for Progressive Capitalism. http://progressive-capitalism.net/2016/07/the-explosive-concoction-of-globalisation-and-the-rising-cost-of-housing/.

Barnes, P. (1984). *Building Societies: The Myth of Mutuality*. London: Pluto Press.

BBC News. (2017, October 17). *Are House Prices Back from the Crash?* http://www.bbc.co.uk/news/business-41582755.

Belfield, C., Chandler, D., & Joyce, R. (2015). *Housing: Trends in Prices, Costs and Tenure* (IFS Briefing Note BN161). London: Institute for Fiscal Studies. https://www.ifs.org.uk/publications/7593.

Bellamy, J., & Magdoff, F. (2009). *The Great Financial Crisis: Causes and Consequences*. New York, NY: Monthly Review Press.

Berry, F. (1974). *Housing: The Great British Failure*. London: Charles Knight and Co.

Birch, J. (2017, July 25). The Trouble with Leasehold. *Inside Housing*. https://www.insidehousing.co.uk/comment/comment/the-trouble-with-leasehold-50392.

Bourdieu, P. (1984). *Distinction*. London: Routledge.

Bowie, D. (2017). *Radical Solutions to the Housing Supply Crisis*. Bristol: Policy Press.

British History Online. (2017). *Survey of London, Volume 39, the Grosvenor Estate in Mayfair (Part 1)*. http://www.british-history.ac.uk/survey-london/vol39/pt1/pp1-5.

Cabinet Office. (2017). *Gender Pay Gap Report 2017: The First Cabinet Office Report on Gender Pay Gap Data*. London: Cabinet Office. https://www.gov.uk/government/publications/gender-pay-gap-report-2017.

Chadwick, E. (1842). *Report on the Sanitary Condition of the Labouring Population of Great Britain*. London: HMSO.

Charlesworth, S. J. (2000). *A Phenomenology of Working-Class Experience*. Cambridge: Cambridge University Press.

City A.M. (2017, July 24). The Number of People Moving Out of London Has Risen 80 Per Cent in Five Years. http://www.cityam.com/269004/exodus-number-people-moving-out-london-has-risen-80-per.

Commission on Social Justice. (1994). *Social Justice: Strategies for National Renewal*. London: Vintage.

Corlett, A., & Judge, L. (2017). *Home Affront: Housing Across the Generations*. London: Resolution Foundation. http://www.resolutionfoundation.org/publications/home-affront-housing-across-the-generations/.

Cribb, J., Keiller, A. N., & Waters, T. (2018). *Living Standards, Poverty and Inequality in the UK: 2018*. London: Institute for Fiscal Studies.

Crisis. (2018). *Everybody In: How to End Homelessness in Britain*. London: Crisis. https://www.crisis.org.uk/media/238959/everybody_in_how_to_end_homelessness_in_great_britain_2018.pdf.

Daily Express. (2017, August 16). Prices Up By £10,000. https://www.express.co.uk/news/uk/841593/House-price-rise-across-UK-since-Brexit.

Daily Express. (2018, April 10). Giant Rebound in House Prices Sees Biggest Rise in Six Months. https://www.express.co.uk/life-style/property/943886/property-prices-house-price-index-latest-brexit.

Daily Mail. (2017, November 19). Hammond Says Budget Will Have Proposals to Help Build 300,000 Homes Annually. http://www.dailymail.co.uk/wires/pa/article-5097115/Philip-Hammond-aims-fix-housing-market-amid-push-300-000-new-homes-year.html#ixzz4z3FAQ7Yl.

Daily Mail. (2018, February 16). End of the Home Owning Dream: End of the Home Owning Dream: 20 Years Ago, Two Thirds of Average Earners Aged Up to 34 Could Afford Their Own House… Now It's Just One in Four. http://www.dailymail.co.uk/news/article-5397697/Home-owner-crisis-just-one-four-afford-home.html.

Daily Mirror. (2016, August 2). UK Housing Crisis Now a "National Emergency" as Number of Homeowners Plummets to 30-Year Low. http://www.mirror.co.uk/news/uk-news/uk-housing-crisis-now-national-8542855.

Darling, A. (2011). *Back from the Brink: 1000 Days at Number 11*. London: Atlantic Books.

Dawes, M. (2017, February 22, Wednesday). *Evidence to Public Accounts Committee: Housing: State of the Nation*. HC 958, Question 132. http://data.parliament.uk/writtenevidence/committeeevidence.svc/evidencedocument/public-accounts-committee/housing-state-of-the-nation/oral/47584.html.

DCLG. (2017a). *English Housing Survey 2015/16 Headline Report, Table FA1201 (S106): Age of Household Reference Person by Tenure, 2015–16*. London: DCLG. https://www.gov.uk/government/statistics/english-housing-survey-2015-to-2016-headline-report.

DCLG. (2017b). *Fixing Our Broken Housing Market* (Cm 9352). London: DCLG. https://assets.publishing.service.gov.uk/government/uploads/system/uploads/attachment_data/file/590464/Fixing_our_broken_housing_market_-_print_ready_version.pdf.

DeFazio, K. (2014). Red Vienna, Class and the Common. In B. Fraser (Ed.), *Marxism and Urban Culture* (pp. 159–190). New York: Lexington Books.

Delft University of Technology. (2011). *Housing Statistics in the European Union*. Delft, The Netherlands. https://www.bmdw.gv.at/Wirtschaftspolitik/Wohnungspolitik/Documents/housing_statistics_in_the_european_union_2010.pdf.

Deloitte. (2016). *Property Index: Overview of European Residential Markets* (5th ed.). London: Deloitte. https://www2.deloitte.com/content/dam/Deloitte/cz/Documents/survey/Property_Index_2016_EN.pdf.

Dorling, D. (2014). *All That Is Solid: The Great Housing Disaster*. London: Allen Lane.

Dorling, D., Pattie, C. J., & Johnston, R. J. (1999). *Voting and the Housing Market: The Impact of New Labour*. London: Council of Mortgage Lenders. http://www.dannydorling.org/wp-content/files/dannydorling_publication_id4095.pdf.

Edwards, M. (2016). The Housing Crisis: Too Difficult or a Great Opportunity? *Soundings* (62). https://www.lwbooks.co.uk/soundings/62/the-housing-crisis-too-difficult-or-great-opportunity.

Eichler, W. (2016). *IPPR: Lessons from German Housing Market Could Benefit UK*. London: LocGov. https://www.localgov.co.uk/IPPR-Lessons-from-German-housing-market-could-benefit-UK-/42169.

Engels, F. (1872). *The Housing Question Part Two: How the Bourgeoisie Solves the Housing Question*. https://www.marxists.org/archive/marx/works/1872/housing-question/.

Farha, L. (2014). *Special Rapporteur on Adequate Housing as a Component of the Right to an Adequate Standard of Living, and on the Right to Non-Discrimination in This Context, Ms. Farha*. Geneva: United Nations Human Rights, Office of the High Commissioner. https://www.ohchr.org/en/issues/housing/pages/leilanifarha.aspx.

Fields, D. J., & Hodkinson, S. N. (2018). Housing Policy in Crisis: An International Perspective. *Housing Policy Debate, 28*(1), 1–5.

Financial Times. (2017). Which Cities Are the Next UK Property Hotspots? Liverpool, Glasgow, Birmingham and Manchester Tipped for Price Growth. https://www.ft.com/content/a38aced2-8662-11e6-8897-2359a58ac7a5.

Financial Times. (2018, June 23). Buy-to-Let Landlords Cool on Property Purchases. https://www.ft.com/content/4d8e2002-75f2-11e8-b326-75a27d27ea5f.

Fitzpatrick, S. (2017, July 28). Let's Be Honest—If You're Middle Class, You're Less Likely to Become Homeless. *Guardian*. https://www.theguardian.com/housing-network/2017/jul/28/middle-class-homelessness-myth-poverty-racism-structural-issues.

Fitzpatrick, S., & Watts, B. (2018). Taking Values Seriously in Housing Studies. *Housing, Theory and Society, 35*(2), 223–227.

Gallent, N. (2016). *Whose Housing Crisis*. London: University College London. http://www.ucl.ac.uk/grand-challenges/sustainable-cities/our-work-so-far/rethinking-housing/whose-housing-crisis.

Gardiner, L. (2016). *VOTEY McVOTEFACE: Understanding the Growing Turnout Gap Between the Generations.* London: Resolution Foundation. http://www.resolutionfoundation.org/publications/votey-mcvoteface-understanding-the-growing-turnout-gap-between-the-generations/.

Ginsburg, N. (1992). Racism and Housing: Concepts and Reality. In P. Braham, A. Rattans, & R. Skellington (Eds.), *Racism and Antiracism* (pp. 109–133). London: Sage.

Global Property Guide. (2018). *German House Prices Are Accelerating!* https://www.globalpropertyguide.com/Europe/Germany/Price-History.

Gov.uk. (2017). *Ethnicity Facts and Figures.* https://www.ethnicity-facts-figures.service.gov.uk/.

Green, A. (2017). *The Crisis for Young People: Why Housing Is the Key to Social Mobility.* https://ioelondonblog.wordpress.com/2017/07/04/the-crisis-for-young-people-why-housing-is-the-key-to-social-mobility/.

Guardian. (2014, February 3). Ministers Savage UN Report Calling for Abolition of UK's Bedroom Tax. https://www.theguardian.com/society/2014/feb/03/ministers-savage-un-report-abolition-bedroom-tax.

Guardian. (2016, August 2). Home Ownership Is Unrealistic: Five Readers on England's Housing Crisis. https://www.theguardian.com/uk-news/2016/aug/02/home-ownership-is-unrealistic-five-readers-on-englands-housing-crisis.

Guardian. (2017a, March 27). Dog Kennel Flats in Barnet Will Be 40% Smaller Than Travelodge Room. https://www.theguardian.com/society/2017/mar/27/dog-kennel-flats-barnet-house-smaller-than-travelodge-room.

Guardian. (2017b). UK Gender Pay Gap Narrows to Lowest for 20 Years—But Is Still 9.1%. https://www.theguardian.com/business/2017/oct/26/uk-gender-pay-gap-narrows-to-lowest-for-20-years-but-is-still-91.

Harari, D., & Ward, M. (2018). *Regional and Country Economic Indicators* (House of Commons Briefing Paper No. 06924). London: House of Commons. https://researchbriefings.parliament.uk/ResearchBriefing/Summary/SN06924.

Hirsch, F. (1977). *Social Limits to Growth.* Abingdon: Routledge.

HM Land Registry. (2018). *UK House Price Index for March 2018.* https://www.gov.uk/government/news/uk-house-price-index-for-march-2018.

Homeowners Alliance. (2012, November). *The Death of a Dream: The Crisis in Homeownership in the UK* (A Homeowners Alliance Report). London: Homeowners Alliance. https://hoa.org.uk/wp-content/uploads/2012/11/HOA-Report-Death-of-a-Dream.pdf.

Hudson, N. (2015). *Land Market Note: The Value of Land.* London: Savills. http://www.savills.co.uk/research_articles/186866/188996-0.

Independent. (2009). It's Time to Give Up the Dream of Homeownership Says Minister. https://www.independent.co.uk/news/uk/politics/its-time-to-give-up-the-dream-of-home-ownership-says-minister-1838189.html.

Independent. (2018, May 18). UK Facing Its Biggest Housing Shortfall on Record with Backlog of 4m Homes, Research Shows. https://www.independent.co.uk/news/uk/home-news/housing-homeless-crisis-homes-a8356646.html.

Intermediary Mortgage Lenders Association. (2014). *Reshaping Housing Tenure in the UK: The Role of Buy to Let.* London: Intermediary Mortgage Lenders Association. http://www.imla.org.uk/perch/resources/imla-reshaping-housing-tenure-in-the-uk-the-role-of-buy-to-let-may-2014.pdf.

Javid, S. (2017a). *Sajid Javid's Speech to the National Housing Federation Conference 2017.* https://www.gov.uk/government/speeches/sajid-javids-speech-to-the-national-housing-federation-conference-2017.

Jenkins, S. (2006). *Thatcher & Sons: A Revolution in Three Acts.* London: Allen Lane.

Jones, R. (2017, February 11). Welcome to Rabbit-Hutch Britain, Land of the Ever-Shrinking Home. *Guardian.* https://www.theguardian.com/money/2017/feb/11/welcome-rabbit-hutch-britain-land-ever-shrinking-home.

Jones, R. (2018, June 25). Single First-Time Buyer in London Needs 17 Years to Find 15% Deposit—Report. *Guardian.* https://www.theguardian.com/business/2018/jun/25/single-first-time-buyer-in-london-needs-17-years-to-find-15-deposit-report.

Joseph, K., & Sumption, J. (1979). *Equality.* London: John Murray.

Joseph Rowntree Foundation. (2018). *UK Poverty 2018: A Comprehensive Analysis of Poverty Trends and Figures.* York: Joseph Rowntree Foundation. https://www.jrf.org.uk/report/uk-poverty-2018.

Leahy, P. (2018, April 12). Fix the UK Housing Problem to Help the Ailing Retail Sector. *Financial Times.* https://www.ft.com/content/ce944972-3c06-11e8-bcc8-cebcb81f1f90.

Liverpool Victoria Insurance. (2014). *Shrinking Family Home Drives a Surge in Overcrowding.* http://www.lv.com/about-us/press/article/shrinking-family-home-overcrowding.

Malpass, P. (1986). (Ed.). *The Housing Crisis.* London: Routledge.

May, T. (2017). Foreword to *Fixing Our Broken Housing Market.* London: Department for Communities and Local Government. https://www.gov.uk/

government/uploads/system/uploads/attachment_data/file/590464/Fixing_
our_broken_housing_market_-_print_ready_version.pdf.

McCann, P. (2017). *The UK Regional-National Economic Problem: Geography, Globalisation and Governance.* Abingdon: Routledge.

McGuiness, F. (2018). *Household Incomes by Region* (Briefing Paper No. 8191). London: House of Commons. https://researchbriefings.parliament.uk/ResearchBriefing/Summary/CBP-8191.

Ministry of Housing, Communities and Local Government (MHCLG). (2018a). *English Housing Survey 2016 to 2017: Headline Report.* London: MHCLG. https://www.gov.uk/government/statistics/english-housing-survey-2016-to-2017-headline-report.

MHCLG. (2018b). *Live Tables on Homelessness.* London: MHCLG. https://www.gov.uk/government/statistical-data-sets/live-tables-on-homelessness.

MHCLG. (2018c). *English Housing Survey 2016 to 2017: Headline Report, Section 1, Household Tables, Section 2, Housing Stock Tables, Figure 2.3.* London: MHCLG. https://www.gov.uk/government/statistics/english-housing-survey-2016-to-2017-headline-report.

Mulheirn, I. (2017, November 13). Parrots, Housing and Redistribution. *Financial Times.* https://medium.com/@ian.mulheirn/parrots-housing-and-redistribution-419b36a72e52.

Mulheirn, I. (2018, March 23). *Two Housing Crises.* London: Resolution Foundation. http://www.resolutionfoundation.org/media/blog/two-housing-crises/.

Munro, M. (2018). House Price Inflation in the News: A Critical Discourse Analysis of Newspaper Coverage in the UK. *Housing Studies, 33*(7), 1085–1105.

Murray, C. K. (2010). *Housing Investment Is Not Productive.* http://www.fresheconomicthinking.com/2010/02/housing-investment-is-not-productive.html.

National Centre for Social Research. (2016). Social Class Identity, Awareness and Political Attitudes: Why Are We Still Working Class? In *British Social Attitudes 33* (pp. 1–17). London: National Centre for Social Research. http://www.bsa.natcen.ac.uk/latest-report/british-social-attitudes-33/introduction.aspx.

Nationwide. (2018). *Affordability Estimates.* https://www.nationwide.co.uk/about/house-price-index/download-data.

New Economics Foundation. (2018). *How the Broken Land Market Drives Our Housing Crisis.* London: New Economics Foundation. https://neweconomics.org/2018/04/broken-land-market.

Nozick, R. (1981). *Anarchy, State and Utopia*. London: Wiley-Blackwell.

Office for National Statistics (ONS). (2003). *Labour Force Survey*. London: Office for National Statistics. https://discover.ukdataservice.ac.uk/catalogue/?sn=5422.

O'Grady, S. (2016, August 2). Newsflash, Young People: Owning Your Own Home Isn't a Human Right—Your Sense of Entitlement Won't Solve This Crisis. *Independent*. http://www.independent.co.uk/voices/newsflash-young-people-owning-your-own-home-isnt-a-human-right-leave-your-entitlement-at-the-door-a7167961.html.

ONS. (2012). *Ethnicity and National Identity in England and Wales: 2011*. London: Office for National Statistics. https://www.ons.gov.uk/peoplepopulationandcommunity/culturalidentity/ethnicity/articles/ethnicityandnationalidentityinenglandandwales/2012-12-11.

ONS. (2017). *International Migration and the Changing Nature of Housing in England—What Does the Available Evidence Show?* London: Office for National Statistics. https://www.ons.gov.uk/peoplepopulationandcommunity/populationandmigration/internationalmigration/articles/internationalmigrationandthechangingnatureofhousinginenglandwhatdoestheavailableevidenceshow/2017-05-25.

ONS. (2018). *Wealth in Great Britain Wave 5: 2014 to 2016: Main Results from the Fifth Wave of the Wealth and Assets Survey Covering the Period July 2014 to June 2016*. London: Office for National Statistics. https://www.ons.gov.uk/peoplepopulationandcommunity/personalandhouseholdfinances/incomeandwealth/bulletins/wealthingreatbritainwave5/2014to2016.

Osborne, G. (2015). *Chancellor George Osborne's Spending Review and Autumn Statement 2015 Speech*. www.gov.uk/government/speeches/chancellor-george-osbornes-spending-review-and-autumn-statement-2015-speech.

Oxford Dictionaries. (2017a). https://en.oxforddictionaries.com/definition/crisis.

Oxford Dictionaries. (2017b). https://en.oxforddictionaries.com/definition/ethnicity.

Oxford Economics. (2016). *Forecasting UK House Prices and Homeownership: A Report for the Redfern Review into the Decline of Homeownership*. Oxford: Oxford Economics. https://www.oxfordeconomics.com/my-oxford/projects/351906.

Posen, A. (2013, July 26). The Cult of Home Ownership Is Dangerous and Damaging. *Financial Times*. https://www.ft.com/content/00bf5968-f518-11e2-b4f8-00144feabdc0.

Preece, J. (2018). *Is It Time For a Right to Affordable Housing?* UK Collaborative Centre for Housing Evidence. http://housingevidence.ac.uk/is-it-time-for-a-right-to-affordable-housing/.

Rampen, J. (2016, August 2). The Property-Owning Democracy Is Dead—So Build One for Renters Instead. *New Statesman*. http://www.newstatesman.com/politics/staggers/2016/08/property-owning-democracy-dead-so-build-one-renters-instead.

Rawls, J. (1971). *A Theory of Justice*. Harvard: Harvard University Press.

Renwick, C. (2017). *Bread for All: The Origins of the Welfare State*. London: Allen Lane.

Resolution Foundation. (2017a). *Diverse Outcomes: Living Standards by Ethnicity*. London: Resolution Foundation. http://www.resolutionfoundation.org/publications/diverse-outcomes-living-standards-by-ethnicity/.

Resolution Foundation. (2018). *The Future Fiscal Cost of 'Generation Rent'*. London: Resolution Foundation. http://www.resolutionfoundation.org/media/blog/the-future-fiscal-cost-of-generation-rent/.

Rowntree, S. (1901). *Poverty: A Study in Town Life*. London: Macmillan and Co.

Rugg, J., & Rhodes, D. (2018). *The Evolving Private Rented Sector: Its Contribution and Potential*. York: Centre for Housing Policy, University of York. http://www.nationwidefoundation.org.uk/wp-content/uploads/2018/09/Private-Rented-Sector-report.pdf.

Ryan-Collins, J. (2018). *Why Can't You Afford a Home?* Bristol: Policy Press.

Savage, M., Cunningham, N., Devine, F., Friedman, S., Laurison, D., Mckenzie, L., et al. (2015). *Social Class in the 21st Century*. London: Pelican.

Scanlon, K., & Whitehead, C. (2016). *The Profile of Mortgage Lenders*. London: Council of Mortgage Lenders. file:///C:/Users/User/Downloads/the-profile-of-uk-private-landlords-20170118.pdf.

Shaw, V. (2017, June 30). *First-Time Buyers Need Average Deposit of £33,000, Finds Housing Market Report*. http://www.independent.co.uk/news/business/news/first-time-buyers-uk-homes-deposit-average-33000-housing-market-report-mortgage-a7816321.html.

Sheffield Political Economy Research Institute. (2016). *Public and Private Sector Employment Across the UK Since the Financial Crisis*. Sheffield: Sheffield University. http://speri.dept.shef.ac.uk/wp-content/uploads/2015/02/Brief10-public-sector-employment-across-UK-since-financial-crisis.pdf.

Shelter. (2016a). *The Living Home Standard*. London: Shelter. https://england. shelter.org.uk/__data/assets/pdf_file/0010/1288387/FINAL_Living_home_ standard_report.pdf.

Shelter. (2016b). *Living Home Findings*. London: Shelter. https://england.shelter.org.uk/__data/assets/pdf_file/0011/1288388/FINAL_Living_home_ standard_Findings_report-insert.pdf.

Shelter. (2017). *Fair Rent Homes: An Affordable Alternative for Hard-Pressed Renters*. London: Shelter.

Shelter. (2018). *Shelter Research: In Work But Out of a Home*. London: Shelter. https://england.shelter.org.uk/__data/assets/pdf_ file/0004/1545412/2018_07_19_Working_Homelessness_Briefing.pdf.

Shrinkthatfootprint. (2018). *How Big Is a House? Average House Size by Country*. http://shrinkthatfootprint.com/how-big-is-a-house#PVoATV52pvKb6L8W.99.

Somerville, P. (2018). Housing and Social Justice. In G. Craig (Ed.), *Handbook on Global Social Justice* (pp. 371–384). Cheltenham: Edward Elgar.

Spiers, S. (2018). *How to Build Houses and Save the Countryside*. Bristol: Policy Press.

Statista. (2018). *Share of Employees on a Zero Hours Contract in United Kingdom (UK) from April to June 2018, by Region*. https://www.statista.com/statistics/398592/share-of-employed-population-zero-hour-contracts-region/.

Stephens, M., Perry, J., Wilcox, S., Williams, P., & Young, G. (2018). *UK Housing Review 2018*. London: Chartered Institute of Housing.

Sun. (2018, February 17). *Tories Are Failing to Fix Britain's Housing Crisis and Can't Take on Opponents in Order to Stand Up for the Middle-Earners*. https://www.thesun.co.uk/news/5599624/sun-says-housing-crisis-tories-are-failing/.

Taylor, H. (2018). *Social Justice in Contemporary Housing: Applying Rawls' Difference Principle*. Abingdon: Routledge.

Taylor, M. (2015, August 16). Housing Is the Nation's Most Urgent and Complex Challenge. Yet We're Paralysed. *Guardian*. https://www.theguardian.com/commentisfree/2015/aug/16/matthew-taylor-we-must-face-difficult-truths-to-solve-housing-crisis.

Teixeira-Mendes, R. (2017, April). Dissecting the Housing Crisis: Radical Progressive Policy Solutions for Britain's Housing Market. *Incite*. https://incitejournal.com/opinion/dissecting-the-housing-crisis-radical-progressive-policy-solutions-for-britains-housing-market/.

Telegraph. (2017, March 20). £92,000: The Average Cost of a Care Home in Britain's Costliest Regions. http://www.telegraph.co.uk/money/consumer-affairs/92000-average-cost-care-home-britains-costliest-regions/.

Telegraph. (2018, November 19). Amber Rudd Accuses United Nations of political Attack on UK Government Over Damning Poverty Report. https://www.telegraph.co.uk/politics/2018/11/19/amber-rudd-accuses-united-nations-political-attack-uk-government/.

Tunstall, R. (2015). Relative Housing Space Inequality in England and Wales, and Its Recent Rapid Resurgence. *International Journal of Housing Policy, 15*(2), 105–126.

Valentine, D. R. (2015). *Housing Crisis: An Analysis of Investment Demand Behind the UK Affordability Crisis.* London: Bow Group. https://www.bowgroup.org/sites/bowgroup.uat.pleasetest.co.uk/files/The%20Bow%20Group%20-%20The%20UK%20Housing%20Crisis%20%282015%29%20FINAL.pdf.

Valuation Office Agency. (2018). *Check the Register of Fair Rents.* https://www.tax.service.gov.uk/check-register-fair-rents/search?q=OL1&page=2.

Walker, R. (2016). The Inequality Machine. In R. Walker & S. Jeraj (Eds.), *The Rent Trap: How We Fell into It and How We Get Out of It* (pp. 113–133). London: Pluto Press.

Willetts, D. (2011). *The Pinch: How the Baby Boomers Took Their Children's Future—And Why They Should Give It Back.* London: Atlantic Books.

Williams, K. (2009). Space Per Person in the UK: A Review of Densities, Trends, Experiences and Optimum Levels. *Land Use Policy, 26*(Suppl. 1), 83–92.

Wilson, W., Barton, C., & Smith, L. (2018). *Tackling the Under-Supply of Housing in England* (Briefing Paper No. 07671). London: House of Commons. https://researchbriefings.parliament.uk/ResearchBriefing/Summary/CBP-7671.

Wood, J., & Clarke, S. (2018). *House of the Rising Son (And Daughter): The Impact of Parental Wealth on Their Children's Homeownership.* London: Resolution Foundation. https://www.resolutionfoundation.org/publications/house-of-the-rising-son-or-daughter/.

Zoopla. (2018, February 8). *When Could Your Home Be Worth £1m?* https://www.zoopla.co.uk/discover/property-news/when-could-your-home-be-worth-1m/#vbU7O8SWRmMfMicA.97.

2

The Slow-Burning Fuses

The current housing crises have deep roots, intertwined in changing demographics and the power balance between capital and labour. Capital, although increasingly divided between landed and industrial capital, was dominant in the nineteenth century but, in the twentieth century, the Labour movement's industrial and political clout helped to produce extensive state intervention in the housing market. This state involvement has been rolled back in the last forty years and the market—characterised by privatisation, commodification and financialisation—is now the primary mechanism determining housing outcomes. 82% of the UK housing stock is privately owned and subject to market forces with the remainder, labelled 'social housing', increasingly being driven towards mimicking the market. There are seven elements in the slow-burning fuses that ignited into the contemporary housing crises: building industry capacity; the growth in private renting; housing financialisation; the demise and stigmatisation of social housing, especially the homes supplied by local government; lack of investment in the existing housing stock; demographic change and the planning system.

© The Author(s) 2019
B. Lund, *Housing in the United Kingdom*,
https://doi.org/10.1007/978-3-030-04128-1_2

Building Industry Capacity

During the nineteenth century most building was undertaken by small local firms who needed to sell their houses quickly to acquire capital for new projects. The building industry was 'speculative', depending on anticipated profits, and according to Tames (1972, p. 40) 'The workers got what was left over', because builders focused on more profitable ventures such as factories, warehouses, docks and public buildings'.

Land value was an important element in profitability. As Wellings (2006, p. 10) notes, 'builders have two ways of making a profit… directly on their building activities or indirectly through land development profit or speculation'. The speculative housing market was subject to the prevailing economic climate and demand was very volatile. Such capricious demand could involve builders in declining land prices and unsold homes. The severest building slump was from 1902 to 1913 with, as examples, the number of new houses built in Newcastle down from 472 in 1902 to 37 in 1913, in Birmingham down from 3429 to 1331 and, in Derby, from 728 to 114 (Lewis 1965, pp. 307–312). At each market downturn there was a tendency for the smaller, local builders—the dominant nineteenth century providers—to cease trading or merge with larger companies.

From 1919 to 1933, the private building industry was supported by the state via direct subsidies to private builders and contracts from local government to build central state-assisted council houses. John Wheatley formulated his 1924 Housing Act through a committee consisting entirely of building industry representatives and trade union officials, promising building firms full order books in return for 'fair' behaviour and the trade unions stable employment for reducing restrictive practices. 1933–1939 were 'golden years' for private housebuilding. Axing the 1924 Housing Act 'general needs' subsidies in 1933 reduced local authority direct labour house production; low-interest rates; cheap suburban land—almost free from planning legislation—and a finance flood into the building societies combined to produce an average 263,000 houses per year delivered directly by the private sector, mainly without subsidy (Bowley 1946). However, most houses were for owner-occupation and, although more better paid skilled workers acquired such homes, those who could not afford to buy were excluded from better housing. Small companies still had a large market share with the largest ten builders constructing only about 7% of the new houses (Wellings 2006, p. 34). New private housebuilding was concentrated in the South East that absorbed 44.5% of the new houses. Local authority housing was directed towards slum clearance and overcrowding.

From 1945 to 1954 the residential construction industry had to rely on local government contracts but, post 1955, a 'dual market'—similar to the 1930s—emerged. State housing was concentrated on the requirements arising from slum clearance, encouraged by special subsidies for high-rise, targeted at inner cities. Such state housing was a part of 'high modernism'—'a strong, one might say muscle-bound, version of the self-confidence about scientific and technical progress… and, above all, the rational design of social order commensurate with the scientific understanding of natural laws' (Scott 1999, p. 4). As Dunleavy (1981) has demonstrated, new building techniques such as system building—prefabricated slabs slotted into steel structures—favoured the large-scale builders. However, as Merrett (1982, p. 26) claimed, 'with respect to private housing, it was essentially a matter of unleashing the industry'. Houses built for homeowners, aided by tax relief on mortgage interest, increased. In the process, small scale builders lost ground to the volume builders whose market share had increased to about 20% by the mid-1970s.

The Thatcher/Major governments concentrated new housebuilding on private sector construction for homeownership. New private enterprise completions fluctuated according to the building cycle, ranging from 207,000 to 130,000 per year but, overall, 159,495 houses per year were built by the private sector from 1979 to 1997 compared to 165,800 between 1970 and 1979. Social sector new house construction plummeted from 148,500 per year in the 1970s to 42,000 per year between 1979 and 1997. Under New Labour, UK private sector housebuilding gradually increased from 155,800 in 1998 to 195,800 in 2007 but social sector completions continued to decline, averaging only 22,900 per year from 1998 to 2007. When the recession came, only 105,230 private sector houses were completed in 2010 (MHCLG 2018a). Smaller scale builders were hid badly by the slump and the number of building firms declined.

The historical statistical evidence demonstrates that private enterprise, operating through the market, cannot produce the houses necessary to meet requirements, especially the needs of low-income households. The residential construction industry has been subject to mounting criticism for its poor output and productivity (see Chapter 7). The volume builders now have a large market share, the top ten builders with 47% of the market. Clive Betts, Chair of the House of Commons Housing, Communities and Local Government Select Committee stated 'Smaller builders are in decline and the sector is over-reliant on an alarmingly small number of high-volume developers, driven by commercial self-interest and with little incentive to build any quicker' (quoted in BBC News 2017).

Company amalgamations have produced fewer homes than before mergers (Archer and Cole 2016). A greater profit share is now derived from land speculation and financialisation, such as selling new homes as leasehold rather than freehold and, when sold as freehold, including long-term service charges in the contract (see Chapter 6). Build quality is unsatisfactory with Wilson and Rhodes (2018) reporting:

> MPs are encountering constituents who have bought new homes, and who are struggling to achieve satisfactory resolution when defects are reported to builders…There have been some high profile examples of blocks facing demolition/major repair work only a short time after completion due to construction defects…

Stimulated by the Help to Buy scheme, the prices charged for new houses by the volume builders houses have been increasing faster than average house prices (Archer 2017) and there is evidence that volume builders are managing site build-out rates to sustain profits (see Chapter 7).

Private Landlordism

In the nineteenth century, builders sold houses to private landlords who realised their investment by long-term renting. Private landlords possessed over 80% of the housing stock but the sector's ownership structure was opaque. Freehold land holdings were highly concentrated and the landowners—well aware that, over the long-term, land was a secure investment—were reluctant to sell outright. Rights to use land were layered, with the leasehold—conveying time-limited use rights—passing through a number of landlords making it difficult to separate owners from tenants. Rent collecting, a tough business in inner cities, was usually delegated to agents and sub-agents.

Private Landlords and Slums

In the late nineteenth century, attention focused on the 'slum' as a housing crisis symbol. The 'slum' was portrayed not only as a single dwelling 'unfit for human habitation' but as a closed area, teeming with overcrowded, densely packed, insanitary houses accessed by foot via narrow alleys. It was regarded as the epicentre of social evils—crime, immorality, mob violence and disease. In his *Report on the sanitary condition of the labouring population of Great Britain*, Edwin Chadwick (1842) warned politicians that, if the sanitary condition of the labouring classes was not improved, the moral, physical and military prowess of the nation would fade, a theme taken up by Disraeli (1872, p. 2) when, in declaring 'Sanitas sanitatum, omnia sanitas', stated: 'If the population every ten years decreases, and the stature of the race every ten years diminishes, the history of that country will soon be the history of the past' (Disraeli 1872, pp. 1–2).

The blame for the overcrowded slum was mainly directed at the slum dweller with, for example, *Sir* Charles Dilke, a member of the Royal Commission on the Housing of the Working Classes (1885) alleging that the poor had a 'disposition to overcrowding' (quoted in Stedman Jones, p. 224). *However*, 'house farmers' were deemed partially culpable. Houses declined in value as the leasehold on the land ran down and 'house farmers' bought the lease cheaply, making profits by 'sweating' the property through multi-occupation and overcrowding. Slum landlords, often called 'house knackers', had a poor reputation in respectable society with Octavia Hill condemning them as 'unfit and improper persons' to manage urban housing because they were interested only in profit and not in how tenants behaved. Slum clearance and railway extension exacerbated the problem because few houses were constructed to replace the lost homes and those that were built were beyond the incomes of the slum inhabitants. George Haws (1900, p. 81) reported an East London meeting of 2000 people who unanimously passed a resolution in protest against:

> The inhuman behaviour of the new extortionist landlords, who are systematically raising the rents of the houses thereby causing misery and privation amongst the unfortunate tenants whom circumstances force to remain in the districts affected.

The Social Democratic Federation, then England's leading socialist organisation, led the opposition to landlord exploitation. It organised rent strikes and demonstrations that could become violent. The agitation became so serious that a Royal Commission was set up with a membership including Lord Salisbury, the Prince of Wales and Cardinal Manning but even Lord Salisbury's meek proposal—cheap Treasury loans to local government—encountered enmity as 'sailing into the turbid waters of State Socialism' (*Pall Mall Gazette*, 1884, quoted in Roberts 1999, p. 283). Thus, although 1885 Housing of the Working Classes Act allowed local authorities to obtain Treasury loans to build houses, the interest rate charged was almost the commercial rate.

'Creeping' Decontrol

Rent discontent continued to simmer in the early twentieth century and erupted during the First World War. Worker movement into the munitions factories in 1914/1915 produced rent increases that led to rent strikes and threats of industrial action with protest at its most intense in Glasgow. Rent and mortgage interest control plus security of tenure were imposed by the government. Such regulation was intended to last only until the war was over but, with franchise enlargement, it was difficult to roll back. The 1920 Housing Act allowed rents to be increased by up to 40%, phased over three years, and the 1923 Rent and

Mortgage Restrictions Act allowed 'creeping decontrol', that is, ending rent control on a tenancy change. Dissatisfaction generated by this legislation was a factor in the Conservative loss of Mitcham to Labour in a 1923 by election—dubbed the 'housing by election' (Pathé News 1923)—and Labour gains in the 1923 General Election. Following this setback, the Conservative Party became far more circumspect on rent decontrol, even removing poor quality private rented accommodation from creeping decontrol under 1933 Rent and Mortgage Restrictions Amendment Act. By 1939 many houses occupied by the working class were let at rents well below the market level. Landlords sold to owner-occupiers on vacant possession or to sitting tenants. From 1914 to 1938 there were 1.1 million sales from the private landlord sector to owner-occupiers (Department of the Environment 1977).

When the Second World War started strict rent control was reintroduced and rent levels were almost static until the 1957 Rent Act decontrolled all houses above a specified rateable value and allowed other houses to become decontrolled on vacant possession. The 'creeping' decontrol on vacant possession erupted as a political issue when the activities of Perec Rachman—a London slum landlord—were revealed. Rachman, unlike many other landlords, did not discriminate but his agents intimidated sitting tenants to leave their homes and, with vacant possession, Rachman let them to migrants at high rents (Green 1979). 'Rachmanism' became a major issue in the 1964 General Election. The Labour Government's 1965 Rent Act introduced regulated tenancies with long-term security of tenure accompanied by 'fair' rents assessed by independent rent officers with appeal to a Rent Assessment Committee. In assessing 'fair' rents scarcity value had to be ignored. Neither the 1957 Rent Act nor the 1965 Rent Act stemmed the sales flow to owner-occupiers: 1.1 million houses were sold by private landlords to owner-occupiers from 1960 to 1975 (Department of the Environment 1977). Although the Conservatives made changes to private landlord regulation in the early 1980s, fair rents and tenure security survived until new tenants were required to pay market rents and their tenure security was severely restricted under the 1988 Housing Act. For a few years the new 'creeping' decontrol had little effect but, post 1997, the private landlord sector started to expand.

Several factors contributed to this growth. Migration, with the new-comers needing rapid access to accommodation, was important, there being an association—of course not necessarily causal—between the acceleration in private lettings post 2004 and migration growth. The growing student population, increasing difficulty in saving for the deposit necessary for homeownership and Rent to Buy—the mortgage lenders' agreement to lend to landlords on terms close to those for owner-occupation—contributed. These causes were augmented by the impact the 1988 Housing Act, indeed, some larger landlords—notably Grainger PLC, now the largest UK private residential landlord, acquiring regulated property knowing that, in time, it could charge market rents. Many landlords bought property, often flats that had limitations in selling to owner-occupiers, first sold to sitting tenants under the Right to Buy. Moreover, private landlords had considerable tax advantages. As businesses, landlords could counterbalance mortgage interest payments against tax liability—wealthier landlords received relief at 40%. They also gained from a tax offset worth 10% of their annual net rental income covering 'wear and tear' on furniture and fixtures. Other claimable expenses included broker and arrangement fees; letting agent fees; advertising; tenant credit checking; obtaining references; deposit protection costs; insurance premiums; maintenance and repairs; ground rent and service services and the direct costs of letting the property such as phone calls and the business costs of travelling between different properties. Although liable to pay Capital Gains Tax—not paid by own-er-occupiers—HM Revenue and Customs claimed that only 500,000 private landlords regularly filed self-assessment tax returns (Guild of Residential Landlords 2015).

Private landlordism developed its own impetus. As property values increased and cash from rents poured in, some landlords acquired more houses and were able to buy homes without mortgages. Landlords were competing in the same market as first-time buyers and, for a time, the restrictions on mortgage access to owner-occupation applied by the Bank of England to dampen the housing market—affordability tests and limiting the number of mortgages more than four-and-a-half times a borrower's income—did not apply to buy-to-let loans. This meant that a high proportion of the finance released by Quantitative Easing and Funding for Lending was taken up by private landlords, not by potential first-time buyers (Robinson 2018).

The rapid rise in private renting has produced new issues and old issues are being revisited. When market rents were introduced, Housing Minister, Sir George Young, said that Housing Benefit would 'take the strain' from higher rents (quoted in Birch 2013) but, despite a £8.6 billion 2016/2017 spend (Department for Work and Pensions [DWP] 2018) mean after benefit rent payments still absorbed 46% of private tenants' weekly household income (DCLG 2017). Nineteenth century 'house farmers'—now labelled 'rogue landlords'—have re-emerged with conversions of three bedroom family houses into six self-contained flats a new 'house farming' marker. Wall (2018, p. 1) states:

> Three-bed houses, where the maximum weekly housing benefit for flat-sharers is under £100 a person, are being converted into as many as six tiny self-contained studios – as little as 10 sq m in size. Each then qualifies for housing benefit of £181 a week, enabling a landlord to squeeze £56,000 a year in rent from a property on London's fringes, all paid from public funds. The £56,000 compares with the typical £6200 annual rent on a three-bed council house.

Housing Financialisation

In the late nineteenth century new housebuilding was financed by banks, wealthy individuals, often landowners, and investment clubs organised by local solicitors but building societies had started to become increasingly important. Building societies started as working class self-help organisations, terminating when all the members were housed but, by the start of the twentieth century, 'permanent' societies—taking savings from people not requiring housing—had become dominant. As 'mutuals', without shareholders, they claimed to be interested only in the reciprocal welfare of their investors and mortgage holders. Their aura was buttressed through promoting a 'property-owning democracy' as the path to full citizenship. Harold Bellman, Director of the Abbey Road Building Society, asserted:

The man who has something to protect and improve—a stake of some sort in the country—naturally turns his thoughts in the direction of sane, ordered and perforce economical government. (Bellman 1927, p. 65)

By the 1930s savings were pouring into the societies and, to make use of these funds, the societies encouraged the better paid members of the working class in secure employment to become homeowners. The deposit was reduced—sometimes to as low as 5%—and repayment periods were increased to up to 27 years. The 'builders' pool—builders agreeing to be responsible for properties coming into repossession by setting aside a 'fund pool' for building society use if a loss was made—supported over half the new houses built in the 1930s. Local authorities also supplied mortgages to purchase low-cost houses and, by 1939, 150,000 loans had been advanced by local government. Scott (2013) claims that, in the 1930s, up 50% of new owners were from the working class.

Following the Conservative government's post-1954 support for homeownership, with the 1963 abolition of Schedule A tax on the imputed rental income obtained through homeownership being a major boost, building societies thrived and their cartel in setting mortgage rates meant there was a direct relationship between the savings deposited in the societies and mortgage finance available to enhance housing supply. The state intervened from time to time by giving loans to the societies when finance—hence housing building—was slow. However, by the early 1980s building societies were subject to mounting criticism with the building society cartel in setting mortgage interest rates the principal indictment.

Competition

The building society cartel was ended in the mid-1980s by the abolition the 'corset' on bank lending thereby allowing banks and fringe mortgage lenders full access to the residential mortgage market. Building societies complained about their limited access to wholesale funds and, in response, the government allowed building societies to become banks under 1986 Building Societies Act. This became a slow-burning fuse, well illustrated by Northern Rock. On becoming a bank, Northern Rock floated on the London Stock Market. It aggressively expanded its mortgage market share by borrowing on wholesale markets using 'securitisation'—selling on the loans—as collateral and attracting new mortgage business through deals such as its 'Together' loan—up to 125% of house value and six times the borrower's annual income (Brummer 2008). Only 25% of its funds came from the retail market with 40% obtained from securitisation and 24% from wholesale unsecured borrowing (Milne 2009). As the credit crunch spread from the United States (see Chapter 4), Northern Rock suffered a bank run and was taken into public ownership in 2008. Other banks encountered severe problems and later it was revealed that some were heavily involved in irresponsible lending and securitisation. For example, the Royal Bank of Scotland was fined £4.3 billion by the US Department of Justice for the mis-selling $32 billion of US sub-prime mortgages (*Guardian* 2017a). The state was forced to intervene via an expensive bank rescue package in the forms of government-backed mergers; a range of short-term loans and guarantees of inter-bank lending; guarantees for customer deposits and up £50 billion of direct state investment in the banks. At its peak, state support to banks amounted to £1029 billion in guarantee commitments and £133 billion in cash outlays (National Audit Office 2017). Government intervention stabilised the banking industry but at the cost of adding to public debt with the subsequent austerity agenda producing cutbacks in state expenditure.

The Demise of Council Housing

Rise

In the 1890s local government started to add housebuilding to its long list of municipal activities but the number of homes built was small. The Conservative Party and mainstream Liberals were suspicious of local government involvement in housebuilding especially if subsidies were involved, viewing such state intervention as 'socialism'. Authorities were not allowed to make a loss on any scheme, albeit that this restraint was sometimes bypassed by writing down land acquisition costs and was ended in 1901. Social unrest during the First World War led Lloyd George to promise 'a land fit for heroes to live in' (Lloyd George 1918) and, post 1919, housing projects were subsidised through central grants and local rate contributions with central state assistance acting as a 'butterfly valve' (Merrett 1979) to direct local authorities to build for 'general needs' or to rehouse slum inhabitants.

The Conservative Party disliked local authority housebuilding and initially Conservative ministers in the 1918–1922 coalition opposed the generous state subsidies included in the 1919 Housing and Planning Act until Lloyd George warned about a Bolshevik revolution (Lund 2016). The Conservative's 1923 Housing Act gave lower subsidies than the 1919 Act to both private enterprise and local government, restricting local authority activity to situations where it could be demonstrated that private enterprise could not produce sufficient supply. However, the minority Labour government's 1924 Housing Act was retained by subsequent Conservative governments although subsidy levels were reduced until, in 1933, all general needs subsidies were abolished. Subsequently the local government's housing role was confined to 'public health'—slum clearance and abating overcrowding—with the subsidies made available under the 1930 and 1935 Housing Acts.

Between 1945 and 1954 local government delivered the overwhelming majority of new houses. Aneurin Bevan, responsible for the Labour government's housing programme regarded local authorities as 'plannable instruments', capable of delivering new homes quickly in planned environments with mixed communities and allocating these home directly to people in need. Harold Macmillan, Minister for Housing and Local Government in the post-1951 Conservative government realised private enterprise was incapable of delivering the 300,000 houses per year promised in the 1951 Conservative Party Manifesto so he also relied on local government. When the 300,000 housing target was met in 1954, the public sector supplied 221,000 of the houses. However, Macmillan encountered demands from his party to increase homeownership and started work on a 'grand design' for housing, involving promoting owner-occupation by ending 'general needs' subsidies to local government. The 1933 policy was repeated: local government would house people removed from the slums, private enterprise would meet all other requirements. This approach was maintained from 1954 to 1979 albeit that, in 1961, general needs subsidies—lower than in the early 1950s—were restored. Between 1964 to 1970 and 1974 to 1979, Labour governments build a substantial number of homes on 'periphery estates', but most new homes were flats for inner-city inhabitants displaced by slum clearance. Between 1945 and 1950, 10.5% of the accommodation constructed by local authorities was in flats, by 1966–1970, it was 50.6%, rising to 90% in inner cities (Dunleavy 1981).

Whenever local authorities built for 'general needs' the houses were good quality but standards declined when new-build was concentrated on constructing houses to replace the slums. By 1979, local government owned 31% of the housing stock but the local authority housing image had become tarnished by its association 'high rise', 'deck access' and 'Tower and Slab' brutalism architecture (Urban 2011). Moreover, the sector was becoming 'residualised' (Forrest and Murie 1983), that is, increasingly supplying accommodation only to poor people.

Fall

Margaret Thatcher regarded local authority housing as socialist woodworm eroding the nation's moral fabric. She claimed that all council estates were bad (Jenkins 2006, pp. 125–126) and reduced the role of council housing through a variety of stratagems: Right to Buy; stock transfer via Tenant's Choice and Housing Action Trusts plus severely limiting local government's financial ability to build new homes and improve their stock. HB cost was added to local authority housing revenue accounts putting them into deficit and the role of local authority direct labour organisations in providing houses was curtailed.

New Labour restricted the Right to Buy during its second term in office and injected resources into upgrading the local authority housing stock. However, this upgrading was part of a stock transfer programme to housing associations and the number of new local authority homes continued on the downward path established by Thatcher. In 1996 only 1670 council houses were built in the UK but local authority output had slumped to 560 in 2009. The coalition government 'revitalised' the Right to Buy in England through higher discounts but, Cameron's one for one replacement commitment on the additional homes sold under the 'revitalised' Right to Buy was broken. By 2018 only 15,981 had been built or acquired compared to the 17,072 required to meet the promise to replace all *additional* homes sold within three years of introducing the revitalised Right to Buy with only 48% for social rent. Between 2012 and 2017 councils sold 63,518 homes under the Right to Buy (Apps 2018).

Housing Associations

Housing associations are not-for-profit organisations. By the early twentieth century, they consisted of 'charitable' societies set up to help the poor, financed by donations and/or by philanthropic investors limiting their return to 5%. The non-profit designation also covered cooperatives—sometimes called co-partnerships—and the organisations set up to create and manage new towns. Until the post-1919 expansion of local government involvement in the housing market, housing associations were the major not-for-profit housing suppliers but their contribution was small—about a 0.5% market share—and concentrated in London.

From 1919 until the early 1970s housing associations had a minor role in housing provision—they owned only 1.5% of the housing stock in 1973—but the 1974 Housing Act supplied the platform for a major advance in their activities. Introduced as a bill by a Conservative government, but passed and implemented by Labour, the Act provided associations with generous subsidies to refurbish older homes and build new ones assisted by government loans delivered by the Housing Corporation. By 1979 housing associations had increased their stock to 471,000 homes—2.2% of the UK housing—but Margaret Thatcher distrusted them as contributing to public sector debt and as cushioned from economic realism by government grants. Charitable associations escaped the Right to Buy only by a House of Lords rebellion (Murie 2008). Housing associations responded to the new Conservative regime by promoting low-cost homeownership schemes but, between 1980 and 1987, housing association output declined from 21,480 per year to 13,150.

'Entrepreneurial' Housing Associations

Salvation came from housing associations becoming part of the 'entrepreneurial' private sector with a larger slice of their investment coming from private sources, reclassifying housing association debt as private not public and by higher rents, gradually moving to market rents with HB allegedly 'taking the strain' from low-income households. Housing associations were also assisted by legally enforceable planning obligations entered into under Section 106 of the 1990 Town and Country Planning Act allowing a local planning authority to negotiate an 'affordable' housing proportion on a site in the planning approval process. In 1997 housing association output reached 28,240 but this was mainly the outcome of John Major's attempt to kick start the building industry by bringing forward future allocated resources thereby providing housing associations with the finance to buy up unsold properties. During the Thatcher/Major years there was a tendency for associations to increase production for low-cost homeownership rather than for rent.

New Labour's 1997 manifesto promised enhanced housing production via 'a three-way partnership' between the public, private and housing association sectors' but initially the government concentrated resources on refurbishing the existing social housing stock via stock transfer from local government. Housing associations had the necessary finance to complete upgrades because they were unconstrained by rules on public sector borrowing. New housing association production declined, reaching 17,630 in 2003, restricted by lower central grants relative to costs and linked to the market via reliance on private sector profitability through Section 106 agreements. By 2007, output was higher at 27,430 but stock transfer—often whole stock transfer to housing associations specially created to receive the stock—had created more players in the development process. The sharp fall in market sector production following the 'credit crunch' prompted New Labour to inject more cash into housing associations to counter the building slump but the coalition government's austerity agenda meant fewer central resources for housing associations. By pushing new home rents to 80% of market level—labelled 'affordable'—and encouraging existing stock sales and the conversion of existing homes to 'affordable' rent levels, the government hoped that new house production in England at below-market rent could be sustained.

Housing associations have been called 'hybrids'—neither state nor private. Their ambiguous nature has enabled their activities to be moulded by the state and, in recent years, they have appealed to all political parties as vehicles for housing delivery. The Liberal Party has always viewed housing associations favourably as a means to create a more mutual society and the Liberal Democrats in the coalition government attempted to support their activities. In the past, the Labour Party's position has been more ambivalent, encouraging cooperative forms of association but suspicious of the 'lady bountiful' charitable organisations and wary lest they become substitutes for local government supply. However, New Labour embraced housing associations with enthusiasm: they were 'social entrepreneurs', 'social hearted and commercially minded' (Chevin 2013).

'Old' Labour's misgiving that housing associations would be used to replace local government was justified. The Conservative Party has had a long-standing ambition to achieve this substitution (see Moyne 1933) and, assisted by New Labour, the mission is now well on the way to attainment. In the process, the essence of housing associations has been transformed. They have become market orientated and frequently used to mop up private sector capacity during recessions. New build is dominated by large associations with a national rather than local orientation and the 'commercial mind' is prevailing over the 'social' heart. Despite internal divisions within the housing association movement, associations are imitating private landlords. Rents on new properties can be set at up 80% of the market rent with, in 2016/2017, 22,113 new housing association starts for letting at such 'affordable' rents compared to only 944 at social rent (Homes and Communities Agency 2017). Despite a government imposed restriction on social rent increases housing associations made a record operating profit of £3.5 billion in 2017 via reducing spending on repairs, producing houses for market sale or for market—or near-market—rent and by selling off its existing stock. The *Guardian* (2018) reported:

> Housing associations have made at least £82.3 m from auctioning homes in five London boroughs since 2013…. The true figures are likely to be much higher as the data only covers sales made by one agency. The auctions are part of a wider trend of some housing associations selling off social housing in expensive central London to fund new developments, which tenants say are unaffordable or far removed from their families, schools and work.

There are doubts about whether profits are being used to support social housing as some housing associations claim (Wiles 2018; Crook and Kemp 2018).

Housing associations, the chosen vehicles for new social housing supply, have proved unable to deliver the housing volume required to compensate for the decline in local authority production. Moreover, as their activities have become market-oriented their products have become less accessible to households in need. Low-cost home ownership is beyond the means of low-income households in higher priced areas and low take-up of the schemes was a reason why the 2015 Conservative government extended income eligibility criteria to £80,000 (£90,000 in London). An increasing number of housing associations lets are being made at 'affordable' levels and some at market rents. There has been a long controversy on the willingness of housing association to accept local authority nominations (Cowan et al. 2007; Heywood 2015). The per cent of lettings made as a result of nominations or referrals by local authorities went down from 55.6% in 2008/2009 to 45.5% in 2015/2016 and the per cent of housing association lettings made to homeless households had been on a descending trend since 2006/2007 (Stephens et al. 2018).

The Decline in Social Housing Supply

The MHCLG publishes two-time series on additional houses in England: a quarterly series covering new builds only and an annual series comprising of overall net supply. The annual net supply series includes new builds, conversions, change of use, demolitions and other changes in the dwelling stock. In recent years the MHCLG has used the annual net supply of additional dwellings in England as its headline figure. In 2016/2017 217,350 net additions were recorded but caveats on net additional dwellings as an output measure are necessary. In 2016/2017 net use change accounted for 37,190 of net additional supply, up from 12,780 in 2012/2013 (MHCLG 2018b). In 2013, by relaxing planning controls, the government made it easier for developers to covert offices to homes. This helped to boost office to home conversions to 18,000 in 2016/2017 but many were very small and research has revealed that developers have avoided the affordable homes required in new-build schemes and that the enhanced profits from conversions have diverted developers from new build (Local Government Association 2018). Moreover, under the 'permitted development' provisions, developers did not have to make Section 106 contributions for social housing (Royal Institute of Chartered Surveyors 2018). Figure 2.1 sets out UK new house output from local government and housing associations alongside private sector supply indicating how housing supply reduction is mainly related to the decline in new social housing output.

In 2017/2018 there were 220,190 net additions to the dwelling stock in England (MHCLG 2018c) with new-build completions at 195,290. 48,000 were deemed affordable by the government but only

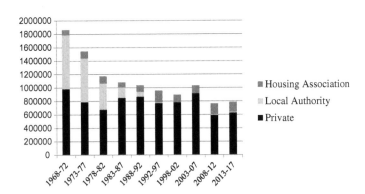

Fig. 2.1 New houses by tenure: UK 1968–2017 (*Source* MHCLG [2018a])

6000 were rented at social rents (MHCLG 2018d). The scarcity of new homes in the social sector, combined with the home loss through the Right to Buy and market sales, has meant that, between 2007/2008 and 2017/2018 new social lettings declined by 15% in England (MHCLG 2018e).

Stigmatising 'Social' Housing

Stigmatising low-income households has a long history. In the nineteenth century those with the lowest-incomes were labelled the 'residuum'—their homes called 'plague spots'; 'rookeries'; 'slums' and 'the Labyrinth'.

In the late nineteenth century, the Eugenics Education Society augmented stigma by associating poverty with inherited intelligence: in the words of the Anglican hymn, 'God had made the poor lowly and had ordered their estate'. Before the 1930s, when local government built for 'general needs', council housing was 'aspirational' (Boughton 2018). However, when the programme was switched to clearance, stigmatisation was applied. Eugenic influence remained influential in the inter-war period with, in 1930, churchman Dean Inge opposing help to the poor as 'subsidising the teeming birth rate of the slums' (quoted in Soloway 1995, p. 214) and *Pringle* (1929) argued that slum inhabitants took their mentality into council housing. In their pursuit of a 'property-owning democracy' the Conservative Party and the building societies constantly emphasised homeownership virtues implying that renters, especially subsidised council tenants, were second class citizens.

Stigmatising council tenants in the 1950s and 1960s became more difficult because the sector housed a fairly representative sector of the population and the subsidised, 'dependent' critique could be countered by pointing the homeowners' tax relief on mortgage interest. However, as the consequences of high-rise and other modernist building forms became apparent, local authority housing started to have an image problem. The tendency for council 'estates' to become the places where low-income households lived was magnified from the 1980s and the better quality houses were sold under the Right to Buy.

Corralling low-income households into geographically defined 'estates' made it easier to shame social tenants. Hanley (2007) said 'You only have to say the word "estates" for someone to infer a vast amount from it….It's a bruise in the form of a word'.

The term 'social' housing started to enter the housing lexicon in the early 1990s, gaining impetus when John Major abandoned Thatcher's policy of moving all rents to market levels. Rather than being categorised—alongside private landlords—as part of the 'independent' sector (Department of the Environment 1987), housing associations were bracketed with local authorities as social housing. New Labour embraced the term social housing to encourage stock transfer to housing associations and also introduced regulations to align local authority and housing association rents by a formula setting rents in both sectors. Although intended to reduce the 'spoiled identity' linked to living in a council house, blurring the distinction between council and housing association housing did little to mitigate stigma. 'Social' has warm nuances linked to 'community', 'shared' and 'togetherness' but, like 'welfare' it also has negative tones associated with dependency. When asked the question in a Fabian Society poll (Fabian Society 2014) 'which two or three words do you associate with 'social housing"? 49% answered 'benefits' (53% owner-occupiers, 50% private tenants and 29% social tenants).

Picking up on the negative tone surrounding the term 'welfare', the coalition government adopted a restrictive welfare definition, akin to the US interpretation. According to Laws (2016, p. 97):

> George Osborne saw 'welfare' as a big political dividing line. He wanted Labour to be seen as the party of 'welfare scroungers', and he hoped that the Conservatives could position themselves as the party of the strivers

Stereotyping council tenants intensified in the media with television programmes—*Shameless* and *Benefits Street* for example—adding to newspaper headlines such as 'Unrepentant father-of-eight immigrant who turned down a 'too small' five-bed council house defends his life on hand-outs' (*Daily Mail* 2016) and 'Turkish pensioner who blagged a council house and £170 k in benefits jailed' (Sun 2017).

Conservative politicians promoted the stigma. The Centre for Social Justice—a think tank co-founded in 2004 by Iain Duncan Smith and Tim Montgomerie—Iain Duncan Smith claimed 'The levels of dependency among social housing renters is quite staggering … This is not a situation that will resolve itself. How can we expect different from those who never see anything different?' (Duncan Smith 2008, p. 5). When Secretary of State for Work and Pensions, Duncan Smith redefined poverty away from relative income measures towards a series of indicators including exam results and whether parents are in work (Duncan Smith 2015; *Telegraph* 2015). New Labour was not immune from promoting stigma. Caroline Flint, then Minister for Housing, wanted new tenants to sign 'commitment contracts' to actively seek work when obtaining a tenancy as a way to counter the culture of 'no one works around here' (Flint 2008, quoted in Wintour 2008). However, as the Chartered Institute of Housing (2018) has pointed out: 43% of social housing tenants are working; only 8% are registered unemployed; 28% of tenants are retired and 17% are registered as disabled with almost 50% of all households reporting at least one member of the household as experiencing a long-term illness or disability.

Investment in the Existing Housing Stock

In the middle 1980s Margaret Thatcher's government announced that homeowners 'must carry the primary responsibility for keeping their property in good repair' (Department of the Environment 1985). State help, directed to maintaining and improving the existing housing stock was made more selective and resources were cut. New Labour prolonged this policy in the private sector although it targeted more resources to upgrading social housing. State capital and human resources aimed at home improvement continued to decline under the post-2010 Conservative-led governments. Most of the state resources spent on upgrading homes have been directed to improving energy efficiency but, in recent years, progress has stalled (Elmhurst Energy 2017). Given that residential property contributes 17% of all greenhouse gas emissions and higher energy efficiency reduces household bills this hiatus in progress is disappointing. Private sector investment, stimulated by increases in house prices, has helped to upgrade the existing stock but has also produced a shift in the tenure structure and higher rents (see Chapter 6).

Demographic Change

Total population increase relative to houses built is charted in Fig. 2.2. Figure 2.3 sets out the natural increase and net migration contributions to population change.

From 1979 to the early 2000s, despite a sharp fall in new housing output, population growth was lower than new house construction. Although there was a change in the age structure leading to higher household formation—more people in the 65+ age group and a tendency for young people and couples experiencing relationship breakdown to form separate households—the demographic trend provided an opportunity for housing conditions to improve. Larger house sub-division into flats added to accommodation availability. From 1981 to 2001, the people who bought their local authority homes under the

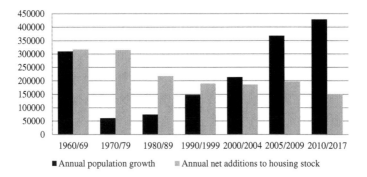

Fig. 2.2 Population growth per annum and annual increase in new dwellings: UK 1960–2017 (selected time intervals) (*Notes* In the 1960s and 1970s slum clearance reduced the dwelling stock, but, although some of the demolished dwellings might have been capable of improvement, most were grossly unfit for human habitation; New dwelling supply was supplemented by conversions) (*Sources* ONS [2017b]; MHCLG [2018a])

Right to Buy would not have moved so the Right to Buy did not make an immediate impact on new social housing lettings but, as new social housing completions declined and homes were lost via the Right to Buy, new social lettings started to decline; down from 370,000 in 1995/1996 to 251,999 in 2007/2008 (Stephens et al. 2018).

Housing amenity availability improved between 1981 and 2001. In 1981 twelve million dwellings lacked central heating but this was down to five million by 2001. Overcrowding, as measured by the bedroom standard, waned, reaching 2.4% in 2001. Trends recorded by home-lessness statistics reflect legislative changes and central guidance to local government on implementing this legislation but the number of house-holds living in temporary accommodation declined in the early and middle 1990s. Indeed, by 2001, the abatement in the housing problem in some areas was sufficient for New Labour to identify 'low demand'—mainly along the M62 corridor—and introduce the Housing Market Pathfinders Initiative.

However, as can be seen from Fig. 2.3, under New Labour's watch the demographics changed. The net migration increase started in 1998 when more asylum seekers started to arrive in the UK but accelerated in 2004 when ten countries joined the EU. New Labour anticipated only

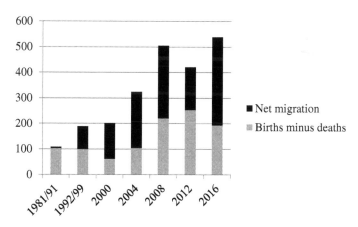

Fig. 2.3 Population change: UK 1981–2016 (000s): net migration and births minus deaths (selected time intervals) (*Note* The 1981/1991 and 1992–1999 figures are annual averages) (*Sources* Beaumont [2011]; ONS [2017a, b])

a modest increase in net migration—between 5000 and 13,000—from the new EU member states (Watt and Wintour 2015) and the UK was one of only three member states, alongside Sweden and Ireland, to open its labour market to these new EU citizens immediately.

Post 2004 natural increase (births minus deaths) gathered momentum as did net migration. In 2003 EU net migration contributed 15,000 to UK population growth and net migration from outside the EU 224,000 but, by 2007, the figures were 127,000 (EU) and 204,000 (non EU). During the recession both EU and non-EU net migration fell from the 2007 highpoint but by 2015 EU net migration had climbed to 184,000 and non-EU migration to 189,000 (Migration Observatory at the University of Oxford 2018). In 2017, net migration started to fall reaching 283,000 in a year to December 2017, mainly due to a reduction in net migration from the EU (ONS 2018). Migration has been unevenly distributed across the UK with Hawkins (2018) recording that, in 2015, 25.7% of London's population was born outside the UK in non-EU countries and 10.8% in EU countries compared to 3.6% (non-EU) and 1.9% (EU) in the North East.

The impact of migration on house prices is disputed. In an interview published in the *Sunday Times* (2018), the Housing Minister at the time—Dominic Raab—claimed that, between 1991 and 2016, immigration had pushed house prices up by 20%. In response to demands for data to support this claim, the MHCLG (2018f) released *Analysis of the Determinants of House Price Changes*. On the basis of an econometric model used by the National Housing Planning Advice Unit (2007) that estimated the relationship between housing supply and affordability through the interplay of demographic trends, incomes, the labour market and the housing market, the MHCLG report concluded that between 1991 and 2016 total population growth, translated into household growth increased real house prices by 32% (£17,000) of which 21% could be attributed to international migration. Income increases pushed house prices up by 150% (£80,000) and the increase in housing supply reduced prices by 21%. Of course, these estimates are influenced by the validity of the model used and the time spans under examination. Using household growth is questionable because housing supply influences household formation (see Chapter 5) and the time span in the analysis includes a long period when net migration was low. Starting in 2003 would have produced different outcomes. Exploration of the regional and area variations in house prices in relationship to the interplay of demographic trends, incomes and the labour market would have refined the analysis.

Shriver (2018) has attributed the housing crisis to 'mass migration' arguing that 'Oxford demographer David Coleman estimates that 85% of the UK's population increase from 2000 to 2015 is explained by migrants and their children' and that 'the housing crunch is further complicated by the fact that so many immigrants settle in the southeast, where residential shortages are keenest'.

However, migration is a 'soft target' as a cause of housing crises. The Migration Advisory Committee (2018, p. 3) stated:

> Our analysis suggests that migration has increased house prices. The impacts of migration on house prices cannot, however, be seen in isolation from other government policies. The evidence points towards a higher impact of migration in areas with more restrictive planning policies in which it is harder for the housing stock to increase in line with demand.

Government failure to increase housing overall supply, the reduction in social housing availability and the reliance on private landlords charging market rents, to meet housing demand from migrants (most without a vote in Parliamentary elections) were the primary contributions to the housing crises experienced by people lacking economic power.

Planning

The 1909 Housing and Planning Act gave local authorities the power, but not the duty, to plan future development and 1932 Town and Country Planning Act extended these powers although very few local authorities used the legislation because they had to pay compensation if planning permission was refused. Lack of planning control assisted suburban development but building on greenfield sites encountered mounting resistance. The Council for the Preservation of Rural England was set up in 1926, with Patrick Abercrombie as its Honorary Secretary, to enlist rural interest groups in campaigning for green belts. Clough William-Ellis (1928, p. 3) asserted that suburbia was an 'octopus strangling England' and a 'Beast' destroying the countryside (William-Ellis 1937). There was a 'high brow' disdain for suburbia and its inhabitants. Leading architects condemned suburban homes as 'Mock Tudor' and in *Coming Up for Air* in 1939, George Orwell was disgusted by the same 'long, long rows of little semi-detached houses And, God! The dreadful things that dwell within'. This fear of suburbia was reflected in the 1935 Restriction of Ribbon Development Act, a modest response to the campaign to stall urban growth that makes new building within 220 feet of classified roads subject to planning control. It was justified as protecting 'natural beauty' (Hore-Belisha 1935) and coincided with the move to build flats for slum inhabitants in inner cities.

Although primarily an attempt to protect the interests of established residents in rural areas there was a socialist element in the call to contain urban growth linked to the desire to plan, to ensure that development gain was retained by the community and to supply a 'green lung' for urban dwellers. Indeed, the first UK green belt was devised by Herbert Morrison, Labour London County Council Leader in the late 1930s. The Greater London Plan, 1944, prepared by Sir Patrick Abercrombie, included a 'Green Belt Ring' intended to stop speculative developers and councils building more houses (Grindrod 2017).

The 1947 Housing and Town Planning Act took development rights into public ownership. Henceforth, all new developments required permission from the designated local planning authority. Post 1968 permissions were to be granted according to structure plans produced by county authorities in conjunction with districts. Unitary authorities produced a single plan. Structure plans were alleged to be rationally compiled documents, looking forward up to 20 years and showing future land use, transport and environmental proposals. In fact, plan production process was in constant flux. Structure plans took years to prepare and, if ever complete, were out of date. Local plans were in a similar state of instability. This meant that granting specific planning permissions was usually an 'ad hoc' decision.

Sharp, Middle-Class Elbows

Local authorities had little to gain in granting planning permission with the extra rates (later council tax) meagre in relationship to government grants that balanced needs and resources. Politically they had much to lose. The 1971 Town and Country Planning introduced public participation into the planning process. Labour was sceptical about such public involvement in planning: according to Shapely (2014, p. viii), 'Many, including [Harold] Wilson, felt that only a few interfering members of the middle class, who were hostile to Labour, really wanted participation'.

The 1971 Town and Country Planning Act coincided with homeownership becoming the majority tenure and sparked a 'vicious circle between homeownership and housing supply' (Ortalo-Magné and Prat 2007, p. 4). Whitehead et al. (2015) list the potential costs of new residential development to 'established' homeowner households as:

- loss of amenity which not only reduces individual welfare but may also reduce property values;
- pressure on local services;
- pressure on infrastructure, causing congestion, pollution, and road safety issues;
- adverse consequences of ill-designed buildings that fail to foster community, these include social as well as economic and environment costs all of which can reduce property values and most directly; and
- additional supply may generate lower house prices reducing wellbeing among those already living in the neighbourhood.

The list of potential benefits included:

- the provision of more and better housing to accommodate additional households;
- the possibility of increased property values if new development is well designed and complements existing housing;
- the possibility that development brings in new infrastructure;

- longer term improvements in affordability across the housing market; and
- additional spending and investment in local shops and services.

Despite the list of benefits, they are long-term, uncertain and general with part of the Community Infrastructure Levy (CIL)—allowing local authorities to obtain a general payment from developers in return for planning permission—paid to local communities not individuals. The costs are immediate and individually experienced. Successfully opposing a new development is a win/win for homeowners.

A poll by the Policy Exchange (2018) found that 49% of respondents said that nationally too few homes were being built but this fell to 31% when asked if too few houses were being built in their neighbourhoods and opposition to new development is likely to increase when a scheme is proposed for the immediate vicinity.

Each planning application requires specific consideration by the planning authority, when vociferous local objections can crowd out the more general benefits. Individual ward councillors worry about the electoral backlash approval could provoke and may seek alliances with other councillors promising support for refusal should a planning application be made in their wards. An application for a large development may affect many wards and a political party's attitude to development, accumulated over time, may be important in influencing general as well as local elections. The Liberal Party, later the Liberal Democrat Party, used 'community politics' as a means to secure political power. Formally adopted by the Liberal Party in 1970 (Meadowcroft 2012) and coordinated through the Association of Liberal Councillors, 'community politics' targeted wards and neighbourhoods via its *Focus* newsletters, usually opposing planning applications. NIMBY—not in my backyard—entered the media lexicon to which David Cameron, in housebuilding mood in 2006, added 'BANANA—Build Absolutely Nothing Anywhere Near Anyone' (Cameron 2006, quoted in *Telegraph* 2006).

New Labour, under the 2004 Planning and Compulsory Purchase Act, abolished county structure plans replacing them with Regional Spatial Strategies, prepared by Regional Development Agencies consisting of civil servants and co-opted members. Regional Spatial Strategies encountered the same problems as structure plans. Local opposition and long delays in preparation were supplemented by regional strategies being ignored by local planning authorities when preparing their local development plans.

'Middle England'

Cameron's support for new building evaporated when he fought for the 'middle England' vote in the 2010 General Election campaign. Both the Conservatives and the Liberal Democrats opposed Regional Spatial Strategies and, in their 2010 manifestos, promised to return planning decisions to elected local authorities, a policy set out in detail in *Open Source Planning* (Conservative Party 2010). This commitment was confirmed in the coalition government's *Our programme for government* (HM Government 2010) and implemented in the 2011 Localism Act. However, HM Treasury, worried about a stagnant economy and a sharp fall in planned housebuilding, provoked a rethink. Although a somewhat diluted version of the original proposals published in the *Draft National Planning Framework* (DCLG 2011) the *National Planning Framework* (DCLG 2012a) contained robust measures to promote land release: a requirement on local authorities to produce up to date local plans with a rolling programme of specific, deliverable sites that had to approved by the National Planning Inspectorate. In the absence of a 'fit for purpose' plan planning applications there should be a 'presumption in favour of sustainable development' when planning applications were considered. For a short time government policy became pro-development and Nick Boles, a passionate development advocate, was appointed as planning minister. However, as the 2015 General Election approached and with Conservative MPs, faced with a UKIP challenge, objecting to new building in their backyards, the Conservative Party leadership modified its stance. Boles was sacked from his Planning Minister post, having been asked to apologise for losing Tory seats (*Telegraph* 2014). Little pressure was applied to local authorities to produce an up to date plan and Eric Pickles, then Secretary of State for

Communities and Local Government, blocked the production of 9200 homes in the run up to the General Election (*Inside Housing* 2015).

The long-run price responsiveness of supply to demand is low in the UK compared to other countries (Sánchez and Johansson 2011). Cheshire and Sheppard (1989) have demonstrated how planning restraints have restricted new house production and Hilber and Vermeulen (2015, p. 400), in their conclusion to a study of supply constraints on house prices, state:

> Our findings point to the English planning system as an important causal factor behind the crisis. Moreover, recent studies have suggested that regulatory constraints have become more binding over the last few decades.

The planning system has also contributed to land price increases. Postwar Labour governments—following Lloyd George's futile land tax idea—tried to tax the 'betterment' accruing from land price hikes but with little success (Tichelar 2018), the principal drawback being the ability of landowners to delay selling until a future Conservative government abolished the taxes.

Conclusion

The slow-burning fuses—always generating housing crises for many working class people—started to ignite in the mid-2000s. The UK population increased rapidly after 2004 and the long-term demise in new house construction by local government was not replaced by housing associations as state housing support to producers was reduced and resources switched to means-tested consumer subsidies in the form of HB. New house construction became the unchallenged speculative private housebuilder's domain with the market increasingly dominated by the larger building firms—morphing into a near monopoly—with few incentives to promote efficiency and design improvements. The planning system severely restricted new housebuilding especially in high-demand areas. Finance came from a more competitive mortgage market producing irresponsible lending that fuelled house prices.

The long-term dearth in new house construction was accompanied by a marked tenure shift. Between 2004 and 2017 home ownership declined and social housing as a per cent of the housing stock fell from 18.5 to 16.8, a decline accompanied by more aggressive stigmatisation. 2.6 million extra households rented from private landlords.

Private landlordism is now characterised by high rents and low security, with, at the lower end of the market, 'rogue' landlords letting sub-standard properties and hindering quiet home enjoyment. As the social sector has declined, its share of low-income households has increased and tenants have been subject to stereotyping as subsidised, dependent and lazy. Some commentators linked the 2017 Grenfell Tower fire tragedy to entrenched attitudes to social housing (Abbott 2017; *Guardian* 2017b) and, after the fire, Theresa May said 'For too long in our country, under governments of both colours, we simply have not given enough attention to social housing' (May 2017).

All the slow-burning fuses are related to ways that housing has been subjected to financialisation and privatisation. The housing crisis is not a crisis for all which partially explains why it exists. There have been gains for the 'rentiers' living off existing assets: established property and landowners, banks and the 'exchange' organisations operating the system.

References

Abbott, D. (2017, June 26). Hundreds Died in the Grenfell Tower Fire, Says Shadow Home Secretary, Diane Abbott: The MP for Hackney North and Stoke Newington Also Blames the Disaster on Tory Attitudes Towards Social Housing. *Independent*. http://www.independent.co.uk/news/uk/politics/grenfell-tower-fire-diane-abbott-victims-number-hundreds-labour-shadow-home-secretary-a7806106.html.

Apps, P. (2018). Government Breaks Promise on Right to Buy Replacements. *Inside Housing*, 28 March 2017. https://www.insidehousing.co.uk/news/government-breaks-promise-on-right-to-buy-replacements-55559.

Archer, T. (2017). *Why Are the Major Housebuilders Growing Revenues Faster Than Output?* https://twitter.com/tomhousing?t=1&cn=ZmxleGlibGVf

cmVjcw%3D%3D&refsrc=email&iid=6f76ec2d76854b1e823521f40e-0fa917&uid=728533290110603264&nid=244+272699403.

Archer, T., & Cole, I. (2016). *Profit Before Volume? Major Housebuilders and the Crisis of Supply.* Sheffield: Sheffield Hallam University. https://www4.shu.ac.uk/research/cresr/sites/shu.ac.uk/files/profits-before-volume-housebuilders-crisis-hous.

BBC News. (2017, April 29). *MPs Say "Dominance" of Big Home-Building Firms Must End.* https://www.bbc.co.uk/news/business-39752869.

Beaumont, J. (2011). Population. In J. Beaumont (Ed.), *Social Trends 41.* London: Office for National Statistics.

Bellman, H. (1927). *The Building Society Movement.* London: Methuen.

Birch, J. (2013, April 10). Taking the Strain. *Inside Housing.* https://www.insidehousing.co.uk/home/home/taking-the-strain3-35246.

Boughton, J. (2018). *Municipal Dreams: The Rise and Fall of Council Housing.* London: Verso.

Bowley, M. (1946). *Housing and the State 1919–1944.* London: Allen & Unwin.

Brummer, A. (2008). *The Crunch: The Scandal of Northern Rock and the Escalating Credit Crisis.* London: Random House Business.

Chadwick, E. (1842). *Report on the Sanitary Condition of the Labouring Population of Great Britain.* London: HMSO.

Chartered Institute of Housing. (2018). *Rethinking Social Housing: Final Report.* Coventry: Chartered Institute of Housing. http://www.cih.org/Rethinkingsocialhousing.

Cheshire, P., & Sheppard, S. (1989). British Planning Policy and Access to Housing: Some Empirical Estimates. *Urban Studies, 26*(5), 469–485. http://journals.sagepub.com/doi/abs/10.1080/00420988920080541?journalCode=usja.

Chevin, D. (2013). *Social Hearted, Commercially Minded: A Report on Tomorrow's Housing Associations.* London: The Smith Institute. http://www.smith-institute.org.uk/book/social-hearted-commercially-minded-a-report-on-tomorrows-housing-associations/.

Conservative Party. (2010). *Open Source Planning Green Paper.* London: Conservative Party. https://issuu.com/conservatives/docs/opensourceplanning.

Cowan, D., McDermont, M., & Morgan, K. (2007). *'Problematic Nominations': Final Report.* School of Law, University of Bristol, in Partnership with Shelter, the Local Government Association and the National Housing Federation.

Crook, A. D. H., & Kemp, P. A. (2018, June 17). In Search of Profit: Housing Association Investment in Private Rental Housing. *Housing Studies*. https:// www.tandfonline.com/doi/abs/10.1080/02673037.2018.1468419? journalCode=chos20.

Daily Mail. (2016, February 18). The Rise of Millionaire's Row: Could House Prices Really Double to £560k by 2030 and the Number of £1m Homes Triple? http://www.dailymail.co.uk/property/article-3451304/How-higher-house-prices-New-report-claims-values-double-560K-2030-number-homes-worth-1m-triple.html.

DCLG. (2011). *Draft National Planning Policy Framework*. London: DCLG. https://www.gov.uk/government/consultations/draft-national-planning-policy-framework.

DCLG. (2012a). *National Planning Policy Framework*. London: DCLG. https://www.gov.uk/government/publications/national-planning-policy-framework-2.

DCLG. (2017). *Fixing Our Broken Housing Market* (Cm 9352). London: DCLG. https://assets.publishing.service.gov.uk/government/uploads/system/uploads/attachment_data/file/590464/Fixing_our_broken_housing_market_-_print_ready_version.pdf.

Department of the Environment. (1977). *Housing Policy Review: Technical Volume Part 111*. London: Department of the Environment.

Department of the Environment. (1985). *Home Improvement: A New Approach* (Cmnd 9513). London: HMSO.

Department of the Environment. (1987). *Housing: The Government's Proposals* (Cm 214). London: Department of the Environment.

Disraeli, B. (1872). *Speech of B. Disraeli at the Free Trade Hall, Manchester, April 3, 1872*. Bristol Pamphlets: University of Bristol. https://history-atwoodlands.wikispaces.com/file/view/Speech+of+B.+Disraeli+at+the+Free+Trade+Hall%252c+Manchester%252c+April+3%252c+1872.pdf.

Duncan Smith, I. (2008). Foreword. In *Breakthrough Britain: Housing Poverty, from Social Breakdown to Social Mobility*. London: Centre for Social Justice.

Duncan Smith, I. (2015). *Government to Strengthen Child Poverty Measure*. London: Department of Work and Pensions. https://www.gov.uk/ government/news/government-to-strengthen-child-poverty-measure.

Dunleavy, P. (1981). *The Politics of Mass Housing in Britain: A Study of Corporate Power and Professional Influence in the Welfare State*. Oxford: Clarendon Press.

DWP. (2018). *Benefit Expenditure and Caseload Tables 2018*. London: DWP. https://www.gov.uk/government/publications/benefit-expenditure-and-caseload-tables-2018.

Elmhurst Energy. (2017). *The Energy Efficiency of English Homes Has Stalled*. London: Elmhurst Energy. https://www.elmhurstenergy.co.uk/the-energy-efficiency-of-english-homes-has-stalled.

Fabian Society. (2014). *Silent Majority: How the Public Will Support a New Wave of Social Housing*. London: Fabian Society. https://fabians.org.uk/publication/silent-majority/.

Forrest, R., & Murie, A. (1983). Residualisation and Council Housing: Aspects of the Changing Social Relations of Housing Tenure. *Journal of Social Policy, 12*(4), 453–468.

Green, S. (1979). *Rachman*. London: Michael Joseph.

Grindrod, J. (2017). *Outskirts: Living Life on the Edge of the Green Belt*. London: Sceptre.

Guardian. (2017a, February 24). Losses of £58bn Since the 2008 Bailout—How Did RBS Get Here? https://www.theguardian.com/business/2017/feb/24/90bn-in-bills-since-2008-how-did-rbs-get-here-financial-crisis-.

Guardian. (2017b, June 25). Grenfell Tower Tragedy Shows Social Housing System Has Failed UK Citizens. https://www.theguardian.com/politics/queens-speech.

Guardian. (2018, June 13). Fury as Housing Associations Redevelop and Sell Affordable Homes. https://www.theguardian.com/society/2018/jun/13/fury-affordable-homes-redeveloped-sold-housing-associations.

Guild of Residential Landlords. (2015). *HMRC Upset About Landlord Tax Avoidance and Offers Easy Payments*. http://www.landlordsguild.com/hmrc-upset-about-landlord-tax-avoidance-and-offers-easy-payments/.

Hanley, L. (2007). *Estates: An Intimate History*. London: Granta.

Hawkins, O. (2018). *Migration Statistics* (Briefing Paper No. SN06077). London: House of Commons. http://researchbriefings.parliament.uk/ResearchBriefing/Summary/SN06077.

Haws, G. (1900). *No Room to Live: The Plaint of Overcrowded London*. London: Wells Gardner, Darton and Co.

Heywood, A. (2015). *Working Together—Thinking Alike: What Do Councils and Local Enterprise Partnerships Expect from Housing Associations?* London: Smith Institute.

Hilber, C. A. L., & Vermeulen, W. (2015). The Impact of Supply Constraints on House Prices in England. *Economics Journal, 126*(591), 358–405.

HM Government. (2010). *The Coalition: Our Programme for Government*. https://www.gov.uk/government/uploads/system/uploads/attachment_data/file/78977/coalition_programme_for_government.pdf.

Homes and Communities Agency. (2017). *Housing Statistics Tables June 2017*. https://www.gov.uk/government/statistics/housing-statistics-1-april-2016-to-31-march-2017.

Hore-Belisha, L. (1935, June 25). *Restriction of Ribbon Development Bill [Lords.]*. HC Deb vol 303 cc957–1069. http://hansard.millbanksystems.com/commons/1935/jun/25/restriction-of-ribbon-development-bill.

Inside Housing. (2015, April 10). Pickles Blocks 9,200 Homes in Build Up to Election. https://www.insidehousing.co.uk/news/news/pickles-blocks-9200-homes-in-build-up-to-election-43297.

Jenkins, S. (2006). *Thatcher & Sons: A Revolution in Three Acts*. London: Allen Lane.

Laws, D. (2016). *Coalition: The Inside Story of the Conservative-Liberal Democrat Coalition Government*. London: Biteback Publishing.

Lewis, J. P. (1965). *Building Cycles and Britain's Growth*. London: Macmillan.

Lloyd George, D. (1918, November 24). *Prime Minister David Lloyd George, Speech in Wolverhampton*. http://ww1centenary.oucs.ox.ac.uk/body-and-mind/lloyd-georges-ministry-men/.

Local Government Association. (2018). *More Than 423,000 Homes with Planning Permission Waiting to Be Built*. London: Local Government Association. http://home.bt.com/news/uk-news/more-than-423000-homes-with-planning-permission-waiting-to-be-built-study-11364250837993.

Lund, B. (2016). *Housing Politics in the United Kingdom: Power Planning and Protest*. Bristol: Policy Press.

May, T. (2017, June 22). *PM Commons Statement on Grenfell Tower*. https://www.gov.uk/government/speeches/pm-commons-statement-on-grenfell-tower-22-june-2017.

Meadowcroft, J. (2012). Community Politics. *Liberal History: The Website of the Liberal Democrat History Group*. http://www.liberalhistory.org.uk/history/community-politics/.

Merrett, S. (1979). *State Housing in Britain*. Abingdon: Routledge & Kegan Paul.

Merrett, S., with Gray, F. (1982). *Owner-Occupation in Britain*. Abingdon: Routledge & Kegan Paul.

MHCLG. (2018a). *Live Tables on House Building: New Build Dwellings*. London: MHCLG. https://www.gov.uk/government/statistical-data-sets/live-tables-on-house-building.

MHCLG. (2018b). *Components of Housing Supply: Net Additional Dwellings: England 2006–7 to 2016–7.* London: MHCLG. https://www.gov.uk/government/statistical-data-sets/live-tables-on-net-supply-of-housing.

MHGLG. (2018c). *Table 120: Components of Housing Supply: Net Additional Dwellings, England 2006/7 to 2017/8.* London: MHGLG. https://www.gov.uk/government/statistical-data-sets/live-tables-on-net-supply-of-housing.

MHCLG. (2018d). *Affordable Housing Supply: April 2017 to March 2018: England.* London: MHGLG. https://assets.publishing.service.gov.uk/government/uploads/system/uploads/attachment_data/file/758389/Affordable_Housing_Supply_2017-18.pdf.

MHCLG. (2018e). *Social Housing Lettings: April 2017 to March 2018.* London, UK: MHCLG. https://assets.publishing.service.gov.uk/government/uploads/system/uploads/attachment_data/file/759738/Social_Housing_Lettings_April2017_to_March2018_England.pdf.

MHCLG. (2018f). *Analysis of the Determinants of House Price Changes.* London: MHCLG. https://assets.publishing.service.gov.uk/government/uploads/system/uploads/attachment_data/file/699846/OFF_SEN_Ad_Hoc_SFR_House_prices_v_PDF.pdf#.

Migration Advisory Committee. (2018). *EEA Migration in the UK: Final Report.* London: Migration Advisory Committee. https://assets.publishing.service.gov.uk/government/uploads/system/uploads/attachment_data/file/740991/Final_EEA_report_to_go_to_WEB.PDF.

Migration Observatory at the University of Oxford. (2018). *Net Migration in the UK.* Oxford: Migration Observatory at the University of Oxford. https://migrationobservatory.ox.ac.uk/resources/briefings/long-term-international-migration-flows-to-and-from-the-uk/.

Milne, A. (2009). *The Fall of the House of Credit: What Went Wrong in Banking and What Can Be Done to Repair the Damage?* Cambridge: Cambridge University Press.

Moyne, W. E. (Chair). (1933). *Report of the Departmental Committee on Housing* (Cmd 4397). London: HMSO. https://www.conservativehome.com/thetorydiary/2016/07/delivering-a-one-nation-housing-policy.html.

Murie, A. (2008). *Moving Homes: The Housing Corporation 1964–2008.* London: Politicos.

National Audit Office. (2017). *Taxpayer Support for UK Banks.* London: National Audit Office. https://www.nao.org.uk/highlights/taxpayer-support-for-uk-banks-faqs/.

National Housing Planning Advice Unit. (2007). *Affordability Matters.* London: National Housing Planning Advice Unit. http://www.wiltshire.

gov.uk/corestrategydocument?directory=Studies%2C%20Surveys%20 and%20Assessments&fileref=3.

ONS. (2017a). *International Migration and the Changing Nature of Housing in England—What Does the Available Evidence Show?* London: Office for National Statistics. https://www.ons.gov.uk/peoplepopulationandcommunity/ populationandmigration/internationalmigration/articles/internationalmigra-tionandthechangingnatureofhousinginenglandwhatdoestheavailableevidence-show/2017-05-25.

ONS. (2017b). *National Population Projections: 2016-Based Statistical Bulletin.* London: Office for National Statistics. https://www.ons.gov.uk/peoplepop-ulationandcommunity/populationandmigration/populationprojections/ bulletins/nationalpopulationprojections/2016basedstatisticalbulletin.

ONS. (2018). *Migration Statistics Quarterly Report: July 2018 (Rescheduled from May 2018).* London: Office for National Statistics. https://www. ons.gov.uk/peoplepopulationandcommunity/populationandmigration/ internationalmigration/bulletins/migrationstatisticsquarterlyreport/ july2018revisedfrommaycoveringtheperiodtodecember2017.

Ortalo-Magné, F., & Prat, A. (2007, January). *The Political Economy of Housing Supply: Homeowners, Workers, and Voters* (Discussion Paper No. TE/2007/514). London School of Economics and Political Science: Suntory-Toyota International Centers for Economics and Related Disciplines. http://citeseerx. ist.psu.edu/viewdoc/download?doi=10.1.1.368.6964&rep=rep1&type=pdf.

Pathé News. (1923). *The Housing Problem By-Election. 1923.* https://www.you-tube.com/watch?v=zhORGbDEGvM.

Policy Exchange. (2018). *Building More, Building Beautiful: How Design and Style Can Unlock the Housing Crisis.* London: Policy Exchange. https://pol-icyexchange.org.uk/wp-content/uploads/2018/06/Building-More-Building-Beautiful.pdf.

Pringle, J. C. (1929). Slums and Eugenics. Review of *The Slum Problem* by B.S. Townroe. *Eugenics Review, 20*(4), 273–274.

Roberts, A. (1999). *Salisbury: Victorian Titan.* London: Phoenix.

Robinson, M. (2018, January 29). *How Much Use Is a Magic Money Tree Anyway?* London: BBC. http://www.bbc.co.uk/news/business-42835758.

Royal Commission on the Housing of the Working Classes. (1885). *Reports, with Minutes of Evidence.* London: HMSO.

Royal Institute of Chartered Surveyors. (2018). *Assessing the Impacts of Extending Permitted Development Rights to Office-to-Residential Change of Use in England.* London: RICS. http://www.rics.org/Global/PDR%20 Research%20trust%20reports/22790%20RICS%20Assessing%20

Impact%20of%20Office-to-Residential%20REPORT-WEB%20(without%20notice).pdf.

Sánchez, A. C., & Johansson, A. (2011). *The Price Responsiveness of Housing Supply in OECD Countries*. Paris: Organisation for Economic Co-Operation and Development. http://www.oecd-ilibrary.org/economics/the-price-responsiveness-of-housing-supply-in-oecd-countries_5kgk9qhrnn33-en?crawler=true.

Scott, J. C. (1999). *Seeing Like a State: How Certain Schemes to Improve the Human Condition Have Failed*. New Haven, CT: Yale University Press.

Scott, P. (2013). *The Making of the Modern British Home: The Suburban Semi and Family Life Between the Wars*. Oxford: Oxford University Press.

Shapely, P. (2014). *People and Planning: Report of the Skeffington Committee on Public Participation in Planning with an Introduction by Peter Shapely*. Abingdon: Routledge.

Shriver, L. (2018, March 17). How Mass Immigration Drives the Housing Crisis: It's the One Reason for This Worsening Problem That Blinkered Liberals Choose to Ignore. *Spectator*. http://archive.is/gH5c4#selection-1463.0-1469.87.

Soloway, R. A. (1995). *Demography and Degeneration: Eugenics and the Declining Birthrate in Twentieth Century Britain*. Chapel Hill: University of North Carolina Press.

Stephens, M., Perry, J., Wilcox, S., Williams, P., & Young, G. (2018). *UK Housing Review 2018*. London: Chartered Institute of Housing.

Sun. (2017, January 31). *Turkish Pensioner Who Blagged a Council House and £170k in Benefits Jailed*. https://www.thesun.co.uk/news/2751315/turkish-pensioner-blagged-council-house-170k-benefits-pretending-scottish-jailed/.

Sunday Times. (2018, April 8). Tory Housing Minister Dominic Raab Warns That Immigration Has Pushed Up House Prices. https://www.thetimes.co.uk/article/tory-housing-minister-dominic-raab-warns-that-immigration-has-pushed-up-house-prices-n27b7lq8j.

Tames, R. (1972). *Economy and Society in Nineteenth Century Britain*. Abingdon, OX: Routledge.

Telegraph. (2006, March 27). Cameron's Housing Plan Signals Fall of the NIMBY. http://www.telegraph.co.uk/news/uknews/1514056/Camerons-housing-plan-signals-fall-of-the-nimby.html.

Telegraph. (2014, May 6). Nick Boles Told to Apologise for "Costing Tories Seats". http://www.telegraph.co.uk/news/earth/greenpolitics/planning/10809862/Nick-Boles-told-to-apologise-for-costing-Tories-seats.html.

Telegraph. (2015, July 1). Child Poverty Definition Changed by Iain Duncan Smith. https://www.telegraph.co.uk/news/politics/conservative/11710995/Child-poverty-definition-changed-by-Iain-Duncan-Smith.html.

Tichelar, M. (2018). *The Failure of Land Reform in Twentieth-Century England: The Triumph of Private Property.* Abingdon: Routledge.

Urban, F. (2011). *Tower and Slab: Histories of Global Mass Housing.* Abingdon: Routledge.

Wall, T. (2018, January 13). Rogue Landlords Making Millions Out of Housing Benefits. *Guardian.* https://www.theguardian.com/money/2018/jan/13/landlords-housing-benefit.

Watt, N., & Wintour, P. (2015, March 24). How Immigration Came to Haunt Labour: The Inside Story. *Guardian.* https://www.theguardian.com/news/2015/mar/24/how-immigration-came-to-haunt-labour-inside-story.

Wellings, F. (2006). *British Housebuilders: History and Analysis.* London: Blackwell.

Whitehead, C., Sagor, E., Edge, A., & Walker, B. (2015). *Understanding the Local Impact of New Residential Development: A Pilot Study, Final Report 2015.* London: London School of Economics. http://eprints.lse.ac.uk/63390/1/Understanding_the_Local_Impact_of_New_Residential_Development.pdf.

Wiles, C. (2018, February 28). Housing Associations' Record Profits Are No Reason to Rejoice. *Guardian.* https://www.theguardian.com/housing-network/2018/feb/28/housing-associations-record-profits-affordable-homes.

Williams-Ellis, C. (1928). *England and the Octopus.* London: Council for the Protection of Rural England.

Williams-Ellis, C. (Ed.). (1937). *Britain and the Beast.* London: J.M. Dent and Sons.

Wilson, W., & Rhodes, C. (2018). *New-Build Housing: Construction Defects— Issues and Solutions* (No. 07665). London: House of Commons. https://researchbriefings.parliament.uk/ResearchBriefing/Summary/CBP-7665.

Wintour, P. (2008, February 5, Tuesday). Labour: If You Want a Council House, Find a Job. *Guardian.* https://www.theguardian.com/politics/2008/feb/05/uk.topstories3.

3

Housing Crises

Entrenched social and economic cleavages have generated diverse housing crises. This chapter examines the class, gender and ethnicity dimensions to these crises whereas Chapter 4 explores the spatial variable. All the dimensions interact but data restrictions make it difficult to identify the relative importance of each variable.

Owner-Occupation: Acquiring; Managing; Using and Transferring

Homeownership decline dominates the current narrative on the age group divide. The Intergenerational Commission (2017, p. 4) has claimed that 'many disparities exist' between the generations but 'none is as acutely felt than the question of housing'. The think tank, *Resolution Foundation*, has made the generation divide its principal research focus. Its Chair, former Conservative cabinet minister, David Willetts (2017) has said that generation rent 'is not voting for a massive transformation of British society; what they're wanting, actually is classic Tory aspirations. It's a property-owning democracy'.

© The Author(s) 2019
B. Lund, *Housing in the United Kingdom*,
https://doi.org/10.1007/978-3-030-04128-1_3

Acquiring

Köppe and Searle (2017) identify four stages in the pathways into and through homeownership: acquiring; managing; using and transferring. Acquiring is about getting on the owner-occupation ladder. The average age at which people became homeowners was 25 in 1969. This had increased to 29 by 1989, falling back to 28 in 1994, but then moving upwards to 32 in 2016 (Rivera and Lee 2016). House prices rises have made a major contribution to homeownership decline amongst young people. Cribb et al. (2018b, p. 2) state:

> Mean house prices were 152% higher in 2015–16 than in 1995–96 after adjusting for inflation. By contrast, the real net family incomes of those aged 25–34 grew by only 22% over the same twenty years. As a result, the average (median) ratio between the average house price in the region where a young adult lives and their annual net family income doubled from 4 to 8, with all of the increase occurring by 2007–08.

However, first-time buyers do not typically buy average priced houses and usually have lower incomes than other purchasers, so a more appropriate affordability indicator is the ratio of lower quartile house prices to lower quartile earnings. In 2002 this was 5.12 for England and Wales, by 2017 it was 7.91 (ONS 2018a), varying, across England from 3.68 to 31.86 (Local Government Association 2018).

Mortgage rates vary in relationship to factors such as fixed or variable, risks as perceived by mortgage lenders and how the Bank of England's views future inflation when setting the base rate. Post-2007, mortgage interest rates were on a downward trend with, for example, fixed five-year mortgages at an average 6.1% in 2007 but 1.99% in 2017 (*Telegraph* 2016; Statista 2018). Since 2009, despite the house price hike in some areas, there has been a tendency for mortgage holders' housing outlays to fall. Belfield et al. (2015, p. 1) state 'On average, real housing costs for owner-occupiers with a mortgage fell by 38% between 2007–2008 and 2012–13....' Nonetheless, owner-occupation amongst younger households continued to decline and deposit size became regarded as the major obstacle. This prompted the coalition government to introduce its Help to Buy scheme. Help to Buy was started in 2013 with two elements. The Mortgage Guarantee took the form of guarantees to lenders with the government accepting some of the risk involved in low deposits from purchasers. It was available for both new build and existing homes with £600,000 maximum purchase price. This initiative was abandoned in December 2016. The Help to Buy Equity Loan was restricted to new-build homes up to £600,000. Under this scheme the buyer was only required to raise 5% of the property value as a deposit with the government offering a further loan of up to 20% in return for an equity share, making a combined deposit of up to 25%. The government loan was interest-free for five years and then 1.5% in the form of a fee, subsequently rising by 1% above inflation.

Although Help to Buy helped to push up house prices for first-time buyers, together with a post-2014 tendency for mortgage lenders to demand lower down-payments, it helped to lower deposits to 16% in 2017 but with large area variations ranging 30–12% (Which 2018).

As discussed in Chapter 1, declining homeownership may not be a concern—the age on becoming a homeowner is higher in other countries such as Germany, USA, Spain and Switzerland. However, in the UK there is a powerful desire to be a homeowner: in 2016, 81% of 25/34-year-olds, 75% of 35/44-year-olds and 80% of 45/54-year-olds wanted to be homeowners in two years and 71% of private renters aspired to homeownership within ten years (Council of Mortgage Lenders 2016). Despite rollercoaster fluctuations, over time house prices have exceeded inflation and, although these gains have often been government induced for electoral reasons, there is much to be said for joining the majority tenure when political parties respond to dominant electoral concerns. Moreover, although private renting does not have to be so insecure, UK private renters have had very limited tenure security since 1989.

English Housing Survey data (DCLG 2017b) demonstrated that it costs more to rent a home than it does to pay a mortgage—on average around £25 week extra. In every age group, renters pay more than homeowners. Buying over a lifetime is far cheaper than lifetime renting—in 2012, Barclay's Mortgage estimated that the *lifetime* rental cost was £200,000 more than owning (Topham 2012)—an issue often ignored in UK/Germany comparisons. According to Eurostat statistics, whereas the per cent of households with a 'housing cost overburden'—total housing costs net of allowances more than 40% of disposable income—paying market rents in Germany is 23.1% compared to 33.2% in the UK, the per cent of the *total* population with a housing cost overburden is 15.9% in Germany compared to 12.1% in the UK, reflecting the UK's higher homeownership rate (Eurostat 2017).

Managing: Staying on and Climbing the Ladder

Stepping on the lower rungs of the owner-occupation ladder is only part of the homeowner issue: 'managing' homeownership—keeping on and climbing the ladder—is important. Mortgage foreclosure pushes people off the ladder. In the early 1990s recession, mortgage repossessions accelerated from 16,000 in 1989 to 75,000 in 1992 (Council of Mortgage Lenders 2016). A similar increase was expected when house prices started to decline in 2008 but, despite the predictions, the 2008 credit crunch did not produce a large increase in UK mortgage foreclosures comparable to 1992. Mortgage foreclosures increased from 26,000 in 2007 to 38,000 in 2010 but were down to 7700 by 2016 (Council of Mortgage Lenders 2017), although in 2017 they started to move upwards. Taking a lesson from US experience—mortgage foreclosures had accelerated the downward spiral in house prices—New Labour acted quickly to prevent a similar climb in the UK. New mortgage rescue schemes were introduced and resources allocated to social housing were brought forward to 'kick-start' the market. Finance was injected into the banking system, the Bank of England reduced its base rate from 5.75% in July 2007 to 0.5% in August 2009 and the money supply was augmented. With some modifications, the coalition government continued New Labour's measures, and the continuing trend for mortgage interest rates to decline has had a major impact on containing mortgage foreclosures. However, repossession is only one reason for movement away from owner-occupation as many people leave voluntarily before formal foreclosure and others, finding it difficult to take the second step on the housing ladder have moved into the private landlord sector.

In 1969 first-time buyers had made their first move up the ladder by the age of 28. This had increased to 34 by 1989 and had reached 39 by 1999 before falling back to 35 in 2009. In 2013 it was 42 (Ideal Home 2013). This significant increase in 'second stepper' age reflects the increasing affordability problems involved in securing extra space when the family increases. Noting that homeowners are now moving half as often as before the 2008 recession, BBC News (2018a) quoted Savills as stating 'Those not trading up are the forgotten people of the housing market....We've concentrated on first-time buyers. They get the concessions and all the focus has been on getting people onto the housing ladder'.

Many first-time buyers have stretched their resources to get onto the first rung of the homeowner ladder and, although their first purchase may produce extra equity if prices have increased, in relative terms it is likely that the larger house they want to buy has increased by more than their present home. Moreover, in many parts of the UK house prices have declined in real terms since 2007 (BBC News 2017) with the homes bought by first-time buyers declining by relatively more than the houses they want to move into thus leaving potential movers short on equity. Lloyds Bank (2018) reported that the average price gap between the existing residence of potential second steppers and the required property to accommodate an expanding family was £135,985, varying from £77,449 in Northern Ireland to £300,599 in Greater London. An average of £85,877 equity in existing homes reduced the standard cost of a move. The problem has been compounded by the Financial Conduct Authority's affordability test that was stepped up after the 'credit crunch' and is now codified in the Financial Conduct Authority's Handbook (Financial Conduct Authority 2018). The test compares income and expenditure (including child care costs that can be high) and involves an assessment of the mortgage applicant's ability to afford possible future interest rate increases.

Mortgage availability also restricts finance for extensions. To acquire extra space, more households with children have had to live in the rented sector, that, although more expensive in the long run, is easier to access and offers the opportunity to claim HB—now called Local Housing Allowance (LHA) when claimed by privately renting tenants—that is unavailable to working owner-occupier households. According to the English Housing Survey, the number of households moving from homeownership each year into the private rented sector (PRS) increased from 129,000 in 2003/2004 to 170,000 in 2013/2014. Hence, homeownership exit has not been caused mainly by mortgage foreclosures but by the inability of couples with children to find suitably sized affordable accommodation in the owner-occupied sector. This problem seemed to abating—in 2015/2016 135,000 homeowners moved into the private landlord sector—but the number increased to 143,000 in 2016/2017 (MHCLG 2018a). Thus whereas, after a long decline, the proportion of younger people becoming homeowners has started to increase—up by 3% for 25–34-year-olds since 2016 (Tomlinson 2018)—potential 'second steppers' are dropping off the owner-occupation ladder.

Generation rent is getting older as private renting moves up the age scale. In 2003/2004, 8.6% of 35/44-year-olds in England were renting privately as were 5% of those aged 45–54 and 4% of those aged 55–64. By 2016/2017 the figures were 28.5 (35/44), 16% (45/54), and 9.6% (55–64) (MHCLG 2018c). By 2017—labelled 'silver renters'—almost half of all UK private renters were aged over 46 (*City A.M.* 2016). In the past, those aged 40–65 would have been securely locked into owner-occupation with about 78% being homeowners in 2001, partially the outcome of Margaret Thatcher's Right to Buy. However, marked differences within the cohort are emerging. In 2015 74% of those aged 60–64 were homeowners but only 60% of those aged 40–44 (Brinded 2016). Projecting the current trend towards private renting produces dire predictions for state spending on HB as renters move into the retirement. The Resolution Foundation (2018) has linked the rise of generation rent to future higher costs to the state. On a 'pessimistic' scenario that economic conditions will not change, it estimates that the cost of HB for pensioners will increase from £6.3 billion per year in 2016 to £16.0 billion per year in 2060. On an 'optimistic' scenario—'a return to economic conditions similar to those that existed when it was a lot easier to purchase one's home'—the HB bill increases from 6.3 billion in 2016 to 12.2 billion to 2060.

Using and Transferring

Unlike renters, homeowners can use the equity in their homes for other purposes. At the house price boom zenith in 2006 equity withdrawal contributed 5.48% to consumer spending but, since 2008, house price falls in many parts of the country plus mortgage holders taking advantage of low-interest rates to pay off mortgage debt has reversed equity release (Stephens et al. 2018). Equity can only be used when house prices have increased and, despite the higher deposits demanded after the 2008 house price crash, an estimated 500,000 UK households were in negative equity in 2014 (BBC News 2014). Negative equity varies according to when a house was purchased and by location. In 2017 the highest negative equity rates were in Northern Ireland, the North East and South Wales (Tatch 2018) but the rollercoaster housing market has now put some London homeowners in jeopardy.

As the 'baby boomers' have reached retirement—often early on final salary schemes—their mortgages have been paid and some are inheriting housing assets from their parents. Moreover, many do not need to tap their housing wealth for day-to-day expenses. Several factors—occupational pension availability, the 'triple lock' on state pensions and free travel—have combined to boost older people's incomes. In 2002/2003, median pensioner income as a percentage of median non-pensioner income was 81%, but it was 101% in 2016/2017 (Cribb et al. 2018a). The Resolution Foundation (2017) estimated that, overall, the median equivalised disposable income of pensioners after housing costs increased by £1500 between 2009 and 2016 whereas the after housing costs incomes of working age people increased by only £200.

Households containing older people are faring much better than in the past. In England, 76% of older (aged 65+) households were owner-occupiers compared with 53% of younger households. Some 62% of older households owned outright compared to 9% of younger households. Older households had a median income of £22,300 after housing costs compared with £19,000 for younger households. Living space for older households is now higher than for younger households. In 1996, average floor area had been similar for older and younger households but, in 2012/2013, it was 95 m² for older people compared to 85 m² for younger people (DCLG 2014). 10% of 25–34-year-olds and 15% of 35–44-year-olds under occupied their homes compared to 32% of 55–64-year-olds and 47% of people over 65 (Gov.uk 2017).

Savills (2018) have estimated that the over 50s hold 75% of housing wealth. In Great Britain, on average, the over 65s owned 1566 billion in housing wealth, those aged 35–49 £701 billion and the under 35s £214 billion. The age gap in housing wealth has been accelerating but it is possible that, in future, wealth inheritance will modify the wealth distribution and put younger people in a better position to become homeowners. Gardiner (2017, p. 4) comments:

> … fast-rising home ownership rates for the baby boomers and the silent generation (born 1926-45) before them mean that, as well as bigger total inheritances each year, a greater share of young people today are likely to benefit from inheritances than did in the past. With home-ownership rates now around 75 per cent among the baby boomers, most millennials might expect to get a share of a parental home eventually.

The ways that wealth cascades through the generations are complicated, depending on such factors as grandparents' willingness to pass on their wealth to their grandchildren rather than their children and equity release use to maintain living standards in old age. Most people retain their housing wealth with children inheriting when the second partner dies (Crawford 2018). According to Gardiner (2017, p. 35), the most common inheritance age is expected to be 61 for people now aged 20–35, a full 30 years after the age at which they will typically start having children' so 'wealth transfers cannot be relied upon to ensure entry into home ownership for many millennials'.

Variations in Old Age

There is a tendency to amalgamate all older people in a 65+ category but 'old age' includes a wide age range and disaggregating the 'old age' category reveals substantial inequality. Although the Gini Coefficient has declined in the working age group, it has increased amongst older people.

Between 2009/2010 and 2015/2016 the Gini Coefficient for retired households moved from 24.3 to 27.1, a reflection of a division between the 'baby boomers', now entering old age, and the cohorts born earlier. Households containing a person retiring in 2015/2016 had an average weekly income after housing costs of £357 but those aged over 75 had an average weekly income after housing costs of £258 (DWP 2017). The per cent of pensioners in absolute poverty after housing costs declined from 33% in 2001/2002 to 15% in 2014/2015 whereas relative poverty declined from 26 to 16% in 2014/2015. However, the relative poverty percentage reached a plateau in 2008/2009 and, post-2013/2014, started to increase, reaching 17% in 2016/2017 (McGuiness 2018a), suggesting that 'baby boomer' generation entering retirement gains are being matched by losses by older people. As might be expected, there is an age-related gradient in wealth and income. At £230,000, households where the oldest person was aged 65–74 had the highest median equity compared with £220,000 for all older people aged over 65. The older the household, the lower the median income with and those aged 85 and over having the lowest median income (DCLG 2016a).

Overall, at 19%, the proportion of non-decent homes inhabited by older and younger households is similar but living in a non-decent home increases within old age reaching 29% for households where the oldest household member is over 85 (DCLG 2016a). As age increases, so does the likelihood that the household contains at least one person with a long-term illness or disability—40% (65–74) and 50% (75–84). Almost two-thirds of households were the oldest person was 85 or over had at least one person in their home with a long-term illness or disability. A lower proportion of older people lived in homes with an energy efficiency rating A-C but a higher proportion (6.5% for those aged over 60 and 3.5% for those under 60) lived in homes rated F-G (MHCLG 2018d).

Independent Age (2018, p. 3) noted:

As social housing has become more inaccessible, many renters, including older renters, have been forced to turn to the private rented sector....An estimated 500,000 older people are privately renting. This is 1 in 10 of all private rented households.

According to the Independent Age report:

- Poverty levels among older private renters are higher than older people in other housing situations. A third of older private renters are living below the poverty threshold after they have paid their rent;
- As many as 4 out of 10 older private renters live in non-decent housing;
- Over a third of people aged 75 and over who required an adaptation to their house didn't have it…;
- Nearly 1 in 3 (32%) private renters felt their accommodation was unsuitable. (Independent Age 2018, p. 5)

Many people in the 'forgotten' generation category live in sheltered accommodation provided by local authorities and housing associations. Levels of decency and energy efficiency are higher in sheltered housing than in other accommodation but about 13% of older people living in sheltered accommodation live in non-decent homes (DCLG 2016a).

Class

One of the few recent studies to link housing with class, Shelter's examination of housing outcomes according to five living home standards—'affordability', 'decent', 'space', 'stability' and 'neighbourhood' (Shelter 2016a, b)—revealed sharp social class cleavages on every standard. As examples, 35% of social class E fell below the affordability standard compared to 18% of social class A and 18% of social class E lacked adequate space compared to 8% in social class A. From the 1920s to the early 1970s there was a robust association between housing tenure and class (see Lund 2017) but homeownership growth and changes in private landlord and social housing sectors have modified this association.

Homeownership and Class

Differentiation and fragmentation in homeownership was identified by Forrest et al. (1990) but contemporary information on the issue in relationship to class is in short supply. Place is an important house price determinant but, unsurprisingly, the type of home in each locality and the space within it also affect house prices. Between 2007 and 2017 detached houses increased in price by 21.7%, semi-detached houses by 22.5%, terraced houses by 18.8% and flats by 15.6% (Zoopla 2017), albeit that these changes were influenced by the housing market in London. Between 2007 and 2015, in the North West, flats declined in price by 19%, terraced by about 10% and semi-detached houses and detached houses by 5% (Nationwide 2017).

Access to homeownership has become more difficult for all social classes since the early 2000s but getting on the homeownership ladder is becoming increasingly class stratified. The class dimension in homeownership access has been demonstrated by Green (2017) (see Chapter 2). Class analysis is sparse in the English Housing Survey publications but the income/tenure examination for 2016/2017 (MHCLG 2018e) showed that less than 4% of mortgagors were in the lowest income quintile and 10% in quintile two whereas 37% were in the top quintile. Cribb et al. (2018b, p. 1) state:

> In 2014–17, 30% of 25- to 34-year-olds whose parents were in a low occupational class (e.g. delivery drivers or sales assistants) owned their home, compared with 43% of those whose parents were in a high occupational class (e.g. lawyers, teachers or estate agents).

Government help has benefited higher earners. Judge's research on Help to Buy found:

> Those who have purchased a property with a HTB equity loan have an income significantly higher than the median – indeed, 40 per cent of HTB loans have gone to those with annual incomes of £50,000-plus. Unsurprisingly, DCLG's own assessment of the policy suggests that 35 per cent of HTB recipients could have bought a home in the absence of the subsidy (albeit perhaps a smaller property or one in a less desirable neighbourhood). (Judge 2017, p. 1)

Help from 'the bank of Mum and Dad' plus the 'Bank of Granddad and Grandma' has become an important factor in this class divide and the class factor in access to higher education compounds the inequality. Wood and Clarke (2018) note:

Our analysis reveals two key findings. The first is that at the age of 30 those without parental property wealth are approximately 60 per cent less likely to be homeowners. Secondly we find that the amount of property wealth your parents have increases the chances that you yourself will become a homeowner. Moving from the median amount of property wealth up to the 75th percentile increases the probability that someone's children will, in a given year, become a homeowner by over 11 per cent. Moving down to the 25th percentile reduces the probability by approximately 7 per cent.

In the future, wealth inheritance will compound the housing class divide. An examination of current inheritance receipts revealed that:

the highest-income fifth of 40-59 year olds inherited nearly three times as much as the bottom 20 per cent did in the two years to 2012-14. The total value of inheritances is set to double over the next two decades, and 'future intergenerational transfers look set to vastly increase absolute wealth gaps between millennials. (Gardiner 2017, pp. 5–6)

Private Renting

Associations between class and private renting are obscured by the relationship between age and tenure. Governments have constantly stressed the 'flexibility' involved in renting privately with ease of access making the tenure suitable for mobile young people. In 2016, 65% of 16–24-year-olds rented privately as did 42% of 25–34-year-olds but the 10% of 16–24 and 39% of 25–34-year-olds in owner-occupation probably reflects the social class divide. 23% of 35–44-year-old householders now rent privately as do 13% of those aged 45–54 (Barton 2017). The figures were 9 and 5% in 2001. The difficulties in securing a home in the owner-occupied sector, suited to family size, and the restrictions on access to social renting has meant that more low-income households are renting privately. Coulter (2016, p. 18) notes:

Although young adults heading all types of families became considerably more reliant on the PRS between 2001 and 2011, this trend was more pronounced for lone parents and couples with routine and manual occupations than for dual-earning couples with "salariat" jobs.

The English Housing Survey (MHCLG 2018f) records satisfaction with private landlord accommodation at 83.6% but expectations can be low and the opinion relates to the property's physical condition not value for money. When asked by the English Housing Survey in 2014/2015 (DCLG 2016b) if their form of tenure was 'a good way of occupying their home', only 53% of private renters agreed, compared 94% of owner-occupiers and 80% of social renters. For most, private renting is not a choice and having to be a private tenant creates discontent. A qualitative study involving in depth interviews with 16 young people (aged 35 and under) living in the PRS who were not in full-time education and who had low to middle incomes revealed that the majority wanted to be home owners with a smaller number aspiring to social housing but 'private renting was regarded as their only option in the short-term due to an inability to realise these goals'. Private renting was discussed 'largely negatively' (McKee and Soaita 2018, p. 3).

The class/income factors influencing access to home ownership are also the drivers that push different income group classes into private renting, especially when children are born. However, the social security system makes a contribution. LHA is not available to homeowners. Thus, low-income households, especially those with children, are steered into renting with LHA offering a degree of protection from income fluctuations. However, this protection is limited with 79.7% of couples with dependent children living in the PRS not claiming HB (MHCLG 2018g). According to figures set out in *Fixing Our Broken Housing Market* (DCLG 2017a) mean private rent payments as a per cent of weekly household income only dropped from 53 to 45% after benefits had been taken into account. A Chartered Institute for Housing analysis found that 90% LHA rates fail to cover the rent of the cheapest 30% of private rented homes (Chartered Institute of Housing 2018).

High private rents have become especially problematic for low-income households with children. Cribb et al. (2018a, p. 37) comment:

In 2002–03, 15% of children living in the poorest 20% of households lived in private rented accommodation, and this figure rose to 36% in 2016–17. This has pushed up average housing costs because private renting is the tenure with the highest housing costs. Mean housing costs among this group of private renters stood at £136 in 2016–17 (£92 net of housing benefit), in comparison to £115 (£53) in 2002–03.

Rhodes (2015) identified a steep location gradient in the increase in private renting growth from 2001 to 2011 with private renting increasing by 37.5% in the least deprived 10% of districts, but by 89.5% in the most deprived 10% of districts. If local authorities are ranked by levels of multiple deprivation, there is a gradient from 13% privately renting in the least deprived local authorities to 21% in the most deprived authorities (Rugg and Rhodes 2018).

In 2016/2017 17% of people living in the PRS (all ages) were in relative poverty before housing costs but this increased to 35% after housing costs. The per cent of children in relative poverty in privately rented accommodation increased from 23% before housing costs to 48% after housing costs (McGuiness 2018b). With 4.8 million people living in the private landlord sector below the relative poverty line in 2015/2016—up from 2.6 million in 2006/2007 (Joseph Rowntree Foundation 2017a)—the *Guardian* (2016) labelled private renting 'the new home of poverty'.

Private renters not only face affordability problems. The PRS is very diverse in terms of conditions and landlord behaviour ranges from cordial to deplorable. Rented homes have to conform to the Housing Health and Safety Rating system but the standard is very low and patchily enforced by local government. The Housing, Communities and Local Government Committee (2018) noted that that Birmingham City Council had only five EHOs to cover a city of 1.1 million people and six out of 10 councils had not prosecuted a single landlord in 2016. 800,000 private rented homes in England have at least one Category One hazard (Housing, Communities and Local Government Committee 2018) and 500,000 children live in a privately rented home that is physically unsafe (New Policy Institute 2016). In 2016, 26.8% of private rented homes were 'non-decent' compared to 19.7% in the owner-occupied sector, 13.6% of local authority homes and 11.9% of the housing association stock (MHCLG 2018h). In 2015–16, 415,000 working-age households in the PRS (36%) were in receipt of HB and living in non-decent homes (Dawes 2018).

The 'quiet enjoyment' of a home depends on security. The 'assured shorthold' tenancy became the norm for new tenants under the 1988 Housing Act and it was made the default tenancy under the 1996 Housing Act. Effectively the tenant has six months tenure security. Whereas most landlords want to retain good tenants, short-term tenancies promote feelings of insecurity. Private renters move ten times more frequently than homeowners (Shelter 2013) with consequences for participation in neighbourhood activities and for 'social capital'—defined by Bourdieu and Wacquant 1992, p. 119) as:

> the sum of the resources, actual or virtual, that accrue to an individual or a group by virtue of possessing a durable network of more or less institutionalized relationships of mutual acquaintance and recognition.

Although length of stay by private tenants is increasing—a quarter of households in private rented accommodation had lived in the sector for between five and nine years and a similar proportion had been there for over a decade (MHCLG 2018i)—frequent movement seriously affects electoral participation Apostolava et al. (2017, p. 13) comment:

> The Electoral Commission notes that in part, lower levels of registration among young people are explained by the fact that young people move house more often, and this has a strong impact on registration.

Repeated moves make voter registration difficult for private tenants with attachment to a particular area—likely to promote election participation—impeded. A high proportion of younger voters are private renters and the Resolution Foundation (2016, p. 12) noted 'first-time eligible turnout has been falling: it was 65 per cent in 1992 but, by 2015, it had dropped to just 46 per cent'. This dearth in private tenant electoral participation extends up the age scale. Voter turnout in elections up to 2015 was 20% above the norm for 'baby boomer' owner-occupiers aged 62 but 32% below the norm for a 46-year-old generation X renters and 37% below the norm for a 30-year-old generation X renters (Resolution Foundation 2016).

Regular flitting has a strong impact on children. Shelter (2013), noting that one-third of private renters had children, stated:

- 1 in 10 renting families (10%) have had to change their children's school due to moving, with moves causing stress and upset for some children;
- Renting families are nine times as likely to have moved in the last year than families who own their homes;
- Nearly three quarters of families (72%) are struggling or falling behind with their rent (compared to 63% of all renters), with many cutting back on essentials to stay in their homes;
- In 2012, 28% of families have not had repairs carried out or poor conditions dealt with by their landlord or letting agent.

Moreover, as Coulter (2016, p. 5) states:

Renting privately can pose extra challenges for families above and beyond the more general issues of constrained affordability and poor dwelling conditions that disproportionately afflict the PRS …Although housing insecurity can be problematic for anyone, the expiry of short contracts or brinkmanship by landlords seeking to raise rents between leases may be especially detrimental for families if this makes it difficult for them to avoid making costly and disruptive residential moves ….

He cites sources such as Oishi and Talhelm (2012) suggesting 'that such mobility can—in some circumstances and especially if it occurs frequently—adversely affect children's educational outcomes, socialization and health' (Coulter, 2016, p. 5). Parents tolerate long commutes, higher rents or a less desirable house so their children can stay in the same school. Moreover, private letting involves direct costs. In addition to a deposit these may include inventory, agreement, reservation and administrative fees plus moving in and out charges that can amount to over £800 in high demand areas. Letting agent fees were banned in Scotland in 2012 and are scheduled to end in England but Generation X's frequent movement in the private landlord sector, each time paying letting agent fees, has helped to undermine the ability of tenants to save for a deposit. Limited tenure security in the private landlord sector impedes tenants in improving their housing conditions due to fear of 'revenge evictions', that is, evictions following complaints about repairs etc. The 2015 Derogation Act gave tenants some protection from such 'revenge evictions' but, as with other measures aimed at rascal landlords, its impact has been limited due to the shortage of local authority officials to enforce the legislation (Tombs 2015; Whitworth 2017). 44% of tenants said a fear of retaliatory eviction would stop them from making a complaint to their landlord and 200,000 tenants reported having been abused or harassed by a landlord (Housing, Communities and Local Government Committee 2018).

Social Renters

Social renting now has a close association with class. Over the past fifty years there has been a powerful trend towards low-income households to become concentrated in social housing. This process, often called 'residualisation' (Forrest and Murie 1983)—an unfortunate term given its association with 'residue' the nineteenth-century term for the 'underclass'—has meant been that, whereas, in 1972, the average income of household heads living in a local authority house was 56.4% of those buying with a mortgage, in 2016 it was 32.5% (Stephens et al. 2018). The average income of household heads living in a housing association home was 35.3% of households buying with a mortgage. Table 3.1 gives household income according to tenure in 2016/2017.

The proportion of households with children in the lowest income distribution quartile (after housing costs) living in social housing declined from 48–36% between 2002/2003 and 2016/2017, the outcome of an increase in the proportion living in the private landlord sector, up from 14% in 2002/2003 to 38% in 2016/2017 (Cribb et al. 2018a).

The historical processes influencing the concentration of low-income households in social housing have been examined in Chapter 2. Cameron's 2015 Conservative government wanted to reinforce the tendency for social housing to become 'welfare' housing. Under the 'pay to stay', policy households with a combined income of £40,000 and above

Table 3.1 Gross weekly income: household reference person and partner by tenure, 2016/2017 (%)

	<£15K	£15K–£30K	£30K–£40K	£40K–£50K	>£50K
Own outright	22.3	35.2	14.1	9.8	18.5
Buying with mortgage	5.1	18.9	17.1	16.7	42.3
Local authority	49.9	38.4	7.7	2.7	1.4
Housing Association	46.8	37.9	9.6	3.2	2.8
Private renter	23.5	37.6	14.6	9.9	14.4

Source MHCLG (2018j)

in London, and £31,000 in the rest of England, would be classified as 'high-income tenants' and have to pay rent increases of 15p for every pound they earned above the high-income thresholds. However, as part of her concern for 'just about managing' families, Theresa May placed this policy on the back burner.

Hills (2014) has highlighted how social classifications based on 'us' and 'them' notions neglect the fluidity involved in giving and receiving through the welfare state over a lifespan. Thus, the notion of a long term, social tenant economic housing interest may be fanciful despite the fact that 58% of tenants currently living in the social sector have lived in their homes for more than ten years (MHCLG 2018k). As Chancellor of the Exchequer, George Osborne attacked social housing as subsidised stating 'social housing is subsidised because the price of private rental stock is the real price, reached by logic of the market' (Osborne 2015). But subsidies to existing homeowners are not gauged according to whether they are paying the current market price for their properties. Moreover, viewed in relationship to historic costs plus maintenance and management charges, local authority tenants, as a group, are not subsidised.

Despite the £42 billion in capital receipts acquired by the Treasury in asset stripping local authority housing, the sector still pays its way. The tangled rules governing local authority housing revenue accounts operations make surpluses and deficits difficult to assess but between 1995/1996 and 2015/2016 the Treasury gained an average of £250 million per year from local authority housing (Stephens et al. 2018). The Localism Act 2011 started a process of redistributing debt between local authorities with the aim of removing the need for revenue subsidies to some local authorities. By 2015, local authority housing had become 'self-financed': no subsidies, no Treasury surplus purloining. However, between 2012 and 2015 the Treasury took £800 million of the £3.5 billion raised in Right to Buy receipts (Apps and Barnes 2017). Given the loss of local authority homes to the private landlord sector and the demolition of council houses to be replaced by expensive housing (Lees 2018), 'accumulation by dispossession' (Harvey 2005) seems an appropriate idea to apply to the process.

Data limitations mean that estimating the subsidy to housing association tenants—now the majority of social tenants—is even more difficult than assessing the subsidy to local authority tenants. Despite extensive stock transfer from local authorities—44% of housing association homes have been acquired from local government—housing association houses are newer than those owned by local government, so housing associations have benefited less from houses built at the low costs obtainable before the house price hikes in the 2000s. However, questions have been raised about the willingness of some housing associations to use their surpluses to benefit low-income families (see Chapter 2). Housing Benefit is distributed on a means-tested basis but, even after this and other benefits had been taken into account, according to *Fixing Our Broken Housing Market* (DCLG 2017a), housing association tenants paid 32% of mean weekly income in housing costs compared to 18% for homeowners.

As demonstrated in Chapter 2, the Conservative Party has a long track record in stigmatising council tenants but, when Cameron was Prime Minister, the stigmatisation intensified. Not only were social tenants condemned as 'subsidised', HB cuts and the ways that Universal Credit is being implemented (National Audit Office 2018) makes it more difficult to pay the rent and, on eviction, tenants have been denounced as 'scroungers' (Cooper and Paton 2017). A few housing associations followed their political masters and adopted the 'conditionality' programmes characteristic of 'welfare' housing in the United States. Yarlington Housing Association's 'household ambition plans' could include, as tenancy conditions, contributing no less than eight hours of community service work per month and requiring tenants to stay fit, quit smoking and look for work (Johnson 2013). The designate

Deputy Chief Executive of a proposed new housing association—a merger of three existing large associations—published *Knuckle Down,* where she stated:

> We have been responsible and are partly to blame for the dependency culture we have created but in future we will be asking our residents to take more personal responsibility in respecting their homes and making an effort to help themselves. (Bailey 2016)

Housing and Inequality

Rising housing costs have augmented inequality in the UK. In 1979, the Gini Coefficient, both before and after housing costs, was 25 but, by 2016, it had reached 35 before housing costs and 39 after housing costs (McGuiness 2018c). Being an overall inequality indicator, the Gini Coefficient can mask differences between the rich and the poor. The P90/10 ratio—the ratio of the ninth decile, that is, the 10% of people with highest income, to that of the poorest first decile;—reveals the rich/poor gap. In 1979, the P90/10 ratio was 3 for both before and after housing costs but, by 2016, it had increased to 3.9 before housing costs and 5.1 after housing costs (McGuiness 2018c).

Housing Wealth and Class

Housing wealth is a potent class inequality indicator. Academic interest in housing wealth intensified following the publication of Piketty's *Capital in the Twenty-First Century* (Piketty 2013) where he claimed that the rate of capital return in developed countries had been persistently greater than the rate of economic growth, and that this trend had caused wealth inequality to increase However, Rognie maintained that Piketty's rising inequality explanation underplayed the role of housing scarcity. He states:

> … the rise in housing's contribution to the capital share can be explained in part as the result of scarcity. The rising real cost of residential investment and the limited quantity of residential land have conspired to make

housing more expensive, and given low elasticities of substitution this has meant a rise in housing's share of income. (Rognlie 2014, p. 51)

According to Savills (2017), UK private housing equity exceeded £5 trillion. Housing equity is closely related to location (see Chapter 4) and the age of the homeowner. Moreover, the expansion in private landlordism has been a 'double whammy' for 'generation rent'. High rents make it difficult to save for a mortgage deposit hence renters lose the opportunity to acquire wealth. Indeed high rents relative to income have meant that more young people—labelled the 'boomerang generation'—are spending more time in the parental home. Tosi (2018, p. 3) states:

> The cost of housing and job insecurity means that, according to the most recent data from the Office for National Statistics, about a quarter of young adults in the UK are living with their parents—the highest number since records began in 1996. The trend is echoed all over Europe.

Research by Tosi and Grundy (2018) revealed that older children living in the parental home negatively influenced the parents' perceptions of well-being.

In the absence of the compulsory registration in England, the total number of landlords is unknown although it has been estimated that 2.3 million adults in England are private landlords (Rugg and Rhodes, 2018). An investigation by Shelter (2016c) revealed that 82% were from social classes ABC, 29% had an annual income of more than £70,000 per year and 20% between £50,000 and £69999. On the ACORN Group classification, private landlords were over-represented in the 'lavish lifestyle', 'executive wealth', 'mature money', 'city sophisticates', 'successful suburbs' categories. 45% had no mortgages. A survey of private landlords by the MHCLG (2019) revealed that landlords received 42% of their total gross income from rental property; the mean estimated value per rental property for all landlords was £261, 900, compared to the £243,600 average house price in England in April 2018 and 48% of landlords had terraced houses in their portfolios, 35% semi-detached houses and 18% detached.

Ownership in the private landlord sector is diverse. Rugg and Rhodes (2018) identify 'episodic' or temporary landlords, often letting as a result life course events; pension plan landlords, seeking income for

retirement and 'portfolio landlords' building up their housing investment. The larger housing associations, local government and institutional investors are moving into the private rented market.

A study by HomeLet (2015) found that 32% of landlords were
aged over 60 whereas 5% of older people rented privately. A survey by
Scanlon and Whitehead (2016) revealed that the landlord median gross
income band, including rental receipts, was £60,000—69,999 with
18% of buy-to-let landlords having an income of more than £100,000
per year. For comparison, at the time, UK median household income
was £25,700. Moreover, the average private landlord property portfolio is increasing with, in 2017, landlords holding £1.3 trillion in net
housing equity—the portion of a home that is owned rather than mortgaged—compared to £1.2 trillion in mortgaged homes with their owners in residence (Savills 2018).

In exploring total wealth—including housing wealth—Atkinson
(2015) concludes that the wealth owned by the UK's top 1% fell by
17% between 1950 and 1975, before increasing by 2% between the
early 1980s and 2000s. He states that although 'we need to be cautious
in drawing conclusions about any upturn in wealth concentration', we
can 'conclude that the trend to less wealth concentration came to an
end' (Atkinson 2015, p. 62). In 2014/2016, UK housing wealth had
increased by 17% since 2012/2014. This was 36% of all UK wealth with
the Gini Coefficient reaching 67 for housing wealth compared to 62 for
total wealth. In 2014/2016, the top decile of housing wealth holders had
£1823 billion and the fifth decile £242 billion (ONS 2018b). The poorest
29% had no or negative housing wealth, the 10th percentile £480,000
and the richest 1% £1,400,000 (National Housing Federation 2018).

Statistics on housing wealth by social class are scarce. Banks and Tetlow
(2008) recorded the mean wealth distribution of people aged over 50.
Excluding pension wealth but including personal wealth such as share
holdings and housing wealth, they found a progression from unskilled
manual workers holding £78,300 to the professional and managerial class
holding £381,700 in personal wealth. Their figures relate to 2006 and the
spatial trends in house prices since the 'credit crunch' are likely to have
magnified these class differences in wealth. The ONS (2018c) classifies
socio-economic position into ten categories with the 23% of the 'Large

employers and higher managerial' category having net property wealth of over £500,000 and the 'Higher Professional' category with 17% having net property wealth of over £500,000. In contrast, only 15% of the semi-routine category and 9% of the routine grouping owned more than £250,000 in net property wealth. In their account of *Social Class in the 21st Century* (2015) Savage et al. identify an 'elite' with large quantities of social and cultural capital plus economic capital from homeownership worth almost double that of the 'established middle class'.

Land

Land value is crucial to the accumulated wealth locked into houses with land yielding 'economic' rent, defined by Ryan-Collins et al. (2016, p. xvii) as: 'Any return derived from the possession of a scare or exclusive factor in production in excess of the cost of bringing it into production' adding that 'since land has no cost of production, any payment given for its use can be considered economic rent'. Land durability makes it a good investment vehicle and its visibility makes it suitable as security for loans.

Numerous economists and philosophers have raised objections to the 'undeserved' benefits acquired by 'rentiers' from landownership.

> The first man, who, having enclosed a piece of ground, bethought himself of saying 'this is mine' and found people simple enough to believe him, was the real founder of civil society …. You are undone if you once forget that the fruits of the earth belong to us all, and the earth itself to nobody. (Jacques Jean Rousseau 1762, p. 84)
> As soon as the land of any country has all become private property, the landlords, like all other men, love to reap where they have never sowed, and demand a rent even for its natural product. (Adam Smith 1776, p. 56)
> Landlords grow richer, as it were in their sleep, without working, risking, or economising. (John Stuart Mill 1848, p. 28)

Residential land prices vary according to location and density (see Chapter 4) but the UK land price trend has been upwards since the early 1930s when land constituted less than 10% of the cost of a new house. A major acceleration occurred in the late 1950s after Duncan Sandys introduced his green belt policy (Gleeson 2017). By the late 1980s real residential land prices were more than four times higher than in the late 1950s before falling back in the middle 1990s recession (Evans and Hartwich 2005). Then there was a twelve-year hike in residential land prices with real prices rising fourfold between 1996 and 2008 (Ryan-Collins et al. 2016). After the 'credit crunch' land prices declined but, since 2010 land prices in London have increased to 20% above their 2007 peak albeit prices were flat in 2018. Although increasing in many parts of the UK, outside London land prices are still below the 2007 maximum. Knoll et al. (2015) estimated that, between 1950 and 2012, 74% of house price increase could be attributed to changes in land prices. In England, residential land value per hectare was estimated at £6,900,000 (Kent Business Intelligence Statistical Bulletin 2016). At 32 'addresses per hectare', the current density in England, the average plot cost is £215,625. Residential densities in elevated land cost areas such as London are much higher than the England average. In 2015/2016 'addresses per hectare' ranged from 71 to 140 in inner London (DCLG 2017c) with very high densities in tower block flats balancing the low-density mansions. The New Economics Foundation has linked high land prices to the dearth of affordable housing. Land speculators, having acquired land at high prices, resist requirements to provide social housing on the sites so:

> The top 10% of local authorities in terms of land prices experienced a 70% drop in the numbers of new affordable/social rent homes between 2011/2012 and 2014/2015. This compares to a drop of 20% in the rest of England. (New Economics Foundation 2018, p. 2)

An investigation of the land market by the Institute for Public Policy Research Commission on Social Justice (IPPRCSJ 2018a, pp. 2–3) stated:

> The broken land market is the driving force behind England's broken housing market. In 1995, the price paid for a home was almost evenly

split between the value of the land and the property. In 2016, the cost of the land had risen to over 70 per cent of the price paid for a home.... The land value uplift that arose from the awarding of planning permission in 2014/2015 was £12.4 billion, but the combined receipts captured by development measures were less than a quarter of that at £2.7 billion. It is estimated that the amount lost could accumulate to £185 billion over the next two decades.

The Institute for Public Policy Research Commission on Social Justice (IPPRCSJ) (2018b, p. 196) has drawn attention to a 'negative feedback loop' in which 'the high cost of land is driven by the shortage of homes, but as land prices rise it becomes more expensive to build, thus driving prices up further'.

In 2017, land owned by UK households was worth £4.1 trillion and land owned by other landowners was worth £1.3 trillion. The ONS (2018d) noted:

UK net worth more than trebled between 1995 and 2017, but much of this was from growth in the value of land. Land accounts for 51% of the UK's net worth in 2016, higher than any other measured G7 country.

Land Ownership

There is no comprehensive land ownership inventory in the UK: a testimony to the landowners' political power. The blog 'Who Owns England?' offers sketchy information revealing for example, that 50 companies, including water utilities, mining corporations, aristocratic estates and offshore companies own over a million acres of England and Wales but such statistics tell us little about the value of the land and its development potential. The banks with secured mortgages own a large slice of UK land and 34% of UK households are outright houseowners—mainly over 65—giving them a substantial share of land value. As Mount (2005, p. 65) has commented, the planning system manages land prices in 'the way De Beers keeps up the price of diamonds, by controlling the supply and releasing gems onto the market in carefully calculated batches so that the price is never in danger of collapse'.

Gender

Changing domestic relationships makes it difficult to disentangle the impact of gender on housing pathways across the life cycle but examining housing outcomes when a man is absent from the household, such as single women with or without children and older women whose male partner has died, helps in understanding the gender variable.

Younger Single Women (Without Children)

Access to homeownership now mainly depends on two incomes. The English Housing Survey 2014/2015 (DCLG 2016c, p. 1) commented:

> The proportion of first-time buyers that were single households halved from 29% in 1994-95 to 14% in 2014-15. Therefore, 80% of all first-time buyers were couple households, a marked change since 1994-95 (63%) and 2004-05 (62%). This may be due to an increasing need for two incomes to be able to buy.

The gender pay gap (see Chapter 1) permeates differences between single men and single women in homeownership access. Calculations by the Resolution Foundation (2017) revealed that the current gender pay gap between men and women increases with age. For example, by the age of 42, the gender pay gap for the generation born between 1966 and 1980 is 27% compared to 5% for men and women in their 20s (Inman and Walker 2017). By examining the relationship between pay for men and women and house prices, Emoove (2017) found that the average affordability gap between men and women in acquiring a home had fallen from 15% in 2006 to 12% in 2016.

Single Parents

Single parenthood starkly reveals the gender pay gap and partner dependency. The long-term social housing shortage, the credit crunch, subsequent recession and government austerity measures have had disproportionate impact on single parents. This is revealed in the homelessness figures. In 2017 30,000 single parents were made homeless—up 8% on the 2012 figure (BBC News 2018b). The Joseph Rowntree Foundation referred to 'the lone parent penalty', noting:

> Nearly half of children in lone-parent families live in poverty (49%) compared with one in four of those in couple families (25%). This disparity has increased over the last five years; poverty rates for children in lone-parent families have risen by around twice as much as those for children in couple families….Higher poverty among lone parents is driven by their disproportionate concentration in low-paid work, the high cost of housing (due to needing the same size home as couple parents) and cuts to benefits and tax credits. (Joseph Rowntree Foundation 2018, p. 5)

In 2012, 66% of single parents were in the two lowest income quintiles *before* housing costs compared to 40% for couples with children. The proportion increased to 71% for single parents *after* housing costs but reduced to 24% for couples with children (Culliney et al. 2014), a reflection of the homeowner/renting divide. Although single parents remain disproportionately represented in the social housing sector there has been a rapid increase in single parents renting from private landlords that has increased poverty after housing costs amongst single-parent households. Tables 3.2 and 3.3 set out the housing tenure of lone parents and couple households in 2008/2009 and 2015/2016.

Older Women

In 2014/2015, 21% of people aged over 85 were in relative poverty, compared to 14% of 75–84-year-olds and 12% of 65–74-year-olds. Whereas the proportion in poverty amongst those aged below 84 has reduced substantially since 2004/2005, it has remained static for the 85 plus group where women predominate with, in 2016/2017, 17% of people aged 85+ below the poverty threshold (Age UK 2014, 2018). Amongst all pensioners, poverty rates were highest for single women and private renters (Age UK 2018). The Joseph Rowntree Foundation (2018, p. 5) noted:

Table 3.2 Tenure: households with dependent children 2008/2009 (%)

	Single parents	Couples
Own outright	6.8	9.4
With mortgage	26.8	65.8
Private renter	22	11.8
Social housing	44.4	13

Source MHCLG (2018b)

Table 3.3 Tenure: households with dependent children 2015/2016 (%)

	Single parents	Couples
Own outright	5.8	9.6
With mortgage	19.3	55.8
Private renter	35.9	21.8
Social housing	39	12.8

Source MHCLG (2018b)

Poverty among pensioners in the private rented sector is now 36% (up from 27% in 2007/08). For social renters, poverty has risen from 20% to 31% since 2012/13. Eligible rent – the amount that Housing Benefit will cover – has been falling behind actual rents paid by low-income pensioners due to changes in the rules governing eligible rents since 2010/11... Of the 330,000 additional pensioners in poverty since 2012/13, 60,000 are private renters and 130,000 are social renters.

The 2011 Census recorded 407,000 men and 847,000 women aged 85 or older. There were 150,000 men and 474,000 women aged 85 or over living alone. Statistics on the housing conditions of those aged over 85 are sparse because this age group are usually placed in the broad 'over 65' category. At 10%, households where the oldest person was aged 85 years or over were most likely to live in the homes with the lowest efficiency bands F and G (DCLG 2016a).

Ethnic Minorities

Tenure divisions according to selected ethnicities are recorded in Table 3.4.

Table 3.4 Tenure by ethnicity

	% Homeowners	% Private renters	% Social housing
White British	68	16	16
Bangladeshi	39	19	42
Indian	68	25	7
Pakistani	64	26	11
Black African	21	31	48
Black Caribbean	39	17	45

Source Gov.uk (2017)

There has been a marked change in ethnic minority housing tenure since 1991. Finney and Harries (2013, p. 1) note:

> Increased private renting and decreased home ownership between 1991 and 2011 was a common experience across ethnic groups' with the fall in home ownership proportionately greatest for the Pakistani (-18%), Chinese (-17%) and Indian (-16%) groups and least for the White and Bangladeshi groups (-3% each).

41% of foreign born UK residents live in the PRS compared to 15% of UK born inhabitants (Migration Observatory at the University of Oxford 2017). The high proportion of established ethnic minorities housed in the private landlord sector is, in part, the outcome of the difficulties in accessing owner-occupation related to the economic positions of some ethnic minorities. The Cabinet Office (Gov.uk 2017), in setting out the economic circumstances of ethnic minorities, included:

- In 2016, just over 4% of White people were unemployed, which is lower than the rate of unemployment for people from all Other ethnic groups;
- the 'employment rate gap'—the difference between the employment rate for the whole population and that for all ethnic minorities (other than White ethnic minorities)—has decreased over time, from 15 percentage points in 2004 to 10 percentage points in 2016;
- Other ethnic and Black households were the most likely to have a weekly income of less than £400;

- In the last 3 months of 2016, the average hourly pay for White employees was £13.75, whilst the average hourly pay for employees from other ethnic groups was £13.18.

The proportion of households with children below the relative poverty line before and after housing costs in three out of the last four years up to 2015/2016 according to ethnicity is given in Table 3.5. The Gov.uk figures use broad categories but other data indicates that Bangladeshi households experience the highest before and after housing costs (Joseph Rowntree Foundation 2017b).

Although the private landlord sector is important to ethnic minorities in securing accommodation there are barriers to such access. There is a long history of racial discrimination by private landlords (Lund 2017) and, although much reduced, the Joint Council for the Welfare of Immigrants (2017) found contemporary evidence of its existence. Policies aimed at restricting illegal migrants' access to housing may also create barriers for migrants. The 2014 Immigration Act, for example, requires landlords in England to check new tenants' right to be in the UK before granting a tenancy and the Joint Council for the Welfare of Immigrants (2017) found that 42% of the landlords it surveyed said that, because of the scheme, they were less likely to rent to anyone without a British passport.

Ethnic minority housing disadvantage is reflected in other statistics. A selection is given in Table 3.6.

Table 3.5 Poverty: households with children 2015/2016: before and after housing costs (ethnicity)

	Before housing costs	After housing costs
White British	10	15
Asian	25	31
Black	20	22
Mixed	11	15

Source (Gov.uk 2017)

Table 3.6 Ethnic minority housing conditions

	% Homeless[1,2]	% Overcrowded	% Non-decent homes	Damp problems
White British	59	2	19	4
Bangladeshi	9.5	30	17	6
Indian	9.5	8	19	3
Pakistani	9.5	15	29	11
Black African	17	15	20	12
Black Caribbean	17	8	19	6

Source (Gov.uk 2017)
Notes
[1]Homeless refers to households that local authorities have a duty to find accommodation
[2]The figures relate to the per cent in each category of the total number of homeless households. The homeless statistics use 'Asian', 'Black', 'Mixed', 'White', 'Other' and 'Unknown'. In the above table 'Asian' is Bangladeshi, Indian and Pakistani, 'Black' is Black African and Black Caribbean and 'White' is White British. The information is taken from a Cabinet Office website that supplies information on other minorities such as the Chinese community and contains other facts and figures on housing and ethnicity

Conclusion

Examining the housing crisis by how it is experienced by different demographic and socio-economic groups demonstrates how the broad category, 'generation rent', masks other variables in housing circumstances. Generation rent is becoming more diverse as renters progress through the life span and exploring gender highlights the increasingly difficult housing situations faced by single-parent families as more and more are forced into renting from private landlords. The ethnicity variable permeates housing disadvantage via discrimination albeit that settlement patterns and length of residence in the UK influences outcomes. Social housing tenants have been subject to higher rents and increasing stigma. Class, under-researched in housing outcome analysis, but important in the 2016 European Union referendum and the 2017 General Election (see Chapter 8) pervades housing outcomes with land ownership the most important factor in class inequality.

References

Age UK. (2014). *Age UK: Evidence Review: Poverty in Later Life*. London: Age UK. http://www.futureyears.org.uk/uploads/files/Age%20UK%20on%20poverty%20in%20old%20age.pdf.

Age UK. (2018). *Poverty in Later Life*. London: Age UK. https://www.ageuk.org.uk/globalassets/age-uk/documents/reports-and-publications/reports-and-briefings/money-matters/rb_apr18_poverty_in_later_life.

Apostolava, V., Uberoi, E., & Johnston, N. (2017, April 26). *Political Disengagement in the UK: Who Is Disengaged?* (House of Commons Briefing Paper No. CBP7501). http://dera.ioe.ac.uk/29007/1/CBP-7501.pdf.

Apps, P., & Barnes, S. (2017, March 2). Barwell Under Pressure Over £800m Right to Buy Receipts Kept by Treasury. *Inside Housing*. https://www.inside-housing.co.uk/news/news/barwell-under-pressure-over-800m-right-to-buy-receipts-kept-by-treasury-49992.

Atkinson, A. B. (2015). *Inequality: What Can Be Done?* Cambridge, MA: Harvard University Press.

Bailey, E. (2016, February 6). Knuckle Down. *Inside Housing*.

Banks, J., & Tetlow, G. (2008). *The Distribution of Wealth in the Population Aged 50 and Over in England* (IFS Briefing Note BN86). London: Institute for Fiscal Studies. https://www.ifs.org.uk/bns/bn86.pdf.

BBC News. (2014). *Negative Equity Afflicts "Half a Million Households"*. https://www.bbc.co.uk/news/business-26389009.

BBC News. (2017, October 17). *Are House Prices Back from the Crash?* http://www.bbc.co.uk/news/business-41582755.

BBC News. (2018a, March 28). *Almost 30,000 Lone Parent Families Made Homeless in England in 2017*. https://www.bbc.co.uk/news/education-43503102.

BBC News. (2018b). *Moving Home Is "Becoming a Rarity"*. http://www.bbc.co.uk/news/business-43541990.

Belfield, C., Chandler, D., & Joyce, R. (2015). *Housing: Trends in Prices, Costs and Tenure* (IFS Briefing Note BN161). London: Institute for Fiscal Studies. https://www.ifs.org.uk/publications/7593.

Bourdieu, P., & Wacquant, L. (1992). *An Invitation to Reflexive Sociology*. Cambridge: Polity Press.

Brinded, L. (2016, April 27). *Britain Is Crashing into the End of the Homeownership Era*. http://uk.businessinsider.com/resolution-foundation-uk-property-prices-housing-ownership-and-income-research-2016-4.

Chartered Institute for Housing. (2018). *Benefit Freeze Puts Private Renting Out of Reach for Low-Income Tenants and Risks Fuelling Homelessness.* Coventry: Chartered Institute of Housing. http://www.cih.org/news-article/display/vpathDCR/templatedata/cih/news-article/data/Benefit_freeze_puts_private_renting_out_of_reach_for_low-income_tenants_and_risks_fuelling_homelessness.

City A.M. (2016, September 28). Opinion: The Private Rented Sector Needs to Be Vibrant and Consistent Enough to Cater for a Wide Range of Needs. http://www.cityam.com/250326/opinion-private-rented-sector-needs-vibrant-and-consistent.

Cooper, V., & Paton, K. (2017). The New Urban Frontier of Everyday Evictions: Contemporary State Practices of Revanchism. In A. Abel & B. Núria (Eds.), *Gentrification as a Global Strategy: Neil Smith and Beyond* (pp. 142–151). London: Routledge.

Coulter, R. (2016). Social Disparities in Private Renting Amongst Young Families in England and Wales, 2001–2011. *Housing Theory and Society, 34*(3), 297–322. http://www.tandfonline.com/doi/full/10.1080/14036096.2016.1242511.

Council of Mortgage Lenders. (2016). *Homeownership or Bust?* London: Council of Mortgage Lenders. https://www.cml.org.uk/.../home-ownership-or-bust/20161017-home-ownership-or-b.

Council of Mortgage Lenders. (2017). *Arrears and Possessions.* London: Council for Mortgage Lenders. https://www.cml.org.uk/policy/policy-updates/all/arrears-and-possessions/.

Crawford, R. (2018). *The Use of Wealth in Retirement* (IFS Briefing Note BN237). London: Institute for Fiscal Studies. https://www.ifs.org.uk/uploads/publications/bns/BN237.pdf.

Cribb, J., Keiller, A. N., & Waters, T. (2018a). *Living Standards, Poverty and Inequality in the UK: 2018.* London: Institute for Fiscal Studies.

Cribb, J., Hood, A., & Hoyle, J. (2018b). *The Decline of Homeownership Among Young Adults* (IFS Briefing Note BN224). London: Institute for Fiscal Studies. https://www.ifs.org.uk/publications/10505.

Culliney, M., Haux, T., & McKay, S. (2014). *Family Structure and Poverty in the UK: Report to the Joseph Rowntree Foundation.* Lincoln: University of Lincoln. http://eprints.lincoln.ac.uk/14958/1/Family_structure_report_Lincoln.pdf.

Dawes, M. (2018). *Working Age Housing Benefit and Non-decent Homes in the Private Rented Sector 2015–16.* London: MHCLG. https://www.

parliament.uk/documents/commons-committees/public-accounts/ Correspondence/2017-19/mhclg-gcgp-housing-300118.pdf.

DCLG. (2014). *English Housing Survey Profile of English Housing 2013.* London: DCLG. https://assets.publishing.service.gov.uk/government/ uploads/system/uploads/attachment_data/file/445370/EHS_Profile_of_ English_housing_2013.pdf.

DCLG. (2016a). *English Housing Survey Housing for Older People Report, 2014–15.* London: DCLG. https://assets.publishing.service.gov.uk/government/uploads/system/uploads/attachment_data/file/539002/Housing_for_ Older_People_Full_Report.pdf.

DCLG. (2016b). *2014-Based Household Projections in England, 2014 to 2039.* London: DCLG. https://www.gov.uk/government/ statistics/2014-based-household-projections-in-england-2014-to-2039.

DCLG. (2016c). *New Homes Bonus: Sharpening the Incentive Government Response to the Consultation.* London: DCLG. https://assets.publishing. service.gov.uk/government/uploads/system/uploads/attachment_data/ file/577904/NHB_Consultation_Response_Doc.pdf.

DCLG. (2017a). *Fixing Our Broken Housing Market* (Cm 9352). London: DCLG. https://assets.publishing.service.gov.uk/government/uploads/system/ uploads/attachment_data/file/590464/Fixing_our_broken_housing_market_-_print_ready_version.pdf.

DCLG. (2017b). *English Housing Survey Housing Costs and Affordability, 2015–16.* https://assets.publishing.service.gov.uk/government/uploads/system/ uploads/attachment_data/file/627683/Housing_Cost_and_Affordability_ Report_2015-16.pdf.

DCLG. (2017c). *Planning for the Right Homes in the Right Places: Consultation Proposals.* London: DCLG. https://www.gov.uk/government/consultations/ planning-for-the-right-homes-in-the-right-places-consultation-proposals.

Department for Work and Pensions (DWP). (2017). *Pensioners' Incomes Series: Financial Year 2015/16.* https://www.gov.uk/government/uploads/ system/uploads/attachment_data/file/600594/pensioners-incomes-series-2015-16-report.pdf.

EMoov. (2017). *The Gender Property Gap: Male Mortgage Affordability 15% Higher Over the Last 10 Years.* https://www.emoov.co.uk/news/2017/09/15/ gender-property-gap-male-mortgage-affordability-15-higher-last-10-years/.

Eurostat. (2017). *Housing Cost Overburden Rate by Tenure Status.* http:// ec.europa.eu/eurostat/tgm/refreshTableAction.do?tab=table& plugin=1&pcode=tessi164&language=en.

Evans, A. W., & Hartwich, O. M. (2005). *Bigger Better Faster More: Why Some Countries Plan Better Than Others*. London: Localis. https://www.localis.org.uk/wp-content/uploads/2005/06/Evans-A.W-Hartwich-O.M-Bigger-Better-Faster-More.pdf.

Financial Conduct Authority. (2018). *FCA Handbook*. London: Financial Conduct Authority. https://www.handbook.fca.org.uk/.

Finney, N., & Harries, B. (2013). *Understanding Ethnic Inequalities in Housing: Analysis of the 2011 Census*. London: Race Equality Foundation. www.raceequalityfoundation.org.uk/resources/downloads/understanding-ethnic-inequalities-housing-analysis-2011-census.

Forrest, R., & Murie, A. (1983). Residualisation and Council Housing: Aspects of the Changing Social Relations of Housing Tenure. *Journal of Social Policy, 12*(4), 453–468.

Forrest, R., Murie, A., & Williams, P. (1990). *Home Ownership Transition: Differentiation and Fragmentation*. Abingdon: Routledge.

Gardiner, L. (2017). *The Million Dollar Be-Question: Inheritances, Gifts and Their Implications for Generational Living Standards*. London: Resolution Foundation. https://www.resolutionfoundation.org/publications/the-million-dollar-be-question-inheritances-gifts-and-their-implications-for-generational-living-standards/.

Gleeson, J. (2017). *Historical Housing and Land Values in the UK*. https://jamesjgleeson.wordpress.com/2017/04/03/historical-housing-and-land-values-in-the-uk/.

Gov.uk. (2017). *Ethnicity Facts and Figures*. https://www.ethnicity-facts-figures.service.gov.uk/.

Green, A. (2017). *The Crisis for Young People: Why Housing Is the Key to Social Mobility*. https://ioelondonblog.wordpress.com/2017/07/04/the-crisis-for-young-people-why-housing-is-the-key-to-social-mobility/.

Guardian. (2016, July 20). Private Rental Sector Is the "New Home of Poverty" in the UK. https://www.theguardian.com/housing-network/2016/jul/20/private-rental-sector-poverty-housing-joseph-rowntree.

Harvey, D. (2005). *The New Imperialism*. Oxford: Oxford University Press.

Hills, J. (2014). *Good Times, Bad Times: The Welfare Myth of Them and Us*. Bristol: Policy Press.

HomeLet. (2015). *Landlord Survey 2015*. https://homelet.co.uk/homelet-rental-index/landlord-survey-2015.

House of Commons Housing, Communities and Local Government Committee. (2018). *Private Rented Sector: Fourth Report of Session 2017–19 Report, Together with Formal Minutes*. London: House of Commons.

https://publications.parliament.uk/pa/cm201719/cmselect/cmcom-loc/440/440.pdf.

Ideal Home. (2013). *Want to Buy Your Second Home? You'll Have to Wait Until You're 42.* http://www.idealhome.co.uk/news/second-time-buyers-42184.99.

Independent Age. (2018). *Unsuitable, Insecure and Substandard Homes: The Barriers Faced by Older Private Renters.* London: Independent Age. https://www.independentage.org/unsuitable-insecure-and-substandard-homes-barriers-faced-by-older-private-renters.

Inman, P., & Walker, P. (2017, January 4). Gender Pay Gap Down to 5% Among UK Workers in Their 20s, Study Finds. *Guardian.* https://www.theguardian.com/society/2017/jan/04/gender-pay-gap-down-to-5-among-uk-workers-in-their-20s-study-finds.

Institute for Public Policy Research Commission on Social Justice. (2018a). *The Invisible Land: The Hidden Force Driving the UK's Unequal Economy and Broken Housing Market.* London: Institute for Public Policy Research. https://www.ippr.org/research/publications/the-invisible-land.

Institute for Public Policy Research Commission on Social Justice. (2018b). *Prosperity and Justice; A Plan for the New Economy: The Final Report of the IPPR Commission on Economic Justice.* London: Institute for Public Policy Research. https://www.ippr.org/files/2018-08/1535639099_prosperity-and-justice-ippr-2018.pdf.

Intergenerational Commission. (2017, September). *Home Affront: Housing Across the Generations.* London: Intergenerational Commission. http://www.resolutionfoundation.org/publications/home-affront-housing-across-the-generations/.

Johnson, A. (2013, April 26). Social Housing Residents Told to Sign "Ambition" Plan as Part of Tenancies. *Independent.* http://www.independent.co.uk/news/uk/politics/social-housing-residents-told-to-sign-ambition-plan-as-part-of-tenancies-8590713.html.

Joint Council for the Welfare of Immigrants. (2017). *Passport Please: The Impact of Right to Rent Checks on Migrants and Ethnic Minorities in Britain.* London: Joint Council for the Welfare of Immigrants. https://www.jcwi.org.uk/sites/jcwi/files/201702/2017_02_13_JCWI%20Report_Passport%20Please.pdf.

Joseph Rowntree Foundation. (2017a). *Numbers in Poverty: Housing Tenure.* York: Joseph Rowntree Foundation. https://www.jrf.org.uk/data/numbers-poverty-housing-tenure.

Joseph Rowntree Foundation. (2017b). *Poverty Rate by Ethnicity*. York: Joseph Rowntree Foundation. https://www.jrf.org.uk/report/poverty-ethnicity-labour-market.

Joseph Rowntree Foundation. (2018). *UK Poverty 2018: A Comprehensive Analysis of Poverty Trends and Figures*. York: Joseph Rowntree Foundation. https://www.jrf.org.uk/report/uk-poverty-2018.

Judge, L. (2017). *Helping or Hindering? The Latest on Help to Buy*. London: Resolution Foundation. http://www.resolutionfoundation.org/media/blog/helping-or-hindering-the-latest-on-help-to-buy/.

Kent Business Intelligence Statistical Bulletin. (2016). *Estimated Residential Land Values: Kent Local Authorities as at 1st March 2015*. https://www.kent.gov.uk/__data/assets/pdf_file/0008/53882/Land-prices.pdf.

Knoll, K., Schularick, M., & Steger, T. (2015). *No Price Like Home: Global House Prices, 1870–2012*. http://eh.net/eha/wp-content/uploads/2015/05/Knoll.pdf.

Köppe, S., & Searle, B. A. (2017). Housing, Wealth and Welfare Over the Life Course. In C. Dewilde & R. Ronald (Eds.), *Housing Wealth and Welfare* (pp. 85–107). Cheltenham: Edgar Allen.

Lees, L. (2018, March 16). Challenging the Gentrification of Council Estates in London. *Urban Transformations*. http://www.urbantransformations.ox.ac.uk/blog/2018/challenging-the-gentrification-of-council-estates-in-london/.

Lloyds Bank. (2018). *Equity Gains Help Second Steppers Fund the £136,000 Price Gap to Trade Up*. http://www.lloydsbankinggroup.com/globalassets/documents/media/press-releases/lloyds-bank/2018/030318_lb_ss1.pdf.

Local Government Association. (2018). *Ratio of Lower Quartile House Price to Lower Quartile Gross Annual (Workplace-Based) Earnings in Eilean Siar*. London: Local Government Association. http://lginform.local.gov.uk/reports/lgastandard?mod-area=S12000013&mod-group=AllSingleTier-AndCountyLaInCountry_England&mod-metric=75&mod-type=namedComparisonGroup.

Lund, B. (2017). *Understanding Housing Policy* (3rd ed.). Bristol: Policy Press.

McGuiness, F. (2018a). *Household Incomes by Region* (Briefing Paper No. 8191). London: House of Commons. https://researchbriefings.parliament.uk/ResearchBriefing/Summary/CBP-8191.

McGuiness, F. (2018b). *Poverty in the UK: Statistics* (Briefing Paper No. 7096). London: House of Commons. https://researchbriefings.parliament.uk/ResearchBriefing/Summary/SN07096.

McGuiness, F. (2018c). *Income Inequality in the UK* (Briefing Paper No. 7484). London: House of Commons. https://researchbriefings.parliament.uk/ResearchBriefing/Summary/CBP-7484#fullreport.

McKee, K., & Soaita, A. M. (2018). *The 'Frustrated' Housing Aspirations of Generation Rent.* UK Collaborative Centre for Housing Evidence, University of Glasgow. http://housingevidence.ac.uk/wpcontent/uploads/2018/08/R2018_06_01_Frustrated_Housing_Aspirations_of_Gen_Rent.pdf.

Mill, J. S. (1848). *Principles of Political Economy with Some of Their Applications to Social Philosophy.* http://www.econlib.org/library/Mill/mlP.html.

Ministry of Housing, Communities and Local Government (MHCLG). (2018a). *English Housing Survey 2016 to 2017: Headline Report.* London: MHCLG. https://www.gov.uk/government/statistics/english-housing-survey-2016-to-2017-headline-report.

MHCLG. (2018b). *Affordable Housing Supply: April 2017 to March 2018: England.* London: MHGLG. https://assets.publishing.service.gov.uk/government/uploads/system/uploads/attachment_data/file/758389/Affordable_Housing_Supply_2017-18.pdf.

MHCLG. (2018c). *Tenure Trends and Cross Tenure Analysis.* London: MHCLG. https://www.gov.uk/government/statistical-data-sets/tenure-trends-and-cross-tenure-analysis.

MHCLG. (2018d). *English Housing Survey 2016: Energy Efficiency.* London: MHCLG. https://www.gov.uk/government/statistics/english-housing-survey-2016-energy-efficiency.

MHCLG. (2018e). *English Housing Survey 2016 to 2017: Home Ownership.* London: MHCLG. https://www.gov.uk/government/statistics/english-housing-survey-2016-to-2017-home-ownership.

MHCLG. (2018f). *Attitudes and Satisfaction.* London: MHCLG. https://www.gov.uk/government/statistical-data-sets/attitudes-and-satisfaction.

MHCLG. (2018g). *Social and Private Renters.* London: MHCLG. https://www.gov.uk/government/statistical-data-sets/social-and-private-renters.

MHCLG. (2018h). *Stock of Non-Decent Homes, England 2001–2017.* https://www.gov.uk/government/uploads/system/uploads/attachment.../LT_119.xlsx.

MHCLG. (2018i). *English Housing Survey 2016 to 2017: Private Rented Sector.* London: MHCLG. https://www.gov.uk/government/statistics/english-housing-survey-2016-to-2017-private-rented-sector.

MHCLG. (2018j). *Tenure Trends and Cross Tenure Analysis.* London: MHCLG. https://www.gov.uk/government/statistical-data-sets/tenure-trends-and-cross-tenure-analysis.

MHCLG. (2018k). *Housing Need Assessment.* London: MHCLG. https://www.gov.uk/guidance/housing-and-economic-development-needs-assessments.

MHCLG. (2019). *English Private Landlord Survey 2018: main report—Findings from the English Private Landlord Survey 2018*. London: MHCLG. https://www.gov.uk/government/publications/english-private-landlord-survey-2018-main-report.

Migration Observatory at the University of Oxford. (2017). *Migrants and Housing in the UK: Experiences and Impacts*. Oxford: Migration Observatory at the University of Oxford. https://migrationobservatory.ox.ac.uk/resources/briefings/migrants-and-housing-in-the-uk-experiences-and-impacts/.

Mount, F. (2005). *Mind the Gap: The New Class Divide in Britain*. London: Short Books.

National Audit Office. (2018, June 15). *Rolling Out Universal Credit*. HC 1123 SESSION 2017–2019. London: National Audit Office. https://www.nao.org.uk/report/rolling-out-universal-credit/.

National Housing Federation. (2018). *Demographic Change and Housing Wealth*. https://www.housing.org.uk/resource-library/browse/demographic-change-and-housing-wealth/.

Nationwide. (2017). *House Price Index: By Property Type*. https://www.nationwide.co.uk/about/house-price-index/download-data#xtab:regional-quarterly-series—by-property-age-group-data-available-from-1991-onwards.

New Economics Foundation. (2018). *What Lies Beneath: How to Fix the Broken Land System at the Heart of Our Housing Crisis*. London: New Economics Foundation. https://neweconomics.org/uploads/files/what-lies-beneath.pdf.

New Policy Institute. (2016). *A Nation of Renters: How England Moved from Secure Family Homes Towards Rundown Rentals*. London: New Policy Institute. http://www.npi.org.uk/publications/housing-and-homelessness/nation-renters-how-england-moved-secure-family-homes-towards/.

Oishi, S., & Talhelm, T. (2012). Residential Mobility: What Psychological Research Reveals. *Current Directions in Psychological Science, 21*(1), 425–430. http://journals.sagepub.com/doi/full/10.1177/0963721412460675.

ONS. (2018a). *House Price to Workplace-Based Earnings Ratio*. London: Office for National Statistics. https://www.ons.gov.uk/peoplepopulationandcommunity/housing/datasets/ratioofhousepricetoworkplacebasedearningslowerquartileandmedian.

ONS. (2018b). *Property Wealth: Wealth in Great Britain*. https://www.ons.gov.uk/peoplepopulationandcommunity/personalandhouseholdfinances/incomeandwealth/datasets/propertywealthwealthingreatbritain.

ONS. (2018c). *The National Statistics Socio-Economic Classification (NS-SEC)*. London: Office for National Statistics. https://www.ons.gov.uk/methodology/classificationsandstandards/otherclassifications/thenationalstatisticssocioeconomicclassificationnssecrebasedonsoc2010.

ONS. (2018d). *The UK National Balance Sheet Estimates: 2018.* London: Office for National Statistics. https://www.ons.gov.uk/economy/nationalaccounts/uksectoraccounts/bulletins/nationalbalancesheet/2018.

Osborne, G. (2015). *Chancellor George Osborne's Summer Budget 2015 Speech.* www.gov.uk/government/speeches/chancellor-george-osbornessummer-budget-2015-speech.

Piketty, T. (2013). *Capital in the Twenty-First Century.* Cambridge, MA: The Belknap Press of Harvard University.

Resolution Foundation. (2016). *VOTEY McVOTEFACE: Understanding the Growing Turnout Gap Between the Generations.* London: Resolution Foundation. http://www.resolutionfoundation.org/publications/votey-mcvoteface-understanding-the-growing-turnout-gap-between-the-generations/.

Resolution Foundation. (2017). *Living Standards 2017: The Past, Present and Possible Future of UK Incomes.* London: Resolution Foundation.

Resolution Foundation. (2018). *The Future Fiscal Cost of 'Generation Rent'.* London: Resolution Foundation. http://www.resolutionfoundation.org/media/blog/the-future-fiscal-cost-of-generation-rent/.

Rhodes, D. (2015). The Fall and Rise of the Private Rented Sector in England. *Built Environment, 41*(2), 258–270.

Rivera, L., & Lee, S. (2016). *Average Age of First-Time Buyers Rises to 30 in the UK and 32 in London.* London: Homes and Property. https://www.homesandproperty.co.uk/property-news/buying/first-time-buyers/average-age-of-firsttime-buyers-rises-to-30-in-the-uk-and-32-in-london-a102966.html.

Rognlie, M. (2014, June 15). *A Note on Piketty and Diminishing Returns to Capital.* http://gabriel-zucman.eu/files/teaching/Rognlie14.pdf.

Rousseau, J. J. (1762). *On the Social Contract.* Amsterdam. https://www.ucc.ie/archive/hdsp/Rousseau_contrat-social.pdf.

Rugg, J., & Rhodes, D. (2018). *The Evolving Private Rented Sector: Its Contribution and Potential.* York: Centre for Housing Policy, University of York. http://www.nationwidefoundation.org.uk/wp-content/uploads/2018/09/Private-Rented-Sector-report.pdf.

Ryan-Collins, J., Lloyd, T., & Macfarlane, L. (2016). *Rethinking the Economics of Land and Housing.* London: Zed Books.

Savage, M., Cunningham, N., Devine, F., Friedman, S., Laurison, D., Mckenzie, L., et al. (2015). *Social Class in the 21st Century.* London: Pelican.

Savills. (2017). *Spotlight 2017: Investing to Solve the Housing Crisis.* London: Savills. https://www.savills.co.uk/research_articles/229130/224869-0.

Savills. (2018, April 4). *Over 50s Hold 75% of Housing Wealth, a Total of £2.8 Trillion (£2,800,000,000).* http://www.savills.co.uk/_news/article/72418/239639-0/4/2018/over-50s-hold-75–of-housing-wealth–a-total-of-%C2%A32.8-trillion-(%C2%A32-800-000-000).

Scanlon, K., & Whitehead, C. (2016). *The Profile of Mortgage Lenders.* London: Council of Mortgage Lenders. file:///C:/Users/User/Downloads/the-profile-of-uk-private-landlords-20170118.pdf.

Shelter. (2013). *Growing Up Renting: A Childhood Spent in Private Renting.* London: Shelter. https://england.shelter.org.uk/__data/assets/pdf_file/0005/656708/Growing_up_renting.pdf.

Shelter. (2016a). *The Living Home Standard.* London: Shelter. https://england.shelter.org.uk/__data/assets/pdf_file/0010/1288387/FINAL_Living_home_standard_report.pdf.

Shelter. (2016b). *Living Home Findings.* London: Shelter. https://england.shelter.org.uk/__data/assets/pdf_file/0011/1288388/FINAL_Living_home_standard_Findings_report-insert.pdf.

Shelter. (2016c). *Research Report: Survey of Private Landlords.* London: Shelter. https://england.shelter.org.uk/professional_resources/policy_and_research/policy_library/policy_library_folder/research_report_survey_of_private_landlords.

Smith, A. (1776). *An Inquiry into the Nature and Causes of the Wealth of Nations.* London: W. Strahan and T. Cadell.

Statista. (2018). *Average Interest Rates for Mortgages in the United Kingdom (UK) as of March 2014 and June 2017, by Type of Mortgage.* https://www.statista.com/statistics/386301/uk-average-mortgage-interest-rates/.

Stephens, M., Perry, J., Wilcox, S., Williams, P., & Young, G. (2018). *UK Housing Review 2018.* London: Chartered Institute of Housing.

Tatch, J. (2018). *A Closer Look at Mortgage Arrears and Possessions.* London: UK Finance. https://www.ukfinance.org.uk/a-closer-look-at-mortgage-arrears-and-possessions/.

Telegraph. (2016, February 8). Mortgage Rates Hit Nine-Year Low. http://www.telegraph.co.uk/finance/bank-of-england/12146448/Mortgage-rates-hit-nine-year-low.html.

Tombs, S. (2015). *Social Protection After the Crisis: Regulation Without Enforcement.* Bristol: Policy Press.

Tomlinson, D. (2018). *Home Ownership Is Rising, But the Crisis Is Far from Over.* London: Resolution Foundation. https://www.resolutionfoundation.org/media/blog/home-ownership-is-rising-but-the-crisis-is-far-from-over/.

Topham, G. (2012, June 18). Home Ownership £200,000 Cheaper Than Lifetime of Renting, Study Finds. *Guardian*. https://www.theguardian.com/money/2012/jun/18/home-ownership-cheap; https://www.theguardian.com/money/2012/jun/18/home-ownership-cheaper-renting-studyer-renting-study.

Tosi, M. (2018, March 8). *Parents' Lives Made More Miserable by Boomerang Generation*. http://www.lse.ac.uk/News/Latest-news-from-LSE/2018/03-March-2018/Boomerang-generation.

Tosi, M., & Grundy, E. (2018). Returns Home by Children and Changes in Parents' Well-Being in Europe. *Social Science and Medicine, 200,* 99–106.

Which. (2018). *How Much Deposit Are First-Time Buyers in Your Area Paying? Average First-Time Buyer Deposits Range from £13,700 to £175,000 by Area*. https://www.which.co.uk/news/2018/02/how-much-deposit-are-first-time-buyers-in-your-area-paying/.

Whitworth, D. (2017, February 9). *Revenge Eviction Law Not Working*. BBC News. http://www.bbc.co.uk/newsbeat/article/38795177/revenge-eviction-law-not-working.

Willetts, D. (2017, September 29). Tories Risk Permanent Loss of Youth Vote, Says Willetts. *Guardian*. https://www.theguardian.com/politics/2017/sep/29/tories-risk-permament-loss-of-youth-vote-says-willetts.

Wood, J., & Clarke, S. (2018). *House of the Rising Son (And Daughter): The Impact of Parental Wealth on Their Children's Homeownership*. London: Resolution Foundation. https://www.resolutionfoundation.org/publications/house-of-the-rising-son-or-daughter/.

Zoopla. (2017). *House Prices UK*. http://www.zoopla.co.uk/house-prices/uk/?num_months=240.

4

Location, Location, Location

This chapter scrutinises housing crises according to place. It begins by examining globalisation's impact and then explores variations in housing conditions in the four 'home nations' before analysing regional, district and neighbourhood differences in England and the impact of government policies aimed at tackling housing deprivation on an area basis.

Globalisation

Some commentators attach high significance to the globalisation's growing influence on national housing outcomes. Paris (2017a, p. 66; emphasis original) states:

> It would be absurd to suggest that a fully global system of housing investment, production and consumption has emerged but there has been strong growth of *transnational* housing investment, production and consumption (using transnational as in the Oxford Dictionary: 'extending or operating across national boundaries). Thus, any assumption that housing markets or housing systems are constrained by national boundaries can no longer be considered valid.

© The Author(s) 2019
B. Lund, *Housing in the United Kingdom*,
https://doi.org/10.1007/978-3-030-04128-1_4

Securitisation

The 2008 credit crunch is regarded as the prime example of how globalisation affects national housing systems. Between 2001 and 2007 global house prices increased by 60% (International Monetary Fund 2017) with the USA, Australia, Spain, Ireland and the UK in the house price inflation vanguard. In 2007, the USA housing bubble burst with repercussions in other countries. The main problem was 'securitisation', that us, taking illiquid assets and, via complex financial processes, transforming them into a 'security' to be sold on the global market, thereby transferring debt between nation states (see Chapter 2).

From the late 1980s, the US Central Bank met financial jolts such 9/11 crisis by lowering interest rates. Low-interest rates made property-ownership more appealing and excess demand over supply led to accelerating house prices. This house price boom was fuelled by 'sub-prime' mortgages, encouraged by President Clinton and President Bush to promote the homeownership 'American Dream'. They set goals for 'Fannie Mae' and 'Freddie Mac'—mortgage-buyers under-writing the mortgage industry—that at least 42% of the mortgages they purchased and re-circulated should be targeted on borrowers with a household income below the area median. The 2003 American Dream Downpayment Act granted Federal assistance to finance mortgage deposits to first-time buyers. Mortgage suppliers and banks identified profits to be obtained by fuelling the 'American Dream'. 'Affordability products' were offered with low 'teaser' introductory interest rates followed by a sharp increase. Interest only and 100% mortgages—sometimes more—were made available. Mortgage brokers sold sub-prime mortgages to banks that resold them in packages—often bundled with 'prime' mortgages and given AAA status by the credit rating agencies—on the global financial market. This 'initiate and distribute' strategy meant that the initial mortgage supplier had every incentive not to check the borrower's credit history.

By 2007 sustained house price inflation had pushed up supply and the Federal government's interest rate, at a 1% low-point in 2004, had started to increase. When the 'teaser' rates finished, mortgage foreclosures soared and abandoned houses helped to produce a multiplier effect on prices. The bursting housing bubble prompted an international financial crisis. 'Securitised' mortgages became poisonous and, because banks did not know who owned the flawed debt, they refused to lend to each other producing a 'credit crunch', steep house price falls in many countries and a recession. Yet, some countries did not experience housing booms and busts. Why? In part, the answer can be found in financial management. The Economist's house price index (*Economist* 2017) set at 100 for 2000, showed, by 2007, an increase to 219 in the UK, in the USA to 182, in Spain to 267 and in Ireland to 220. In contrast, the Switzerland index increased to 120 and, in Germany and Japan, prices declined. The highest house price inflation countries were reckless in credit control. The United States' negligence has been recorded above but, under New Labour, UK financial regulation became 'light touch' with interest rates set according to indicators disregarding most housing costs. In the USA, UK, Ireland and Spain securitisation was used extensively (Millán 2014). When the housing bubbles ruptured, prices declined rapidly. The Economist's house price index fell to 190 (UK); 144 (USA) 199 (Spain) and 152 (Ireland). There were particular, 'embedded' reasons why some countries avoided the extreme boom/bust cycle. Germany, for example, kept tight control on credit expansion (Waffel 2008) and its large private rented sector (PRS) helped to restrain a dash for wealth through homeownership. Following the bust, large scale international and national government intervention helped housing markets to recover. By 2015 the index was 264 (UK) and 176 (USA). Spain continued on the downward spiral until 2016 when prices started to increase and, in 2017, the Spanish housing market recorded the highest growth in a decade, with prices rising by 4.47%. In Ireland the market recovery started in 2014 with prices increasing by 7% in 2017 (Global Property Guide 2018).

Real Estate Speculation and the Super Rich

Although technological developments such as Airbnb are making an impact on housing availability driving up real estate prices in global tourism cities, today, globalisation's main impact occurs through real estate speculation and 'super-rich' behaviour. Real estate speculation and 'trophy home' acquisition by the 'super-rich' are connected because they often occur through off-shore companies thereby making transactions difficult to track. Banks, pension and hedge funds, private equity firms and individuals have identified housing in selected cities as a secure haven to park capital. Real estate is traded like gold. This extreme housing financialisation is mainly directed at 'alpha cities', attractive to the rich. Norges Bank (2015, p. 1) stated:

> The main impact of globalisation on real estate has been the growing importance of a relatively small number of 'global cities' with transnational functions and specific real estate requirements. These markets tend to be driven more by global economic factors.

The *Financial Times* (2018) noted the emergence of 'one global city' as house prices in prime city markets across the world were synchronising. Wealth X. (2017) ranked London as the top 'alpha city' followed by New York, Tokyo, Sydney and Paris. In London it has been estimated that 32% of homes in 'prime' London areas are owned by people with non-UK nationalities with 5% purchasing for investment purposes (Wilson and Barton 2017). Christie's International Real Estate (2013) claimed: '… the higher the price of the property, the less likely the buyers to arrange traditional mortgage finance for the home acquisition' with the result that 'Such transactions … never enter "national" accounting systems and play no part in many accounts of aggregate "national" house price trends' (quoted in Paris 2017b, p. 259). According to Sassen (2012, p. 10), the emergence of the international property market 'means that real estate prices in the centre of New York City are more connected to prices in Central London or Frankfurt than to the overall real estate market in New York's metropolitan areas'. Although the super-rich and the investment markets appear to be highly concentrated they have implications for the domestic market with prime sites taken by large houses and expensive apartment blocks, sometimes with empty flats and local authorities finding it difficult to secure affordable homes in the new flat developments (see Chapter 7).

United Kingdom Devolution

Scotland, Wales and Northern Ireland have had varying degrees of de facto and de jure independence in shaping housing policy with, until direct Westminster rule was imposed in 1973, Northern Ireland having the most autonomy. In the years following the formal devolution in the late 1990s, New Labour's dominance in Scottish and Welsh politics generated policy convergence whereas the specific politics of Northern Ireland, punctuated by periods of direct Westminster control, influenced housing policy inputs and outcomes. Post-2010, Conservative-dominated governments have pushed housing policy in England towards a greater reliance on market forces but in Scotland and Wales and, to a lesser extent in Northern Ireland, market forces have been resisted. Indeed, to some commentators, England is now an 'outlier' in housing policy (McKee et al. 2017, p. 60).

Scotland

Before devolution, there were variations in housing policy between England and Scotland, located in different housing conditions, class politics and Scottish identity. This produced divergence in housing outcomes with the local authority housing stock proportion the most marked disparity. In 1979, before UK Right to Buy, 54% of households in Scotland occupied local authority housing but this had declined to 12.3% by 2016. The housing association stock increased from less than 1% in 1979 to 10.8% in 2016. In 2016, 60.7% of homes in Scotland were owner-occupied and 16.1% private rented (Stephens et al. 2018).

Housing was included in the responsibilities transferred to the Scottish Parliament but many of the economic levers necessary to boost housing supply remained at Westminster as did HB policy. Overall spending in Scotland is determined by Westminster via the Barnett formula. In 2016/2017 public spending per person in Scotland, at £13,000 was 16% above the UK average (Keep 2018).

New Labour was dominant in the Scottish Parliament until 2007 when the Scottish National Party acquired control, albeit in a minority administration. It gained an absolute majority in 2011 but, in 2016, fell short by two seats. When New Labour was in control at Westminster and in the Scottish Parliament, housing policy in Scotland—with the exception of homelessness policy—was similar to policy in England. Indeed, in some ways it was less radical. The Right to Buy, for example, was restricted for new social tenants but existing tenants could use the Right to Buy on more generous terms than in England. Stephens et al. (2018) recorded that, in 2010, the average Right to Buy discount was 53% in Scotland but 26% in England and 20% in Wales.

The Scottish National Party (SNP)

The SNP wrapped itself in the Saltire. As Clegg (2016, p. 249) has remarked 'The SNP has skilfully positioned itself as the party that "belongs" to Scotland and that authentic Scottishness "belongs" to it'. Although action has been modest, the SNP has highlighted traditional Scottish concerns on land ownership and in 2017, under the Land Reform (Scotland) Act 2016, the Scottish Land Commission was set up to review law and policy and make recommendations to the Scottish government. There is no private landlord compulsory registration in England but, in Scotland, compulsory registration was introduced in 2006 by New Labour. The SNP has stepped up the regulations on private renting with the Private Housing (Tenancies) (Scotland) Act 2016 allowing local authorities in Scotland to implement rent caps in designated areas where there are unwarranted rent increases and gives tenants greater tenure security. In Scotland, landlords using existing assured tenancies have a duty to provide new tenants with a pack containing information on renting in the private sector.

Since 2007/2008, an average of 3.2 new houses per 1000 population have been supplied—a far better record than in England where, on average, 2.4 per 1000 population have been delivered. Moreover, in Scotland, 0.86 per 1000 population homes were social sector whereas, in England, only 0.48 per 1000 population social housing homes were constructed. Local authority house completions—increasing from only 28 in 2007 to 1125 in 2016 (Stephens et al. 2018)—made a useful contribution to Scotland's total. Relative to population, in Scotland ten times more local authority houses than in England have been built over the last ten years.

Historically, local authority rents have been lower in Scotland than in England and, in 2016, local authority rents absorbed 11.1% of average weekly earnings in Scotland compared to 13% in England with housing association assured rents taking 12.8% of average weekly earnings (13.6% in England). However, although using 'intermediate' rents, Scotland has not adopted the English move to affordable rents at up to 80% of the market rent that, in 2016, were 18.8% of average weekly earnings (Stephens et al. 2018). The approach adopted in Scotland is reflected in poverty as measured before and after housing costs (see Table 4.1).

Although, in the past, Scotland's high local authority housing percentage has minimised the gap between child poverty before and after housing costs—the gap was only 3% in 2003 (Cribb et al. 2018)—but Scotland's before/after housing cost child poverty gap has not increased by as much as in English Regions. For example, the gap in the North East in 2003 was 3%.

Table 4.1 Child poverty: per cent below relative poverty line before and after housing costs 2015/2016

	Child Poverty % BHC	Child Poverty % AHC	Gap %
North East	20	28	8
North West	21	30	9
Yorks and Humberside	22	29	7
East Midlands	21	29	8
West Midlands	23	33	10
East of England	16	25	9
London	17	37	20
South East	13	25	12
South West	17	26	9
Wales	20	30	10
Scotland	17	23	6
Northern Ireland	23	26	3

Source McGuiness (2018)

Scotland's 'Housing Crisis'?

To some, there is a 'housing crisis' in Scotland (BBC News 2016). The housebuilding rate has not recovered to pre 'credit crunch' levels with 6.5 new builds per 1000 households in 2015/2016 compared to 11.1 per 1000 households in 2007/2008. 16209 new houses were built in 2015/2016 but the Commission on Housing and Wellbeing (2015) considered 23,000 new-build houses per annum as necessary. In 2016, 6472 homes at sub-market cost were completed, 60% being 'social' housing, the rest at 'intermediate' rent or for low-cost homeownership. According to Shelter Scotland (2016) about 12,000 affordable houses per annum are required over five years. Yet, despite this 'crisis' narrative, if housing policy outcomes are judged in terms of John Rawls' notion of justice—organising society to produce 'the greatest benefit of the least-advantaged members of society' (Rawls 1971, pp. 42–43)— then Scotland's performance compared to England and Wales is good. 'Headline' figures, such as homelessness acceptances and numbers in temporary accommodation, can distort homelessness reality. Scotland's more liberal attitude to homelessness acceptances and greater temporary accommodation use can put more people on a path to secure accommodation. Moreover, 'prevention' strategies to trim the homelessness figures have been less robust in Scotland than in England. There has been more acceptances and more households in temporary accommodation per 1000 population in Scotland but, in 2016/2017, 51.2% of all new local authority lettings in Scotland were allocated to homeless households (16% in England) and 33.1% of housing association lettings were made to homeless households compared to 21% in England (Stephens et al. 2018). In terms of other housing outcomes, Scotland has produced more houses per 1000 population than England, more social housing—in 2016, 25% of the new houses in Scotland were produced by local government and housing associations compared to 18.5% in England—and rents are lower. In 2017, the Scottish Government committed itself to building 50,000 affordable homes up to 2021—a 67% increase in affordable housing supply on previous five year period's achievement—with at least 35,000 of them to be socially rented. To achieve this goal, an estimated £3 billion of public funds has been identified for the five-year programme as a whole (Scottish Government 2017). Young and Donohoe (2018, p. 6), on the basis of an examination of local authority data on housing programmes, concluded that the 50,000 target 'is potentially within reach'.

Wales

In the past, housing policy in Wales was more aligned to English policy than in Scotland with local government owning 30% of the housing stock in 1979 compared to 29% in England. In 2016, Wales had the highest owner-occupation proportion but, at 69%, it was down from its 2005 highpoint at 75.1%. In 2016, 13% of homes were rented privately, 11% rented from housing associations and 7% rented from local government (Statistics for Wales 2018). Local authority rents were 14.1% of average incomes, housing association assured rents 14.6% and private landlord rents 20.4% (Stephens et al. 2018).

Housing responsibility devolution to Wales was slower than in Scotland with Wales not acquiring primary housing legislative powers until 2012. When Labour was dominant in the National Assembly for Wales and at Westminster, housing policy in Wales followed policy in England with 'Welsh' attached to new policy initiatives. However, after 2010, policy started to diverge from England. In Wales, tight conditions were applied to Right to Buy discounts for new and existing tenants, whereas, in England, discounts were expanded with the outcome that, in 2015, the average discount in Wales was 20% compared to 45% in England. In 2017 the Right to Buy was abolished in Wales. The 2014 Housing *(Wales) Act*, made the private landlord registration and licensing compulsory. Although a Help to Buy scheme was introduced in Wales, the National Assembly for Wales did not adopt the English 'affordable' rent policy and Wales introduced a more preventative approach to homelessness, later adopted, with amendments, in England. In 2015/2016, 26.1% of new local authority and 14.7% of housing associations lets were to homeless households (Stephens et al. 2018).

In 2017, the average house price in Wales was £143,964, the second lowest in the UK regions and, in 2016, the mortgage cost-to income-ratio for first-time buyers was 14 in Wales (Stephens et al. 2018). The gap between the per cent of children in relative poverty before and after costs, at 10% in Wales, is surpassed only by London (20%), the South West (13%) and the South East (12%).

Since 2001, an average of 2.4 new homes per 1000 population have been built in Wales but, post-2010, housing output in Wales fell below output in England—an average of 2.2 per 1000 population in England between 2010 and 2016 compared to 1.9 in Wales. This prompted fierce attacks on Labour-dominated Wales from the Conservative Secretary of State for Communities and Local Government, Eric Pickles said that, in Wales:

> Labour has failed to boost house-building starts by a mere 1% as com-pared to 19% in England. Labour in Wales hit the housing market with extra red tape, adding £13,000 to the cost of building a new home in comparison with England. (Pickles 2013)

The red tape accusation was related to the Welsh requirement that sprinklers had to be installed in all new and converted housing with the Westminster Secretary of State for Wales declaring that 'Regulations on builders are considerably more onerous than in England including the bizarre proposal to fit every house with a sprinkler system' (David Jones 2013, quoted in Ifsec Global 2013). This assault reflected the nature of devolution. Wales chose quality rather than quality and, given the Grenfell Tower fire, the policy orientation in Wales is under-standable albeit that quality and quantity would have been preferable. In 2016/2017, 6833 houses were completed in Wales—2.2 per 1000 population—with 18%, all built by housing associations, in the 'social' sector. Unlike in England net additions via conversions etc. are not recorded in Wales but the overall new house building rate is well below the rate necessary to keep up with household projections.

Northern Ireland

In Northern Ireland housing policy has been influenced by the divide between *Irish* nationalist/republicans (mainly Roman Catholic) and unionist/loyalist (mainly Protestant). Housing issues were a major catalyst in the civil disturbances of the late 1960s and the Northern Ireland Housing Executive (NIHE) was set up that assumed the housing responsibilities of 65 local authorities and the New Town Development Commissions to become Northern Ireland's single comprehensive housing authority. From the formal abolishment of the Northern Ireland Parliament, the NIHE was under direct Westminster control but, following the 1998 Good Friday Agreement, it became accountable to the Northern Ireland Assembly. The Assembly has been suspended on several occasions, the longest deferral being from 14 October 2002 until 7 May 2007 and, when the Assembly is inoperative, responsibility for housing policy in Northern Ireland eventually moves with Westminster.

The tenure division in Northern Ireland in 2017/2018 was 69% owner occupied; 14% private rented; 12 NIHE and 4% housing association (Northern Ireland Department for Communities 2018). In 2014/2015 NIHE rents were 12% of average earnings, housing association rents (net of service charges) 14.5% and private rents 18% (Stephens et al. 2018). In recent years house prices in Northern Ireland, linked partially to prices in Ireland, have been volatile. This has been reflected in mortgage cost to income ratios. In 2007 the ratio of first-time buyer mortgage costs to incomes was 25.1 (in London at 25.6) but steep falls in house prices reduced the ratio to 12.7 in 2016 compared to 16.6 in London (Stephens et al. 2018). Wallace et al. (2014, p. 30) note that 'Northern Ireland homeowners contain larger proportions of people in routine and manual occupations, whereas in Great Britain many of these people have been squeezed out of the tenure'.

Despite long periods under direct Westminster control, there have been significant policy variations between England and Northern Ireland. Northern Ireland has its version of the Right to Buy and also adopted the English Help to Buy and Mortgage Guarantee schemes but, although new social housing has become a housing association responsibility, stock transfer to housing associations has not been significant. The major difference between Northern Ireland and Great Britain has been the level of government resources available to housing. A 1974 housing survey revealed housing conditions in Northern Ireland as 'the worst in Britain and amongst the worst in Europe' (NIHE 2011, p. 19). Such housing pressures fuelled sectarian divisions. However, since the

1970s, there have been sustained high levels of investment in Northern Ireland housing, reflected in new housing production. From 2001 to 2007, new housing output per thousand population averaged 8.1 compared to 3 in England and, although much reduced, housing output relative to population is still higher than in England. This long-term high Northern Ireland housing investment level impact is revealed in the before and after housing costs child poverty figures: although, at 23%, child poverty in Northern Ireland before housing costs is very high, its increase after housing costs is only 3%, the lowest increase in the UK.

England: Regional, Local Authority and Neighbourhood Dimensions: London

In 1830, William Cobbett nicknamed London 'the great wen', a putrid cyst disfiguring England. Today, London dominates media and academic narratives on the UK housing crisis with most housing 'horror' stories located in London. 'Rogue landlord squeezes 35 men into three-bedroom home' (Metro 2017). 'Immigrants packed in squalid '£850-a-month' sheds and garages of West London' (Sun 2017).

In 1993 the average house price gap between London and the East Midlands was £21,627, by 2017, the gap was £260,000 (Nationwide 2017). Although house prices declined in London after the credit crunch, they soon recovered. A BBC News investigation found that in 99% of London wards prices had increased in real terms since 2007 compared to seven regions were, in the majority of wards, prices had declined with 95% of wards in the North East experiencing a price decline (BBC News 2017a).

The magnitude of the London problem in accessing homeownership was expressed in the *Financial Times* (Brooker 2017):

> There is a studio flat for sale on Holloway Road, north London.... It is on the market with Harris Brown for £250,000, making it among the cheapest homes in inner London. So, imagine you are 25 and want to buy this property. Presuming you earn the median wage for Londoners — for those aged 22 to 29 that is about £29,900 gross, according to the

Office for National Statistics — presuming you can get a 4.5 times salary mortgage; and presuming you can save 20 per cent of your take-home pay every month after tax, student loan repayments and rent for a room in a shared flat nearby, how long would it take, hypothetically, to save for the deposit? Forty-one years and five months. And that is if you're a man. If you're a woman, based on median earnings figures from the ONS, it will take you an extra nine years.

Between 2000 and 2014 the homeowner proportion in London fell from 58.7 to 48% with the private renter percentage increasing from 15.2 to 28% (Mayor of London 2017). In 2016/2017 the mean London rental price was £1748 per month, more than double the English mean rent (National Housing Federation [NHF] 2018). The mean rental price in the housing association sector was £135 in London and £129 in the local authority sector In England (excluding London) mean rents were £100 for a housing association home in 2016/2017 and £87 in the local authority sector (MHCLG 2018a).

The impact of high-London housing costs is demonstrated by the before and after housing costs child poverty statistics with the London 20% gap in child poverty before and after housing costs far exceeding the next highest, 12% in the South East and the UK 10% average (McGuiness 2018). Moreover the London before/after child poverty gap has been accelerating; in 2003 it was 13% (Cribb et al. 2018).

Overcrowding and homelessness statistics also reflect London's housing problem. London has the highest overcrowding rate in England with 8%, of all households lacking one or more bedrooms on the bedroom standard compared to 2% in the rest of England (Wilson and Fears 2016). Statutory homelessness acceptances in London increased by 33% between 2008/2009 and 2016/2017 with eviction from private landlord accommodation as the immediate cause of homelessness accelerating to 36% of all recorded reasons. 75% of all households living in temporary accommodation provided under the 1996 Housing Act are in Greater London and the number of households living in such accommodation increased from 39,030 in 2010 to 54,540 in 2018 with 87,310 children living in temporary accommodation (MHCLG 2018b).

What Has Caused the London Housing Crisis?

In 1981, London's population was 6.7 million. By 2001, it was 7.2 million, in 2011 8.2 million and, in 2016, it reached 8.8 million (Trust for London 2018). This rapid population expansion has reflected the capital's economic growth. Between 2010 and 2016 economic growth in London, as measured by Gross Value Added (GVA) per head, averaged 3.2% per year, compared to 1.9% in the UK and only 0.7% in the North East (Harari and Ward 2018). This economic activity has attracted international migration that, between 2004 and 2014, contributed 60% to London's population growth each year, adding to natural increase, with births in London outnumbering deaths by 80,000 per year. About 38% of people living in London were born outside the UK, compared with 14% for the UK as a whole and 33% of EU nationals living in the UK were living in London, around 1.2 million people (Hawkins 2018).

Since 2007 new house completions in London have averaged about 21,000 per year but population size has been increasing at 122,000 per year. House extensions and flat conversions have helped to mitigate the London housing dearth but, what little is known about housing space availability in London, suggests not only a large rise in officially recognised overcrowding but also a general decline in rooms per person—down from 1.99 in 2001 to 1.88 in 2011 (Mayor of London 2017). Although space standards in the owner-occupied sector have increased in London—from 34.3 m^2 per person in 1996 to 37.3 m^2 per person in 2013, space per person has declined in the PRS from 31 to 23.1 m^2 and in the 'social' housing sector from 26.4 to 25.2 m^2 over the same time span (Belfield et al. 2015). Concern about housing space availability prompted the London Mayor to introduce minimum space standards for new houses (excluding conversions) in 2010 that were set at about the same level as the national standards established in 2015 (Park 2017).

Accelerating demand for accommodation in London and the dearth in new supply have not been the only factors contributing to London's housing woes. The UK rise in house prices up to 2007 was, in part, caused by a 'feeding frenzy' as people tried to occupy a rung on the housing ladder before prices accelerated beyond their means.

In London, prices recovered quickly from the post-2008 price slump and there was another Gadarene rush to get on the housing ladder. Swelling property prices were augmented by private landlords purchasing more London properties and greater mortgage finance availability via Funding for Lending and Help to Buy. That the 'Bank of Mum and Dad' has higher assets in London may have contributed to the house price hike and gearing—using enhanced property prices to obtain a higher mortgage for a move—could also have had an impact. In addition, foreign investment, mainly concentrated on London, added to the 'feeding frenzy'. The London housing market's bubble traits indicates a future bust and, in October 2017, prices started to decline despite, from February 2016, Help to Buy providing a 40% mortgage in London on a new property with a price tag up to £600,000.

The extreme social housing scarcity in London relative to need has added to the crisis. Waiting lists are a poor guide to housing need due to local authority variations in how they are compiled but, in London, local authority housing waiting lists increased from 250,000 in 2004 to 375,000 in 2013 before government promoted changes in how waiting lists are complied influenced the figures (Migration Watch 2014). Social lettings to new tenants in London declined from 33,900 in 2000/2001 to 17,417 in 2016/2017 (Stephens et al. 2018) meaning an average waiting list stay of over 10 years. London's housing problems are reflected in child poverty as measured before and after housing costs (see Table 4.1). London is the most unequal city in the western world (Dorling 2015) and, whilst London does not have the highest spatial segregation by income in Europe (Tammaru et al. 2016), there are marked variations in housing conditions and policy outcomes between the London boroughs.

London Differences

Housing outcome differences in London are illustrated by the contrasts between four London boroughs set out in Table 4.2.

There are stark contrasts in housing outcomes *within* the London boroughs. Overall, Richmond upon Thames is ranked 296 out of 326 local authorities in terms of low deprivation but, although it contains

Table 4.2 Variations within London

	Richmond	Tower Hamlets	Newham	Wandsworth
Mean house price (2016/2017)	781,260	526,978	384,651	788,501
Ratio of house price to income	16.3	13.6	14.1	17.7
% detached or semi-detached	33	6	17	9.9
Mean monthly private sector rent (2016/2017)	1830	1853	1391	1801
Owner-occupied (%)	67	27	29	52
Social housing (%)	9	40	32	19
Private rented (%)	21	33	39	29
Child poverty before housing costs (%)	9.4	38	29	19
Child poverty after housing costs (%)	15	53	43	30
Overcrowded % (2011 Census)	10	34.8	25	20
Future housing requirement	1709	4873	3840	2414
Housing completions per 1000 households	0.5	12	13.6	1.8
Housing completions per 1000 pop	0.7	4.9	3.8	1.7
Population	195,800	304,900	341,000	316,100

Sources National Housing Federation (2018), End Child Poverty (2018), ONS (2013), DCLG (2017), and MHCLG (2018c)

no areas in falling into England's 10% most deprived districts, parts of the borough are in the 20% most deprived areas in England. The child poverty rate after housing costs between Richmond's wards ranged from 5.7 to 31.7% (End Child Poverty 2018). Richmond explains its very low new building rate relative to its housing requirements as a consequence of 'more than two thirds of its land is protected by either open space or conservation area status, resulting in both the highest land values of any outer London borough and limited sites to build on' (London Borough of Richmond Upon Thames (2018, p. 5).

In Wandsworth, there are wide variations in incomes and housing conditions with, in 2014, 9.8% having a household income of less than

15K, 16.9% between £15K and £25K and, at the other end of the scale, 6.9% with £70–80K and 8.7% with more than £85K. Although the average child poverty rate by ward after housing costs was 30.2%, the child poverty varied extensively between wards ranging from 11.5 to 45.4%.

Tower Hamlets is the seventh most deprived local authority area in the country. In 2015, 24% of all Tower Hamlets' Lower Level Super Output Areas (with a minimum population of 1000 a mean of 1500) were in the UK's most deprived 10% areas (Tower Hamlets 2016) with the most deprived areas clustered in the east of the borough. The incidence of child poverty after housing costs across the borough was uniform, ranging from 46.4 to 57.4% with an average of 53.4% (End Child Poverty 2018).

The Outer North East London Strategic Market Assessment (Opinion Research Services 2016) calculated that Newham required 22,220 new affordable houses from 2011 to 2033 with the current need backlog taking 9952 of this total. 24,000 households were on the local authority waiting list. Between 2001 and 2011 Newham experienced one of the highest increases in private landlord lettings in London—up by 16.1%—in part an outcome of private landlords buying property sold under the Right to Buy with Newham owning 15.000 leasehold properties rented by private landlords. At 40%, Newham now has the highest proportion of private rented accommodation in the UK (East 2014). Overcrowding in the private landlord sector became very high at 50.2% in 2011 on the Census room standard, an increase from 35.6% in 2001. The number of multi-occupied properties increased from 20 to 35% between 2001 and 2011. The problems generated by this growth in private landlordism prompted Newham to introduce the first borough-wide private landlord registration scheme in England. The implementation of scheme added to the London housing 'horror' stories. 'Two tenants were renting a commercial walk-in freezer in a basement'; 'Building site occupied by 11 tenants. No roof, no windows to the first and second floors, floors surfaces were missing and live wires exposed' (East 2014). In 2013, 5600 warning letters were sent and over 1800 joint operational visits made with the Police forcing 4500 landlords to licence. There were possibly '1500 beds in sheds' in Newham with the conditions reminiscent of 'Tom-All-Alone's', the slum area occupied by Jo, the road crossing sweeper, in Dickens' *Bleak House*. The incidence of child poverty across the wards in Newham after housing costs was similar ranging from 35.9 to 49.7% with an average of 43.2% (End Child Poverty 2018).

Other English Regions

Housing outcomes vary between the English regions. Some of these differences are set out in Table 4.3.

Table 4.3 Regional variations in housing outcomes

	Mean house price	Mean private sector rent	House price/income ratio
North West	183,340	584	7.1
North East	157,512	539	6.3
East of England	310,966	835	10.7
Yorks. and Humberside	181,740	573	7.3
East Midlands	200,029	584	7.7
West Midlands	209,164	623	8
South East	361,026	994	11.7
South West	270,054	770	10.6
London	584,873	17,487	16.4

Sources National Housing Federation (2018), End Child Poverty (2018), ONS (2013), and DCLG (2017)

The regional figures mask considerable inter-region variations at local government level and stark divides within local authority boundaries. Such differences will be explored by comparing less and more affluent local authorities within selected regions and then examining the variations in housing conditions inside local government boundaries (Table 4.4).

Table 4.4 Variations in housing outcomes: Oldham and Cheshire East

	Oldham	Cheshire East
Mean house price (2016/2017)	145,974	263,253
Ratio of house price to income	5.9	9.1
% detached or semi-detached	43	67
Mean monthly private sector rent (2016/2017)	538	748
Owner-occupied (%)	65	76
Social housing (%)	20	11
Private rented (%)	14	12
Child poverty before housing costs (%)	27.3	11.2
Child poverty after housing costs (%)	40.7	18.2
Overcrowded % (2011 census)	6.6	2.2
Future housing requirement	716	1142
Housing completions per 1000 households 2015/2016	5.2	5.4
Mean Housing completions per 1000 pop (2013/2017)	170	1310
Population	232,700	376,700

Sources National Housing Federation (2018), End Child Poverty (2018), ONS (2013), and DCLG (2017)

The North West: Oldham and Cheshire East

With 65% of its neighbourhoods in the 20% of the most deprived areas nationally, Oldham has been labelled 'the most deprived town in England' (Independent 2016). However, 35% were not and Oldham Metropolitan District contains some affluent districts. Indeed, in 2011 Oldham's Gini Income coefficient was 39.1, one of the highest in the North West and Bradshaw and Bloor (2016) ranked Oldham as England's 23rd most unequal borough. North Saddleworth, the most affluent local authority ward has a £40,000 median household income compared to £17,335 in Coldhurst, the poorest ward. Overcrowding in North Saddleworth is low at 2.9% compared to Coldhurst at 21.6%, with a very marked contrast in the per cent of children living in over-crowded houses (43.1% in Coldhurst, 6% in North Saddleworth). 77% of the households in North Saddleworth can afford to keep their homes in a decent condition but only 34% in Coldhurst. In North Saddleworth the anti-social behaviour rate was 190 per 10,000 inhabitants compared to 800 in Coldhurst (all statistics from Oldham Partnership, 2016). In 2016, the average house price in Saddleworth

North was three times higher than in Coldhurst. Renting a two bedroom house would cost £625 per month in North Saddleworth, £475
in Coldhurst. In North Saddleworth 98.5% of the population was classified 'white', in Coldhurst 27.1%. An analysis of child poverty before
and after housing costs, using a different methodology to that used to
compile the official poverty figures (Valdez -Martinez and Hirsch 2018),
found that the per cent of children in poverty living in Coldhurst
increased from 46.7% before housing costs to 62.1% after housing
costs, the highest rate in the UK. In contrast the per cent of poor children was 5.66 (before housing costs) and 9.17 (after housing costs) in
Saddleworth North (End Child Poverty 2018).

Cheshire East has the sixth least affordable housing in the North West
with, in 2012, a lower quartile house price/annual gross income ratio of
6.6 (Cheshire East 2013). An annual income of £38, 571 was required in
2017 to afford a house in the lower quartile house price range (Cheshire
East 2018). The level of dissatisfaction with existing accommodation was
more than twice as high in the private and social sectors than in the owner-occupied sector and overcrowding increased from 4748 to 5681 households over the 10-year period 2001–2011. The number of households on
the waiting list climbed from 7000 to 12,100 between 2010 and 2013
but dropped to 6000 in 2014 following a revision in the criteria used for
compiling the waiting list. In Cheshire East the overall child poverty incidence after housing costs was 18.1% but the ward variations were wide,
ranging from 3.3 to 41.2% (End Child Poverty 2018) (Table 4.5).

West Midlands: Solihull and Walsall

Solihull Observatory (2017, p. 15) describes Solihull as:

> 50% of Solihull residents live in a cluster that can be described as
> 'Prosperous Suburbs', compared with 25% across the region as a whole.
> This group predominates in the urban west, south of the Warwick Road
> (A41) and parts of the semi-rural south and east. The next most com-
> mon groups in Solihull are those described as 'Typical Traits' (14.4%) and
> 'Blue Collar Communities' (13.9%), although in both of these Solihull
> has a lower proportion of residents than the West Midlands average.

Table 4.5 Variations in housing outcomes: Solihull and Walsall

	Solihull	Walsall
Mean house price (2016/2017)	294,186	166,887
Ratio of house price to income	8.3	7.4
% detached or semi-detached	65	61
Mean monthly private sector rent (2016/2017)	851	543
Owner-occupied (%)	74	63
Social housing (%)	16.6	25
Private rented (%)	9.4	12
Child poverty before housing costs (%)	13.2	23.7
Child poverty after housing costs (%)	21.1	36.2
Overcrowded % (2011 census)	2.4	5.2
Future housing requirement	732	881
Housing completions per 1000 households 2015/2016	4.9	6
Housing completions per 1000 pop (2013/2017)	560	540
Population	211,800	278,500

Sources National Housing Federation (2018), End Child Poverty (2018), ONS (2013), and DCLG (2017)

Solihull is a polarised borough, at the top of a list prepared by Bradshaw and Bloor (2016) of the most unequal local authorities. Most deprivation is concentrated in North Solihull, now designated a regeneration area, with three wards in the bottom 3% nationally. In North Solihull, only 20% are very satisfied with the area, compared to 55% elsewhere in Solihull; one ward has only 1.6 hectares of green space per 1000 population whereas, the most affluent ward it is 11 hectares per 1000 population. Weekly incomes in North Solihull are about half of the incomes in the prosperous suburbs and the proportion of children below the poverty line after housing costs in Solihull ranged from 7.8% to 38.1% (End Child Poverty 2018). The per cent of social housing varies from over 70% in North Solihull to less than 1% in more prosperous areas. The incidence of anti-social behaviour is far higher in the most deprived wards.

The extreme concentration of deprivation in Solihull is not present in Walsall, indeed, Walsall Borough Council (2015, p. 3) commented:

Walsall ranks very well on barriers to housing and services deprivation, and has no LSOAs in the most deprived 10% nationally; this domain is

Table 4.6   Variations in housing outcomes: Wokingham and Slough

	Wokingham	Slough
Mean house price (2016/2017)	458,595	319,475
Ratio of house price to income	12.9	11.6
% detached or semi-detached	74	37
Mean monthly private sector rent (2016/2017)	1202	873
Owner-occupied (%)	81	52
Social housing (%)	7	20
Private rented (%)	12	28
Child poverty before housing costs (%)	6.5	19.2
Child poverty after housing costs (%)	10.8	29.8
Overcrowded % (2011 census)	1.7	12.6
Future housing requirements	876	913
Housing completions per 1000 households 2015/2016	8.1	6.7
Housing completions per 1000 pop (2013/2017)	640	130
Population	161,900	147,200

Sources National Housing Federation (2018), End Child Poverty (2018), ONS (2013), and DCLG (2017)

made up of geographical barriers to services, and wider barriers including overcrowding or homelessness — in Walsall, neighbourhoods do not tend to experience both of these types of deprivation in combination, so the overall score is low.

This is reflected in the incidence of child poverty after housing costs. Although the ward outliers are 9.2 and 45.3%, across the borough the child poverty per cent is relatively uniform with a ward average of 36.2% (End Child Poverty 2018) (Table 4.6).

South East: Wokingham and Slough

According to the *Wokingham Housing Strategy 2015-18* (Wokingham Borough Council 2015, p. 4):

The population of the Borough is largely affluent, with high levels of house owner-occupation and car ownership with a high percentage of residents work in managerial and professional occupations and unemployment is consistently low.

Wokingham has the third lowest child poverty incidence (after housing costs) in the UK (Valadez -Martinez and Hirsch 2018). At 5.59 its Index of Multiple Deprivation score placed Wokingham as the least deprived local authority in England although one ward has a deprivation score twice the Wokingham average and 4.1% of households in this ward were overcrowded. The child poverty rate is relatively uniform across the borough but one ward has an incidence of 24% after housing costs. Of the Wokingham housing stock, only 1% is non-decent. One reason for the high housing standards in Wokingham is that high prices keep low to middle-income households out of the borough. Over the period 2001/2011 population growth was only 5.1%. Just 11% of the private rented stock is private rented only 6.4% is social housing thus making it difficult for people to gain a foothold in the borough. In the consultation on the Berkshire Strategic Housing Market Assessment (GL Hearn 2016) local estate agents, said those purchasing properties were usually families looking for larger family homes and that the Wokingham market would benefit from having more flats or 1 to 2-bedroom houses for first-time buyers.

Giving evidence to the House of Commons South East Regional Committee in 2010 Wokingham Council said:

> Although it may be acceptable to consider revising the level of proposed housing growth in some suitable areas in the South East, the specific constraints of Wokingham Borough would indicate that no additional housing should take place in Wokingham Borough and it must be made abundantly clear that Wokingham Borough Council will not support any additional development in Wokingham Borough in the period to 2026. (House of Commons South East Regional Committee 2010, para. 81)

However, shortly after this statement, there was a change in attitude. Wokingham Borough Council established a Local Housing Company, Wokingham Housing Limited to build social and market housing and, in 2014, Loddon Homes was set up to own and manage homes developed by its parent company, Wokingham Housing Limited.

In 2016/2017, the average house price in Slough, eighteen miles from Wokingham, was £318,475, but, in Slough 37.5% of properties were detached or semi-detached properties, compared 74% in Wokingham. At 24%, Slough has a large percentage of houses rented by private landlords and its social sector is double the Wokingham proportion. The high proportion of cheaper (often multi-occupied) private landlord property in Slough has allowed more people to obtain a foothold in the area. Indeed 40% of Slough's population was born outside the UK, compared to 14% in Wokingham (ONS 2018). An income of £23,100 was required to obtain a private rented property in the lower quartile price of houses rented privately. However, easier access to living in Slough has compounded Slough's housing problems. From 2001, population growth was particularly strong (an 18.6% increase), much higher than Wokingham (5.1%). Slough has high level of overcrowding housing with one ward where over 34.4% of households are overcrowded. Housing pressures are reflected in homelessness statistics with the use of temporary accommodation rising rapidly—from 156 in March 2015 to 300 September 2016. The average waiting time for a three bedroom house in the social sector was 3.9 years (Slough Borough Council 2016). The rate of child poverty after housing costs ranges from 19.9 to 38% (End Child Poverty 2018) (Table 4.7).

North East: Northumberland and Middlesbrough

Variations in housing outcomes between local authorities in the North East are small when compared to other regions in England. In 2016/2017 mean house prices varied from £193,994 in Northumberland to 129,187 in County Durham and mean monthly rental prices from £739 in Newcastle upon Tyne to £457 in Hartlepool. The house price to income ratio ranged from 7.5 in Northumberland to 5.0 in County Durham. The percentage of people living in the 20% most deprived areas in England was 17% in Northumberland compared to 55% in Middlesbrough, with other North East local authority areas varying between 23 and 46% (Voluntary Organisations Network North East 2015).

In the most deprived Northumberland ward, 97.3% of the population was classified as 'white', the tenure composition 46%

Table 4.7 Variations in housing outcomes: Northumberland and Middlesbrough

	Northumberland	Middlesbrough
Mean house price (2016/2017)	193,994	148,175
Ratio of house price to income	7.5	6.6
% detached or semi-detached	61	53
Mean monthly private sector rent (2016/2017)	523	474
Owner-occupied (%)	66	61.4
Social housing (%)	18.6	22
Private rented (%)	15.2	16.6
Child poverty before housing costs (%)	15.2	25
Child poverty after housing costs (%)	24.2	38.3
Overcrowded % (2011 census)	2.1	4.5
Future housing requirement	707	267
Housing completions per 1000 households 2015/2016	8.6	7.4
Housing completions per 1000 pop (2016/2017)	1200	440
Population	316,000	140,400

Sources National Housing Federation (2018), End Child Poverty (2018), ONS (2013), and DCLG (2017)

owner-occupation, 29% social rented, 24% private rented and 73% of all the houses were flats or terraced. In the least deprived ward, 72% of properties were detached or semi-detached, 6.9% were in the private landlord sector, 16% social housing and the rest owner-occupied (Northumberland Knowledge 2015). There were large variations between Northumberland's 65 small wards in child poverty after housing costs ranging from 3.1 to 40.1% with a 24.2% average (End Child Poverty 2018).

Half of Middlesbrough's 20 wards were ranked in the top 10 most deprived wards in England but 5 were ranked above the 5000 most deprived wards. The most deprived ward in Middlesbrough ranked number two nationally, the least deprived at 7024. This was reflected in the incidence of child poverty that, after housing costs, ranged from outliers at 7.3 to 52.1% with a 38.3% average (End Child Poverty 2018). In the most deprived ward, 35% of households rented privately and 21.5% were social tenants compared to the least deprived ward where only 2% were social tenants and 4.5% of tenants rented privately.

In the most deprived ward 75% were classified as having semi-routine, routine or as unemployed, in the least deprived ward, 18%.

Area-Based Housing Policies

As demonstrated above, large housing outcome variations occur between and within local authorities. The 2016/2017 English Housing Survey report on stock condition noted:

> Irrespective of tenure, households with relative low-income were more likely to live in deprived areas. Almost a third (31%) of all households with relative low income lived in deprived areas compared with 17% of other households....Households with relative low income were also more likely than other households to live in poor housing (34% compared with 25%). (MHCLG 2018d, p. 25)

Central resource direction towards deprived areas within local authorities has a long history dating back to slum clearance programmes, the Urban Programme, Housing Action Areas, General Improvement Areas, Housing Priority Areas and the Community Development Projects (see Lund 2017). Under Margaret Thatcher, area-based programmes were curtailed but New Labour revived the approach, declaring its aim was to 'narrow the gap between the most deprived areas and the rest of the country' (HM Treasury 2000, p. 1). Several programmes were set up to further this aim with a mix of improving 'human' and 'social' capital in the areas selected plus physical improvement and reducing crime rates. The major schemes were *New Deal for Communities, The Neighbourhood Renewal Fund* and *The Housing Market Renewal Pathfinders Initiative*. In addition, New Labour's nationwide tax credit system would help low-income households in deprived areas with its decent homes programme contributing to improving social housing.

Over £4 billion was spent by New Labour on specific area programmes but the evidence on their impact is mixed. Place changing initiatives (crime, inadequate housing and poor physical environment) seem to have had more impact than people changing (educational underachievement, poor health and worklessness) schemes (Crisp et al. 2015). Some specific scheme evaluations showed improvements in the targeted areas but, when comparator areas were included in assessments, the measured gains in areas with special initiatives were significantly reduced (Centre for Regional Economic and Social Research, Sheffield Hallam University 2010a, b).

According to a DCLG analysis (DCLG 2012) the gap in income deprivation between the lowest decile SLOA and the 50–60% decile reduced by 3% between 1999 and 2008 but then—illustrating economic impacts—the gap increased as the recession hit. Difference in deprivation amongst children reduced by less than for the overall population and, by 2009, it was back to its 1999 level.

In contrast to these somewhat negative assessments, Lupton (2013, p. 2) states:

> There is a myth that Labour spent a lot and achieved nothing. The evidence shows that outcomes improved and gaps narrowed on virtually all the socio-economic indicators that were targeted. Labour left the Coalition with a legacy of more equal outcomes on many measures, less poverty and expanded public services.

On the available evidence, it is difficult to disentangle the impact of specific schemes from changes in the social security system, particularly tax credits, and in public sector job expansion, important to the more deprived parts of England. There is scant information on the 'value for money' of the interventions.

New Deal for Communities and *The Neighbourhood Renewal Fund* came to their scheduled ends in 2010. *The Housing Market Renewal Pathfinder Initiative* was axed by the Coalition government long before its scheduled end, leaving only a small 'transition fund' to 'help families trapped in abandoned streets resulting from the pathfinder demolition schemes' (Shapps 2011). There are now no specific area-based initiatives leaving deprived communities reliant on 'trickle down' from city-based programmes.

From the 1960s various forms of special schemes, especially the Urban Programme, were directed to help districts affected by immigration. In 2009–2010 the then Labour Government introduced a £35 million Migration Impacts Fund (MIF) worth £35 million per year and aimed at assisting public service providers to deal with the transitional migration pressures. It was a small gesture but was axed by the coalition Government who claimed that it was ineffective (House of Commons Home Affairs Committee 2018). To some, ending this fund was a symbol that the government did not care about the differential impact of migration. The Cambridge Centre for Housing and Planning Research (2008) recorded a real increase in rents of 40.3% in South Holland and 34.7% in Boston between 1996/1997 and 2006/2007 with the acceleration occurring post-2003.

When many of the districts most affected by migration voted leave in the 2016 European Union Referendum the government announced a Controlling Migration Fund aimed at 'mitigating the impacts of immigration on local communities' (Home Office 2016). The Fund has two parts:

A local service impacts part of £100m, to help English local authorities and their communities experiencing high and unexpected volumes of immigration to ease pressures on local services.
An enforcement part worth £40m to direct enforcement action against people in the UK illegally in order to reduce the pressure on local areas. (Home Office 2016, p. 4)

Locking the Brexit door after the horse had bolted?

Conclusion

To some, uncontrollable globalisation forces are responsible for the UK housing crisis but the housing stock is spatially fixed and this sets limits globalisation's impact. Even the 2008 credit crunch had a variable influence across countries depending on securitisation use and how nation states managed their economies. Governments can control housing outcomes. Indeed, in Scotland, devolution—even without full nation state powers—has made a significant difference. With a bespoke

Scottish party in control, higher overall housing production and greater social housing availability has enabled Scotland to pursue a rights-based approach to homelessness and achieve a lower gap in the incidence of child poverty before and after housing costs than in the North East of England.

The most important location dimension at regional and local authority levels relates to employment opportunities. Some regional economies have not recovered from the decline in heavy industries that started in the 1920s. McCann (2017) has demonstrated that regional inequalities in the UK are large by international standards and, with the exception of Scotland, regions outside of London and the South have productivity levels akin to the poorer regions in Central and Eastern Europe. The performance of cities is crucially dependent on the performance of the region in which they are located and there is scant evidence that other regions have benefited from London's growth.

Area reputation also influences the appeal of a house. For example, a survey of attitudes to housing in Wales found that 45% of all respondents agreed with the statement 'I would never want to live in social housing' but 'people who actually have some experience of living in social housing have much more positive perceptions of it than home owners or private renters' (Awan-Scully 2018, p. 5). Amenities, especially schools, are connected to district desirability with a Department of Education inquiry finding that, in 2016, proximity to a good primary school adds 8% to house prices and a good secondary school 6.8% (BBC News 2017b). Cultural and social capital are involved in the location dimension. In *Social Class in the 21st Century* Savage et al. (2015) draw attention to the links between economic, social and cultural capital. Interactions between people possessing social and cultural capital augment their economic power and they defend this economic power via social and cultural interventions such as participation in the planning system to stop new development in their districts.

Place variables indicate solutions to the housing crisis not usually associated with housing policy. The 'Northern Powerhouse' and 'Midlands Engine' have salience in generating economic growth outside the South and relieving housing pressure in London and its hinterland (see Chapter 8). Making the distribution of good schools more equal would have an impact and new initiatives, targeted on job growth, better housing and crime reduction in deprived areas are necessary. The current planning process, loaded in favour of status quo defenders, also requires reform (see Chapter 7).

References

Awan-Scully, R. (2018). *Public Attitudes to Social Housing in Wales: Report for the Chartered Institute of Housing Cymru*. Cardiff: Chartered Institute of Housing Cymru. https://omghcontent.affino.com/AcuCustom/Sitename/DAM/097/CIH_Cymru_public_perceptions_report.pdf.

BBC News. (2016, April 26). *Is There a Housing Crisis in Scotland?* http://www.bbc.co.uk/news/election-2016-scotland-35928391.

BBC News. (2017a, October 17). *Are House Prices Back from the Crash?* http://www.bbc.co.uk/news/business-41582755.

BBC News. (2017b, April 29). *MPs Say "Dominance" of Big Home-Building Firms Must End*. https://www.bbc.co.uk/news/business-39752869.

Belfield, C., Chandler, D., & Joyce, R. (2015). *Housing: Trends in Prices, Costs and Tenure* (IFS Briefing Note BN161). London: Institute for Fiscal Studies. https://www.ifs.org.uk/publications/7593.

Bradshaw, J., & Bloor, K. (2016). *Which Local Authorities Are Most Unequal?* York: University of York and Social Policy Research Unit. https://pure.york.ac.uk/portal/en/publications/which-local-authorities-are-most-unequal(e-ba28517-2c13-4bf9-b8d0-e71a13201340).html.

Brooker, N. (2017, April 21). London Housing: Too Hot for Young Buyers. *Financial Times*. https://www.ft.com/content/a0182e62-25e4-11e7-a34a-538b4cb30025.

Cambridge Centre for Housing and Planning Research. (2008). *Private Rents and Rates of Return 1996/7 to 2006/7*. Cambridge: Cambridge Centre for Housing and Planning Research. https://www.cchpr.landecon.cam.ac.uk/Projects/Start-Year/2007/Comparative-analysis-of-private-and-social-sectors-rates-of-return/Rents-rates-of-return-1998-99-to-2006-07/PRS-Report.

Centre for Regional Economic and Social Research (CRESR), Sheffield Hallam University. (2010a). *Making Deprived Areas Better Places to Live: Evidence from the New Deal for Communities Programme. The New Deal for Communities National Evaluation: Final Report—Volume 3*. London:

DCLG. http://extra.shu.ac.uk/ndc/downloads/general/Volume%20 three%20-%20Making%20deprived%20areas%20better%20places%20 to%20live.pdf.

Centre for Regional Economic and Social Research, Sheffield Hallam University. (2010b). *Making Deprived Areas Better Places to Live: Evidence from the New Deal for Communities Programme. The New Deal for Communities National Evaluation: Final Report—Volume 4*. London: DCLG. https:// extra.shu.ac.uk/ndc/downloads/general/Volume%20three%20-% 20Making%20deprived%20areas%20better%20places%20to%20live.pdf.

Cheshire East. (2013, September). *Strategic Housing Market Assessment: 2013 Update Report for Cheshire East Council*. Sandbach: Cheshire East. http:// www.cheshireeast.gov.uk/planning/spatial_planning/research_and_evi- dence/strategic_housing_market_assmt.aspx.

Cheshire East. (2018). *Housing Strategy 2018–2023 (Draft for Consultation)*. Sandbach: Cheshire East. http://www.cheshireeast.gov.uk/housing/strate- gic_housing/housing-strategy-2018-2023-consultation.aspx.

Clegg, N. (2016). *Politics: Between the Extremes*. London: Bodley Head.

Commission on Housing and Wellbeing. (2015). *A Blueprint on Housing and Well-Being: Housing as 'Home'*. http://www.housingandwellbeing.org/ housing-as-home.

Cribb, J., Keiller, A. N., & Waters, T. (2018). *Living Standards, Poverty and Inequality in the UK: 2018*. London: Institute for Fiscal Studies.

Crisp, R., Pearson, S., & Gore, T. (2015). Rethinking the Impact of Regeneration on Poverty: A (Partial) Defence of a 'Failed' Policy. *Journal of Poverty and Social Justice, 23*(3), 167–187.

DCLG. (2012). *Tracking Economic and Child Income Deprivation at Neighbourhood Level in England: 1999 to 2009*. London: DCLG. https:// www.gov.uk/government/statistics/tracking-economic-and-child-in- come-deprivation-at-neighbourhood-level-in-england-1999-to-2009.

DCLG. (2017). *Land Use Change Statistics in England: 2015–16*. London: DCLG. https://assets.publishing.service.gov.uk/government/uploads/sys- tem/uploads/attachment_data/file/595749/Land_use_change_statistics_ England_2015-16_-_2_March_2017_version.pdf.

Dorling, D. (2015). *Income Inequality in the UK: Comparisons with Five Large Western European Countries and the USA*. http://www.dannydorling.org/ wp-content/files/dannydorling_publication_id4756.pdf.

East, J. (2014). *Improving the Private Landlord Sector*. London: Newham Borough. http://www.cih.org/resources/PDF/CIH%20London%20-%20 PRS%203%20-John%20East%20Presentation.pdf.

Economist. (2017). Location, Location, Location, Global House Prices: The Economist's Interactive Guide to Global Housing Markets. https://www. economist.com/blogs/dailychart/2011/11/global-house-prices.

End Child Poverty. (2018). *Poverty in Your Area.* http://www.endchildpoverty. org.uk/poverty-in-your-area-2018/.

Financial Times. (2018, March 14). How the Financial Crash Made Our Cities Unaffordable. https://www.ft.com/content/cc77babe-2213-11e8-add1-0e8958b189ea.

GL Hearn. (2016). *Berkshire (Including South Bucks) Strategic Housing Market Assessment.* http://www.reading.gov.uk/media/2959/Housing-Market-Assessment/pdf/Berkshire_Strategic_Housing_Market_Assessment_Feb_2016.pdf.

Global Property Guide. (2018). *Irish House Prices Will Outpace All Europe Over Next 2 Years.* https://www.globalpropertyguide.com/Europe/Ireland/.

Harari, D., & Ward, M. (2018). *Regional and Country Economic Indicators* (House of Commons Briefing Paper No. 06924). London: House of Commons. https://researchbriefings.parliament.uk/ResearchBriefing/Summary/SN06924.

Hawkins, O. (2018). *Migration Statistics* (Briefing Paper No. SN06077). London: House of Commons. http://researchbriefings.parliament.uk/ResearchBriefing/Summary/SN06077.

HM Treasury. (2000). *2000 Spending Review: Prudent for a Purpose: Building Opportunity and Security for All.* London: HM Treasury. https://www.gov. uk/government/uploads/system/uploads/attachment_data/file/265996/csr2000.pdf.

House of Commons Home Affairs Committee. (2018). *Immigration Policy: Basis for Building Consensus* (Second Report of Session 2017–2019). London: House of Commons. https://publications.parliament.uk/pa/cm201719/cmselect/cmhaff/500/500.pdf.

House of Commons South East Regional Committee. (2010). *Housing in the South East, Oral Evidence.* London: House of Commons. https://publications.parliament.uk/pa/cm/cmseast.htm.

Home Office. (2016). *Controlling Migration Fund: Mitigating the Impacts of Immigration on Local Communities.* London: Home Office. https://assets. publishing.service.gov.uk/government/uploads/system/uploads/attachment_data/file/566951/Controlling_Migration_Fund_Prospectus.pdf.

Ifsec Global. (2013, October 3). *Decline in House Building Blamed on Sprinkler Regulations.* https://www.ifsecglobal.com/decline-in-house-building-blamed-on-sprinkler-regulations/.

Independent. (2016, March 19). Oldham Tops List of Most Deprived Towns in England. http://www.independent.co.uk/news/uk/home-news/oldham-tops-list-of-most-deprived-towns-in-britain-a6940696.html.

International Monetary Fund. (2017). *Global Housing Watch.* http://www.imf.org/external/research/housing/.

Keep, M. (2018). *Country and Regional Public Sector Finances* (Briefing Paper No. 8027). London: House of Commons. https://researchbriefings.parliament.uk/ResearchBriefing/Summary/CBP-8027#fullreport.

London Borough of Richmond Upon Thames. (2018). *Richmond Housing & Homelessness Strategy 2018–2023.* London: London Borough of Richmond Upon Thames. https://www.richmond.gov.uk/media/16179/housing_and_homelessness_strategy_2018_to_2023.pdf.

Lund, B. (2017). *Understanding Housing Policy* (3rd ed.). Bristol: Policy Press.

Lupton, R. (2013). *Did Labour's Social Policy Programme Work?* London: Nuffield Foundation. http://www.nuffieldfoundation.org/news/did-labour%E2%80%99s-social-policy-programme-work.

Mayor of London. (2017). *Housing in London: The Evidence Base for the Mayor's Housing Strategy.* London: Mayor of London. https://files.datapress.com/london/dataset/housing-london/2017-01-26T18:50:00/Housing-in-London-2017-report.pdf.

McCann, P. (2017). *The UK Regional-National Economic Problem: Geography, Globalisation and Governance.* Abingdon: Routledge.

McGuiness, F. (2018). *Poverty in the UK: Statistics* (Briefing Paper No. 7096). London: House of Commons. https://researchbriefings.parliament.uk/ResearchBriefing/Summary/SN07096.

McKee, K., Muir, J., & Moore, T. (2017). Housing Policy in the UK: The Importance of Spatial Nuance. *Housing Studies, 32*(1), 60–72.

Metro. (2017, September 20). *Rogue Landlord Squeezes 35 Men into Three-Bedroom Home.* http://metro.co.uk/2017/09/20/rogue-landlord-squeezes-35-men-into-three-bedroom-home-6942510/.

Migration Watch. (2014). *Housing Demand in London.* https://www.migrationwatchuk.org/briefing-paper/339.

Millán, I. R. (2014). *Securitization in Spain: Past Developments and Future Trends.* https://www.bbvaresearch.com/wp-content/uploads/2014/09/EW_Securitization-in-Spain1.pdf.

Ministry of Housing, Communities and Local Government (MHCLG). (2018a). *English Housing Survey 2016 to 2017: Headline Report.* London: MHCLG. https://www.gov.uk/government/statistics/english-housing-survey-2016-to-2017-headline-report.

MHCLG. (2018b). *Live Tables on Homelessness*. London: MHCLG. https://www.gov.uk/government/statistical-data-sets/live-tables-on-homelessness.

MHCLG. (2018c). *English Housing Survey 2016 to 2017: Private Rented Sector*. London: MHCLG. https://www.gov.uk/government/statistics/english-housing-survey-2016-to-2017-private-rented-sector.

MHCLG. (2018d). *Tenure Trends and Cross Tenure Analysis*. London: MHCLG. https://www.gov.uk/government/statistical-data-sets/tenure-trends-and-cross-tenure-analysis.

National Housing Federation (NHF). (2018). *Home Truths 2017/18: The Housing Market in London*. London: National Housing Federation. https://www.housing.org.uk/resource-library/home-truths/.

Nationwide. (2017). *House Price Index: By Property Type*. https://www.nationwide.co.uk/about/house-price-index/download-data#xtab:regional-quarterly-series—by-property-age-group-data-available-from-1991-onwards.

Norges Bank. (2015). *Global Market Trends and Their Impact on Real Estate* (Discussion Note 2). https://www.nbim.no/contentassets/c199863ae8374916ac15e780662db960/nbim_discussionnotes_2-15.pdf.

Northern Ireland Department for Communities. (2018). *Northern Ireland Housing Statistics 2017–8*. Belfast: Northern Ireland Executive. https://www.communities-ni.gov.uk/publications/northern-ireland-housing-statistics-2017-18.

Northern Ireland Housing Executive. (2011). *More Than Bricks: Forty Years of the Housing Executive*. Belfast: Northern Ireland Executive. https://www.nihe.gov.uk/more_than_bricks.pdf.

Northumberland Knowledge. (2015). *Research Report: English Indices of Deprivation 2015: Northumberland*. https://www.northumberland.gov.uk/NorthumberlandCountyCouncil/media/Northumberland-Knowledge/NK%20place/Indices%20of%20deprivation/Northumberland-ID-2015.pdf.

ONS. (2013). *Nomis Census 2011 Table Links*. London: Office for National Statistics. https://www.nomisweb.co.uk/census/2011/all_tables?release=3.2a.

ONS. (2018). *Population of the UK by Country of Birth and Nationality: July 2017 to June 2018*. London: Office for National Statistics. https://www.ons.gov.uk/peoplepopulationandcommunity/populationandmigration/internationalmigration/bulletins/ukpopulationbycountryofbirthandnationality/july2017tojune2018.

Opinion Research Services. (2016). *The Outer North East London Strategic Market Assessment.* https://www.redbridge.gov.uk/media/3006/lbr-2011-north-east-london-shma-executive-summary-2016.pdf.

Paris, C. (2017a). The Super-Rich and Transnational Markets: Asians Buying Australian Housing. In R. Forrest, S. Y. Koh, & B. Wissink (Eds.), *Cities and the Super-Rich: Real Estate, Elite Practices and Urban Political Economies* (The Contemporary City) (pp. 63–84). Abingdon: Routledge.

Paris, C. (2017b). The Residential Spaces of the Super-Rich. In I. Hay & J. V. Beaverstock (Eds.), *Handbook on Wealth and the Super-Rich* (pp. 244–263). Cheltenham: Edward Elgar.

Park, J. (2017). *One Hundred Years of Housing Space Standards: What Next?* http://housingspacestandards.co.uk/.

Pickles, E. (2013). *Pickles Attacks Labour's Housing Record in Wales.* London: Conservative Home. http://conservativehome.blogs.com/localgovernment/2013/05/pickles-attacks-labours-housing-recordin-wales.html.

Rawls, J. (1971). *A Theory of Justice.* Harvard: Harvard University Press.

Sassen, S. (2012). *Cities in the World Economy.* London: Sage.

Savage, M., Cunningham, N., Devine, F., Friedman, S., Laurison, D., Mckenzie, L., et al. (2015). *Social Class in the 21st Century.* London: Pelican.

Scottish Government. (2017). *Affordable Housing Supply Programme.* Edinburgh: Scottish Government. https://www.gov.scot/policies/more-homes/affordable-housing-supply/.

Shapps, G. (2011). *House of Commons Debates, 24 November, c30-1WS.* London: Hansard. https://publications.parliament.uk/pa/cm201011/cmhansrd/cm111124/wmstext/111124m0001.htm.

Shelter Scotland. (2016). *Affordable Housing Need in Scotland: Final Report— September 2015.* http://scotland.shelter.org.uk/__data/assets/pdf_file/0009/1190871/7909_Final_Housing_Needs_Research.pdf/_nocache.

Slough Borough Council. (2016). *Housing Strategy 2016 to 2021: Consultation Draft.* Slough: Slough Borough Council. http://www.slough.gov.uk/Moderngov/documents/s44921/Housing%20Strategy%20Document.pdf.

Solihull Observatory. (2017). *People and Place Summary, Solihull.* Solihull Metropolitan Borough Council. http://www.solihull.gov.uk/portals/0/key-stats/solihullpeopleandplace.pdf.

Statistics for Wales. (2018). *Welsh Housing Conditions Survey, 2017/8: Headline Report.* Cardiff: Welsh Government. https://gov.wales/statistics-and-research/welsh-housing-conditions-survey/?lang=en.

Stephens, M., Perry, J., Wilcox, S., Williams, P., & Young, G. (2018). *UK Housing Review 2018*. London: Chartered Institute of Housing.

Sun. (2017, November 4). *Immigrants Packed into Squalid "850-a-Month" Sheds and Garages of West London*. https://www.thesun.co.uk/news/4839267/immigrants-sheds-garages-southall-west-london/.

Tammaru, T. Marcińczak, S., van Ham, M., & Musterd, S. (2016). *Socio-Economic Segregation in European Capital Cities: East Meets West*. Abingdon: Routledge.

Tower Hamlets. (2016). *Deprivation in Tower Hamlets: Analysis of the 2015 Indices of Deprivation Data*. London: Tower Hamlets Council. https://www.towerhamlets.gov.uk/Documents/Borough_statistics/Income_poverty_and_welfare/Indices_of_Deprivation_High_resolution.pdf.

Trust for London. (2018). *London's Population Over Time*. https://www.trustforlondon.org.uk/data/londons-population-over-time/.

Valadez-Martinez, L., & Hirsch, D. (2018). *Compilation of Child Poverty Local Indicators, Update to September 2017*. Loughborough: Centre for Research in Social Policy, Loughborough University. www.endchildpoverty.org.uk/…/Local_child_poverty_indicators-2018report-3.docx.

Voluntary Organisations Network North East. (2015). *North East Index of Multiple Deprivation*. https://www.vonne.org.uk/resources/north-east-index-multiple-deprivation-2015.

Waffel, M. (2008, May 28). Why the Global Housing Market Boom By-Passed Germany. *Speigel Online*. http://www.spiegel.de/international/business/real-estate-doldrums-why-the-global-housing-market-boom-by-passed-germany-a-552901.html.

Wallace, A., Jones, A., & Rhodes, D. (2014). *Financial Resilience and Security: Examining the Impact of Falling Housing Markets on Low Income Homeowners in Northern Ireland Final Report*. York: University of York. https://www.york.ac.uk/media/chp/documents/2014/Financial%20Resiliance%20and%20Security%20Report.pdf.

Walsall Borough Council. (2015). *Deprivation in Walsall: September 2015*. Walsall: Walsall Borough Council. file:///C:/Users/User/Downloads/lMD%20Summary%202015%201.0.pdf.

Wealth, X. (2017). *The Global Property Handbook*. http://www.wealthx.com/wp-content/uploads/2017/01/Wealth-X_Warburg-Barnes_2017.pdf.

Wilson, W., & Barton, C. (2017, July 17). *Foreign Investment in UK Residential Property* (House of Commons Briefing Paper, Number 07723). London: House of Commons. file:///C:/Users/User/Downloads/CBP-7723.pdf.

Wilson, W., & Fears, C. (2016, November 14). *Overcrowding (England)* (Briefing Paper No. 1013). file:///C:/Users/User/Downloads/SN01013%20 (1).pdf.

Wokingham Borough Council. (2015). *Wokingham Housing Strategy 2015–18.* Wokingham: Wokingham Borough Council. www.wokingham.gov.uk/ EasySiteWeb/GatewayLink.aspx?alId=151687.

Young, G., & Donohoe, T. (2018). *Review of Strategic Investment Plans for Affordable Housing.* Edinburgh: Shelter Scotland. https://scotland.shelter.org.uk/professional_resources/policy_library/policy_library_folder/ review_of_strategic_investment_plans_for_affordable_housing.

5

Future Housing Requirements

Need, Demand and the Market

In estimating future housing requirements it is conventional to make a distinction between need and demand. Need is a normative concept related to a housing consumption level deemed desirable but not yet attained. Bramley et al. (2010, p. 25) define demand as 'the quantity and quality of housing which households will choose to occupy given their preferences and ability to pay (at given prices)'. The *London Strategic Housing Market Assessment* (Mayor of London 2013) distinguished need from demand as: '…(1) housing need, which is the housing that households require even if they cannot afford it, and (2) housing demand, which is the housing that households are able to afford even if they don't need it'.

Neoliberal economists allege that the market, provided that land release is not impeded by state intervention, will always cater for demand whereas other economists believe that state action is necessary to stimulate housing supply. Need fulfilment involves intensive state involvement aimed at promoting supply at a consumer cost enabling lower-income households to afford decent housing. Policy initiatives

© The Author(s) 2019
B. Lund, *Housing in the United Kingdom*,
https://doi.org/10.1007/978-3-030-04128-1_5

aimed at obtaining this objective include producer subsidies and/or imposing requirements on developers to include an affordable house proportion in new housing schemes. Ensuring that part of the stock is allocated according to non-market criteria via social housing suppliers is another dimension to meeting need, as is consumer support through supplementing low-incomes.

The demand/need distinction has been undermined in recent years by incorporating housing requirement assessments into the planning system. Indeed the MHCLG (2018b, p. 1) now states 'Housing need is an unconstrained assessment of the number of homes needed in an area'.

Planning restraints on new developments have led to nationally demanded but locally implemented housing requirement calculations that the private sector will be *allowed* to meet, not what it *could* supply. Thus, need and demand have been mingled in local Strategic Housing Market Assessments (SHMAs), prepared by local planning authorities. Within SHMAs the necessity for 'affordable' housing has had to be assessed, that is, the housing requirement that cannot be met by the market and will, therefore, involve the types of state intervention outlined above. Unfortunately, there is no concord on the intervention required to produce affordable housing because there is no agreed, robust affordability definition.

In the nineteenth and early twentieth centuries, 'one week's pay for one month's rent' was a frequently used affordability rule of thumb. The National Federation of Housing Associations (NFHA)—now the National Housing Federation (NHF)—resurrected the 25% yardstick. Its 'affordability test' was based on the assertion that 'rents are affordable if the majority of working households taking up new tenancies are not caught in the poverty trap (because of dependency on Housing Benefit) or paying more than 25% of their income in rent' (Wilson 1998).

Shelter enlisted public perceptions to identify affordability. To be affordable a home had to meet the essentials of 'can meet the rent or mortgage payments on the home without regularly having to cut spending on household essentials like food or heating' and not cause worry and 'that rent or mortgage payments could rise to a level that would be difficult to pay', plus one of two 'tradables': 'features many people believed were important, but they were not universally applicable to or equally desired by everyone' (Shelter 2016a). These were 'can meet rent or mortgage payments on the home without regularly preventing participation in social activities' or 'can meet the rent or mortgage payments on the home without regularly being prevented from putting enough money aside to cover unexpected costs'. On this definition, 27% of all UK homes were not affordable (Shelter 2016b).

Other current affordable definitions include a 'housing cost overburden', set at 40% or more of equivalised disposable income spent on housing (Eurostat 2018). In 2016, 35.4% of UK market renters experienced a 'housing cost overburden'—the 6th highest rate in the EU-28. The US Department defines affordable as housing costs not exceeding 30% of gross incomes and the 'living rent' idea in the UK is usually set at 33% of median rent (Mayor of London 2018). In Australia a 30:40 indicator is used in identifying households as having an affordability problem when the household has an income level in the bottom 40% of Australia's income distribution and is paying more than 30% of its income in housing costs. Its basic assumption is that those above the 40% bottom of the income distribution choose to spend more on housing and that such housing costs have little or no impact in their use of basic essentials such as food, health care and education (Australian Housing and Urban Research Institute 2018). Meen (2018) adopts a variation on the Australian indicator.

Not only do affordable housing definitions differ, but their applications are also diverse. Some include the impact of housing benefits whilst others do not, the housing cost norm can vary from average prices to the lowest quartile and housing costs can include or exclude interest rates.

Post-2010, Conservative-led governments directed state intervention to the supply of new affordable housing defined as up to 80% of the market price both in the rented and owner-occupation markets. Starter homes, targeted at first-time buyers, was a major homeownership scheme of the 2015 Cameron government but the White Paper *Fixing Our Broken Housing Market* (DCLG 2017a) 'marked a shift in the Government's housing policy from a strong focus on starter homes, to delivering a wider range of affordable housing' (Cromarty 2018,

p. 39). Although some starter homes are in the pipeline, delivery has been slow and, by July 2018, no starter home had been completed. Cameron's government defined social housing as homes let at social rents, that is, rents set by guideline target rents determined through the government's rent policy. Some commentators refer to such rents as 'genuinely affordable' to contrast them with rents set at up to 80% of the market rent. In 2018, there was a 40% gap between affordable and social rents. Theresa May's government adopted revised affordable housing definitions in a 560-word statement contained in an annex to *Fixing Our Broken Housing Market* (DCLG 2017a) with below 80% of the market price being the theme in the long narrative. No rationale was given for this norm and, in the glossary to the *National Planning Policy Framework* (MHCLG 2018c), 'the rent is set in accordance with the Government's rent policy for Social Rent' was added to the affordability definition.

Local Plans

Until the early 2000s, local housing strategies were the major documents setting out local authority proposals to satisfy local housing requirement assessments, but, in recent years, these have been overshadowed by local plans, focused on estimating need and demand and setting out future land release proposals. We do not have local plans limiting the supply of motor cars, beer, books etc. but politics—at central and local levels—determine the number of houses produced by the private market. Unlike the vast majority of privately supplied goods, land use is controlled and regulated by the local democratic process mediated by the central government. Lord Porter, commenting on local development plans, stated:

> You don't actually need a plan to be able to build houses; you need a plan to stop building houses. The idea of a local plan is to control development, not to enable development. That is the whole point of the plan. (House of Commons, Public Accounts Committee 2017, Question 17)

As the planning system's grip on new housing supply tightened and the local authority housing direct provider role faded, there was greater emphasis on attempting to use development control to satisfy housing requirements not met by the market. Agreements under Section 106 of the 1990 Town and Country Planning Act allowed local authorities to capture 'planning gain' in the form of affordable housing. In order to make these agreements, it was necessary for the local authority to assess the need for affordable housing hence estimating local housing need entered the planning process. New Labour attempted to cajole local authorities to prepare more robust local plans—then called Local Development Plans—via Regional Housing Strategies and a stress on market signals in assessing total housing requirements but, in pursuit of a 'localism', the 2011 Localism Act abolished regional spatial strategies and added neighbourhood planning. As recorded in Chapter 2, Treasury concern about the fall in house numbers projected by local authorities led to the publication of the *National Planning Framework* (DCLG 2012). For the next five years, the DCLG attempted to influence local government to plan for more houses via guidance on preparing local plans and repeated warnings—usually not acted on—that failure to deliver an up-to-date plan in accordance with national guidelines would result in developers winning planning appeals and in New Homes Bonus reductions.

Assessing Housing Requirements

The National Planning Policy Framework (DCLG 2012) required local planning authorities to identify the objectively assessed need for housing in their areas and prepare local plans to translate this need into land supply targets. Local authorities could agree to submit joint plans but, if not, then, in line with the duty to co-operate, local authorities should join forces with their neighbours to ensure that needs assessments covered market areas crossing local authority boundaries. Accordingly, the relevant geographical boundary in assessing need was the Strategic Housing Market Area (SHMA).

Housing need appraisals had to be informed by robust and proportionate evidence. Central government guidance made a distinction between overall housing need and affordable housing need with overall housing need referring to the total number of net additional dwellings to be provided over the plan period, both in the market and affordable sectors. In assessing overall housing need, central government guidance indicated the starting point should be the household projections published by the DCLG but it noted that such projections are trend-based—they project forward past demographic trends—thus they should be altered to take account of factors such as past undersupply, market signals and anticipated employment growth. The total estimated need had to be disaggregated by factors such as age, household type, bedroom number, special requirements, tenure and housing type (DCLG 2015).

Household Projections

The White Paper *Fixing Our Broken Housing Market* stated:

> Since the 1970s, there have been on average 160,000 new homes each year in England. The consensus is that we need from 225,000 to 275,000 or more homes per year to keep up with population growth and start to tackle years of under- supply. (DCLG 2017a, p. 9)

The 225,000–275,000 homes per year target is described as a consensus but other estimates give 300,000 or more. Given that, according to 2014-based projections (DCLG 2016a), 210,000 houses per year were needed to meet the new household formation, at 275,000 per year this leaves only a maximum of 65,000 houses per annum to fulfil the needs backlog. No wonder the DCLG used the phrase 'to start to tackle years of under supply'!

The MHCLG projections are 'rear-view mirror' estimates based on trends in birth rates, death rates, net migration and past household formation rates. The 2014-based projections (DCLG 2016a) envisaged an increase in households from 22.7 million in 2014 to 28.0 million in 2039. Annual average household growth was indicated as 210,000 per year between 2014 and 2039 with average household size falling from 2.35 in 2014 to 2.21 in 2039 and net migration accounting for 37% of household growth. However, household formation rates are influenced by housing supply. The 2006 projections, for example, prepared when net additional housing supply was increasing in England by over 200,000 per year, anticipated a 247,000 per year growth in household formation up to 2013. Compared to 2006, the projections based on 2014 data, using household formation rates between 2001 and 2011 estimated 37,000 fewer households forming per year up to 2039, despite a larger population and an average net house addition 97,000 per year below the 247,000 per year household formation projected in 2006. When the 2014 household projections were made there were only 136, 610 net annual new additions to the housing stock in England (MHCLG 2018a). Lack of supply suppresses household formation. This is revealed in 'concealed' households, that is, potential separate households currently living in other households. Fitzpatrick et al. (2018, p. xvii) comment:

> The numbers of concealed households remain high in England despite ostensibly favourable employment conditions and a recovering housing market. There were 2.32 million households containing concealed single adults in England in early 2017, in addition to 282,000 concealed couples and lone parents. The number of adults in these concealed household units is estimated at 3.38 million.

The rate at which younger adults form separate households has continued to fall across England and has dropped by nearly 40% in London since the early 1990s. The sharing household per cent is 4.2% for single adults, 2.1% amongst couples and 1.6% amongst lone parents (Fitzpatrick et al. 2018). Research by Heriot-Watt University cited by Crisis (2018) estimated that the housing need backlog in Great Britain was 4.75 million dwellings consisting of:

- concealed family or concealed single (including nondependent children) wanting to move;

- overcrowded houses according to the bedroom standard;
- serious affordability problems based on combination of ratio measures and subjective payment difficulties;
- serious self-reported physical condition problems;
- accommodation unsuitable for families such as high-rise or no garden/yard;
- core and wider homelessness;
- older households with suitability needs; and
- households whose housing costs are unaffordable.

According to Heriot-Watt University's calculations meeting this backlog over 15 years would require 383,000 homes per year across Great Britain, 343,000 in England, 14,000 in Wales and 26,000 in Scotland. Presumably, the Heriot-Watt University's figure was based on allowing for future household formation in its need backlog estimates.

Affordable Housing Requirements

The DCLG guidance on assessing the local need for affordable housing began with estimating numbers of households currently in need, such as homelessness, overcrowded households, disabled people living in unsuitable dwellings, households lacking basic facilities and 'households containing people with particular social needs (e.g. escaping harassment) which cannot be resolved except through a move' (DCLG 2015, para. 23). This calculation—often referred to as the 'needs' backlog—had to be supplemented by a future affordable need estimate.

Belatedly, after the National Planning Policy Framework had been in operation for four years, the DCLG set up an expert group to investigate its operation. Although the complex and disputed nature of assessing housing need was identified as a major obstacle to timely local plan production, the Local Plans Expert Group identified 'a lack of political will and commitment' (Local Plans Expert Group 2016, p. 1). The group said 'some SHMAs do not reach clear conclusions at the apparent request of commissioning authorities where politicians wish to influence the reported OAN (objectively assessed need) to its lowest potentially credible level' (Local Plans Expert Group 2016, p. 18). Moreover,

> We heard evidence, however, of certain HMAs being politically defined.... and even of some authorities treating their own administrative boundaries as the extent of their housing market area, which seems inherently unlikely to be the case. (Local Plans Expert Group 2016, p. 19)

Neighbourhood planning provided an additional platform for development resistance. Neighbourhood plans—put forward in a Conservative Party green paper, published just before the 2010 election—promised that 'local people in each neighbourhood will be able to specify what kind of development and use of land they want to see in their area' (Conservative Party 2010, p. 8). Far more neighbourhood plans have been prepared in affluent areas than in poor areas (Kaszynska et al. 2016) with most anti-development (Turley Planning Consultants 2014). Brownhill and Bradley (2017) record that only just over half the neighbourhood plans designated housing sites although most had policies on housing and specifically on affordable housing. They state 'many plans made explicit their opposition to the dominant housing market model and the speculative approach of the volume house-builders' (Brownhill and Bradley 2017, p. 63). Small brownfield sites, custom build and community land trusts were preferred. An examination of neighbourhood plans by Nathaniel Litchfields and Partners (2018) found only 15 of the 330 Neighbourhood Plans scrutinised proposed more housing than the Local Plan with the average increase in these 15 plans being 3%.

A poll carried out on behalf of the Policy Exchange (2018) found that attitudes to development were strongly influenced by unhappiness on the design and style of modern houses and the government has appointed the philosopher Sir Roger Scruton to be chair of a government housing commission to promote 'building better, building beautiful'.

However, such declared responses may be a rationalisation of more venal attitudes such as potential lower house prices, the inconveniences of congestion and pressure on local services (see Chapter 2).

Conservative-led governments have varied in their support for neigh-bourhood planning. In 2014 the Secretary of State for Communities and Local Government ruled that the neighbourhood's right to deter-mine the location of a development outweighed the need to ensure housing growth. However, under Theresa May's government, neigh-bourhood powers are being contained with the *National Planning Policy Framework* (MHCLG 2018c, p. 10) stating 'Neighbourhood plans should not promote less development than set out in the strategic poli-cies for the area, or undermine those strategic policies'.

Planning for the Right Homes in the Right Places

The White Paper *Fixing Our Broken Housing Market* (DCLG 2017a) announced:

> The Government believes that a more standardised approach would pro-vide a more transparent and more consistent basis for plan production, one which is more realistic about the current and future housing pressures in each place....

Proposals on a new standardised approach were put forward in *Planning for the Right Homes in the Right Places: Consultation Proposals* (DCLG 2017b).

In 2017, 40% of local authorities did not have an up-to-date plan and, according to *Planning for the Right Homes in the Right Places: Consultation Proposals* (DCLG 2017b, para. 29):

> At the moment, it is not always clear to local communities or developers how many homes their local area is planning for, let alone needs. These figures are often buried deep in technical reports and hidden away on local authority websites. It can take several hours to track down exactly how many homes a local planning authority has decided it needs — and even then it might not be clear.

The new, standardised approach to assessing housing requirements was set out involving:

- A demographic baseline of the annual average household growth in a local planning area over a ten year period.
- Taking market signals into account. The market signal proposed was 'the workplace-based median house price to median earnings ratio from the most recent year for which data is available' and the assumption would be made that 'each 1 per cent increase in the ratio of house prices to earnings above four results in a quarter of a per cent increase in need above projected household growth'. Thus, in any area where the average house prices are more than 4 times average earnings, the number of homes needed to be planned for increases by 0.25% for every 1% the affordability ratio rises above 4 (DCLG 2017b, para. 18).
- The area used for estimating requirements would be the local planning authority area and, where requirements crossed boundaries, 'housing need for the defined area should be the sum of the local housing need for each local planning authority. It will be for the relevant planning authorities or elected Mayor to distribute this total housing need figure across the plan area' (para. 31).
- Because the new approach to assessing housing requirements would result in some areas having a large increase in housing need, expectations of future supply would be limited to 40% above supply already planned.

Planning for the Right Homes in the Right Places: Consultation Proposals did not give local estimates of social rent or affordable homes requirements, indicating a central government concern with demand rather than need. It would be up to local planning authorities—subject to central guidance—to disaggregate their housing requirements as set by central government into the different sizes, types, tenures required in their local areas (DCLG 2017b, p. 29). This lack of central government guidance on the proportion of affordable homes in local plans has been criticised by the Institute for Public Policy Research Commission on Social Justice (2018b) which stated:

> government should set new guidelines in England for the minimum proportion of new housing developments which must be genuinely

affordable. Our view is that one-third of all new housing should be social housing for rent; one-third genuinely affordable (in perpetuity) for sale; and one-third for sale at market prices. (IPPRCSJ 2018b, pp. 197–198)

The requirement for below market price housing has been estimated at 142,202 per annum including 91,000 at social rent (Crisis 2018).

Promise and Delivery

Planning for the Right Homes in the Right Places: Consultation Proposals (DCLG 2017b) was a 'technical fix' to conflicts between the central government's views on the number of new homes required and local resistance to new housebuilding. It forms the basis of a 'Delivery Test' that, when implemented, will give the DCLG a figure, independent of locally made assessments, on the total new housing supply in each local authority deemed necessary against which performance can be assessed. However, Alex Morton (2016, p. 1), having left his position as housing advisor to the Prime Minister, said:

> When I was in Number 10 and dug out the figures (which officials were not keen to share) fewer than ten councils (out of 326) turned out to have an up to date local plan and deliver their housing need. A similar number do so without an up to date local plan. Thus over 300 councils failed to oversee delivery of housing need. This is the housing crisis in a nutshell.

Government success in cajoling local government to deliver the homes deemed necessary will be the test of the new approach.

New Homes Bonus

The New Homes Bonus (NHB)—an extension of New Labour's Planning Delivery Grant—was introduced by the coalition government to encourage local authorities to grant planning permission for new houses in return for extra resources. By 2016/2017, £4.8 billion had been allocated under the scheme (DCLG 2016b). The NHB gives a central government payment to local authorities for each extra house for six years. The distribution calculation is based on the new dwellings' council tax band with each additional 'affordable' home attracting augmentation at flat rate £350 per annum. An empty home brought back into use qualifies for the grant. There is no obligation on local authorities to use the grant for housing purposes.

The NHB has been criticised on a number of grounds. The DCLG's own evaluation found no evidence that the NHB 'was providing an additional incentive in increasing support specifically for more affordable homes' (DCLG 2014, p. 4). The National Audit Office (2013, para. 17) noted that, because the NHB varies with relative house prices via Council Tax bandings, then 'on average local authorities in areas with higher relative house prices receive higher payments for similar new homes'. It also stated:

> Local authorities that earn only low levels of Bonus will not make up their share of the sum deducted from the Formula Grant. These local authorities are usually in areas where developers are less likely to want to build housing, which are more typically in deprived parts of the country or in areas where land can be more expensive to develop. (National Audit Office 2013, para. 21)

The criticism that the NHB does not necessarily lead to greater new home production was partially answered by an announcement from the Minister for Housing, Communities and Local Government that, from 2017, NHB would not be paid on housing growth below 0.4% so that 'the money is used to reward additional housing rather than just normal growth' (Javid, *Hansard* 2016, col. 976). However, it was also announced that NHB would be paid for only five years in 2017–2018 and four years from 2018–2019, with the resources diverted towards social care costs. Thus, resources spend on NHB are being cut thereby reducing the carrot on offer to local authorities to build more homes.

Reforming the System in England

Ensuring that sufficient new homes are available to meet future need involves central government insisting that local planning authorities plan to release enough land and then deliver the promised homes, despite the deep opposition to new development particularly in heartland Conservative areas. Indeed, it has been suggested that the delay in publishing the 2017 Housing White Paper was due to Conservative MPs resisting more radical proposals contained in early versions (Pickard and Evans 2017). Writing in the *Telegraph*, Fraser (2017) suggested that Theresa May 'a former shire councillor from a constituency constrained by the greenbelt' was 'worried about her base of "Nimbys"'.

The proposals in *Planning for the Right Homes in the Right Places: Consultation Proposals* (DCLG 2017b) effectively abandoned localism in assessing total housing requirements. It was reminiscent of New Labour's Regional Strategic Plans, with their market signals, but with housing requirements assessment nationalised through a formula. By applying its formula across England the DCLG was able to assess the housing requirement for England at just over 266,000 homes, including 72,000 in London. Conveniently this was not too far away from the 250,000 per annum promised from 2020 in the 2017 Conservative Party manifesto. This convergence was achieved by the assumptions in the formula. Although recognising that 'housing formation is constrained to the supply of available properties', using the last ten year average in household projections, a period when household formation was severely constrained by a housing shortage relative to population growth, dampened housing requirements. The affordability element in the formula is a proxy for the needs backlog but a very rudimentary substitute for homelessness, overcrowding, concealed households etc. Sajid Javid, when Secretary of State for Housing, Communities and Local Government, argued that placing responsibility on local authorities to set the distribution of new homes between various needs and tenures, such as housing for older and disabled people; families with children; affordable housing and build to rent housing, meant that the government had retained localism (Javid 2017).

Replacing unmet need assessment with an affordability indicator indicates that meeting housing need has become subordinate to responding to market demand in the central government's concerns. In its critique of the DCLG's approach, the Campaign for the Protection of Rural England asserted that it conflates demand and need whereas planning should be concerned with need (Campaign for the Protection of Rural England 2017). Of course, a concern only with need would reduce housing requirements thereby protecting rural England. Unless people are to be denied the chance to express their consumer preferences in housing consumption then both need and demand are necessary ingredients of housing requirement assessments.

The formula used in *Planning for the Right Homes in the Right Places: Consultation Proposals* (DCLG 2017b) produced some curious outcomes. In London, the inner-London boroughs have large requirements for new homes compared to the outer-London boroughs. Hillingdon, for example, with swathes of green belt land and Boris Johnson's constituency within its boundaries, had a housing requirement of 595 houses per year between 2016 and 2026 but Tower Hamlets had a 4873 per year requirement, indicating that high-rise will be necessary if Tower Hamlets and other inner-London boroughs are to attain their targets. Loading new build into inner areas to protect outer areas from new build, with *The National Planning Policy Framework* (MHCLG 2018c) demanding high densities, is reminiscent of Conservative policy in the 1930s and late 1950s. Even the modest proposals for a new building in 'middle England' included in *Planning for the Right Homes in the Right Places: Consultation Proposals* appear to have encountered opposition in the Conservative Party and produced modifications. *National Planning Policy Framework: Draft Text for Consultation* stated that local planning authorities should produce 'a strategy which will, as a minimum, meet *as much as possible* of the area's objectively assessed needs' (MHCLG 2018c, p. 11; emphasis added).

The MHCLG formula freed local government from having to employ expensive consultants to determine total housing requirements but at the cost of a sophisticated analysis of the housing need. Using the formula, the DCLG has a central assessment of overall housing requirements in each area that it can match to delivery to apply any incentives and sanctions it chooses to use. Changes in ways local government will be financed in the future—away from central grants towards reliance on locally generated business rates and revenue from the council tax—will enhance the salience of specific incentive payments such as the New Homes Bonus but resistance to land release in the areas identified as requiring extra homes, especially in the South East—laggards in the past—will be difficult to overcome.

The National Planning Policy Framework (MHCLG 2018c) reiterated that there should be a presumption in favour of sustainable development adding that approvals for development proposals that accord with an up-to-date development plan should be made without delay but gave a let out clause to authorities without an up-to-date plan in stating that:

> where there are no relevant development plan policies, or the policies which are most important for determining the application are out-of-date, granting permission unless:

> i. the application of policies in this Framework that protect areas or assets of particular importance provides a clear reason for refusing the development proposed; or
> ii. any adverse impacts of doing so would significantly and demonstrably outweigh the benefits, when assessed against the policies in this Framework taken as a whole. (MHCLG 2018c, p. 6)

Scotland

The Scottish Government sets outs out the Scottish Government's strategy for Scotland's spatial development for a 20–30 year period in its *National Planning Framework for Scotland* (Scottish Government 2014a). This document, periodically revised, designates national developments and requires planning authorities to take account of government policies when drafting development plans and making development management decisions.

As stated by Audit Scotland (2013, para. 71) 'Local planning arrangements are complicated…. involving Housing Need and Demand

Assessments: Local Housing Strategies; Strategic Housing Investment Plans; Strategic Local Programmes; Local Development Plans; Strategic Development Plans and Single Outcome Agreements'. There are four Strategic Development Planning Authorities (SDPAs) in Scotland located in city regions: Edinburgh and South East Scotland SDPA covers the City of Edinburgh, East Lothian, Midlothian and Fife. Scottish Borders and West Lothian SDPA contains Dundee, Angus, Perth and North Fife. Aberdeen City and Shire SDPA is a partnership between Aberdeen City and Aberdeenshire council and Glasgow with Clyde Valley SDPA comprises of the eight local authorities of East Dunbartonshire, East Renfrewshire, Glasgow City, Inverclyde, North Lanarkshire, Renfrewshire, South Lanarkshire and West Dunbartonshire.

These SDPAs prepare broad strategic plans for their areas but the main responsibility for compiling Housing Need and Demand Assessments (HNDAs) rests with local authorities that are required to produce a local plan.

According to the Scottish Government, the HNDA 'is a key part of the evidence base for both the Local Housing Strategy (LHS) and Strategic and Local Development Plans, and should form the basis for setting the Housing Supply Target' (Scottish Government 2014b, p. 1). HNDAs should be prepared every five years and look forward over twenty years.

The Scottish Government reviews each HNDA and, by December 2012, had assessed all 32 as 'robust and credible' (Audit Scotland 2013, para. 70). However, in recent years, HNDA process has undergone significant change with the Centre for Housing Market Analysis (CHMA) at the Scottish Government developing a HNDA modelling tool to provide a clearer method for estimating housing and working with local authorities to refine local HNDAs.

In 2015, presumably on the basis of HNDAs, in 2015 the Scottish Government set a target of 36,000 homes per year but in 2015 only 15,260 homes were produced (Jones Lang LaSalle [JLL] 2016). Planning for housing in Scotland has concentrated on 'affordable' homes. In 2015 Shelter Scotland commissioned a study of 'affordable' housing requirements in Scotland. The detailed study reached the conclusion that Scotland needs at least 12,000 affordable homes a year from 2015 to 2020 but, at best, existing programmes provided only half the required output (Shelter Scotland 2016). Nonetheless, over the past five years, Scotland's performance in producing new homes and 'affordable' new homes has been far better than in England and Wales indicating that whatever the complexities involved in technical estimates of need and land release the public attitudes and the political will to promote the common good is the influential factor. The National Centre for Social Research (2013, p. 127), notes that 'Scotland stands out for showing overall positive support for new local house building'. Following an independent review (Beveridge et al. 2016) and a consultation process, the 2017 Planning (Scotland) Bill was introduced to Parliament in December 2017. The changes proposed were mainly technical but there was an emphasis on improving community engagement in the planning process.

Wales

The planning system in Wales is similar to system in England with each planning authority having to prepare a local development plan aimed at making 'planned provision for an adequate and continuous supply of land to meet society's needs in a way that is consistent with sustainability principles, as set out in the Well-being of Future Generations (Wales) Act 2015' (Welsh Government 2018). Plans are examined by the Welsh Planning Inspectorate. However, the planning system in Wales is changing with, in some areas, a regional planning tier being established.

As in England, Welsh Government planning policies state that household projections should form the starting point when local planning authorities assess their housing requirements but these projections should be supplemented by other data (Welsh Government 2016). New home delivery has been disappointing in Wales which perhaps explains why in 2014 local planning authorities were required to submit an annual monitoring report to the Welsh Government based on local development plan implementation and performance. The *All*

Wales Planning Performance Annual Report (Welsh Government 2017) revealed that, as of 31 March 2015, 21 of 25 local planning authorities had an adopted development plan but only 28% of local planning authorities had a five-year housing supply.

In 2015 the Public Policy Institute for Wales published estimates of future housing need in Wales from 2011 to 2031, prepared by Holmans (2015). On current levels of household formation, 174,000 new houses were required: 5500 per year in the market sector and 3300 in the 'social' sector. However, because household formation was restricted by the current housing dearth, assuming household growth based on earlier trends would produce an annual 7800 private sector requirement and 4200 in the 'social' sector. Between 2011 and 2015 only 23,003 new dwellings had been built compared to the 34,800 deemed necessary on the lower estimate and 48,000 on the higher estimate.

Like Scotland, Wales has also focused on affordable houses, with, on average, 2301 per year affordable homes delivered from 2011/2012 to 2015/2016 compared to the 4200 per year 'social' sector homes considered necessary by Holmans' higher estimate.

Northern Ireland

In 1972, following the establishment of direct Westminster rule, planning in Northern Ireland was centralised in the Department for the Environment with local councils only able to influence decisions through consultation. Devolution in 1998 brought change but Lloyd (2016, p. 134) commented:

> Remarkably, in this changed political context, land-use planning remained a centralised matter. Indeed there was a further twist: land use planning was effectively broken up into three departmental areas — regional development (strategic planning), social development (regeneration) and environment. (statutory land use planning)

However, the long period of restricted local government involvement in planning and the subsequent 'fragmentation of responsibility' may have been helpful in stimulating housing production in Northern Ireland.

The Northern Ireland Housing Executive, a 'depoliticised', comprehensive housing authority was set up in 1971 to remove discrimination in housing allocation and to improve overall housing conditions. A 1974 House Condition Survey found that Northern Ireland 'had the worst housing conditions in Britain and amongst the worst in Europe' (Northern Ireland Housing Executive 2011, p. 19). The Northern Ireland Housing Executive, relatively unrestricted by planning constraints, and assisted by large resource injections from Westminster, succeeded in boosting housing output. Housebuilding per 1000 population in Northern Ireland had 'achieved parity by the mid-1990s' (Paris 2001, p. 15) and was well in excess of the Great Britain average from the late 1990s (McPeake 2014). Davison et al. (2012) found that the relatively new condition of the Northern Ireland housing stock produced overall standards higher than in Wales and England.

The lack of local authority involvement in planning for housing is changing. Planning powers were devolved to eleven new councils in 2015 producing the Nimbyism spectre in Northern Ireland. A structure for creating local plans accompanied by guidance, very similar to the English guidance, has been established. Since 2016 a Department for Infrastructure has overseen the planning process

Conclusion

The conflict between central and local governments in England on releasing sufficient land for new homes has a long history. The struggle reached a highpoint in the 2000s when New Labour attempted to impose land release targets on local planning through Regional Housing Strategies that used affordability indicators as undersupply measures. The Conservative/Liberal Democrat localism agenda ripped the heart out of this approach and, post-2012, the central government has attempted to coax and cajole local authorities to release more land. This had a limited impact on boosting new development approvals but new construction still failed to meet national requirements. Moreover, the housing completions were not in the districts where they were most needed. As examples, even on the MHCLG's restricted housing need assessment, Kensington and Chelsea ought to be delivering 834 homes per year and Richmond on Thames 1709. In 2016/2017 Kensington and Chelsea produced 110 homes and Richmond on Thames 140 (MHCLG 2018d).

In England, housing output has been disappointingly low when compared to Scotland where the localism agenda has had a far lower profile in the planning process. In terms of assessing total local housing requirements, the wheel has now turned full circle with a national formula containing a nationally determined affordability index now used. To overcome the difficulty that local authority boundaries straggle housing market areas, *Planning for the Right Homes in the Right Places: Consultation Proposals* (DCLG 2017b) simply combiningits assessment for the individual local authorities involved, leaving it to the local authorities to sort out responsibility for meeting the need.

The proposals in *Planning for the Right Homes in the Right Places: Consultation Proposals* (DCLG 2017b) are evocative of Duncan Sandys' promoting green belts whilst simultaneously concentrating new house construction in the form of high-rise in the inner-cities albeit that that the lack of any specific affordable housing requirement figure in the formula application may retard future affordable home supply if local authorities simply accept the total housing requirement and do not attempt to assess their affordable housing need.

Pressure from those with a vested interest in restricting housing supply has severely restrained new housing construction in England. Low levels of land release push up land prices. In 2012 the Treasury wanted a presumption in favour of sustainable development in the absence of an up-to-date local plan but backbench Conservative MP resistance resulted in more time being allowed to prepare plans and Eric Pickles, then Secretary of State for Communities and Local Government, showed no inclination to apply the requirement at appeal stage. Under the government's current plans if, by 2020, housebuilding is below 75% of the government's local target, then developers will be able to build on sites not included in a local plan (Barker 2018). The government's 'delivery test' is scheduled to be applied when new household projections become available and a revised calculation of local needs can be made. Given the past failure to ensure that local government delivers new homes where they are needed most, enforcement of the 'delivery test' will be an indicator of the government's commitment to supply more homes in the right places.

References

Audit Scotland. (2013). *Housing in Scotland*. Edinburgh: Accounts Commission. http://www.audit-scotland.gov.uk/docs/local/2013/nr_130711_housing_overview.pdf.

Australian Housing and Urban Research Institute. (2018). *Understanding the 30:40 Indicator of Housing Affordability Stress*. Melbourne: Australian Housing and Urban Research Institute. https://www.ahuri.edu.au/policy/ahuri-briefs/2016/3040-indicator.

Barker, N. (2018, May 25). Government Targets Mean 165,000 Homes Could Bypass Local Plans, Warns LGA. *Inside Housing*. https://www.insidehousing.co.uk/home/home/government-targets-mean-165000-homes-could-bypass-local-plans-warns-lga-56440.

Beveridge, C., Biberbach, P., & Hamilton, J. (2016, May). *Empowering Planning to Deliver Great Places: An Independent Review of the Scottish Planning System*. Edinburgh: Scottish Government. https://beta.gov.scot/binaries/content/documents/govscot/publications/advice-and-guidance/2016/05/empowering-planning-to-deliver-great-places/documents/1aed2528-cdd6-4100-854e-cb5b4777e0b5/1aed2528-cdd6-4100-854e-cb5b4777e0b5/govscot:document/.

Bramley, G., Pawson, H., White, M., Watkins, D., & Pleace, N. (2010). *Estimating Housing Need*. London: DCLG. https://www.gov.uk/government/publications/estimating-housing-need.

Brownhill, S., & Bradley, Q. (Eds.). (2017). *Localism and Neighbourhood Planning: Power to the People?* Bristol: Policy Press.

Campaign to Protect Rural England. (2017). *Needless Demand: How a Focus on Need Can Help Solve the Housing Crisis*. London: Campaign to Protect Rural England. https://www.cpre.org.uk/resources/housing-and-planning/housing/item/4677-needless-demand-how-a-focus-on-need-can-help-solve-the-housing-crisis.

Conservative Party. (2010). *Open Source Planning Green Paper*. London: Conservative Party. https://issuu.com/conservatives/docs/opensourceplanning.

Crisis. (2018). *Everybody In: How to End Homelessness in Britain*. London: Crisis. https://www.crisis.org.uk/media/238959/everybody_in_how_to_ end_homelessness_in_great_britain_2018.pdf.

Cromarty, H. (2018). *Starter Homes for First-Time Buyers (England)* (Briefing Paper Number 07643). file:///C:/Users/User/Downloads/CBP-7643%20(2).pdf.

Davison, M., Nicol, S., Roys, M., Garrett, H., Beaumont, A., & Turner, C. (2012). *The Cost of Poor Housing in Northern Ireland*. Belfast: Northern Ireland Housing Executive. https://www.nihe.gov.uk/cost_of_poor_ housing_in_ni.pdf.

DCLG. (2012). *National Planning Policy Framework*. London: DCLG. https://www.gov.uk/government/publications/national-planning-policy-framework--2.

DCLG. (2014). *Evaluation of the New Homes Bonus*. London: DCLG. https:// assets.publishing.service.gov.uk/government/uploads/system/uploads/ attachment_data/file/387152/NHB_Evaluation_FINAL_report.pdf.

DCLG. (2015). *Guidance: Housing and Economic Development Needs Assessments*. London: DCLG. https://www.gov.uk/guidance/housing-and-economic-development-needs-assessments.

DCLG. (2016a). *2014-Based Household Projections in England, 2014 to 2039*. London: DCLG. https://www.gov.uk/government/statistics/2014-based-household-projections-in-england-2014-to-2039.

DCLG (2016b) *New Homes Bonus: Sharpening the Incentive Government Response to the Consultation*. London: DCLG. https://assets.publishing. service.gov.uk/government/uploads/system/uploads/attachment_data/ file/577904/NHB_Consultation_Response_Doc.pdf.

DCLG. (2017a). *Fixing Our Broken Housing Market* (Cm 9352). London: DCLG. https://assets.publishing.service.gov.uk/government/uploads/sys-tem/uploads/attachment_data/file/590464/Fixing_our_broken_housing_ market_-_print_ready_version.pdf.

DCLG. (2017b). *Planning for the Right Homes in the Right Places: Consultation Proposals*. London: DCLG. https://www.gov.uk/government/consultations/ planning-for-the-right-homes-in-the-right-places-consultation-proposals.

Eurostat. (2018). *Statistics Explained*. https://ec.europa.eu/eurostat/statis-tics-explained/index.php?title=File:Housing_cost_overburden_rate_by_ tenure_status,_2016_(%25_of_population)_YB18.png.

Fitzpatrick, S., Pawson, H., Bramley, G., Wilcox, S., Watts B., & Wood, J. (2018). *The Homelessness Monitor: England 2018*. London: Crisis. https:// www.crisis.org.uk/media/238700/homelessness_monitor_england_2018. pdf.

Fraser, I. (2017, November 20). Inside the Government's Quarrels on How to Fix the Housing Market. *Telegraph*. http://www.telegraph.co.uk/business/2017/11/20/inside-governments-machinations-solve-uks-housing-crisis-threatening/.

Holmans, A. (2015). *Future Need and Demand for Housing in Wales*. Cardiff: Public Policy Institute for Wales. https://sites.cardiff.ac.uk/ppiw/files/2015/10/Future-Need-and-Demand-for-Housing-in-Wales.pdf.

House of Commons Public Accounts Committee. (2017, February 22). *Oral Evidence: Housing: State of the Nation*. HC 958 Question 17. London: House of Commons. https://publications.parliament.uk/pa/cm201617/cmselect/cmpubacc/958/958.pdf.

Institute for Public Policy Research Commission on Social Justice. (2018b). *Prosperity and Justice: A Plan for the New Economy. The Final Report of the IPPR Commission on Economic Justice* London: Institute for Public Policy Research. https://www.ippr.org/files/2018-08/1535639099_prosperity-and-justice-ippr-2018.pdf.

Javid, S. (2016, October 10). *Hansard*, vol. 615, col. 976. https://hansard.parliament.uk/Commons/2016-10.../NeighbourhoodPlanningBill.

Javid, S. (2017). *Oral Statement to Parliament: Local Housing Need*. https://www.gov.uk/government/speeches/local-housing-need.

Jones Lang LaSalle (JLL). (2016, February). *Scotland Residential Forecast, 2016: Rising to the Challenge*. http://residential.jll.co.uk/new-residential-thinking-home/research/scotland-residential-forecast-february-2016.

Kaszynska, P., Parkinson, J., & Fox, W. (2016). *Re-thinking Neighbourhood Planning: From Consultation to Collaboration*. (A ResPublica Green Paper). https://www.architecture.com/Files/RIBAHoldings/PolicyAndInternationalRelations/Policy/RIBAResPublica-Re-thinkingNeighbourhoodPlanning.pdf.

Lloyd, G. (2016). Land Use Planning in Northern Ireland. In P. Shanks & D. Mullins (Eds.), *Housing in Northern Ireland* (pp. 129–140). London: Chartered Institute of Housing.

Local Plans Expert Group. (2016). *Local Plans Expert Group: Report to the Secretary of State for Communities and Local Government*. London: Department for Communities and Local Government. https://www.gov.uk/government/uploads/system/uploads/attachment_data/file/508345/Local-plans-report-to-governement.pdf.

Mayor of London. (2013). *The 2013 London Strategic Housing Market Assessment: Part of the Evidence Base for the Mayor's London Plan*. London: Mayor of London. file:///C:/Users/User/Downloads/FALP%20SHMA%202013.pdf.

Mayor of London. (2018). *London Living Rent*. London: Mayor of London. https://www.london.gov.uk/what-we-do/housing-and-land/renting/london-living-rent.

McPeake, J. (2014). *The Changing Face of Housing Need in Northern Ireland*. https://www.qub.ac.uk/research-centres/TheInstituteofSpatialand EnvironmentalPlanning/filestore/Filetoupload,759315,en.pdf.

Meen, G. (2018). *How Should Housing Affordability Be Measured?* UK Collaborative Centre for Housing Evidence. http://housingevidence.ac.uk/wp-content/uploads/2018/09/R2018_02_01_How_to_measure_affordability.pdf.

MHCLG. (2018a). *Live Tables on House Building: New Build Dwellings*. London: MHCLG. https://www.gov.uk/government/statistical-data-sets/live-tables-on-house-building.

MHCLG. (2018b). *Housing Need Assessment*. London: MHCLG. https://www.gov.uk/guidance/housing-and-economic-development-needs-assessments.

MHCLG. (2018c). *National Planning Policy Framework*. London: MHCLG. https://assets.publishing.service.gov.uk/government/uploads/system/uploads/attachment_data/file/728643/Revised_NPPF_2018.pdf.

MHCLG. (2018d). *Housebuilding Completions Per 1000 Households*. London: MHCLG. http://opendatacommunities.org/data/house-building/completions-ratio/by-category.

Morton, A. (2016, July 21). How to Deliver a One Nation Housing Policy. *Conservative Home*. https://www.conservativehome.com/thetorydiary/2016/07/delivering-a-one-nation-housing-policy.html.

Nathaniel Litchfields and Partners. (2018). Local Choices?: Housing Delivery Through Neighbourhood Plans. *Insight May*. https://lichfields.uk/media/4128/local-choices_housing-delivery-through-neighbourhood-plans.pdf.

National Audit Office. (2013). *The New Homes Bonus*. London: National Audit Office. https://www.nao.org.uk/wp-content/uploads/2013/03/10122-001-New-Homes-Bonus_HC-1047.pdf.

National Centre for Social Research. (2013). *British Social Attitudes 28*. London: National Centre for Social Research.

Northern Ireland Housing Executive. (2011). *More Than Bricks: Forty Years of the Housing Executive*. Belfast: Northern Ireland Executive. https://www.nihe.gov.uk/more_than_bricks.pdf.

Paris, C. (Ed.). (2001). *Housing in Northern Ireland—And Comparisons with the Republic of Ireland*. London and Coventry: Chartered Institute of Housing.

Pickard, J., & Evans, J. (2017, January 5). UK Housing White Paper Risks "Huge Backlash". *Financial Times.* https://www.ft.com/content/3bffa61a-d280-11e6-b06b-680c49b4b4c0.

Policy Exchange. (2018). *Building More, Building Beautiful: How Design and Style Can Unlock the Housing Crisis.* London: Policy Exchange. https://policyexchange.org.uk/wp-content/uploads/2018/06/Building-More-Building-Beautiful.pdf.

Scottish Government. (2014a). *National Planning Framework 3.* Edinburgh: Scottish Government. http://www.gov.scot/Publications/2014/06/3539.

Scottish Government. (2014b). *Housing Need and Demand Assessment (HNDA): A Manager's Guide.* Edinburgh: Scottish Government. http://www.gov.scot/Topics/Built-Environment/Housing/supply-demand/chma/hnda/ManagerGuide2014.

Shelter. (2016a). *The Living Home Standard.* London: Shelter. https://england.shelter.org.uk/__data/assets/pdf_file/0010/1288387/FINAL_Living_home_standard_report.pdf.

Shelter. (2016b). *Living Home Findings.* London: Shelter. https://england.shelter.org.uk/__data/assets/pdf_file/0011/1288388/FINAL_Living_home_standard_Findings_report-insert.pdf.

Shelter Scotland. (2016). *Affordable Housing Need in Scotland: Final Report—September 2015.* http://scotland.shelter.org.uk/__data/assets/pdf_file/0009/1190871/7909_Final_Housing_Needs_Research.pdf/_nocache.

Turley Planning Consultants. (2014). *Neighbourhood Planning: Plan and Deliver?* London: Turley Planning Consultants.

Welsh Government. (2016). *Planning Policy Wales: Edition 9.* Cardiff: Welsh Government. http://gov.wales/topics/planning/policy/ppw/?lang=en.

Welsh Government. (2017). *All Wales Planning Performance Annual Report.* Cardiff: Welsh Government. http://gov.wales/topics/planning/planningstats/annual-performance-report/?lang=en.

Welsh Government. (2018). *Planning Policy Wales: Edition 10.* Cardiff: Welsh Government. https://beta.gov.wales/planning-policy-wales-edition-10.

Wilson, W. (1998). *Rent Levels, Affordability and Housing Benefit* (Research Paper 98/69). London: House of Commons. file:///C:/Users/User/Downloads/RP98-69%20(2).pdf.

6

Making Better Use of the Existing Housing Stock

At current replacement levels each new home built in England will have to last 2000 years (Local Government Association 2017). In 1968, the most productive new house construction year in England, 353,440 new homes were built adding 2% to the housing stock whereas, in 2016/2017, 183,750 new homes were built contributing only 0.7% to existing supply. This low new housebuilding level means that using the current stock to its full potential is important to improving housing conditions. Public and private initiatives have produced significant changes in how houses are used, not least by house to flat conversions—there were 5680 recorded house to flat conversions in 2016/2017—by extensions to existing dwellings, changing existing building use and, important to believers in a 'property-owning democracy', modifications to the tenure structure. In England, the recent focus on new house production in local plans has tended to obscure upgrading the current housing stock. Stewart and Lynch (2018, p. 2) comment: 'while housing aspects of environmental health are a fundamental part of public health, they are constantly being overlooked in terms of policy development. This has to change'.

© The Author(s) 2019
B. Lund, *Housing in the United Kingdom*,
https://doi.org/10.1007/978-3-030-04128-1_6

Empty Homes

Empty houses can signal a buoyant housing market as more people move home so the number of homes unoccupied for more than six months—designated 'long-term empty'—is a more pertinent statistic to use when exploring the problem. Across England, there were about 216,000 long-term empty homes in 2017 (BBC News 2018b), down from 318,642 in 2005 (Wilson et al. 2018). Long-term empty homes reflect the strength of the regional housing markets, being 1.3% in the North West and North East but only 0.6% in London (Empty Homes Agency 2016).

Over the years, local authorities have been granted several powers to bring empty homes back into use including:

- Compulsory Purchase: regarded as a 'last resort' in solving the problem (Wilson et al. 2016);
- Variations in council tax premiums and exemptions;
- Local government can undertake works and place a charge on the property that can be sold at auction under the Enforced Sales Procedure;
- Empty Dwelling Management Orders (EDMOs) allowing local authorities to take over management if a property has been empty for a specified period;
- A range of other powers such as requiring owners to make a property safe.

The coalition's government stated that it would 'explore a range of measures to bring empty homes into use' (HM Government 2010). Specific funding streams were made available in the Empty Homes Programme—worth £156 million between 2012 and 2015—and £60 million in the Clusters of Empty Homes Programme, aimed at empty home concentrations in low housing demand areas. Empty Homes Loans supplied credit to empty property owners but were soon ended due to low take-up and the coalition's government's austerity agenda. Some of the government money put into these funding schemes was used to alleviate the problems caused by axing the

Housing Market Renewal Pathfinders Initiative (see Chapter 4). In 2015, the Conservative government abolished dedicated funding streams aimed at bringing empty houses back into use but specific bids for schemes to re-occupy vacant houses could be made to the Homes and Communities agency—now named Homes England. Cutbacks in local authority spending have to reduce the human resources available to prepare and implement schemes such as Empty Home Strategies. In 2017, only 19 of the 247 councils responding to a BBC information request in England and Wales had used an Empty Home Management Order in the past five years (BBC News 2018a).

Vacant houses not only waste resources, but their unsightly appearance can also blight an area. Market mechanisms help to reduce vacant properties with private landlords acquiring empty homes but state involvement can steer the market towards social objectives such as promoting homeownership. In the early 1980s, Michael Heseltine introduced 'homesteading' whereby people wanting to become homeowners could locate an empty house and approach a local authority or housing association for help in acquiring and improving it. There is an information shortage on bringing empty homes into use but it seems that, in recent years, private landlords rather than owner-occupiers have been principal participants in the process with implications for the distribution of wealth and long-term spending on means-tested housing allowances.

Living Over the Shop (LOTS)

In the 1980s the Living Over the Shop campaign, organised by a non-profit company, was successful in persuading the government to invest in using the empty spaces above shops for housing. By 1998, 10,000 dwellings above shops had been created, often through Housing Association programmes (Beatley 2000). The Federation of Master Builders (2017) identified the potential to create between 300,000 and 400,000 new homes by converting empty spaces above high street shops. The increasing reliance on the market has limited above shop conversions for social housing but private landlords may now show a greater interest in flats over shops because the hikes in Land

Stamp Duty Tax for second homes do not apply to commercial properties. However, mortgage providers are reluctant to supply mortgages for flats above shops (This is Money 2017), indicating that mortgage underwriting by the state may be necessary to boost over the shop living. The recent decline in retailing—one in seven shops are now vacant (The Home 2017)—has generated interest in 'Living in the Shop', that is the full conversion of shops, especially in town centre retail districts, into homes.

Buy to Leave Empty

In the 1960s, developers leaving commercial properties empty, so they could be sold quickly at a property boom zenith, was highlighted in the media (Scott 1996). The issue re-emerged in 2013, this time in relation to residential property. There were accusations that developers were selling blocks of flats to investors, often from overseas, who kept properties empty being content to make gains through accelerating values. It was alleged that residential property was being traded like gold (Wainwright 2014) and, in 2013, the coalition government introduced an annual tax on enveloped dwellings (ATED), that is, property owned in investment vehicles valued at over £500,000.

The evidence on the extent and location of the buy to leave empty problem is disputed (Spurr 2016) but although property purchase in London by overseas purchasers is extensive—in the City of Westminster 38%, in Kensington and Chelsea 32% between 2014 and 2016—a report commissioned by the Mayor of London found 'there was almost no evidence of [new-build] units being left entirely empty—certainly less than 1%' (Fraser 2017). At the end of 2015, Islington Borough Council required all new homes built within its boundaries to be regularly occupied—a policy to be enforced through a Section 106 agreements and High Court injunctions. Similar action by other local authorities would mitigate the problem. In the 2017 Autumn Budget the Chancellor of the Exchequer announced that local authorities would be able to charge 100% council tax on empty homes, an initiative that a Director of a Chartered Accountant firm said 'risked being a triumph of symbolism over substance' (quoted in Nemeth 2017).

Home Improvement

From the late 1950s to the early 1980s government support for home improvements was robust. To the Conservatives, improvement was a mechanism to forestall demolishing sub-standard houses and their replacement by council housing. In 1959, 'standard' local authority grants for installing basic amenities—bathroom, wash hand basin, hot and cold water supply, WC and food store—became mandatory if a house had a fifteen-year life. This, plus central government loans to building societies to encourage lending on pre-1919 stock, stimulated the sale of houses owned by private landlords to homeowners, often sitting tenants. Such 'standard' grants made a major contribution to improving housing standards in the 1960s and 1970s.

The Labour Party leadership also came to view improvement grants as a way to help its supporters and, under the 1969 and 1974 Housing Acts, resources for improvement became more selective on an area basis, first via Housing Improvement Areas and then through Housing Action Areas. Area improvement was regarded as a way to uplift a district and encourage private investment. 'Enveloping'—renovating the external fabric of a dwelling block, usually terraced houses, by the local authority at no cost to those owners, encouraging the occupants to improve the interiors—was a popular form of intervention.

Although the Conservative government (1979–1997) initially injected more resources into improvement grants, in the middle 1980s, by increasing selectivity on a means-tested income basis, they reduced expenditure. New Labour continued this policy and, by 2010, spending in England on improvement grants was down from £336.7 million in 1995 to £232.1 million (Stephens et al. 2018) albeit that New Labour's area based programmes injected resources into improvement. From the 1990s home improvement gradually became an owner responsibility with only highly selective help, mainly targeted on older people, offered by the state. Private landlords made a contribution to improvement, often through buying older property and upgrading it for letting. Numerous television programmes such as *Property Ladder*, *House Doctor* and *Homes Under the Hammer* encouraged the process. By 2016/2017 the austerity agenda had reduced state spending on improvement to only £61.5 million in England (Stephens et al. 2018).

Value Added Tax (VAT)

VAT on new building is zero-rated whereas improvements, conversions and extensions can be subject to up to 20% VAT. This has led pressure groups, arguing that the system discourages improvement and encourages demolition and new build, to campaign for VAT reductions on improvements. However, given the large revenue obtained through VAT on upgrading property, the Treasury is unlikely to surrender the entire amount. Selective proposals involving VAT relief on the work necessary to achieve the decent home standard would have more chance of obtaining Treasury approval but, given the difficulties that second steppers encounter in acquiring more space for their children, VAT relief on extensions for extra bedrooms may secure Treasury favour (see Chapter 8).

Energy Efficiency

According to the Westminster Sustainable Business Forum (2016, p. 4), increasing home efficiency 'offers a highly cost-effective route to engaging with the three elements of the energy trilemma: decarbonising energy systems, ensuring security of energy supply and ensuring energy is affordable'.

Progress on energy efficiency is measured through the government's Standard Assessment Procedure (SAP), that gives an index on a scale of 1 (highly inefficient) to 100 (zero energy cost). Mean SAP ratings

Table 6.1 Energy efficiency ratings by housing tenure 1996–2016 (England)

	1996	2004	2007	2010	2013	2015	2016
							Mean EER rating
Owner-occupied	43.8	47.5	50.3	54.3	58.5	60.5	60.7
Private rented	40.4	46.0	49.1	53.9	58.4	60.2	60.3
Private sector	**43.3**	**47.3**	**50.1**	**54.2**	**58.5**	**60.4**	**60.6**
Local authority	:	:	:	60.8	64.9	66.2	65.9
Housing association	:	:	:	63.4	66.2	67.7	68.2
Social sector	**48.7**	**54.9**	**58.1**	**62.1**	**65.6**	**67.0**	**67.3**
All tenures	**44.5**	**48.7**	**51.5**	**55.6**	**59.7**	**61.5**	**61.7**

Source MHCLG (2018b)

over time are given in Table 6.1 but the table masks the incidence of very low energy efficient properties with, in 2016/2017, 25% of private rented properties were in bands E-G compared to 8% in the social housing sector (MHCLG 2018a). The rate of progress has been slowing down with very little improvement between 2015 and 2016.

Under the coalition government, energy efficiency was a Liberal Democrat domain and. ensuring that new homes were energy efficient and old homes were retrofitted had a high policy profile. The coalition's flagship initiative, the Green Deal offered loans of £6500 per home for energy saving, to be paid back via reduced energy bills, but the scheme had a low take-up because interest rates were set at 7.9–10.3%. An Energy Company Obligation, based on New Labour schemes and focused on the poorest and most vulnerable households, and those living in 'hard to treat' homes was set up. However, towards the end of the coalition government's term in office, energy efficiency slipped down the political agenda and Cameron's Conservative government reduced state involvement not only by ending the Green Deal (which was subsequently re-launched privately) but by reducing other grants and modifying the obligations placed on energy companies.

Overall, some progress was made up to 2015 in improving energy efficiency but cutting spending and minimising 'regulatory burdens', rather than maximising long-term efficiency, then became the dominant preoccupations and improvement has slowed (National Infrastructure

Commission (2017). There is considerable potential for more energy saving with the UK Energy Research Centre (2017, p. 1) stating that 'Cost-effective investments to 2035 could save around one-quarter of the energy currently used, an average saving of £270 per household per year at current energy prices'. Several policy initiatives are available to cut energy consumption, many not involving additional government spending. A new state version of the Green Deal based on 'pay as you save', with lower interest rates, would be beneficial as would imposing minimum standards in the owner-occupier sector to prevent the sale of property with low energy performance and/or variable Land Tax Stamp Duty rates according to energy efficiency (Houses of Parliament Parliamentary Office of Science and Technology, 2017, p. 2). More robust supplier obligations directed at ending fuel poverty would be a productive initiative. Transfer of homes from landlords to tenants (see below) would probably improve energy efficiency.

Decent Homes

In England, progress in upgrading older property can be monitored via the decent homes standard. This was set in 2002 and updated in 2006. To be decent, a home:

- must meet the current statutory minimum standard for housing: in 2006 this was determined by Housing Health and Safety Rating System (HHSRS);
- must be in a reasonable state of repair;
- must have reasonably modern facilities and services, such as;

  – a kitchen which is 20 years old or less;
  – a bathroom which is 30 years old or less;
  – adequate external noise insulation;
  – a reasonable degree of thermal comfort. (DCLG 2006)

The House of Commons Communities and Local Government Committee (2010, p. 12), praising the progress on decent homes, declared 'the decent homes standard is, nonetheless, a low standard', and the Green Paper on social housing said:

... the Decent Homes Standard has not been revised since 2006, so we believe it should be reviewed to consider whether it is demanding enough and delivers the right standards for social housing alongside other tenures. The standard could also be updated to reflect Government's current and forthcoming priorities. (MHCLG 2018c, p. 24)

Following the Grenfell Tower disaster, fire safety is an obvious addition to the standard.

Local authorities can take action against landlords in breach of the HHSRS element in the decent homes yardstick but local authority landlords cannot be taken to court and, as a result of rent limits that have remained unchanged since the 1950s, the current requirements on fitness standards in the private landlord sector are ineffective. Karen Buck, MP for Westminster North has introduced private member bills to improve basic conditions in the rented sector. Under her Homes (Fitness for Human Habitation) Bill 2017–2019, likely to become law, if a landlord does not maintain a property to a revised 'fit for human habitation standard', tenants will have the right to take action in court.

The per cent of non-decent homes is set out in Table 6.2. It reveals a slowdown in the rate at which homes are becoming decent with an increase in the proportion of non-decent homes in the owner-occupied sector between 2015 and 2016.

Table 6.2   Non-decent homes: England 2006–2016 (%)

	Owner-occupied	Private rented	Social rented
2006	34.4	46.7	28.8
2007	34.1	45.4	29.4
2008	32.3	44.0	27.2
2009	29.3	40.8	23.2
2010	25.6	37.2	19.9
2011	22.3	35.0	16.8
2012	20.3	33.1	15.2
2013	19.4	29.8	14.7
2014	18.6	28.6	14.3
2015	18.3	28.5	13.0
2016	19.7	26.8	12.6

Source MHCLG (2018a)

Because the private landlord sector has grown substantially, there were 1,301,000 private rented homes below the government's decent home standard in 2016 compared to 994,000 in 2004 (MHCLG 2018d). The private landlord sector had the highest severe problem incidence with, as examples, 15.4% having at least one health and safety hazard and 5.1% with excess cold—very important for energy efficiency (MHCLG 2018d). Given the tax breaks available to landlords, the government's £8.6 billion annual spending in the private landlord sector through LHA and that the mean rent in the private landlord rent was £192 per week in 2016/2017 (MHCLG 2018e), the overall performance of private landlordism in providing decent homes is disappointingly poor.

Private landlord regulation is light touch with, no compulsory private landlord registration in England. The only significant policy to induce landlords to upgrade their properties is the requirement that, from April 2018, landlords will have to ensure that their properties reach at least a grade E energy efficiency rating before a new tenancy agreement is made. These requirements will apply to all private rented properties—including already occupied properties—from April 2020. In an answer to a parliamentary question, Richard Harrison, speaking for the Department for Business, Energy and Industrial Strategy, stated:

> Data derived from the 2014 English Housing Survey shows that the average annual cost of heating an E rated home in the private rental sector to an adequate level is £510 cheaper than for an F rated private rented sector home, and £990 cheaper than for a G rated property. (Harrison 2017)

How great would be the benefit of a minimum C rating?

Rather than relying on private landlords to upgrade their properties more assistance could be given to potential homeowners. This would be cheaper for the state than the long-term payment of LHA. Schemes—similar to 'homesteading' for empty houses—involving the sale of non-decent homes to low-income households for owner-occupation, accompanied by state-sponsored mortgages and improvement grants could be introduced.

New Home Energy Efficiency

Compared to older homes, new homes are energy efficient with 80% of new homes rated AB meaning, according to Macbryde Homes (2017), that new build homeowners will spend on average £443.30 a year (£276 heating/£108 hot water/£60 lighting) on energy—well under half the £1072 an owner of an older home can expect to spend and a saving of £629 a year. Enhanced energy efficiency also means low carbon emissions and it is possible to design new homes with zero-carbon emissions. New Labour proposed to phase in enhanced building regulations so that, by 2016, all new homes would be 'zero-carbon', defined as 'over a year, the net carbon emissions from all energy use in the home would be zero'. The Liberal Democrats adopted New Labour's agenda but the Conservatives, were concerned that higher standards would add to new house prices. A *Guardian* report claimed that, when asked about the delay in establishing new standards, a DCLG spokesperson said: 'We want to see greener homes, but we need to avoid excessive regulation which will simply reduce house-building and push up the cost of buying a new home' (Harvey 2013). Free from Liberal Democrat influence, the 2015 Conservative government announced there would be no zero-carbon obligations imposed on developers and stalled moves to ensure that new houses were cheaper to heat. In 2017, 1% of new houses received an A energy efficiency rating (SAP rating) and 82% were awarded a B rating but, disappointingly, 12% were rated C, 4% D and 1% E (MHCLG 2018d).

Fuel Poverty

There are various fuel poverty definitions. Energy UK (2017, p. 1) defines a fuel-poor household as:

> …one which needs to spend more than 10% of its income on all fuel use and to heat its home to an adequate standard, defined in England as 21°C in the living room and 18°C in other occupied rooms.

In 2014 the Energy UK fuel poverty definition was abandoned in England as the official fuel poverty line in favour of the Low-income High Costs (LIHC) indicator. The Department for Business, Energy and Industrial Strategy (2017, p. 3) stated:

> Under the LIHC indicator, a household is considered to be fuel poor if:
>
> - they have required fuel costs that are above average (the national median level)
> - were they to spend that amount, they would be left with a residual income below the official poverty line.

The *Annual fuel poverty statistics report: 2017* (Department for Business, Energy and Industrial Strategy [DBEIS] 2017) estimated the proportion of households in fuel poverty in England at 11% (approximately 2.50 million households). This was an increase from 2.35 million households in 2013. The average fuel poverty gap (the difference between income and amount needed to meet the fuel poverty threshold) was £353.

Fuel poverty is driven by the interaction between a home's energy efficiency; energy costs and household income. In 2014, 28.5% of residents in properties living in G rated homes were classed as fuel poor, compared to 2.5% in C+ rated properties. The fuel poverty gap for G rated properties (£1345) was about seven times higher than for C+ rated (DBEIS 2017).

The depth of fuel poverty was highest in the private landlord sector (£410), followed by £381 for owner-occupiers; £200 for housing association tenants and £175 for local authority tenants (DBEIS 2017). From 2003, the rate of fuel poverty reduction has been lowest in the private landlord sector (ONS 2018). By age group, the highest proportion in fuel poverty was 16%/18% for children under 16 (DBEIS 2017), in part a reflection of the high percentage of children living in the private landlord sector. Fuel poverty is related to premature winter deaths with around 10,000 deaths in 2016–2017 related to cold homes (Institute for Public Policy Research 2018).

The government's statutory fuel poverty target for England is expressed in vague terms, that is, 'to ensure that as many fuel-poor homes as reasonably practicable achieve a minimum energy efficiency rating of a Band C, by 2030' (Department of Energy and Climate Change 2015). The ONS (2018) projected that the long-term trend for fuel poverty to decline would end, partially a consequence of the reductions in the energy efficiency obligations on energy companies as a 'quick fix' to allow the companies to reduce overall energy payments and shoot the Labour Party's fox of an energy price freeze made in the countdown to the 2015 General Election. The profits of the energy companies remain high—five times too high according to Competition and Markets Authority (2016), partially the outcome of loyal customers being placed on the highest energy—the 'standard'—tariff. In 2017, Theresa May announced that there would be a five-year cap on this standard tariff.

The Institute for Public Policy Research has stated that, if the 2030 target is to be realised for all 2.5 million fuel-poor homes, then:

> the scheme will need to undergo substantial changes…based on current rates of installation of energy efficiency measures, reaching all homes with even one measure, let alone sufficient measures to elevate these households to EPC band C, will not be achieved until 2091 at the very earliest. (Institute for Public Policy Research 2018, p. 9)

Scotland, Wales and Northern Ireland

Scotland

The Scottish government has adopted the same broad approach to home improvement as Westminster stating: 'Responsibility for keeping houses in good condition lies mainly with the owner' (Scottish Government 2017). In Scotland, spending on home improvement assistance has declined from £42.9 million in 2009 to £91 million in 2016/2017 (Stephens et al. 2018). Local authorities can provide

Housing Improvement and Repair Grants to help with the cost of bringing private houses up to modern standards and to deal with serious disrepair. Such grants are limited although care and repair services appear to be more robust than in England. As in England, the Green Deal, funded by loans from the Green Deal Finance Company, no longer operates in Scotland but the Scottish government offers help for energy efficiency via schemes, targeted on areas with a high level of fuel poverty, run by local government. The national scheme, *Warmer Homes Scotland* is available to vulnerable private sector households through *Warmworks Scotland*. The Scottish Government also makes available interest-free, unsecured loans of up to £15,000 to install measures such as solid wall insulation, double glazing or a new boiler.

In 2017 there were 37,000 long-term (over 6 months) empty properties in Scotland. Of these over half had been empty for over 12 months (Scottish Empty Homes Partnership 2017). The empty homes problem is being tackled in Scotland via the £4 million Empty Homes Loans Fund offering interest-free loans to bring vacant homes back into use and the Empty Homes Partnership run by Shelter that has brought almost 2500 homes back into use.

Scotland does not have a decent homes standard. Two other measures are used. The Scottish Housing Quality Standard (SHQS) is a collection of five broad housing criteria that must all be met if the property is to pass standard. These criteria comprise 55 elements and nine sub-elements against which properties are measured. The Scottish Tolerable Standard is a very basic fitness level that a home must meet to be deemed habitable. In 2016 1.3% of all dwellings were below the standard, down from 3.6% in 2010 (Stephens et al. 2018). The Scottish Government set a policy target for social landlords to bring their stock up to every element of the SHQS. Private sector landlords and owner-occupied households are not subject to the policy target. In 2016, 45% of all dwellings and 47% of private sector dwellings failed to meet the SHQS with energy inefficiency and not being healthy, safe and secure the principal reasons. 38% of social sector homes did not reach the SHQS. At 14% falling below Shelter's decent condition standard (Shelter 2016a, b) Scotland's performance, relative to England has been sound. Homeowners in Scotland can borrow up to £32,000 interest-free to energy efficiency and other aspects their homes. Between 2010 and 2015 there was improvement in the energy efficiency profile of housing with a 74% increase in the share of the most energy efficient dwellings (rated C or better). The proportion rated F and G dropped from 6% to 3% (Scottish Government 2016).

Wales

In Wales, home improvement is being addressed via a national, interest-free loan scheme, introduced in 2015 and worth £10 million over 15 years. The scheme is delivered by local authorities and is aimed at enabling the owners of sub-standard properties who pass affordability criteria to upgrade their properties. As loans are repaid, the funding is recycled.

To tackle the problem of an estimated 23,000 empty properties in Wales in 2012, the Welsh Government set up a £20 million Houses into Homes scheme offering interest-free loans to bring empty houses or commercial buildings back into use as homes—including dividing them into flats—for sale or rent. 5.8% of the empty homes were re-occupied in 2016/2017 but local authority performance in bringing empty homes back into use was variable (Crisis 2018).

In 2016, the Welsh Government published its first Energy Efficiency Strategy (Welsh Government 2016a). It noted the limited powers of the Welsh Government to promote energy efficiency and its older homes inheritance, stating:

Modelled fuel poverty estimates for 2012 indicate that 386,000 (30 per cent) of all households in Wales were fuel poor. This is an increase of 54,000 households since 2008…. The increase in the number of fuel poor households since 2008 has resulted from significant increases in energy prices during the period, along with falling or flat lining incomes. (Welsh Government 2016b, p. 27)

The strategy endorsed the existing domestic energy efficiency programmes in Wales, notably the *Warm Homes Programme*, providing funding for home energy efficiency improvements to low-income households and people living in deprived communities. In 2017 it was announced that £104 million, with part of the funding coming from the European Union, would be spent over four years on this programme.

Shelter's decent conditions measure, with 28% of households in Wales falling below the threshold (Shelter 2016a, b), higher than all the English regions except London and twice the rate in Scotland, indicated that Wales is a laggard in home improvement, an impression that the preliminary results of the Welsh Housing Conditions Survey 2017–2018 appear to confirm (Statistics For Wales 2018). 82% of houses in Wales were free from category 1 hazards compared to 88% in England. The average SAP rating for a residential dwelling in Wales was 61, slightly lower than in England.

Northern Ireland

From the 1990s to the 2000s major improvements were made in housing conditions in Northern Ireland via new build and upgrading the existing housing stock. Total spending on private sector grants averaged about £43 million per year from 2001/2002 to 2008/2009 but then declined to £12.1 million in 2014/2015 (Frey and Brown 2016) with further cutbacks in the pipeline. In 2017, the Northern Ireland Housing Executive announced:

> Due to the reduction in grants funding, we are currently only accepting applications for mandatory Disabled Facilities and Repair grants. Discretionary Renovation, Replacement and Home Repair Assistance grants are only available in exceptional circumstances…. We are not currently accepting new applications for Houses in Multiple Occupation (HMO), Living over the Shop (LOTS), or Group Repair Schemes. (Northern Ireland Housing Executive 2017, p. 1)

In the 'social' sector, Northern Ireland adopted the English decent homes standard and the injection of resources into meeting this standard resulted in the number of social homes falling below the decent homes standard reducing from 32% in 2001 to 11% in 2011 (Frey and Brown 2016).

In 2014 the Department for Social Development published its *Empty Homes Strategy and Action Plan* (Northern Ireland Department for Social Development 2014) promising to establish a dedicated Empty Homes Unit in the Northern Ireland Housing Executive, assisted by a £4.7 million funding scheme, charged with identifying empty homes and with a target to reduce the number of empty homes by 4% or taking action on 120 homes each year

Green Deal did not operate in Northern Ireland but a number of energy efficiency assistance schemes were in operation. The Affordable Warmth Grant scheme provides a package of energy efficiency and heating measures to owner-occupiers or householder of a privately rented property if gross annual household income is less than £20,000. The Utility Regulator's Northern Ireland Sustainable Energy Programme provides over £7million of funding for energy efficiency work in NI each year through schemes such as CosyHomes and Energyplus. Fuel poverty in Northern Ireland is far higher than in other parts of the UK—42% of households in Northern Ireland, 12% in England, 30% in Wales and 35% in Scotland—(UK Fuel Monitor 2016) mainly due to higher energy costs.

Maximising Space Use

In 2013 the coalition government abolished what it called the 'spare room subsidy' by restricting HB for social tenants to a specified number of bedrooms. The new rules allowed one bedroom for:

- every adult couple (married or unmarried)
- any other adult aged 16 or over
- any two children of the same sex aged under 16
- any two children aged under 10
- any other child (other than a foster child or child whose main home is elsewhere)

- children who can't share because of a disability or medical condition
- a carer (or team of carers) providing overnight care.
- an overnight carer who looks after someone in the home.

In justifying the spare room subsidy abolition—quickly to become known as the 'bedroom tax'—the coalition government argued that it enhanced fairness by aligning social with private tenants and it would help to maximise housing space use by encouraging social tenants to move to smaller properties. However, a report by the DWP (2015) revealed that only 8% of tenants hit by the bedroom tax moved to smaller properties, mainly because smaller homes were unavailable and claimants wanting to stay in their local area. Rather than move, tenants cut back spending on food and energy.

Measured by the bedroom standard, the number of under-occupying households in the owner-occupied sector in England increased between 1995–1996 and 2016–2017 from 39% (5.3 million households) to 50.5% (7.4 million households). In contrast, under-occupation amongst private renters fell from 18% in 1995–1996 to 14.8% in 2015–2016 and under-occupation amongst social renters declined from 12% to 8% (MHCLG 2018a). There are large differences in the percentage of households with two or more spare bedrooms across tenures. Owner-occupied households, at 46.5%, are three times more likely than private renters (15.1%) and four times as more likely than social renters (10.9%) to have two or more spare bedrooms (ONS 2014).

In *All That Is Solid: The Great Housing Disaster* (2014) Daniel Dorling argued that space differences in housing consumption were the outcome of the increase in overall inequality—the wealthy have more money to spend on new large homes and extensions. There have certainly been large number extensions in the owner-occupied sector: 38.2% of the owner-occupied homes had been extended between 1996 and 2015 compared to 4.6% in the social sector and in the 13.4% in the private rented sector (DCLG 2017).

On Dorling's inequality diagnosis, some combination of a mansion tax, capital gains taxation on annual wealth accumulation, a land value tax and far higher rates of council tax on expensive homes would be a remedy. Other ways to reduce under-occupation include:

- Specific local authority down-sizing initiatives targeted on elderly people such as help with moving costs, cash incentives to move from social housing based on the number of bedrooms surrendered, Seaside and Country Homes, offer households living in social rented housing in London the opportunity to move out of the capital to seaside and rural locations;
- Ending the 25% single-occupancy council tax reduction;
- Only 1% of homeowners aged over 65 moved in 2015 (Studd and Parker Estate Agents 2016). Removing Stamp Duty Land Tax on homeowner pensioners who downsize and/or direct state cash incentives would not only increase the supply of larger homes but would release equity to be passed on, via the Bank of Mum and Dad and the Bank of Grandpa and Grandma, to younger households to purchase homes.

Tenure Change

The average rent for a two-bedroom home in the private rented sector was £791 (£1716 in London) per month in 2017 whereas the average rent for a two-bedroom social sector home was £347 (£428 in London) (MHCLG 2018f). Shifting households between tenures could reduce housing expenditure, not only for households but for the state in reducing consumer subsidies. The necessary shift is from private renting with its high rent and long-term support via LHA—to owner-occupation and the social housing sector with rent control a mechanism to promote this change.

A Right to Buy for Private Landlord Tenants

In his 2015 campaign to become Labour Party leader, Jeremy Corbyn proposed a Right to Buy for private landlord tenants, funded by withdrawing the £14 billion tax allowances then given to buy-to-let landlords (*Independent* 2015). Surprisingly, a variation on this proposal was supported by the right inclined think-tank *Civitas*. In his *Civitas* publication, Saunders (2016) lamented the post-2004 decline in UK homeownership stating:

> The spread of home ownership in the twentieth century has distributed ownership of wealth more widely than ever before. It has also strengthened ties of community and rates of civic participation. Mass owner occupation has in these ways benefited individuals and the wider society. (Saunders 2016, p. viii)

Saunders did not place the entire blame for the decline in homeownership on private landlords but he claimed that the sector had to be trimmed. His Right to Buy scheme for private tenants involved:

- five year tenancies for most private lets to prevent evictions undermining the new Right to Buy;
- purchase rights for private tenants on the same terms as the Right to Buy for local authority tenants but with this right ending at the end of the five year tenancy, only available on properties more than 25 years old and the discount never be so high as to impose losses on the landlord;
- exempting landlords from capital gains tax on sales and other penalties, such as extra land stamp duty on second home purchase and the limit on tax relief on mortgage interest, should be revoked.

Rent Control

It is now conventional to divide rent control into two types. 'First generation' rent control, often called 'classic control', consisted of a rent freeze with upward adjustments only when sanctioned by the state. 'Fair rents', introduced in 1965, allowed rent assessment committees to set rents according to the local housing market but ignoring 'scarcity value'. 'First generation' control produced extensive selling to owner-occupiers, often to sitting tenants but free-market economists argued that such control reduced spending on the housing stock, prevented new investment in homes to let and produced a poor rented accommodation supply that restricted labour mobility (Minford et al. 1987). In contrast to classic rent control, so-called 'smart' rent regulation—the system operating in Germany—stabilises rents by allowing rent negotiation when a tenancy starts but control within the five-year tenancy duration. The 2016 Private Housing (Tenancies) (Scotland) Act attempted to create greater rent predictability by allowing landlords only one rent increase rents per year. In addition, local authorities have the power to create designated 'rent pressure zones' and apply a rent cap in these zones.

If the objective is to create a property-owning democracy then 'first generation' rent control is a path to take. When in operation, 4.1 million properties were transferred from private landlords to owner-occupiers—the most effective low-cost homeownership scheme ever!

Taxation Changes

In his 2015 Autumn Statement and Spending Review, George Osborne said:

> Frankly, people buying a home to let should not be squeezing out families who can't afford a home to buy. So I am introducing new rates of Stamp Duty that will be 3 per cent higher on the purchase of additional properties like buy-to-lets and second homes. (Osborne 2015)

He used the same 'squeezing out families' justification for gradually reducing tax relief on buy-to-let mortgages to the standard rate. Osborne's measures are starting to have an impact on buy-to-let mortgages loans down by 19% in March 2018 compared to March 2017. Further changes in taxation are an administratively efficient way to trim private landlordism. Gradual increases in the levy on Land Duty Stamp Duty on second homes and ending tax relief at the standard rate on buy-to-let mortgages are options and, subject impact, could enhance Treasury revenues.

Paying Local Housing Allowance to Low-Income Homeowners

Until April 2018, out of work homeowners received Support for Mortgage Interest (SMI) via Income Support/Universal Credit. SMI paid mortgage interest up to £200,000 of loan or mortgage, with, in 2016, the standard interest rate used to calculate SMI set at 3.12%. It was paid directly to the lender following a waiting period, normally 39 weeks after benefit has been claimed. However, from April 2018 payments were treated as a loan, to be repaid when the house is sold.

In the rented sector, HB/LHA is related to income and rent. The maximum rent on which benefit can be paid is determined by a Local Reference Rent (LRR), set for each broad rental market area, defined as 'an area in which a person could reasonably be expected to live having regard to facilities and services for the purposes of health, education, recreation, personal banking and shopping, taking account of the distance of travel, by public and private transport, to and from those facilities and services' (Fenton 2012). The LRR is set at the 30% percentile (reduced from the 50th percentile in 2011) of the rent levels in the area, excluding exceptionally high and low rents. LRRs for selected broad rental market areas in UK are set out in Table 6.3.

Note: The amount payable is subject to a total 'Benefits Cap'. In 2018 this was:

- £442.31 per week (£1916.67 per month or £23,000 per year) for couples and lone parents in Greater London

Table 6.3   Local reference rents: £s per week (three rooms, 2018)

Barnsley	98.07
Cambridge	247.50
Central London	835
Greater Liverpool	126.92
Inner East London	512.50
North Cumbria	109.61
Scunthorpe	98.65
Solihull	166.73

Source Valuation Office Agency (2018)

- £384.62 per week (£ 1666.67 per month or £20,000 per year) for couples and lone parents outside Greater London
- £296.35 per week (£1284.17 per month or £15,410 per year) for single adults in Greater London
- £257.69 per week (£1116.67 per month or £13,400 per year) for single adults outside Greater London

Allowing low-income homeowners an entitlement to LHA on mortgage payments, perhaps paid directly to the lender, at levels determined by LRRs, would have an impact on the homeownership rates as it would make homeownership more affordable for low-income households, especially those with children. State payments would move from private landlords to homeowners and end when the mortgage has been paid. However, such schemes have a low, almost non-existent, political profile and costs of potential schemes have not been explored. In limited circumstances, Housing Choice Vouchers, the United States equivalent of HB, can be paid to homeowners.

The Right to Buy (RTB) for Social Tenants

From 2004, New Labour placed more restrictions on the RTB and sales in England declined from 69,991 in 2003/2004 to 2739 in 2009/2010 (Stephens et al. 2018). A proportion of the stock sold under the RTB—perhaps 40% (Apps 2015)—has been bought by private landlords so has not been lost to the rented sector but private sector rents are much higher than in the local authority sector and this is reflected in state expenditure on LHA.

The coalition government 'revitalised' RTB in England by increasing discounts and modifying restrictions on resale. By 2015 about £42 billion had been raised in RTB receipts in England but only a small fraction had been spent on new social housing. Indeed, David Cameron's explicit commitment that the capital receipts from the 'revitalised' RTB would be spent by local government to replace the houses sold on a one-to-one basis has not been met (see Chapter 2). The 2015 Conservative Party manifesto announced that the RTB for council house tenants would be extended to housing association tenants and financed by forcing councils to sell their higher value property but this pledge was modified by an agreement with the housing associations to make the new RTB 'voluntary' on the part of associations and phasing in the process. Progress on implementing the idea has been described as 'glacial' (Sky News 2017).

Ending the Right to Buy for social tenants (as in Scotland and Wales) would prevent the loss of about 14,000 houses per year—London has a disproportionally high rate of sales—from the social housing sector.

Conclusion

State spending on improvement has been substantially cut in recent years and Turkington and Watson (2014, pp. 2–3) note that, both in political and academic circles, 'housing renewal tends to be less prominent than other aspects of policy such as new housing and affordability'.

That all the 'home nation' governments have reduced housing renewal spending reflects market reliance and the politics involved in making expenditure cuts: withdrawing money from those who have not yet received it is politically easier than taking money away from current recipients. Reducing 'backroom' staff is also more acceptable than cutting 'frontline' services, albeit that cuts have restricted the enforcement of standards. Given the importance of energy efficiency to alleviating fuel poverty and to climate change, reducing spending on energy efficiency programmes ought to be a last resort but, in England, the 'green agenda' has been diluted.

According to Eurostat's definition, a household is considered 'overburdened' when the total housing costs ('net' of housing allowances) represent more than 40% of disposable income, where housing costs include mortgage or housing loans interest payments for owners and rent payments for tenants. Utilities (water, electricity, gas and heating) and any costs related to regular maintenance and structural insurance are also included (see Pittini 2012). In 2015, the average per cent of households with housing cost overburden in the 28 European Union member states was 6.7% for owners with a mortgage and 5% in the

UK. For 'social' tenants it was 12.4% in the 28 European Union member states and 15.4% in the UK but for private tenants it was 27% in 28 European Union member states and 37.3% in the UK (Eurostat 2017). The lowest quality homes are to be found in the private landlord sector and the cutbacks in the personnel needed to implement standards have meant that enforcement action is rare. The Guardian reported that 'More than one in seven councils in England and Wales have failed to prosecute a single bad landlord over the past three years, despite some having very high numbers of homes classed as "non-decent"' (Wall 2018).

Shifting the tenure balance away from private renting to homeownership—thereby promoting a property-owning democracy—and to social housing would be an effective way to maximise consumer satisfaction in the ways the housing stock is used.

References

Apps, P. (2015, August 14). Right to Buy to Let. *Inside Housing*. https://www.insidehousing.co.uk/insight/insight/right-to-buy-to-let-44479.

BBC News. (2018a). *Moving Home Is "Becoming a Rarity"*. http://www.bbc.co.uk/news/business-43541990.

BBC News. (2018b, January 1). *More Than 11,000 UK Homes Empty for 10 Years*. http://www.bbc.co.uk/news/uk-42536418.

Beatley, T. (2000). *Green Urbanism: Learning from European Cities*. Washington, DC: Ireland Press.

Competition and Markets Authority. (2016). *Energy Market Investigation*. London: Competition and Markets Authority. https://www.gov.uk/cma-cases/energy-market-investigation.

Crisis. (2018). *Everybody In: How to End Homelessness in Britain*. London: Crisis. https://www.crisis.org.uk/media/238959/everybody_in_how_to_end_homelessness_in_great_britain_2018.pdf.

DCLG. (2017). *50 Years of the English Housing Survey*. London: DCLG. https://assets.publishing.service.gov.uk/government/uploads/system/uploads/attachment_data/file/658923/EHS_50th_Anniversary_Report.pdf.

Department for Business, Energy and Industrial Strategy (DBEIS). (2017). *Fuel Poverty Statistics*. London: Department for Business, Energy and Industrial Strategy. https://www.gov.uk/government/collections/fuel-poverty-statistics.

Department for Communities and Local Government (DCLG). (2006). *A Decent Home: Definition and Guidance*. London: DCLG.

Department for Work and Pensions (DWP). (2015). *Evaluation of Removal of the Spare Room Subsidy: Final Report*. https://www.gov.uk/government/publications/removal-of-the-spare-room-subsidy-evaluation-final-report.

Department of Energy and Climate Change. (2015). *Fuel Poverty Strategy for England*. London: Department of Energy and Climate Change. https://www.gov.uk/government/speeches/fuel-poverty-strategy-for-england.

Dorling, D. (2014). *All That Is Solid: The Great Housing Disaster*. London: Allen Lane.

Empty Homes Agency. (2016). *Empty Homes in England*. London: Empty Homes Agency. http://www.emptyhomes.com/assets/empty-homes-in-england-final-september-2016.pdf.

Energy UK. (2017). *Fuel Poverty*. http://www.energy-uk.org.uk/policy/fuel-poverty.html.

Eurostat. (2017). *Housing Cost Overburden by Poverty Status*. http://ec.europa.eu/eurostat/tgm/refreshTableAction.do?tab=table&plugin=1&pcode=tessi163&language=en.

Federation of Master Builders. (2017). *Homes on Our High Streets*. London: Federation of Master Builders. https://www.fmb.org.uk/media/37062/fmb-homes-on-our-high-streets-low-res-final.pdf.

Fenton, A. (2012). *Look-Ups from Local Authority and Postcode Sectors to Broad Rental Market Areas (BRMAs)*. London School of Economics, Centre for Analysis of Social Exclusion. http://eprints.lse.ac.uk/46454/.

Fraser, I. (2017, June 14). 'Almost No Evidence' of London Homes Owned by Foreign Buyers Being Left Empty. *Telegraph*. http://www.telegraph.co.uk/property/house-prices/almost-no-evidence-london-homes-owned-foreign-buyers-left-empty/.

Frey, J., & Brown, J. (2016). Housing Conditions Transformed. In P. Shanks & D. Mullins (Eds.), *Housing in Northern Ireland*. Coventry: Chartered Institute of Housing.

Harrison, R. (2017, September 5). Energy: Private Rented Housing: Written Question—8878. *Hansard*. http://www.parliament.uk/business/publications/written-questions-answers-statements/written-question/Commons/2017-09-05/8878.

Harvey, A. (2013, February 18). Zero-Carbon Home "Dithering" Is Threatening UK Housing Industry. *Guardian*. https://www.theguardian.com/environment/2013/feb/18/zero-carbon-home-housing-industry.

HM Government. (2010). *The Coalition: Our Programme for Government.* https://www.gov.uk/government/uploads/system/uploads/attachment_data/file/78977/coalition_programme_for_government.pdf.

House of Commons Committee on Communities and Local Government. (2010). *Fourth Report: Beyond Decent Homes.* London: House of Commons. https://publications.parliament.uk/pa/cm200910/cmselect/cmcomloc/60/6002.htm.

Houses of Parliament Parliamentary Office of Science and Technology. (2017, February). *Future Energy Efficiency Policy* (POSTNOTE No. 550). http://researchbriefings.parliament.uk/ResearchBriefing/Summary/POST-PN-0550.

Independent. (2015, June 24). Extend Right to Buy to Tenants of Private Landlords, Labour's Jeremy Corbyn Says. http://www.independent.co.uk/news/uk/politics/extend-right-to-buy-to-the-tenants-of-private-landlords-labours-jeremy-corbyn-says-10342824.html.

Institute for Public Policy Research. (2018). *Beyond Eco: The Future of Fuel Poverty Support.* London: Institute for Public Policy Research. https://www.ippr.org/publications/beyond-eco.

Local Government Association. (2017). *Confidence in New Builds Falls as Average House in England Will Have to Last 2,000 Years.* London: Local Government Association. https://www.local.gov.uk/about/news/confidence-new-builds-falls-average-house-england-will-have-last-2000-years.

Macbryde Homes. (2017). *£629 Worth of Savings to Be Made by Investing in Energy Efficient New Build Homes.* https://www.macbryde-homes.co.uk/energy-efficient-new-build-homes/.

Ministry of Housing, Communities and Local Government (MHCLG). (2018a). *English Housing Survey 2016 to 2017: Headline Report.* London: MHCLG. https://www.gov.uk/government/statistics/english-housing-survey-2016-to-2017-headline-report.

MHCLG. (2018b). *Social Housing Lettings: April 2017 to March 2018.* London, UK: MHCLG. https://assets.publishing.service.gov.uk/government/uploads/system/uploads/attachment_data/file/759738/Social_Housing_Lettings_April2017_to_March2018_England.pdf.

MHCLG. (2018c). *A New Deal for Social Housing* (Cm 9571). London: MHCLG. https://assets.publishing.service.gov.uk/government/uploads/system/uploads/attachment_data/file/733635/A_new_deal_for_social_housing_print_ready_version.pdf.

MHCLG. (2018d). *Dwelling Condition and Safety.* London: MHCLG. https://www.gov.uk/government/statistical-data-sets/dwelling-condition-and-safety.

MHCLG. (2018e). *Live Tables on Rents, Lettings and Tenancies.* London: MHCLG. https://www.gov.uk/government/statistical-data-sets/live-tables-on-rents-lettings-and-tenancies.

MHCLG. (2018f). *Social and Private Renters: Demographic and Economic Data on Social and Private Renters*. London: MHCLG. https://www.gov.uk/government/statistical-data-sets/social-and-private-renters.

Minford, P., Peel, M., & Ashton, P. (1987). *The Housing Morass: Regulation, Immobility and Unemployment*. London: Institute for Economic Affairs.

National Infrastructure Commission. (2017). *Congestion, Capacity, Carbon—Priorities for National Infrastructure*. London: National Infrastructure Commission. https://www.nic.org.uk/wp-content/uploads/Congestion-Capacity-Carbon_-Priorities-for-national-infrastructure.pdf.

Nemeth, H. (2017, November 22). Autumn Budget 2017: "Buy-to-Leave" Landlords Face Empty Homes Tax. *Moneywise*. https://www.moneywise.co.uk/news/2017-11-22/autumn-budget-2017-buy-to-leave-landlords-face-empty-homes-tax.

Northern Ireland Department for Social Development. (2014). *Empty Homes Strategy and Action Plan*. Belfast: Northern Ireland Executive. https://www.communities-ni.gov.uk/publications/northern-ireland-empty-homes-strategy-and-action-plan-2013-%E2%80%93-2018.

Northern Ireland Housing Executive. (2017). *Types of Grant Available*. Belfast: Northern Ireland Executive. http://www.nihe.gov.uk/index/benefits/home_improvement_grants/grants_available.htm.

Office for National Statistics (ONS). (2014). *Overcrowding and Under-Occupation in England and Wales*. London: Office for National Statistics. https://www.basw.co.uk/system/files/resources/basw_120028-2_1.pdf.

ONS. (2018). *Fuel Poverty Trends 2018: Long Term Trends Under the Low Income High Costs Indicator (2003–2016 Data)*. London: Office for National Statistics. https://www.gov.uk/government/statistics/fuel-poverty-trends-2018.

Osborne, G. (2015). *Chancellor George Osborne's Spending Review and Autumn Statement 2015 Speech*. www.gov.uk/government/speeches/chancellor-george-osbornes-spending-review-and-autumn-statement-2015-speech.

Pittini, A. (2012, January). *Housing Affordability in the EU: Current Situation and Recent Trends*. Research Briefing, Year 5, No. 1. CECODHAS Housing Europe's Observatory. www.housingeurope.eu/file/41/download.

Saunders, P. (2016). *Restoring a Nation of Home Owners: What Went Wrong with Home Ownership in Britain, and How to Start Putting It Right*. London: Civitas. www.civitas.org.uk/content/files/Restoring-a-Nation-of-Home-Owners.pdf.

Scott, P. (1996). *The Property Masters: A history of the British Commercial Property Sector*. London: Taylor & Francis.

Scottish Empty Homes Partnership. (2017). *Scottish Empty Homes Partnership Annual Report 2016–17*. Edinburgh: Shelter Scotland.

Scottish Government. (2016). *Statistical News Release*. Edinburgh: Scottish Government. https://beta.gov.scot/news/statistical-news-release-2016-12-06/.

Scottish Government. (2017). *Repairs and Improvement*. Edinburgh: Scottish Government. http://www.gov.scot/Topics/Built-Environment/Housing/investment/grants.

Shelter. (2016a). *The Living Home Standard*. London: Shelter. https://england.shelter.org.uk/__data/assets/pdf_file/0010/1288387/FINAL_Living_home_standard_report.pdf.

Shelter. (2016b). *Living Home Findings*. London: Shelter. https://england.shelter.org.uk/__data/assets/pdf_file/0011/1288388/FINAL_Living_home_standard_Findings_report-insert.pdf.

Sky News. (2017). *Right to Buy: Flagship Government Housing Scheme in Trouble*. https://news.sky.com/story/right-to-buy-flagship-government-housing-scheme-in-trouble-11105894.

Spurr, S. (2016, March 9). Is Buy-to-Leave Real? *Estates Gazette*. http://www.estatesgazette.com/blogs/london-residential-research/2016/03/buy-leave-really-new-build-problem/.

Statistics for Wales. (2018). *Welsh Housing Conditions Survey, 2017/8: Headline Report*. Cardiff: Welsh Government. https://gov.wales/statistics-and-research/welsh-housing-conditions-survey/?lang=en.

Stephens, M., Perry, J., Wilcox, S., Williams, P., & Young, D. (2018). *UK Housing Review 2018*. London: Chartered Institute of Housing.

Stewart, J., & Lynch, Z. (2018). *Environmental Health and Housing: Issues for Public Health* (2nd ed.). Abingdon: Routledge.

Studd & Parker Estate Agency. (2016). *Call to Remove Stamp Duty for Downsizing*. https://www.struttandparker.com/knowledge-and-research/call-remove-stamp-duty-downsizing-100915.

The Home. (2017). *Living Over the Shop*. http://www.thehomeonline.co.uk/living-over-the-shop/.

This Is Money. (2017, February 7). *Five People Have Made Offers on Our Flat Only to Be Refused a Mortgage Thanks to a Takeaway Next Door: What Can We Do to Sell?* http://www.thisismoney.co.uk/money/experts/article-4171842/Why-lenders-refuse-mortgage-flat-shop.html.

Turkington, R., & Watson, C. (2014). *Renewing Europe's Housing*. Bristol: Policy Press.

UK Energy Research Centre. (2017). *Policy Briefing: A UKERC/CIED Policy Briefing Unlocking Britain's First Fuel: The Potential for Energy Savings in UK Housing.* London: UK Energy Research Centre. http://www.ukerc.ac.uk/ publications/unlocking-britains-first-fuel-energy-savings-in-uk-housing. html.

UK Fuel Monitor. (2016). *UK Fuel Monitor 2015/6, a Review of Progress Across the Nations.* http://fuelpovertyni.org/wp-content/uploads/FPM_2016_low_ res.pdf.

Valuation Office Agency. (2018, January). *Local Reference Rent Levels Listed by BRMA and Property Size.* London: Valuation Office Agency. www.gov.uk/government/publications/local-reference-rents-listed-by-brma-and-property-size-january-2018.

Wainwright, O. (2014, September 17). The Truth About Property Developers: How They Are Exploiting Planning Authorities and Ruining Our Cities. *Guardian.* https://www.theguardian.com/cities/2014/sep/17/ truth-property-developers-builders-exploit-planning-cities.

Wall, T. (2018, October 24). 53 Councils Have Not Prosecuted a Single Landlord in Three Years: Large Parts of England and Wales with Many 'Non-Decent' Homes Have Had No Convictions. *Guardian.* https://www. theguardian.com/business/2018/oct/24/53-councils-have-not-prosecuted-a-single-landlord-in-three-years.

Welsh Government. (2016a). *Energy Efficiency Strategy for Wales.* Cardiff: WelshnGovernment. http://gov.wales/topics/environmentcountryside/ energy/efficiency/energy-efficiency-strategy-for-wales/?lang=en.

Welsh Government. (2016b). *Planning Policy Wales, Edition 9.* Cardiff: Welsh Government. http://gov.wales/topics/planning/policy/ppw/?lang=en.

Westminster Sustainable Business Forum. (2016). *Warmer and Greener: A Guide to the Future of Domestic Energy Efficiency.* London: Westminster Sustainable Business Forum. http://www.policyconnect.org.uk/wsbf/research/ warmer-greener-guide-future-domestic-energy-efficiency-policy.

Wilson, W., & Fears, C. (2016, November 14). *Overcrowding (England)* (Briefing Paper, No. 1013). file:///C:/Users/User/Downloads/SN01013%20 (1).pdf.

Wilson, W., Cromarty, H., & Barton, C. (2018). *Empty Housing (England)* (Briefing Paper No. 3012). https://researchbriefings.parliament.uk/ ResearchBriefing/Summary/SN03012#fullreport.

7

Increasing New House Supply

Most media pundits and government ministers claim that the solution to the UK housing problem is to boost new home construction.
The *Telegraph* (2016) announced 'It's simple—we need to build more
houses'. John Kay, writing in the *Financial Times* (2017a), said 'So
what should be done? There is only one good answer: build more new
houses' and CityMetric (2018) declared 'Yes, supply is the cause of the
housing crisis'. When Secretary of State for Communities and Local
Government, Sajid Javid, placed the blame for high house prices 'almost
entirely on low rates of house building' (quoted in the *Guardian* 2017).

The assertion that increasing housing supply is a sufficient response
to the housing problem has been disputed (see Chapter 1) but,
although supply scarcity is only one element in the housing crises, relative even to the flawed government assessed requirements, UK new
home output has been seriously deficient for many years, creating a
large backlog of housing need. There are many suggestions on how to
accelerate new home delivery.

© The Author(s) 2019
B. Lund, *Housing in the United Kingdom*,
https://doi.org/10.1007/978-3-030-04128-1_7

New Towns and Villages

New towns developed from Ebenezer Howard's garden city idea put forward in *Garden Cities of Tomorrow* (1902). Howard's vision was located in capturing development gain Nairn (2016, p. 1, emphasis original) comments:

> In fact, most of the book can be read as a business model being pitched to potential investors. He assures interested parties that he can get them a 4.5% return....The financial linchpin of the plan is the fact that all of the land is purchased up front, so that the increase in property values generated by the growth will be captured by the community itself.

Despite successful private ventures in establishing garden cities at Letchworth and Welwyn Garden City, between the wars the Town and Country Planning Association (TCPA) attempted, with little success, to promote state interest in the idea albeit that garden estate, notably Wythenshawe in south Manchester, were developed (Boughton 2018). Garden cities, by 1945 often known as 'new towns', had many attractions to a country needing new homes but worried about urban sprawl and agricultural production. The idea was adopted with enthusiasm by the 1945–1951 Labour government.

New Town Blues

The 1946 New Towns Act made New Town Development Corporations responsible for new towns. The Corporations were appointed by the government, financed by Treasury loans and had planning and compulsory purchase order powers. The 'first wave' of new towns, mainly around London, was designated by the 1945–1951 Labour government. Harold Macmillan, the Conservative Minister of Housing from 1951 to 1954, supported new towns but met Treasury and Conservative Party resistance. The Treasury believed that they were too expensive and elements in Conservative Party thought they were mechanisms to parachute Labour voters into Tory areas. Moreover, 'new town blues'—an imprecise mixture of mental health vulnerabilities experienced by

New Town residents—had started to be identified. No additional new towns were designated until 1961 when a new 'housing crisis' was identified (see Lund 2016). A second new town programme started to be planned in 1961 and this was followed by a 'third wave', designated by the Labour Government from 1967 to 1970. By the late 1970s, new towns—by then viewed as contributing to inner-city decline—had fallen from political favour. The 1946 New Towns Act had incorporated provisions to transfer new town assets to local government when the town was complete but, in 1961, the government set up a Commission for New Towns to manage new town industrial and commercial assets. Later, under the Thatcher/Major governments, all the Development Corporations were dismantled: their business assets and many freehold sites sold to private companies and most of the housing stock transferred to housing associations. This was part of a large-scale exercise in privatising public land that included the transfer of local authority stock to housing associations and the Right to Buy. Christophers (2018) estimates that since 1979 about 10% of the British land mass, including much of its valuable real estate, has passed from public to private hands.

In evidence to the Housing, Communities and Local Government Committee (2018 question 187), Hugh Ellis, Head of Policy at Town and Country Planning Association, said:

> The new towns programme, using development corporations, paid back its entire borrowing for the delivery not just of infrastructure but the whole of the towns, 32 communities and 2.8 million people. It paid back the debt to Treasury at £4.75 billion in 1999 and has gone on yielding, since that time, about £1 billion to what is now Homes England and the Treasury…. The original development corporations were so profitable that they were lending money to other people.

Thatcher's distaste for state organisations helps to explain the new town idea demise but, by the 1980s, local opposition to new town development was becoming more vociferous. In 1983 Consortium Developments Ltd wanted to develop up to 15 privately financed new country towns around London. Four proposals reached the planning stage but all were rejected by the government due to local objections.

In 2007 New Labour revived the new town idea as eco-towns. Eco-towns were to have a population of about 20,000; 30% of the houses built would be affordable; 40% of the site would be open space and the houses would be built to very high energy efficiency standards. Fifteen locations were identified but reduced to four following intense local opposition. In 2017 work on the UK's first *eco-town* in North West Bicester, Oxfordshire commenced.

Initially enthusiastic about new towns, David Cameron's zeal faded as the strength of 'Middle England' opposition became manifest. However, after the election, the Conservative government support for new towns strengthened a little and new villages were added to the agenda. In 2017 the DCLG announced that 14 new garden villages would have access to a £6 million fund over the next two financial years to support their delivery. A few local authorities—some via council led development corporations—started to develop garden village proposals but local opposition was potent (Talbot 2018a). Three new garden towns in Aylesbury, Taunton and Harlow and Gilston received government support. Yet, despite the government's National Infrastructure Commission's call for several new towns to be created between Oxford and Milton Keynes, and Bedford and Cambridge with up 150,000 homes in the largest towns (National Infrastructure Commission 2017), the new town vision lacked robust political backing.

The White Paper *Fixing Our Broken Housing Market* (DCLG 2017a, para. 1.36) announced 'We will also legislate to allow locally accountable New Town Development Corporations to be set up, enabling local areas to use them as the delivery vehicle if they wish to' and, in 2018, new town designation became a local government as well as a central government power—perhaps a response to backbench Conservative MP concerns on nationally designated new town corporations because local designation has become the accepted orthodoxy. Labour has shown more enthusiasm for new towns. Its 2017 Housing Manifesto (Labour Party 2017, p. 11) declared 'We will start work on a new generation of new towns and garden cities within the next Parliament, delivered by New Homes Corporations based on reformed new towns legislation...'

Garden cities, new towns, eco-towns and villages have all been announced since 2007 but, with few exceptions, they have become ghost settlements. Reporting on the 2017 government announcement of a string of new towns and villages Talbot (2018b) noted that six proposals had already been discarded.

All the new settlement initiatives have encountered strident local opposition supported by the Conservative Party and, at local level, by the Liberal Democrats pursuing their 'community politics' agenda, the Green Party and the Labour Party. Yet garden cities, new towns and new villages, built on existing, cheap agricultural land, have the potential to make a major contribution to overcoming UK housing crises. New town economics were well expressed in the winning entry for the 2014 Wolfson Economics Prize submitted by Urban Environment Design. It argued:

> In the absence of large scale subsidy the only solution to the economics of the Garden City is what Ebenezer Howard called the 'unearned increment'.... We have assumed that the land will be brought at an average cost of £350,000 per hectare, 20 times its current agricultural value but only 15% of its value as housing land. The economics of the scheme are based on these differentials.... The Garden City Trust would be vested with the land, would commission masterplanning work and then use the equity of the land to raise a Bond to fund the initial investment in infrastructure. (Urban Environment Design 2014, p. 2)

Social benefits can be added to new town economics. Mixed communities could be created, all the new homes might be super-energy efficient and the new towns could be charged with promoting health (NHS England 2016).

Green Belts

The Green Belt was 1,634,700 hectares in 2017. At 99%, West Lancashire has the highest proportion of green belt land in its area but several districts near London such as Tandridge, Epping Forest, Sevenoaks, Brentwood, South Bucks, Windsor and Maidenhead have more than 80% of their areas designated green belt (Grimwood 2017).

Epping Forest has seven tube stations and Brentwood is getting two stops on Crossrail. They are all delivering far fewer homes than centrally assessed requirements—in Sevenoaks, for example only 230 new homes were constructed in 2016 compared to the 698 deemed necessary (MHCLG 2018a: DCLG 2017b). Many of the green belt areas in and around London have sound rail connection with central London that could be improved and the proximity of green belt areas to commuter hubs has led to suggestions that green belt land should be released around these networks (Centre for Cities 2014: Papworth 2015).

An Ipsos/Mori survey, commissioned by the Campaign to Protect Rural England, asked the question 'To what extent do you agree or disagree, in principle, that existing Green Belt should be retained and not built on'? (Ipsos/Mori 2015, p. 6). 64% wanted the green belt protected but, when asked what they knew about green belts, 25% had never heard of them and a further 35% knew nothing or very little. 42% of those aged 25–34, whose future green belts are intended to protect, knew nothing about green belts. Indeed, public knowledge on developed land in England is low. Although 54% of the public believed that around half of England and 10% that more than 75% is developed (Barker 2006), a BBC News investigation (BBC News 2017) found that 56.7% of UK land was farmland, 34.9% natural, 2.5% green urban and only 5.9% built on.

Many people seem to merge green belts with national parks. A 2009 survey, also commissioned by the Campaign to Protect Rural England (CAPI OmniBus 2009), found that the term 'green belt' evoked images of woodland, nature reserves, country parks, walking and cycling, playing fields and reservoirs. Despite green belt retainers maintaining that all green belt is 'countryside' (Spiers 2018), 37% of green belt land is used for intensive agriculture and some is scrubland (Papworth 2015). The London Green Belt contains airfields, water treatment works and old hospitals. Golf courses comprise 7.1% of London's green belt with more of Surrey now taken by golf courses than by houses (Cheshire 2014).

Despite strong public support for green belts, the majority do not believe that all green belt land is sacrosanct. In CAPI OmniBus 2009 survey, only 30% disagreed with the statement 'While most of the countryside around England's large towns and cities should be protected, some could be used for new housing and other development' (CAPI OmniBus 2009, p. 8) and, in 2006, a survey by Ipsos/Mori, carried out for the Barker Review of Land Use Planning (Barker 2006), found that only 17% respondents thought it was important to protect 'edge of city land'. Ipsos/Mori's 2015 survey found a close relationship between support for green belts and social class with 72% of social classes A and B but only 54% of social classes DE supporting green belts.

London's Green Belt—*Punch* magazine labelled it the 'fairy ring'— was justified in 1935 by the London County Council as preventing urban sprawl and as supplying a green recreational lung for city dwellers. However, it is doubtful if green belts fulfil either of these purposes. Much new development leapfrogs the green belt with implications for commuter journeys. Wiles (2014, p. 1) comments:

> Cambridge is a typical example. It is estimated that 40,000 people commute into the city every day, the majority from beyond its Green Belt, which is 3 to 6 miles wide and over six times larger than the city itself. 74 percent of the Cambridge Green Belt is devoted to intensive farming and has low aesthetic value. Much of it is closed to the public.

Even the Campaign to Protect Rural England (2015, p. 1) recognised the 'leapfrogging' problem but claimed that '"Leapfrogging" is not inherently unsustainable if a good transport network exists'.

In the late nineteenth-century Octavia Hill supported green areas around London so that poor inner-London residents could have access to fresh air (Grindrod 2017), yet most green belt land is in private ownership with restricted entry rights and many city dwellers—by plane, car and public transport—can enjoy rural environments, not necessarily in the UK.

In the 1970s another argument was added to the case for green belts: restricting expansion around a city forced new development into the city thereby encouraging 'an urban renaissance'. New Labour used this argument to promote its 'brownfield first' policy, but as housing prices started to escalate, it started to apply pressure on local authorities to release more greenfield land through Regional Spatial Strategies. After a hiatus when Regional Spatial Strategies were axed and 'localism' prevailed, the coalition government also applied pressure to land release via its National Planning Policy Framework. If local authorities were unable to find sufficient land to meet the National Planning Policy Framework's demands then green belt land would need to be released. David Cameron retreated from this strategy in the countdown to the 2015 General Election and Theresa May's government also strongly supported green belts. *Fixing Our Broken Housing Market* (DCLG 2017a, para. 1.38) declared:

> ...we propose to amend and add to national policy to make clear that authorities should amend Green Belt boundaries only when they can demonstrate that they have examined fully all other reasonable options for meeting their identified development requirements.

At the launch of the draft revised NPPF, in March 2018, Theresa May declared that 'the answer to our housing crisis does not lie in tearing up the Green Belt' (BBC News 2018). However, the CPRE has alleged that May lacks real commitment to protecting green belts, claiming that 'Nearly 400 football pitches worth of green belt land have been lost to housing in the last year alone' (CPRE 2018a, p. 5), with more in the pipeline and that, at 21 dwellings per hectare compared to 32 outside green belts, using green belt land is wasteful. Nothing was said about the amenity value of this lost green belt land which represented 0.05% of total green belt land (DCLG 2017c).

Green belt political salience was starkly revealed in *Planning for the right homes in the right places: consultation proposals* (DCLG 2017b). The formula adopted in the document to assess housing requirements heavily loaded new homes into inner-cities, especially inner London. The Labour Party supported green belts in its 2017 manifesto but there is substantial support for sensitive reappraisals of existing green belt boundaries with green belt land judged according to amenity value (Cheshire 2013) rather than a blanket ban on new development justified as preventing urban sprawl. Indeed, a new pressure group, London YIMBY— 'yes, in my back yard'—has been formed arguing that well designed new homes in selected areas can enhance the current Green Belt.

The CPRE defends all the existing green belt land but the 'green belt' is not a natural entity. It is the sum of green belt boundaries designated by local planners and politicians at different times to restrict urban growth. The 'belt' or 'noose' (Papworth 2015) has been emphasised at the expense of the 'green'. It would take only limited changes in green belt boundaries, releasing land with limited green characteristics, to increase land availability. Centre for Cities (2014, p. 15) states:

> One approach cities could use is to rethink the green belt on a case by case basis....there are 59,600 hectares of green belt land within a 25 minute walk of a train station within our successful cities, and 140,000 hectares including surrounding authorities. There would be no need to 'concrete over' swathes of desirable land as cities can instead designate poor quality green belt land that is suitable for housing close and well-connected to successful cities, while still protecting land which has value to communities.

Land Owners and Land Release

Bentley (2017) argues that the land problem predates the 1947 planning system. Landowners, knowing that land values will increase in certain areas due to economic and population growth are likely to be very reluctant to sell their asset and:

> When a deal is finally struck and land is released for construction, the development will usually be targeted at the more expensive sections of the market. Housing developments of any size will be built slowly, over many years, because the developer must maintain the value of the land so that they are able to pass it on to their customers in the price of a new-build home. (Bentley 2017, p. 2)

Bentley claims that this 'power of constraint' has to changed by reforming the 1961 Land Compensation Act which incorporates the right of landowners to receive 'hope value', that is, possible enhancements in land value arising from future development, in addition to any current use value in the event of compulsory purchase by the state. He states:

The effect would be to give public authorities the power once more to acquire land at prices closer to its current use value rather than its potential residential use value. This would reframe incentives in the operation of the land market. The alternative to settling for lower bids for land would no longer be to wait a little longer; it would be to lose the land to the state at even less profit. (Bentley 2017, p. 85)

The Labour Party has signalled its support for such reforms (*Independent* 2018).

Brownfield Sites

A *brownfield site* is previously developed *land, sometimes contaminated,* that could recycled for new homes. Brownfield land availability, its distribution and the reuse costs are contentious issues. In 2014 the Government argued there was space for only 200,000 homes on brownfield land across England and a study by planning consultancy Barton Wilmore found that the 1246 identified brownfield sites could deliver only 100,103 homes by 2035 (Spencer 2018). In contrast, the Campaign to Protect Rural England, using existing local authority brownfield registers as a baseline, estimated that there was brownfield capacity for 1.1 million homes across (Campaign to Protect Rural England 2018b).

Nonetheless, even if CPRE's 1.1 million estimate is correct, brownfield sites would be sufficient only for a less than a four year housing supply at about the level necessary to accommodate projected household growth, some of the sites are difficult to develop and brownfield site availability does not coincide with the places where houses are required. The CPRE (2018b, para. 3.6) stated that 'all regions across England have enough suitable and deliverable brownfield sites to provide for more than two years of the Government's assessment of their entire housing need'—a limited amount—and Bowman (2016) has claimed 'There is virtually no unused brownfield in London, and the brownfield in the south east is disproportionately in use compared with the rest of the country'. Moreover, build-out on brownfield sites is only half the greenfield site rate (Nathaniel Litchfield and Partners (2016).

When, under the influence of Nick Boles as Planning Minister, the DCLG was in a pro-development mood, it noted that national targets on brownfield land use had negative outcomes, 'resulting in imbalances in housing provision for example between blocks of flats and family homes with gardens' (DCLG 2012a, p. 42). In 2015/2016, brownfield new-build dwelling density was 37 addresses per hectare compared to 26 for non-previously developed land (DCLG 2017d). Although brownfield sites can be landscaped to produce an acceptable environment, some are surrounded by electricity pylons, sewage treatment plants, etc. (*Economist* 2013). Brownfield site use has some attributes of the 1950–1970s 'containment of urban Britain' policy—corralling people in the least desirable neighbourhoods.

Before the White Paper *Fixing Our Broken Housing Market* (DCLG 2017a) was published, the 2015 Conservative government had taken a number of steps to promote the use of brownfield sites. These measures included:

– statutory brownfield registers;
– announcing a range of new permitted development rights, giving permission for specified forms of development such as converting office, retail and agricultural buildings into residential use; and
– designating 26 Housing Zones with the potential to deliver up to 44,000 new homes on brownfield land with the London programme of 31 Zones devolved to the Mayor of London.

The 2017 White Paper (DCLG 2017a, para. 1.25) stated that '… the presumption should be that brownfield land is suitable for housing unless there are clear and specific reasons to the contrary (such as high flood risk)'. However, whatever the merits of using brownfield sites, the emphasis on 'brownfield first' restricts the total land considered to be available for development, thereby increasing the overall price of housing land.

Demand-Side Subsidies

Various demand-side subsidies were available between the wars such as low-interest loans for homeownership supplied by local authorities but the major demand-side initiative started in 1963 when the Conservative government abolished Schedule A Tax—levied on the imputed rental income accruing from home ownership—but retained tax relief on mortgage interest. When the tax relief was automatically deducted from mortgage interest payments the scheme became known as Mortgage Interest Relief at Source (MIRAS) and, until 1988, was available to both joint mortgage holders.

At its zenith, MIRAS averaged £800 per household and cost the Exchequer £7.7 billion. During John Major's term as Prime Minister, tax relief on mortgage interest started to be phased out, a task completed by Gordon Brown when Chancellor of the Exchequer. When it ended, New Labour's help to homeowners became more selective taking the form of diverse and constantly changing low-cost homeownership initiatives with different names, usually supplied by housing associations and focused on first-time buyers and social tenants wanting to become homeowners. 'Homebuy', for example, offered purchasers an interest-free loan of 25% of the home's purchase price and 'Key Worker Living' was targeted at public sector workers in London and the South East.

Help to Buy

Help to Buy Equity Loan is the government flagship scheme to help people onto the housing ladder and marks significant government involvement in the owner-occupation market. An extra £10 billion was injected into the scheme in October 2017 with the government estimating that 130,000 households would be helped to become homeowners by 2021 (HM Treasury 2017). By the end of 2017, 158853 properties had been purchased with an equity loan since its 2013 start. 85% of scheme participants had an income of £30,000 plus with 22% £40–50,000, 15% £50–60,000, 16% £60,000–80,000 and 10% £80,000 plus (MHCLG 2018c). Analysis of Help to Buy's short and long term impact on government debt is sparse. The Office for Budget Responsibility seems to assume that it is neutral.

Means Tested Subsidies

In the 1980s Thatcher's policy was to push all rents towards market levels with highly selective HB helping low-income households. Producer subsidies to housing associations were curtailed and, in the local authority sector, abolished. New Labour halted the move towards market rents, a policy change that had been signalled in the Conservative White Paper (Department of the Environment/Welsh Office 1995). Under the coalition government social rents were increased by more than the inflation rate but this policy was reversed in 2016 when it was announced that, for five years, rents would be reduced by 1% below inflation. However, more homes were let at affordable rents under the new build programme and the policy to convert tenancies to affordable rent on vacant possession has meant that, in 2016/2017, 44,442 lets were at affordable rents (MHCLG 2018d). From 2020 social rents will increase at 1% above inflation and the trend towards affordable conversions is likely to continue.

Rent increases have meant that HB has become important to the living standards of low-income households but eligibility is scheduled to become more restrictive as Universal Credit is rolled out nationally. Although Theresa May stopped George Osborne's plan to restrict social tenants to the caps imposed on Local Housing Allowance—thereby mainly helping tenants living in supported housing—and abandoned Cameron's plan to restrict HB entitlement for those aged 18–21, all benefit payment thresholds to working families are frozen until 2020. Moreover, HB will be paid directly to most social tenants, a policy that has already caused significant transition problems (*Inside Housing* 2017).

Demand Subsidies: Impact and Reform

Since the late 1970s there has been a transfer from producer to consumer subsidies and, in recent years, this shift has gained momentum. Perry and Stephens (2018) have calculated that in 1975/1976 the split between total supply and demand side subsidies was 80/20, by 2000/2001 it was 20.3/79.7 and, in 2015/2016, 4.3/95.7. In 2009, the split between producer and consumer subsidies (in the form of housing allowances) for social housing was 36/64, in 2015 it was 15/85.

The main effect of demand-side subsidies for renting or buying is to stabilise or increase prices. This pleases banks, landowners, private landlords, long-term homeowners, 'exchange professionals' and property developers. The government also gains through Stamp Duty Land Tax and the potential to garner contributions to the cost of social housing from developers. Stamp Duty Land Tax raised 13 billion in 2017/2018 compared to 4.9 billion in 2009/2010 (Statistics Portal 2018) and developer contributions helped to build 43% of the affordable houses produced in 2016/2017 (Perry 2018).

Many politicians and economists object to demand-side subsidies on the argument that they push up house prices. Help to Buy has been condemned as aiming to increase house prices to stimulate a consumer boom. Lambert (2016, p. 1) declared:

> Then in his 2013 Budget, George Osborne rolled the dice on the property market and announced Help to Buy .... knowing that by stoking a mini-house price boom he could raise confidence and get people out spending money on all the things that we know do well when people move home, white goods, furnishings, bathrooms, kitchens and a whole range of consumer goods....

In addition, Quantitative Easing and the Funding for Lending to mortgage suppliers injected finance into the housing market (see Chapter 1). In January 2013 house prices had increased 1.1% on the previous year, by April 2016 annual house price inflation was 8.5% thereby boosting bank assets: 60% of bank assets are in the form of mortgage securities (New Economics Foundation 2015). The volume builders benefited from this house price hike producing headlines such as 'Housebuilders' shares rocket to five-year high' (Construction News 2017). In 2017, the Help to Buy Equity Loan was augmented by exemption from Stamp Duty Land Tax for first-time buyers on properties worth up to £300,000 (with a 5% rate for property value from £300,000 to £500,000). An examination of Help to Buy by Morgan Stanley, revealed that new houses prices, boosted by the government's Help to Buy scheme, had outpaced the prices for second-hand homes by 15% since the start of the scheme (Collinson 2017). Knowles (2018) claimed that the average profit made by volumes housebuilders on each home doubled after the scheme was launched. The Stamp Duty Land Tax exemption for first-time buyers—forecast to cost £1,880 million in the four years to 2020/2021, and £1310 million in the two subsequent years—will also boost house prices, limiting its impact on homeownership access (Joyce 2017). Demand-side subsidies give homeowners an advantage over private landlords and, by boosting the equity of prospective 'second steppers', may help them in moving to a larger house. However, raising the 3% Land Stamp Duty Tax levy on second homes or classic rent control are more effective ways to curtail private landlordism.

The Help to Buy ISA is direct government support to consumers investing in housing. If you're saving to buy your first home, the government will top up your savings by 25% (up to £3,000). In 2017 a Lifetime ISA was introduced allowing people under the age of 40 to contribute up to £4,000 in each tax year with the government providing a 25% bonus on these contributions. The ISA can be used to buy a first home worth up to £450,000 at any time from 12 months after opening the account. There are also the much larger subsidies involved in tax concessions such as exclusion from Capital Gains Tax on the main residence, exemption from Schedule A Tax and Inheritance Tax relief. The Inheritance Tax threshold is £325,000 but this is per person, so for couples the threshold is £650,000. Post-April 2017 there has been an additional threshold allowance for transfers of housing wealth to direct descendants (children or grandchildren). Initially this was fixed at £100,000 per person in 2017/2018, rising to £175,000 in 2020/2021. So by 2020/2021, £1 million of wealth will not involve any liability to

Inheritance Tax. Wilcox and Williams (2018) have calculated that the total net tax reliefs were worth £39,978 million in 2017.

The fiscal subsidies to consumption could be diverted to direct producer incentives linked to new home supply. However, given the electorate's reaction to housing wealth taxation, significant modifications to taxing housing wealth are well away from the political agenda. Older people, the main holders of wealth in homes, vote and they react badly to any suggestion that this wealth might be taken. In his memoirs Tony Blair said 'Your average Rottweiler on speed can be a lot more amiable than a pensioner wronged' (Blair 2011, p. 299). In 2007, when Labour was ahead in the public opinion polls and contemplating a snap general election, the Conservatives announced an increasing the Inheritance Tax threshold from £300,000 to £1 million. Conservative popularity increased in marginal constituencies (Seely 2013) and there was no general election. Some centre-left commentators now regard Inheritance Tax as 'toxic' (Toynbee 2017). The 2017 Conservative Party manifesto declared that care costs, residential and home, would be paid for by the family home leaving £100,000 as to be passed on to the family. There was an immediate backlash, with one Tory MP describing the 'dementia tax' as 'an invitation to commit suicide' (Evans 2017). Conservative poll ratings plummeted.

The impact of state means-tested payments on rental prices has been considered in Chapter 3. The empirical evidence suggests that these consumer subsidies push up rental prices—especially in areas where high proportions of households qualify for benefits—and hence leak into landlord subsidies. Because consumer subsidies can become producer profits, rather than stimulate new supply, a shift from consumer to producer support has been advocated.

The means-tested consumer subsidies in the rental sector could be diverted to producer incentives. In the private rented sector, narrowing the 'broad housing market area' definition or reduced the maximum eligible rent to below the median in the market areas currently used would curtail LHA spending but this would result in severe hardship and low-income households being further corralled in poor neighbourhoods. Rent control (see Chapter 5) therefore seems an appropriate response. It would free some resources used to support private landlordism for higher producer subsidies.

Social Housing Under Threat (2017) maintained that, if the resources used by HB were brought forward to build 'genuinely affordable social housing'—let at 'social' rents—then the breakeven year would 2034/2035 and an analysis by Savills (2017), comparing the costs of housing 100,000 households in the private rented sector and social rented sector found that the social rented choice produced £23.9 billion savings over the long term. Of course, in the short term, the additional government help would add to the public debt, although there is a good case for removing local authority borrowing to build homes from the public sector net debt definition (see below).

Supply-Side Incentives

The growth of demand-side subsidies has been at the expense of a decline in supply-side incentives. Supply-side government support takes a variety of forms.

Infrastructure Investment

Building new homes involves infrastructure investment in new roads; flood protection; land remediation work, new schools, etc. Since the 2008 recession there has been a plethora of central government funding schemes to stimulate infrastructure investment, the latest being the Housing Infrastructure Fund (HIF), scheduled for a £3.1 billion in government grants investment from 2017/2018 to 2020/2021. The HIF, accessed by competitive bidding from local authorities, consists of two elements, a Marginal Viability Fund to provide an infrastructure funding to get additional sites allocated or existing sites unblocked quickly and a 'Forward Fund' for bids up to £250 million for major infrastructure projects. The HIF is supported by other schemes to promote housebuilding such as the Land Assembly Fund, assistance to promote building on small sites and accelerate construction. Although HIF and

associated programmes were the biggest government investment programme for than a decade, there is little evidence available on which to
assess whether the extra government infrastructure funding is sufficient
to ensure that new house building is not hampered by lack of roads,
schools etc. and to allay public concern that development impedes the
well-being of current residents.

Build to Rent

Private landlordism has been long-regarded as a 'cottage industry' to
be shunned by major investors. New Labour regarded private renting
a 'flexible' tenure, well-suited to a mobile workforce in a global market
and it attempted to attract 'institutional' investors into the new housebuilding market—*build* to let rather than *buy* to let. It failed but, in
2011, the coalition government set up a committee to review the barriers to institutional investment in private rented homes. The Montague
Report (DCLG 2012b), recognised that private renting could be attractive to institutional investors stating that the demand for rented accommodation was high and returns on residential property had totalled
9.6% on average between 2001 and 2011. Nonetheless, the report
identified obstacles to institutional investment such as the high profits
necessary to attract institutional investment in this 'novel' area, high
management costs and aspects of the planning system. The government
needed to kick-start institutional investment. In response, the coalition
government set up a £1 billion Build to Rent fund to help finance the
construction of homes until they are let and to create new 'demonstra-
tion' projects. In 2016, this was replaced by the Home Building Fund,
managed by Homes England—providing funding for private sector
development schemes including those for build for rent. In addition, a
£3.5 billion Private Rented Sector Guarantee scheme was established to
underwrite 20% of the finance needed for new private rented homes.
Some of these schemes do not count under the public debt definition but, as with Help to Buy, they expand government risk and the
resources could be diverted to social housing supply incentives. Build
to Rent had generated £15 billion investment by 2016 with a further

expected £50 billion by 2020 (Rugg and Rhodes 2018) although much of this investment has been in office conversions.

Fixing Our Broken Housing Market (DCLG 2017a, para. 3.23) stated the government would:

> change the National Planning Policy Framework so authorities know they should plan proactively for Build to Rent where there is a need, and to make it easier for Build to Rent developers to offer affordable private rental homes instead of other types of affordable housing;

This was accompanied by a commitment to 'ensure that family friendly tenancies of three or more years are available for those tenants that want them on schemes that benefit from our changes' (DCLG 2017a, para. 3.23). The support for new build private landlordism is an attempt to bring institutional investors into the private rented market but rents are high and, given the distribution of the housing crisis government resources would have been more productively used in the social housing sector.

It is difficult to separate demand- and supply-side subsidies (demand-side subsidies help producers) but Wilcox and Williams (2018) have identified £16.5 billion between 2016/2017 and 2020/2021 in what might be labelled government supply-side assistance albeit that about two-thirds is in the form of guarantees and loans.

New Social Housing

In the 1930s it was argued that local authority housing crowded out private enterprise but the as social housing supply has declined, private enterprise has failed to meet the gap.

Housing associations are now the principal social housing producers, assisted by government grants and loan guarantees but, in accordance with the changing nature of government aid, the make-up of their output is changing with more build for sale and more homes let at affordable rents. The available resources for affordable houses could be stretched further by pushing the new house rents to, let's say, 90% of the market rent but at the cost of higher future HB expenditure and extending the 'poverty trap', that is, the disincentive impact of the taper applied to HB claimants. Under the Thatcher/Major governments and New Labour, new local authority housing was severely restricted. In 2008 only 830 local authority houses were built in the UK. During the 2008–2010 recession, New Labour started to stimulate new building by local government via a specific £400 million Local Authority New Build Initiative and promised to reform the operations of the Housing Revenue Account to enable local government to build more new homes. In return for a settlement on housing debt distribution, local authorities would have the freedom to use future rent and Right to Buy income as a base for securing loans for new build. The Liberal Democrats endorsed this proposal in its 2010 manifesto. It was included in the 2010 coalition government agreement and was implemented in 2012 but without Right to Buy receipts. Under the 'reinvigourated' Right to Buy with its promise of one-to-one replacement, local authorities were required to spend their one-for-one Right to Buy receipts within three years otherwise they had to be returned to the government with interest of 4% above base rate and Right to Buy receipts could fund no more than 30% of the cost of a replacement home. Moreover, Treasury borrowing constraints severely restricted the local government's ability to secure loans inside and outside the Housing Revenue Account.

By 2018 about one-third of local authorities had set up local housing companies, mainly operating outside the Housing Revenue Account, to facilitate new house building but many, aware that post 2020 they will have to rely more on income generation (Morphet and Clifford 2017), have concentrating on building for sale or rent using their land banks to 'buddy up' with private developers in the hope of boosting their revenues through the surplus made. Morphet and Clifford (2017) found that only 14% of houses built were for social renting whereas 46% were for sale or renting privately. The White Paper *Fixing Our Broken Housing Market* welcomed local housing companies but said 'we want to see tenants that local authorities place in new affordable properties offered equivalent terms to those in council housing, including a Right to Buy their home' (DCLG 2017a, para. 1.38).

Wilson et al. (2018, p. 25) state 'the delivery of more than 200,000 homes per year in England has, since 1939, only happened largely because of major public sector (local authority) housebuilding programmes'. Perhaps, at last, recognising that, on its historical record, private enterprise alone cannot build sufficient homes to meet housing requirements, the 2017 Conservative Party Manifesto (Conservative Party 2017, p. 71) declared:

> We will never achieve the numbers of new houses we require without the active participation of social and municipal housing providers.... This must not be done at the expense of high standards, however: councils have been amongst the worst offenders in failing to build sustainable, integrated communities. In some instances, they have built for political gain rather than for social purpose. So we will help councils to build, but only those councils who will build high-quality, sustainable and integrated communities.

It announced that a future Conservative government would:

> Enter into new Council Housing Deals with ambitious, pro-development, local authorities to help them build more social housing. We will work with them to improve their capability and capacity to develop more good homes, as well as providing them with significant low-cost capital funding. (Conservative Party 2017, p. 71)

It added, 'In doing so, we will build new fixed-term social houses, which will be sold privately after ten to fifteen years with an automatic Right to Buy for tenants, the proceeds of which will be recycled into further homes' (Conservative Party 2017, p. 71). Local authority interest in participating in such schemes will depend on the terms of the new Right to Buy and the time-period allowed before the stock has to be sold. Ten years does not differ significantly from the current cost floor limit. The abolition of the Right to Buy in England would enable local government to build without concern that they might have to sell their asset at a large discount.

Theresa May's speech to the 2017 Conservative Party conference indicated that some of the additional £2 billion allocated to social housing would be directed to local authorities but the restrictions on local government borrowing and the use of Right to Buy receipts were not relaxed. Indeed, Theresa May's additional £2 billion, over five years, placed in the social housing pot, would add only 5000 new homes per year (Booth 2017).

Conservative governments have been very reluctant to lift local authority borrowing caps with, in 2016, a minister stating: 'There are no plans to lift the caps, which are part of the government's strategy to manage the overall level of public debt' (Hansard 2016). However, in the Autumn 2017 Budget, it was announced that councils in areas with high affordability pressure will be able to bid for increases in their borrowing caps from 2019 to 2020. There is some unused capacity in the existing local authority borrowing caps, partially resulting from their distribution and some commentators have advocated pooling the caps (House of Commons Select Committee on Communities and Local Government 2012; Lyons 2014). The government's 2018 Green Paper on social housing (MHCLG 2018b) indicated future relaxation of local government borrowing controls in selected areas (see Chapter 8) and in late 2018 Theresa May told the Conservative Party 2018 Conference that borrowing caps on new house building by local government would be axed. This will boost new house construction albeit that, having transferred their stock, many local authorities have no assets to use as collateral for borrowing; the Treasury still takes a slice of the capital receipts from Right to Buy sales and having to sell houses under the Right to Buy may inhibit many authorities in building new homes.

There are other mechanisms to promote building by local government. It has been suggested that a National Housing and Infrastructure Bank, funded from hypothecated Housing ISAs, should be set up to enhance the capital available for infrastructure and housing (Shelter and KPMG 2015). Additional capital could also be made available by changing the rules on local authority borrowing. Perry (2014, p. 6) maintains:

> The UK's fiscal rules are based on targets for controlling the level of Public Sector Net Debt (PSND). However, PSND is a uniquely British measure; the main international measure of debt is known as General Government Gross Debt (GGGD)… it is the main measure used for international comparisons by bodies such as the IMF and OECD.

If GGGD was used as a debt measure then borrowing by local government to supply homes would not be recorded in the public sector debt. Perry examines other technical ways to remove local authority building for new homes from the public sector debt definition but, even if local authority borrowing for new homes was not removed from the UK's official debt definition, there are long-term gains from local authority building at social rents in future reductions in HB (see this chapter). Moreover, when £60 billion of housing association debt was added to public sector debt the Office for Budget Responsibility (2015) reported that it would cost £1.2 billion in 2015/2016 indicating that the annual cost of new local authority borrowing would be manageable. Restricting local government housing production is an ideological—not a financial—decision.

Labour's 2018 Green Paper *Housing for the Many* (Labour Party 2018) set out a programme to build 100,000 'genuinely affordable' homes per year over ten years, but such is the precarious state of local authority housing finance—half of local authorities do not have a housing stock asset and the capacity to exclude borrowing from the public debt definition is uncertain—that local government only features as a scale provider towards the end of the ten year programme. However, putting local government into a fit state to deliver more homes is promoted by allowing local government to use the Right to Buy receipts taken by the Treasury until the Right to Buy is suspended and providing resources to allow local authorities without a Housing Revenue Account to create one. Reverse transfer of stock from housing associations to local government to enable local authorities to build up an asset base was absent from Labour's agenda.

Direct Labour Organisations

In 1892, dismayed by the high tender costs submitted by private enterprise, the London County Council established an in-house construction service. The use of Direct Labour Organisations (DLOs) for new-build and maintenance spread rapidly between the wars and, by the late 1960s 178,000 workers were employed (House of Lords 1968).

Unsurprisingly, DLOs were unpopular with private builders and they acquired a reputation for inefficiency. Sandbrook (2012) reports that, in hatching a plan for Harold Wilson to sell council houses, Bernard Donoughue, Wilson's political advisor, said had a brother working as a carpenter for Manchester's direct-labour organisation who confided that he did little work—direct or otherwise! Later, a textbook dismissed DLOs in a sentence stating 'Large municipal created direct labour organisations until their wasteful practices were stopped by compulsory competitive tendering' (Golland and Blake 2004, p. 221). The accuracy of this depiction has been challenged, with Whitehead (1984, p. 121), stating 'Yet what limited evidence there is does not confirm this view ....Rather it shows that productivity is very similar, although it is difficult to adjust for different types and quality'. The Thatcher/Major governments severely curtailed DLOs not only by compulsory competitive tendering but by reducing local authority new build and requiring DLOs to make a specified return on their activities thereby curbing some very good apprenticeship schemes. New Labour did not try to revive DLOs and, in 2017, only a few local authorities were using DLOs for new build under housing company structures (South Cambridgeshire District Council 2017).

Housing associations organise the production of social houses and manage them when built but very few use direct labour to build the homes. However, prompted by the downfall of private maintenance organisations in the recession and a VAT increase on repairs, the use of DLOs for maintenance started to increase. Such DLOs could provide the basis for new house building across the social housing sector to provide a rival to the volume house builders.

The Residential Construction Industry

Restoring social housing DLOs has become salient because the private residential construction industry is under performing. In the 2017 General Election campaign both the Labour Party and the Conservative Party announced a 200,000 per year housing programme up to 2020 in

England, accelerating to 250,000 per year by 2022 and to 300,000 per year by the middle 2020s but the private residential construction industry is the dominant delivery vehicle. Several reports (Egan 1998; Barker 2004; Lyons 2014; Arcadis 2015) have criticised the structure and inefficiency of the residential construction industry pointing to its reliance on large-scale producers—60% of new house-building is undertaken by the ten largest building firms—lack of innovation, dependence on profits from land-banking, reliance on workers from overseas and the slow rate of build-out on sites with planning permission to maintain land values. Fraser (2018, p. 1) claims that:

> Housebuilding methods haven't changed much in 150 years and productivity has flat-lined; build costs are 24 times higher in 2015 than they were in 1971 (a real-terms increase of 1.78), this is largely because homes are hand-built, using labour intensive methods, in largely uncontrolled conditions.

The Ministry of Housing, Communities and Local Government (MHCLG 2018e), in announcing an independent review to tackle barriers to building, said that 'as of July 2016, just over half the 684,000 homes with planning permission had been completed'. The government announcing an inquiry into the unfulfilled planning permission issue. The preliminary enquiry findings stated:

> The fundamental driver of build out rates once detailed planning permission is granted for large sites appears to be the 'absorption rate' — the rate at which newly constructed homes can be sold into (or are believed by the house-builder to be able to be sold successfully into) the local market without materially disturbing the market price. (Letwin 2018a, p. 2)

In other words, builders will only build if they can sell at a price that maintains local market prices and their profits, hence sustained high house prices are necessary to promote new building. Subsequent investigation led Letwin to conclude that the 'absorption rate' was particularly low on large sites and to attribute this to the homogeneous nature of the products on offer.

In his final report Letwin recommended new planning rules to provide incentives to diversify existing sites of over 1500 units in areas of high housing demand and introduce a power for local planning authorities in places with high-housing demand to designate particular areas within their local plans as land which can be developed only as single large sites, and to create master plans and design codes to promote a diversity of housing types. In addition, local authorities should be given clear statutory powers to purchase the land designated for such large sites compulsorily at prices around ten times existing use value 'rather than the huge multiples of existing use value which currently apply' (Letwin 2018b, p. 6).

The Construction Leadership Council, asked by the government to identify actions to reduce the industry's structural vulnerability to skills shortages, diagnosed the industry's problem as 'a deep-seated market failure', with a real ticking 'time bomb' in 'the industry's workforce size and demographic' that, 'based purely on existing workforce age and current levels of new entrant attraction, we could see a 20–25% decline in the available labour force within a decade' (Farmer 2016, p. 8). To some, Brexit will add to the building industry's problems. Maclennan and Gibb (2018, p. 1) assert that 'Reduced UK immigration will adversely affect construction sector capacity', albeit that any reduction in EU construction workers will depend on the terms in the final agreement on the UK's exit and post Brexit immigration policy. There is also an argument that labour availability from outside the UK has hindered improved efficiency in the residential construction industry.

Pre-manufactured Houses

Construction Leadership Council located the building industry's long-term market failure in the cyclical nature of the building industry's activities with the social sector used to try to counter the cycle. It noted 'research showed the percentage of the workforce trained, when compared to other industries, is third lowest with only 53% of the workforce trained in 2015' (Farmer 2016, p. 27) and that the fund accumulated by the government's 0.5% of the payroll apprenticeship levy might be under-utilised. Farmer (2016, p. 10) stated:

Critically, a plan for change needs to recognise, based on past evidence, that the industry will not change itself unilaterally at scale. It needs to be led by clients expressly changing their needs and commissioning behaviours or government acting in a regulatory or strategic initiation capacity to drive positive disruption.

In placing stress on pre-manufactured housing as a response to the workforce problems of the residential construction industry, Farmer emphasised government involvement via the Build to Rent initiative. However, in identifying 'high demand cyclicality' as a principal cause of the residential building industry's problems, it pointed to more certain demand through a sustained programme of social housing stating:

> Government has a strategic choice to make about the future role of grant funded social housing, which has historically been used as a counter-cyclical demand tool. More tenure diversity would immediately imply different supply chain and delivery models that may better promote innovation. In time, this may in turn influence core housebuilder delivery models but it is considered unlikely that large scale innovation will start in the volume housebuilder market. (Farmer 2016, p. 49)

According to Fraser (2018) prefabricated house construction is only cheaper than traditional building when procured at scale hence local authority procurement is probably necessary to kick start the industry.

In 1944 the coalition government promised to build 500,000 prefabricated houses but the programme was axed in 1948 by Aneurin Bevan when only 156,323 houses had been built. In the early 2000s, John Prescott promoted the £60,000 prefabricated house but neglected to include land costs and very few such homes were built. Theresa May's government expressed interest in prefabricated houses with the White Paper (DCLG 2017a, para. 3.37) declaring 'Industry reports suggest homes constructed offsite can be built up to 30% more quickly than traditional methods and with a potential 25% reduction in costs'. An accelerated construction programme, announced in the 2017 White Paper, would include offsite manufacturing in an initiative aimed at delivering 15,000 starts by 2020 on public sector land by partnerships between government and small-and medium-size builders. In addition, the Home Builders Fund, launched in 2016, offered loans at commercial rates for schemes that increased innovation and made greater use of modern methods of construction.

An investigation into the residential construction industry by the House of Commons Committee on Communities and Local Government reached the conclusion:

> The high volume homebuilders dominate the market and are therefore able to shape how it operates. Having purchased land at a given price and devised a scheme that will allow them to recoup their investment and deliver a profit, they will not risk over-saturating a local market to the extent that house prices will fall and their profits decrease. This is rational commercial behaviour and a sound business model. But it is not one that is in the country's best interests. (House of Commons Committee on Communities and Local Government 2017, p. 46)

The committee recognised the land shortage as a major constraint on new building and made a number of useful recommendations on improving the performance of the construction industry such local authority imposition of build out rates on development sites but had no suggestions on how to accelerate production by local authority housing companies.

Small-Scale Builders and Self-Build

Small-and medium-sized companies, defined as those building fewer than 500 properties per year, built two-thirds of new homes in the late 1980s, but, by 2016, this was down to 26%. The major problems in building encountered by small-and medium-sized firms identified by the Home Builders Federation (2016) were planning delays, the tendency for land release to be in larger trances and obstacles in securing finance from banks. The Home Builders Federation's suggested remedies included more government loan guarantee backing, extending the plot site size limits on section 106 payments and reclassifying garden land as available for development. In March 2018, the government announced consultations on revisions to the NPPF to encourage the use of smaller sites including a local planning authority obligation to ensure that at least 20% of sites allocated for residential development should be sites of half a hectare or less. The House of Commons Committee on Communities and Local Government investigation of volume builders (2017) recommended access to credit at more favourable rates for small-scale builders.

According to government sources, at 10% of new build, self-build in the UK is lagging behind other countries (Full Fact 2014). Self-build has the potential to deliver more homes and 2015 Self-build and Custom Housebuilding Act (as amended by the Housing and Planning Act 2016) required local authorities to maintain a register of people wanting to build their own homes and make provision for demand in their local plans. In Oxfordshire, a large site, sufficient for 1900 self-build, 'customised' homes has been designated (*Guardian* 2018). However, given that land prices are a major barrier to all forms of new housebuilding, self-build will only accelerate when land price falls are generated via greater land release.

Powerhouses and Engines

In the coalition government, the Liberal Democrats promoted 'City Deals' involving customised packages, often involving additional resources via a Regional Growth Fund, devolving part of the business rate—pooling it with other resources into a single investment pot—and enhanced local autonomy in return for a local plan to promote economic growth. Devolution received a boost from Lord Heseltine's report *No Stone Unturned: In Pursuit of Growth*, in which he recommended more resource and power devolution especially to the cities outside London. Heseltine argued:

> London will always be an important factor in the economic prosperity of the whole of the UK. However, its success should not be at the expense of the rest of the country.... By focusing on raising our performance in every town and city we will return our economy to sustained, long term growth. (Heseltine 2012, p. 26)

'City Deals' were introduced in 'waves' and, by 2016, covered many cities in the UK.

In 2014, the city deal idea was augmented by Chancellor of the Exchequer, George Osborne. The 'Greater Manchester Agreement' between the ten local authorities in Greater Manchester and the government was signed whereby Greater Manchester would obtain more control of budgets, including the resources allocated to housing and the National Health Service, in return for a Greater Manchester elected mayor (HM Treasury and Greater Manchester Combined Authority 2014).

Following a 2015 announcement by HM Treasury that, by 2020, local government would become 'self-reliant'—all the business rates would be assigned to local government and the government core grant would be axed. Anticipating almost total reliance on economic growth for additional resources for local services via the business rate and council tax, other local authority combinations queued for deals similar to the Greater Manchester's. Each deal was bespoke. In some areas devolution deals brought together city, town and country with, for example, the residents of Bath and North East Somerset, Bristol and South Gloucestershire electing the first ever Mayor for the West of England Combined Authority area in May 2017 with the mayor holding powers, inter alia, over transport, land use planning an investment fund. The West Midland mayor was given similar power s with the West Midlands Combined Authority covering Birmingham, Coventry, Dudley, Sandwell, Solihull, Walsall and Wolverhampton. By 2018, twelve devolution deals were in place, with the North of the Tyne devolution deal involving Newcastle, Northumberland and North Tyneside announced in November 2017.

Heseltine's vision had been grand—a return to the powerful, independent, entrepreneurial cities of the nineteenth century. Indeed, the pamphlet contains a picture of Joseph Chamberlain with his declaration 'Unless I can secure for the nation results similar to those which have followed the adoption of my policy in Birmingham … it will have been a sorry exchange to give up the town council for the cabinet'. Central government was to become a 'catalyst, enabler, and partner' (Heseltine 2012, p. 87).

Devolution deal boundaries differ with some resembling the boundaries and powers of the urban metropolitan county councils, set up in 1974 but abolished in 1985. They remain a far way from Heseltine's vision but devolution is a long journey not a destination and the devolved authorities may evolve into more robust organisations. Greater Manchester—described as the 'Northern powerhouse' although subsequently this term has been applied to combined authorities along the M62 corridor and beyond—has the strongest powers. In the housing domain the mayor oversees the spatial development plan covering the ten metropolitan boroughs in Greater Manchester. Already this plan has encountered opposition with reference to green belt release with the mayor declaring in his election campaign that the draft development plan needed to be 'radically rewritten' (Burnham 2017, quoted by *Manchester Evening News* 2017a). However, with the election over, and with 3960 houses built in 2016 compared to a protected 9600 annual household growth, the 'radical' rewriting may not be so radical. Local opposition to building may be easier to overcome at the Greater Manchester level with its 2,683,000 population: those affected by the development are outnumbered by those unaffected hence new house building on green sites will have a lower political impact. The mayor's influence over NHS finance may enable extra resources to be invested in housing-based community care schemes and Greater Manchester's size should make the creation of a large local government housing company more feasible, perhaps, in time, using direct labour.

Stephen Purvis, chair of Policy North, representing the North East, has described the Northern Powerhouse as a 'concept without content' (quoted in the *Daily Express* 2017). As ever, resource availability is the critical issue. In early 2018, five metro mayors signed a letter protesting that they had received low resources when the Housing Infrastructure Fund was distributed because the brownfield sites in their areas were more expensive to develop than greenfield land in the South of England (Brown 2018). Limited new infrastructure investment in the powerhouses needs to be balanced against the deep cuts in central support for mainstream services. There is an ongoing suspicion that English devolution is a devise for cutting spending with the devolved authorities taking the blame for such cuts—a suspicion augmented by Laws' statement in his insider account of the coalition government.

> ...one seasoned government adviser told me, George's view was that the money will either be wasted by central government or local government. He thinks the only advantage of devolution is that you can slice 10 per cent off the money as you devolve it, so the Treasury has to pay less. (Laws 2016, p. 226)

On the plus side, the principal motive underlying English devolution is to divert economic growth, with its associated population growth and housing pressures, away from London. Manchester's housing problems, although serious, are not as acute as London's. Improved transport across the M62 corridor has been identified as the key to growth and the combined clout of the metro authorities across the corridor may be sufficient to modernise the transport structure. However other regions—especially the struggling North East—are isolated. High Speed Two could have started in Newcastle.

Conclusion

Although boosting housing construction is promoted as the principal remedy to the UK housing crisis, many barriers to expanding new-build remain. The White Paper *Fixing Our Broken Housing Market* (DCLG 2017a) recognised these obstacles and adopted some of the remedies discussed above but in diluted forms. It lacked big ideas to tackle the issue. Commenting on the White Paper, the Institute of Directors said 'we needed more from this white paper' (quoted in the *Financial Times*, 2017b) and the *Telegraph* (2017) asserted the White Paper 'does little to tackle bigger housing issues'.

Inadequate land release is the principal hindrance to new home construction. The land release incentives promoted by central government since 2013—with varying degrees of enthusiasm—are beginning to have an impact (see Chapter 2) but land release politics still impedes their effectiveness. Proposals to build on designated green belt land generate vociferous opposition and the Prime Minister has endorsed the opposition to green belt encroachment in Greater Manchester (*Manchester Evening News* 2017b). Without a wholesale change in planning law severely restricting local authority rights to control land release, new towns are likely to be the most fruitful mechanisms to promote new housebuilding. Yes, there will be local protests, but they will be isolated and, once the New Town Corporation is in place, with the extensive powers under the 1946 New Towns Act, rapid progress is possible. 'Northern powerhouses' and their kind have the potential to boost economic growth outside London and its hinterlands but more infrastructure investment is necessary to stimulate the interaction effect that has enhanced London's growth.

It appears that the coalition and post-2015 Conservative governments have relied on 'filtering'—the trickle down of vacancies created by new build to improve the housing conditions of the 'least advantaged'—but, even in the 1930s when new housebuilding was very high relative to population growth, filtering made little impact on the housing circumstances of lower income groups. In England, social housing contributed only 15% to new house starts in 2017. If the principal victims of the housing crisis are to receive better homes at lower cost, a major boost in social housing with far greater local government involvement in construction is necessary.

References

Arcadis. (2015). *People and Money: Fundamental to Unlocking the Housing Crisis.* https://www.arcadis.com/media/D/B/3/%7BDB3A15FD-23D0-4C95-9578-BBE1611D8A0E%7D9308_People%20and%20Money%20Report_WEB_LR.pdf.

Barker, K. (2004). *Delivering Stability: Securing Our Future Housing Needs; Final Report, Recommendations.* London: HM Treasury. http://webarchive.nationalarchives.gov.uk/+/http:/www.hm-treasury.gov.uk/consultations_and_legislation/barker/consult_barker_index.cfm.

Barker, K. (2006). *Barker Review of Land Use Planning: Final Report Recommendations.* London: HM Treasury. https://www.gov.uk/government/

publications/barker-review-of-land-use-planning-final-report-recommenda-tions.

BBC News. (2017, November 9). *How Much of Your Area Is Built On?* http:// www.bbc.co.uk/news/uk-41901294.

BBC News. (2018, March 5). *Theresa May: Young Are "Right to Be Angry" About Lack of Houses.* https://www.bbc.com/news/uk-politics-43279177.

Bentley, D. (2017). *The Land Question: Fixing the Dysfunction at the Root of the Housing Crisis.* London: Civitas. http://www.civitas.org.uk/content/files/thelandquestion.pdf.

Blair, T. (2011). *Tony Blair: A Journey.* London: Arrow.

Booth, R. (2017, October 5). Theresa May's £2bn for Social Housing Unlikely to Solve Problem. *Guardian.* https://www.theguardian.com/society/2017/oct/04/theresa-mays-2bn-for-social-housing-unlikely-to-solve-problem.

Boughton, J. (2018). *Municipal Dreams: The Rise and Fall of Council Housing.* London: Verso.

Bowman, S. (2016). Brownfield Land Won't Be Enough to Solve London's Housing Crisis. *Londonist.* https://londonist.com/2016/01/brownfield-land.

Brown, C. (2018, February 20). Morning Briefing: Metro Mayors "Demand Better Housing Deal". *Inside Housing.* https://www.insidehousing.co.uk/news/morning-briefing-metro-mayors-demand-better-housing-deal-54810.

Campaign to Protect Rural England. (2015). *Green Belt Myths.* London: CPRE. https://www.cpre.org.uk/what-we-do/housing-and-planning/green-belts/in-depth; http://www.cpre.org.uk/what-we-do/housingand-planning/green-belts/in-depth/item/3027-green-belt-myths#myth7.

Campaign to Protect Rural England. (2018a). *The State of the Green Belt.* London: Campaign to Protect Rural England. https://www.cpre.org.uk/resources/housing-and-planning/green-belts/item/4931-state-of-the-green-belt-2018.

Campaign to Protect Rural England. (2018b). *State of Brownfield 2018: An Analysis Demonstrating the Potential of Brownfield Land for Housing.* London: Campaign to Protect Rural England. https://www.cpre.org.uk/resources/housing-and-planning/housing/item/4769-state-of-brownfield-2018.

CAPI OmniBus. (2009). *Green Belt Omnibus Survey: July & August 2009.* https://www.cpre.org.uk/resources/housing-and-planning/green-belts/item/.../463.

Centre for Cities. (2014). *Delivering Change: Building Homes Where We Need Them.* London: Centre for Cities. http://www.centreforcities.org/publication/delivering-change-building-homes-where-we-need-them/.

Cheshire, P. (2013, September 13). Greenbelt Myth Is the Driving Force Behind Housing Crisis. *The Conversation*. http://blogs.lse.ac.uk/politicsand-policy/greenbelt-myth-is-the-driving-force-behind-housing-crisis/.

Cheshire, P. (2014). Turning Houses into Gold: Don't Blame the Foreigners, It's We Brits Who Did It. *Centrepiece, 19*(1), 14–18.

Christophers, B. (2018). *The New Enclosure: The Appropriation of Public Land in Neoliberal Britain*. London: Verso.

City Metric. (2018, April 3). *Yes, Supply Is the Cause of the Housing Crisis and We Do Need to Build More Homes in Successful Cities*. https://www.citymetric.com/business/yes-supply-cause-housing-crisis-and-we-do-need-build-more-homes-successful-cities-3804.

Collinson, P. (2017, October 21). Help to Buy Has Mostly Helped Housebuilders Boost Profits. *Guardian*. https://www.theguardian.com/money/blog/2017/oct/21/help-to-buy-property-new-build-price-ris.

Conservative Party. (2017). *Forward Together: Our Plan for a Stronger Britain and a Prosperous Future*. London: Conservative Party. https://www.conservatives.com/manifesto.

Construction News. (2017, May 2). *Housebuilders' Shares Rocket to Five-Year High*. https://www.constructionnews.co.uk/markets/sectors/housing/housebuilders-shares-rocket-to-five-year-high/10019498.article.

Daily Express. (2017, June 25). Ditch George Osborne's 'Northern Powerhouse' to Make Best of Brexit, Says Report. https://www.express.co.uk/news/politics/821161/Northern-Powerhouse-Brexit-ditch-George-Osborne.

DCLG. (2012a). *National Planning Policy Framework: Impact Assessment*. London: DCLG.

DCLG. (2012b). *Review of the Barriers to Institutional Investment in Private Rented Homes*. London: DCLG. https://assets.publishing.service.gov.uk/government/uploads/system/uploads/attachment_data/file/15547/montague_review.pdf.

DCLG. (2017a). *Fixing Our Broken Housing Market* (Cm 9352). London: DCLG. https://assets.publishing.service.gov.uk/government/uploads/system/uploads/attachment_data/file/590464/Fixing_our_broken_housing_market_-_print_ready_version.pdf.

DCLG. (2017b). *Planning for the Right Homes in the Right Places: Consultation Proposals*. London: DCLG. https://www.gov.uk/government/consultations/planning-for-the-right-homes-in-the-right-places-consultation-proposals.

DCLG. (2017c). *Local Planning Authority Green Belt: England 2016/17*. London: DCLG. https://assets.publishing.service.gov.uk/government/

uploads/system/uploads/attachment_data/file/642684/Green_Belt_Statistics_England_2016-17.pdf.

DCLG. (2017d). *Land Use Change Statistics in England: 2015–16*. London: DCLG.   https://assets.publishing.service.gov.uk/government/uploads/system/uploads/attachment_data/file/595749/Land_use_change_statistics_England_2015-16_-_2_March_2017_version.pdf.

Department of the Environment/Welsh Office. (1995). *Our Future Homes: Opportunity, Choice, Responsibility: The Government's Housing Policies for England and Wales* (Cm 2901). London: HMSO.

Economist. (2013, May 2). Housing and Planning: The Brownfields Delusion. https://www.economist.com/blogs/blighty/2013/05/planning-and-housing.

Egan, J. (1998). *Rethinking Construction, the Report of the Construction Task Force on the Scope for Improving Quality and Efficiency in UK Construction*. London: Department for the Environment, Transport and the Regions.

Ellis, H. (2018, June 11, Monday). *Oral Evidence to Housing, Communities and Local Government Committee: Land Value Capture*. HC 766. http://data.parliament.uk/writtenevidence/committeeevidence.sc/evidencedocument/housing-communities-and-local-government-committee/land-value-capture/oral/85154.html.

Evans, N. (2017, June 10). 'Tory MP Nigel Evans Lays into His Own Party Over "Awful" Election' Manifesto. *Sky News*. https://www.youtube.com/watch?v=4bXmLLfUzhA.

Farmer, M. (2016). *The Farmer Review of the UK Construction Labour Model: Modernise or Die—Time to Decide the Industry's Future*. London: Construction Leadership Council. https://www.gov.uk/government/publications/construction-labour-market-in-the-uk-farmer-review.

Financial Times. (2017a, November 17). How to Solve the UK Housing Crisis. https://www.ft.com/content/d8854b1e-bf08-11e7-823b-ed31693349d3.

Financial Times. (2017b, February 7). Sajid Javid Sets Out Fix for "Broken" Housing Market. https://www.ft.com/content/dfb68f7c-ec97-11e6-930f-061b01e23655.

Fraser, R. (2018, March 2). Can Offsite Manufactured Housing (OSM) Play a Key Role in Solving the Housing Crisis by Ensuring That New Supply Targets Are Met? *Redbrick*. https://redbrickblog.wordpress.com/.

Full Fact. (2014). *Self-Build Britain: Is the UK Lagging Behind Other Countries?* https://fullfact.org/economy/self-build-britain-uk-lagging-behind-other-countries/.

Golland, A., & Blake, R. (Eds.). (2004). *Housing Development: Theory, Process and Practice*. London: Routledge.

Grimwood, G. G. (2017, November 17). *Green Belt* (House of Commons Briefing Paper No. 00934). London: House of Commons.

Grindrod, J. (2017). *Outskirts: Living Life on the Edge of the Green Belt.* London: Sceptre.

Guardian. (2017, February 7). Stop Dithering and Start Building— Experts on Housing White Paper. https://www.theguardian.com/housing-network/2017/feb/07/start-building-experts-housing-white-paper.

Guardian. (2018, February 10). Is Custom Build the Future of Housing? https://www.theguardian.com/money/2018/feb/10/custom-self-build-housing-graven-hill.

Hansard. (2016). *Council Housing Written Question HL3457.* http://www.parliament.uk/written-questions-answers-statements/written-question/lords/2016-11-23/HL3457.

Heseltine, L. (2012). *No Stone Unturned: In Pursuit of Growth.* London: Department for Business, Education and Skills. https://www.gov.uk/government/uploads/system/uploads/attachment_data/file/34648/12-1213-no-stone-unturned-in-pursuit-of-growth.pdf.

HM Treasury. (2017). *Estimated Costs of Principal Tax Reliefs.* London: HM Treasury. https://www.gov.uk/government/uploads/system/uploads/attachment_data/file/579720/Dec_16_Main_Reliefs_Final.pdf.

HM Treasury and Greater Manchester Combined Authority. (2014). *Greater Manchester Agreement: Devolution to Greater Manchester and Transition to a Directly Elected Mayor.* https://www.gov.uk/government/uploads/system/uploads/attachment_data/file/369858/Greater_Manchester_Agreement_i.pdf.

Home Builders Federation. (2016). *Reversing the Decline of Small Housebuilders: Reinvigorating Entrepreneurialism and Building More Homes.* London: Home Builders Federation. http://www.hbf.co.uk/uploads/media/HBF_SME_Report_2017_Web.pdf.

House of Commons Committee on Communities and Local Government. (2012). *Financing of New Housing Supply Eleventh Report of Session 2010–12.* London: House of Commons. https://publications.parliament.uk/pa/cm201012/cmselect/cmcomloc/1652/1652.pdf.

House of Commons Committee on Communities and Local Government. (2017). *Capacity in the Homebuilding Industry* (Tenth Report of Session 2016–2017). London: House of Commons. https://publications.parliament.uk/pa/cm201617/cmselect/cmcomloc/46/46.pdf.

House of Lords. (1968, February 20). *Local Authorities' Direct—Labour Building Departments*. HL Deb vol 289 cc337–54. https://api.parliament.uk/historic-hansard/lords/1968/feb/20/local-authorities-direct-labour-building-1.

Howard, E. (1902). *Garden Cities of Tomorrow*. London: Faber.

Independent. (2018, February 2). Labour Compulsory Purchase Orders: Could Forced Sales of Undeveloped Land Work and Is 'Land Banking' Really Happening? http://www.independent.co.uk/news/business/analysis-and-features/labour-compulsory-purchase-orders-could-work-undeveloped-land-landbanking-profit-council-housing-a8191671.html.

Inside Housing. (2017, October 18). Gauke: "Unacceptable" for Social Landlords to Evict Universal Credit Tenants. https://www.insidehousing.co.uk/home/gauke-unacceptable-for-social-landlords-to-evict-universal-credit-tenants-52848.

Ipsos/Mori. (2015). *Attitudes Towards Green Belt Land Green Belt: Omnibus Survey, July & August, a Study for the Campaign to Protect Rural England*. https://www.ipsos-mori.com/researchpublications/researcharchive/3611/Attitudes-towards-Green-Belt-land.aspx.

Joyce, R. (2017). *Housing Measures*. London: Institute for Fiscal Studies. https://www.ifs.org.uk/publications/10186.

Knowles, T. (2018, September 8). Help-to-Buy: Scheme Has Helped Biggest Developers to Double Profits. *Times*. https://www.thetimes.co.uk/article/help-to-buy-scheme-has-helped-biggest-developers-to-double-profits-759qq3h7m.

Labour Party. (2017). *Labour's New Deal on Housing*. London: Labour Party. https://labour.org.uk/wp-content/uploads/2017/10/Housing-Mini-Manifesto.pdf.

Labour Party. (2018). *Housing For the Many: Labour Party Green Paper*. London: The Labour Party. https://labour.org.uk/issues/housing-for-the-many/.

Lambert, S. (2016, July 21). Osborne Made Britain's House Price Addiction Worse, It's Time for Hammond to Help Us Go Cold Turkey, Says Simon Lambert. *This Is Money*. http://www.thisismoney.co.uk/money/comment/article-3699739/Osborne-house-price-addiction-worse-Hammond-stop-it.html.

Laws, D. (2016). *Coalition: The Inside Story of the Conservative-Liberal Democrat Coalition Government*. London: Biteback Publishing.

Letwin, O. (2018a, March 9). *Letter to the Rt Hon Philip Hammond MP and The Rt Hon Sajid Javid MP*. https://www.gov.uk/government/uploads/system/uploads/attachment_data/file/689430/Build_Out_Review_letter_to_Cx_and_Housing_SoS.pdf.

Letwin, O. (2018b). *Independent Review of Build Out: Final Report* (Cm 9720). London: Secretary of State for Housing, Communities and Local Government. https://www.gov.uk/government/publications/independent-review-of-build-out-final-report.

Lund, B. (2016). *Housing Politics in the United Kingdom: Power Planning and Protest*. Bristol: Policy Press.

Lyons, M. (Chair). (2014). *The Lyons Housing Review: Mobilising Across the Nation to Build the Homes Our Children Need*. London: Labour Party Forum. https://www.policyforum.labour.org.uk/uploads/editor/files/The_Lyons_Housing_Review_2.pdf.

Maclennan, D., & Gibb, K. (2018). *Brexit and Housing: Policy Briefing*. Heriot Watt University: UK Collaborative Centre for Housing Evidence. http://housingevidence.ac.uk/publications/policy-briefing-brexit-and-housing/.

Manchester Evening News. (2017a). *Andy Burnham Comes Out Against "Unfair and Disproportionate" Green Belt Master Plan*. http://www.manchestereveningnews.co.uk/news/greater-manchester-news/andy-burnham-green-belt-development-12441497.

Manchester Evening News. (2017b). *Could Huge Developments Planned for Green Belt Land Be Radically Scaled Back? Theresa May Reiterated the Tories' Promise That Protected Spaces Are "Safe in the Government's Hands"*. http://www.manchestereveningnews.co.uk/news/greater-manchester-news/could-huge-developments-planned-green-12643835.

MHCLG. (2018a). *Housebuilding Completions Per 1000 Households*. London: MHCLG. http://opendatacommunities.org/data/house-building/completions-ratio/by-category.

MHCLG. (2018b). *A New Deal for Social Housing* (Cm 9571). London: MHCLG. https://assets.publishing.service.gov.uk/government/uploads/system/uploads/attachment_data/file/733635/A_new_deal_for_social_housing_print_ready_version.pdf.

MHCLG. (2018c). *Help to Buy (Equity Loan Scheme) and Help to Buy: NewBuy Statistics: April 2013 to 31 December 2017*. London: MHCLG. https://www.gov.uk/government/statistics/help-to-buy-equity-loan-scheme-and-help-to-buy-newbuy-statistics-april-2013-to-31-december-2017.

MHCLG. (2018d). *Social Housing Lettings: April 2016 to March 2017, England*. London: MHCLG. https://assets.publishing.service.gov.uk/government/uploads/system/uploads/attachment_data/file/677489/Social_housing_lettings_in_England_2016-17.pdf.

MHCLG. (2018e). *Supporting Housing Delivery Through Developer Contributions: Reforming Developer Contributions to Affordable Housing and Infrastructure*. London: MHCLG. https://assets.publishing.service.gov.uk/government/uploads/system/uploads/attachment_data/file/691182/Developer_Contributions_Consultation.pdf.

Morphet, J., & Clifford, B. (2017). *Local Authority Direct Provision of Housing*. London: Royal Town Planning Institute/National Planning Forum. http://rtpi.org.uk/media/2619006/Local-authority-direct-provision-of-housing.pdf.

Nairn D. (2016). *Ebenezer Howards Garden City Concept*. http://discoveringurbanism.blogspot.co.uk/2009/06/ebenezer-howards-garden-city-concept.html.

Nathaniel Litchfield and Partners. (2016). *Start to Finish: How Quickly Do Large-Scale Housing Sites Deliver?* https://lichfields.uk/media/1728/start-to-finish.pdf.

National Infrastructure Commission. (2017). *Interim Report on the Cambridge—Milton Keynes Oxford Corridor*. London: National Infrastructure Commission. https://www.nic.org.uk/publications/national-infrastructure-commissions-interim-report-cambridge-milton-keynes-oxford-corridor/.

New Economics Foundation. (2015). *Inquiry into the Economics of the UK Housing Market: Written Evidence from the New Economics Foundation*. London: King's College. https://kclpure.kcl.ac.uk/portal/en/publications/inquiry-into-the-economics-of-the-uk-housingmarket(0574ae6f-7b80–4c5d-8881–212f7fea17ea).html.

NHS England. (2016). *Healthy New Towns*. https://www.england.nhs.uk/ourwork/innovation/healthy-new-towns/.

Office for Budget Responsibility. (2015). *Economic and Fiscal Outlook—November 2015*. London: Office for Budget Responsibility. http://budgetresponsibility.org.uk/docs/dlm_uploads/EFO_November__2015.pdf.

Papworth, T. (2015). *The Green Noose*. London: Adam Smith Institute. https://www.adamsmith.org/research/the-green-noose.

Perry, J. (2014). *Why Is It Important to Change Local Authority Borrowing Rules?* Coventry: Chartered Institute of Housing. http://www.cih.org/resources/PDF/Policy%20free%20download%20pdfs/Policy%20essay%209%20-%20Why%20is%20it%20important%20to%20change%20local%20authority%20borrowing%20rules%20-%20July%202014.pdf.

Perry, J. (2018, March 19). Developers Are Skimping on Low-Cost Housing. Time to Get Tough. *Guardian.* https://www.theguardian.com/housing-network/2018/mar/19/affordable-homes-low-cost-rent-uk-planning-policy-government-developers.

Perry, J., & Stephens, M. (2018). How the Purpose of Social Housing Has Changed and Is Changing. In M. Stephens, J. Perry, S. Wilcox, P. Williams, & G. Young (Eds.), *UK Housing Review* (pp. 29–39). London: Chartered Institute of Housing.

Rugg, J., & Rhodes, D. (2018). *The Evolving Private Rented Sector: Its Contribution and Potential.* York: Centre for Housing Policy, University of York. http://www.nationwidefoundation.org.uk/wp-content/uploads/2018/09/Private-Rented-Sector-report.pdf.

Sandbrook, D. (2012). *Seasons in the Sun: The Battle for Britain 1974–1979.* London: Allen Lane.

Savills. (2017). *Spotlight 2017: Investing to Solve the Housing Crisis.* London: Savills. https://www.savills.co.uk/research_articles/229130/224869-0.

Seely, A. (2013). *Inheritance Tax* (Standard Note SN93). London: House of Commons. file:///C:/Users/User/Downloads/SN00093.pdf.

Shelter & KPMG. (2015). *Building the Homes We Need: A Programme for the 2015 Government.* London: KPHG. https://england.shelter.org.uk/__data/assets/pdf_file/0004/802570/2014_Building_the_homes_we_need_-_Briefing.pdf.

Social Housing Under Threat. (2017). *Investment to Meet the Housing Crisis Submission for 2017 Budget.* https://d3n8a8pro7vhmx.cloudfront.net/4socialhousing/pages/2160/attachments/original/1506356620/Submission_final.pdf?1506356620.

South Cambridgeshire District Council. (2017). *The Greater Cambridge Housing Development Agency (HDA).* Cambridge: South Cambridgeshire District Council. https://www.scambs.gov.uk/hda.

Spencer, J. (2018, January 8). Brownfield Land Identified for Less Than Half of Housing Need in Greater Manchester. *Inside Housing.* https://www.insidehousing.co.uk/news/brownfield-land-identified-for-less-than-half-of-housing-need-in-greater-manchester-53802.

Spiers, S. (2018). *How to Build Houses and Save the Countryside.* Bristol: Policy Press.

Statistics Portal. (2018). *United Kingdom (UK) HMRC Stamp Duty Land Tax Receipts from Fiscal Year 2000/01 to Fiscal Year 2017/18 (in Billion GBP).* https://www.statista.com/statistics/284328/stamp-duty-land-tax-united-kingdom-hmrc-tax-receipts/.

Talbot, D. (2018a, February 28). *The Garden Village Dream*. https://www.insidehousing.co.uk/insight/insight/the-garden-village-dream-54982.

Talbot, D. (2018b, June 18). UK Government's Garden Towns Plan Flounders. *Forbes*. https://www.forbes.com/sites/deborahtalbot/2018/06/18/uk-governments-garden-towns-plan-flounders/#1278057d3713.

Telegraph. (2016, August 2). It's Simple—We Need to Build More Houses. http://www.telegraph.co.uk/news/2016/08/02/its-simple–we-need-to-build-more-houses/.

Telegraph. (2017, February 7). White Paper Does Little to Tackle Bigger Housing Issues. http://www.telegraph.co.uk/business/2017/02/07/white-paper-does-little-tackle-bigger-housing-issues/.

Toynbee, P. (2017, May 5). Inheritance Tax Is Toxic: We Need New Ways to Tackle Inequality. *Guardian*. https://www.theguardian.com/commentis-free/2017/jan/05/inheritance-tax-inequality-wealth-theresa-may-social-mobility.

Urban Environment Design. (2014). *Wolfson Economics Prize: How We Would Deliver a New Garden City Which Is Visionary, Economically Viable, and Popular*. http://researchprofiles.herts.ac.uk/portal/files/11500394/Parham_et_al_Wolfson_Prize_2014_submission.pdf.

Whitehead, C. (1984). Privatisation and Housing. In J. Le Grand & R. Robinson (Eds.), *Privatisation and the Welfare State* (pp. 116–132). London: Allen & Unwin.

Wilcox, S., & Williams, P. (2018). *Dreams and Reality? Government Finance, Taxation and the Private Housing Market*. Coventry: Chartered Institute of Housing. http://www.cih.org/resources/PDF/Policy%20free%20download%20pdfs/Dreams%20and%20reality.pdf.

Wiles, C. (2014, May 14). Sprawl and the Green Belt. *Inside Housing*. https://www.insidehousing.co.uk/comment/comment/sprawl-and-the-green-belt-39882.

Wilson, W., Barton, C., & Smith, L. (2018). *Tackling the Under-Supply of Housing in England* (Briefing Paper No. 07671). London: House of Commons. https://researchbriefings.parliament.uk/ResearchBriefing/Summary/CBP-7671.

8

Conclusion: The Politics of Change

Housing Politics

General Elections are fought on the national stage in primary colours but political parties also target median voters in marginal constituencies. Of course, housing is only one element in electoral outcomes but political commentary has underplayed its salience. For many years, the political arithmetic involved in gaining and retaining power has taken precedence over the long-term public good. Green belts, greenfield sites and private landlordism are prime examples. Entrenched interests, often concentrated in marginal constituencies, react in the ballot box to new development proposals in their areas. In the 2010 General Election, the Conservatives and the Liberal Democrats—via their community politics—competed for the middle England vote via raucous opposition to New Labour's 'top down' land release programme and the recovery from the 2008/2010 downturn in house construction was seriously affected by Conservative Party reluctance to disturb its heartland voters surrounded by green fields and green belt land. When the Liberal Democrats adopted a strong pro-development position in their

© The Author(s) 2019
B. Lund, *Housing in the United Kingdom*,
https://doi.org/10.1007/978-3-030-04128-1_8

2015 manifesto, despite attempts to face both ways at local level, its stance contributed to the party being defeated by the Conservatives in many 'middle England' seats.

In contrast to private tenants (see Chapter 3), landlords vote. In 2016, Jeremy Corbyn, fretting about private landlord voting power, said:

> You're looking at several million people letting out one or two flats. And they can become a politically significant group. Particularly in marginal constituencies. So you will find all parties trimming towards them: landlords tend to be people who vote. (Corbyn 2016, quoted in Walker and Jeraj 2016, p. 79)

Indeed, in the countdown to the 2017 General Election, a poll—albeit based on a small sample—found that 53.3% of private landlords intended to vote Conservative, 14.5% Labour, 11.8% Liberal Democrat and 7.9% UKIP, with the remainder not voting (National Landlords Association 2017). Perhaps concern about such private landlord ballot power was the reason why Labour's 2017 manifesto was so tepid on private landlordism promising only three-year tenancy agreements on new lets with rents limited to inflation for the contract duration. Corbyn's more radical proposals, such as a Right to Buy for private tenants and a rent cap on all rents (*Independent* 2015) were abandoned.

The 2017 General Election revealed a marked change in housing's political salience. The housing crisis, simmering for many years and, 'always a crisis for the oppressed' (Madden and Marcuse 2016) had spread too far to be contained by marginal constituency politics. The runes were observable in the 2016 European Union referendum.

The 2016 European Union Referendum

The underlying discontent on living standards, growing since the 2008 recession, became manifest in the 2016 European Union referendum. Referendums are not fought in marginal constituencies:

every vote counts and turnout in the 2016 plebiscite was 72.2% compared to a 63% average in the four general elections since 2001 (Economist Intelligence Unit 2017). Of those that did not vote in 2015 but voted in 2016, 60% opted to leave the European Union. The income divide in the leave/remain vote was stark with 65% of people in households with an income lower than £1200 per month voting leave and 68% with an income more than £3701 per month voting remain (Swales 2016). Social classes A and B voted 59–41% to remain, social classes D and E 54–36% to leave (Ipsos/Mori 2016). The highest leave vote by local authority ward was 82.5% in Brambles and Thorntree, Middlesbrough—in the top ten most deprived wards in England.

The growing 'precariat'—those with insecure lives, moving in and out of low-paid jobs (Standing 2014)—had hit back. The Economic Intelligence Unit (2017, pp. 1, 17) labelled Brexit 'the revenge of the "deplorables"' and as 'a revolt by large sections of society who feel they have been abandoned politically, economically, socially and culturally by the mainstream political parties to which they used to give their allegiance'. Working class representation in Parliament is low. In 2015, only 3% of MPs were manual workers, compared to 16% in 1979. 30.7% of MPs came from business backgrounds (22.3% in 1979), 30.1% from the professions and 17% were political organisers compared to 3.4% in 1979 (Audickas and Cracknell 2018). The UK revolt has been associated with Donald Trump's 2016 US Presidential Election victory and the 2018 'gilet jaune' protests in France reflected a similar discontent.

Housing per se was not a major issue in the 2016 European Referendum campaign but, to the public, the 'economy' often means their living standards and housing costs have had a major impact on living standards. Income and class were closely associated with the leave/remain vote indicating a housing factor in voting behaviour. The gap between the Gini Coefficient—a measure of overall inequality—before and after housing costs had been increasing, as had the disparity in the P90/10 ratio—an indicator of inequality between rich and poor. The gap in child poverty before and after housing costs, both in absolute and relative terms, widened. Housing associations tenants voted 68/32 to leave and local authority tenants favoured exit by

70/30, perhaps an indication of how they had been stigmatised and neglected. Moreover, immigration and housing are connected. Evidence indicates that people from overseas do not receive preference in social housing allocation (Battiston et al. 2014) but the Migration Advisory Committee (2018, p. 4) stated:

> Migrants are a small fraction of people in social housing but a rising fraction of new tenants. The share of new tenancies going to migrants from the NMS in particular is rising. Given there is little building of new social housing this is inevitably at the expense of other potential tenants.

An opinion survey revealed that 31% of the electorate agreed with the statement 'the way social housing is allocated is generally unfair'. Only 18% disagreed, the rest being uncertain (Ipsos/Mori 2014). A 2016 Ipsos/Mori poll showed that 33% of the population strongly agreed with the statement that Britain is 'in the throes of a housing crisis' but 54% attributed the crisis to immigration (Tigar 2016). The Resolution Foundation (2016) noted a relationship, on an area basis, between the rate of increase in migration and the leave vote. There is a very strong connection between social class and negative perceptions of migration (Park et al. 2015). For many low-income households immigration became a symbol of their deteriorating economic circumstances, made more potent by the perception that the government did not care: the Migration Impacts Fund was axed; rents were rising and new house-building remained disappointingly low.

'Anywheres' and 'Somewheres'

Influential pundits have downplayed income distribution in explaining the Brexit vote. Goodhart (2017) attributed the 2016 referendum outcome to a cultural cleavage between 'Anywheres' and 'Somewheres'. 'Anywheres' are liberal, cognitive, have received a higher education, outward-looking, at ease with globalisation and immigration and secure in their portable, cosmopolitan identities. In contrast, 'Somewheres' are more socially conservative, unlikely to have acquired a higher education and communitarian by instinct gaining their identities via national and local attachments such as Scottish farmer, working class Geordie and Cornish housewife. Without a portable, cosmopolitan identity, they feel uncomfortable about many aspects of cultural and economic change such as mass immigration and globalisation.

Goodhart's 'Anywhere/Somewhere' distinction, with its cultural emphasis, underplayed the economic variables in the Brexit vote with 'the economy'—high on the list of public concerns—reflecting perceptions of living standards. As Halikiopoulou (2018, p. 2), explaining the rise of populist parties, claims, the assertion that 'the economic insecurity argument is wrong' is a false assumption.

> ... 'cultural indicators' such as immigration, are not exclusively cultural. There are reasons to expect the material aspects of immigration scepticism to still matter....Social groups that have a higher degree of exposure to labour market competition are more likely to have an interest in limiting immigration. (Halikiopoulou 2018, p. 2)

Theresa May seemed to recognise the salience of the economic divide. In her first public speech as prime minister she declared that 'Union' meant not only 'the precious bond between England, Scotland, Wales and Northern Ireland' but a union 'between all of our citizens, every one of us, whoever we are and wherever we're from' interspersing her speech with phrases such as, 'if you're a white, working-class boy, you're less likely than anybody else in Britain to go to university' and 'You have your own home, but you worry about paying a mortgage' (May 2016a, p. 1). She promised that government policy would concentrate on 'just about managing' families—'overlooked yet decisive' (Godson 2017). In her speech to the 2016 Conservative Party Conference May declared that her plan was 'to tackle the unfairness and injustice that divides us, so that we may build a new united Britain, rooted in the centre ground'. She also said 'If you believe you're a citizen of the world, you are a citizen of nowhere' (May 2016b).

The 2017 General Election

The housing dimension to voting behaviour became clearer in the 2017 General Election outcome. Theresa May attempted to contest the election on the platform that she would provide 'strong and stable government' and that she was the best person to negotiate a good Brexit deal. However, although May's chosen territory was salient to the election outcome, other public concerns had an impact. Labour's focus was opposition to austerity and 'for the many not the few' (Labour Party 2017a). The election outcome was a hung Parliament with Labour gaining 30 seats and the Conservatives with a 13 seat net loss. The Conservative vote share was 42.3%, Labour 40%, in part a reflection of the UKIP vote collapse.

May's 'just about managing' families theme was repeated in the Conservative Party's 2017 manifesto that was dedicated to such families. May's problem was that action did not match the rhetoric. The Treasury's Autumn Statement (HM Treasury 2016) indicated only a very modest change in policy direction. Rather than being wiped out by 2020/2021, the budget deficit would increase—to be eliminated in 2024/2025 and the Housing Benefit/Universal Credit taper was reduced by 2%. However, the benefit freezes and cuts set in motion by George Osborne were continued despite the anticipated rise in inflation. Both working and non-working 'just about managing' families were adversely affected by these measures.

Polling companies regularly ask their respondents to state the issues that are most important to them. Just before the 2017 general election housing had fallen from fifth to sixth in the public's most important issues league. Only 16% mentioned housing as an important issue, well below the NHS, immigration, the economy, the European Union and just behind education. However, as in the 2016 European Union Referendum, housing was connected to other issues—the economy and immigration—with the top rankings in public concern and housing had close associations with Labour's slogan 'for the many not the few'.

On some housing policy dimensions both the major political party manifestos were similar. Labour and the Conservatives declared their support for green belts and there was consensus on the new home target—250,000 new per year by 2022—albeit that Labour's commitment came in its specific housing manifesto (Labour Party 2017b)—published after the Conservative Party manifesto—rather than in its main manifesto. Both parties promised tighter controls on rogue landlords but Labour's proposals on rent regulation—three year tenancies on new lets with rent increases limited to inflation for the duration of the contract—were stronger than the Conservative promise to 'improve protections for those who rent, including by looking at how we increase security for good tenants and encouraging landlords to offer longer tenancies as standard' (Conservative Party 2017, p. 59).

The main party division was on social housing as opposed to market supply. Labour promised 'a New Deal on affordable homes to build at least 100,000 genuinely affordable homes to rent and buy a year by the final end of the next Parliament, including the biggest council housebuilding programme in more than 30 years' (Labour Party 2017b, p. 5). Although it was implied that 'affordable' meant social levels rents, 'affordable' was not defined and the extent of local government involvement was opaque. The Conservative Party manifesto was extremely cautious on future local government involvement in housing supply promising only 'a new generation of fixed-term council housing linked to a new Right to Buy' (Conservative Party 2017, p. 62).

Tenure Voting Patterns in the 2017 General Election

Owner-Occupiers

Compared to residents in other tenures, existing homeowners fared well post 2008 with mortgage payments declining—mainly due to historically low-interest rates—whilst rental costs increased (Belfield et al. 2015). Examining the period 2002–2003 to 2016–2017, Cribb et al. (2018a) identified a real average housing cost increase of 20% amongst private renters and 34% amongst social renters, compared to a 14% fall amongst owner-occupiers. The Council of Mortgage Lenders (2016) announced 'the lowest level of difficulty since 1982' with 0.03% of all loans resulting in repossession and 0.91% of mortgages more than 2.5 years in arrears. In comparison, the number of tenants evicted from their homes by bailiffs reached a record high in 2015 of 42,728, 0.48% of UK renting households.

Following the 2008 dip in house prices, outside London the South East and a few other housing hotspots, house prices had been stagnant. Government schemes such as Help to Buy, Funding for Lending—alongside quantitative easing—injected zest to the market in the countdown to the 2017 general election. House prices increased by 8.6% from April 2015 to April 2016, Middlesbrough and Westminster being the only areas where there was a drop in value. From May 2016 to May 2017 house prices increased by 4.7%. The Conservative Party's 2017 Manifesto was robust in defence of green belts that functioning as a property price guardian in Conservative heartland seats. Labour's manifesto announced 'We will prioritise brownfield sites and protect the green belt' (Labour Party 2017b, p. 60) and, later, London mayor Sadiq Khan's stated that he would protect the green belt by concentrating new housing supply in London's existing suburbs, building on small sites—including in back gardens—and upward extensions of existing houses, apartment blocks and shops (*Guardian* 2017a).

Nurturing existing homeowners, especially older homeowners without mortgages who were also likely to be Brexit supporters, produced electoral rewards for the Conservative Party with its lead over Labour amongst people owning their home outright increasing from 21% in 2010 to 24% in 2015 and then to 26% in 2017. However, although increasing from 7 to 8% between 2010 and 2015, the Conservative lead over Labour amongst mortgage holders dropped to 2% in 2017 (Akehurst 2017). Unfortunately, the polling organisations do not supply figures on mortgage holder voting behaviour by age but perhaps the decline in Conservative support amongst mortgagees reflected the problems of 'second steppers' locked into homes with inadequate space (see Chapter 3).

Social Tenants

Historically Labour has always taken the lion's share of the social tenant vote and Margaret Thatcher's Right to Buy was an attempt to attract Labour voters and offer an escape route from the consequences of her aspiration to downgrade council housing (see Lund 2016).

In his coalition government account Nick Clegg said:

> It would have been in a Quad meeting, so either Cameron or Osborne. One of them — I honestly can't remember whom — looked genuinely nonplussed and said, 'I don't understand why you keep going on about the need for more social housing — it just creates Labour voters. (Clegg 2016)

According to David Laws' *Coalition Diaries, 2012–2015* (2017), Cameron wanted to push all social rents to market levels. Between 2010 and 2016 council house rents increased from 12% of average earnings to 13% and housing association social rents from 12.7 to 13.6%. Affordable rents, unknown in 2010, were 18.5% of average earnings in 2016 (Stephens et al. 2018). HB cuts had an impact on both social and private tenants. Under the 'Pay to Stay' banner—plans were put in place to increase rents for households with a household income over £30,000 (£40,000 in London) to market levels. Like Thatcher, Cameron opened up exit opportunities through a 'reinvigourated' Right to Buy for council tenants and the 2015 Conservative Party manifesto had contained a proposal to allow housing association tenants to buy their houses on the same terms as council tenants paid for by selling the more expensive council housing. However, the homeowner aspirations of housing association tenants were soon frustrated. Rather than give housing association tenants a statutory Right to Buy, the government made an agreement with the National Housing Federation, representing the housing associations, to sell discounted homes to tenants on a voluntary basis. Before the 2017 General Election voluntary sales were phased over a long period starting with pilot projects, part of Theresa May's partial withdrawal from Cameron's policies that also included a retreat on 'Pay to Stay'. Despite May reining in some of Cameron's more extreme polices, she inherited the legacy. Between 2009/2010 and 2015/2016, when wages were stagnant, mean council house rents increased by 37.7%, housing association rents by 38.6% and private landlord rents by 16.6% after HB (MHCLG 2018d).

Noting that the proportion of children in the bottom quintile living in the private rented sector rose from 17% in 2005/2006 to 37% in 2016/2017, the Joseph Rowntree Foundation (2018, p. 25) stated:

> Rising housing costs have been driven largely by changes in the proportions of families living in different housing tenures. In particular, the fall in home-ownership and expansion of the private rented sector have affected low-income families far more than those who are better off.

In 2016/2017 the percent of people (all ages) in relative poverty living in social housing was 27% before housing costs and 47% after housing costs. The gap in percent of children in the sector living in poverty before and housing costs was 20% (McGuiness 2018a).

In 2017, Labour's lead over the Conservatives amongst social tenant voters was 31%, down 1% on 2015 (Akehurst 2017). Under Cameron the Conservative Party applied the 'politics of humiliation' to social tenants (Lukes 1997) and, given such condescension, disrespect plus rent increases directed at social tenants by the Conservative Party, Labour winning only 57% of the total social tenant vote was a lacklustre performance. The swing to Labour amongst social tenants since 2015 was about half the swing amongst private tenants.

Answering criticisms that the reference terms for the Grenfell Fire Inquiry were too narrow, Theresa May said: 'I am determined that the broader questions raised by this fire — including around social housing — are not left unanswered' (quoted in *Evening Standard* 2017). She promised a Green Paper on social housing. Published in August 2018, the Green Paper stated:

> Stigma was the most consistent theme raised by residents at the engagement events. Residents told us that they were made to feel like

'second- class citizens'. They reported being treated as 'an underclass' and 'benefit scroungers', rather than hardworking and honest people. Some residents told us of a 'demonisation' of social housing and their communities in the media. (MHCLG 2018c, p. 47)

It declared 'This Government is determined to tackle such prejudice to ensure that the positive contribution that social housing residents make to their communities, and to society as a whole, is recognised' (p. 48) but failed to apologise for the role played by prominent Conservatives in the stigmatisation process. Moreover, its specific proposals for overcoming stigma such as a 'best neighbourhood competition' had a paternalistic aura and the notion that social housing should be 'a springboard to homeownership' (p. 65) seemed to reinforce the idea that social housing was a second class tenure.

The Green Paper also acknowledged that tenants were unhappy with the responsiveness and performance of their landlords. It stated:

Residents should have a stronger voice to influence decisions and challenge their landlord to improve performance. They must also be able to access good complaints processes, as well as swift and effective redress where appropriate. (p. 27)

To promote greater responsiveness to tenants the Green Paper put forward a number of suggestions, including strengthening the complaints procedures and boosting the information available to tenants via league tables on social housing provider performance.

Social tenants are angry with the Grenfell Tower fire a potent symbol of their abandonment. The trend to affordable rents at up to 80% of the market rent has to be stopped and reductions in social rents, scheduled from 2016 to 2020, need to be extended beyond 2020. HB cuts have to be reversed and more, far more low-cost housing has to be built. Greater respect is also necessary. The term 'social housing' needs to be eradicated from housing discourse. Restoring grants to Tenants Voice; boosting resources for the decent homes programme and recognising that social tenants are not subsidised would also be useful steps in a respect agenda.

Private Tenants

In the 2010 General Election, the Conservative Party obtained 4% more private tenant votes than Labour. By 2017, Labour had a lead of 23% amongst private tenants, made more significant by the surge in households renting privately, that, at 21.3% in England was almost the same household proportion as in 1965 when Labour had passed legislation to control rents at 'fair' levels. Young people living outside the parental home are overwhelmingly private landlord tenants. To some, voter turnout amongst young people was the key to Labour's progress. The *Financial Times* (2017) stated that in 2017, 64% of registered voters those aged 18–24 turned out to vote, a 19% increase on 2015, albeit that this figure has been disputed with the British Election Study (2018) finding no evidence of a voting surge by young people. Perhaps Labour's private renter vote surge can be explained by discontent amongst older private renters. Pointing out that turnout was virtually unchanged from 2015 to 2017 amongst homeowners, but increased eight points amongst all renters, and 10 points amongst those renting in the private sector and that Labour's margins widened by 13 points amongst all renters and by 20 points amongst private renters, Singh (2018) declared 'The youthquake was in fact a rentquake'. London, with its high proportion of renters, seemed to signify the political implications of the growing rental sector across the UK. Nationally, Labour lost by 2.5%, but won the capital by 21%.

'Generation rent' had been ageing and the far more children are living in the private rented sector. The number of households with dependent children living in the private landlord sector in England has accelerated. It reached 1777,000 in 2016/2017, a rise of 864,000 since 2008/2009—up from 6.8 to 26.4% (MHCLG 2018e). In 2002–2003, 15% of children living in the poorest 20% of households lived in private rented accommodation, 7% in the second poorest quintile and 4% in the middle quintile. By 2016/2017 these figures were 36% (poorest), 27% (second poorest) and 16% in the middle quintile (Cribb et al. 2018a).

Before the 2017 General Election, housing was the third most important issue for private renters (Akehurst 2017). Nonetheless, voter turnout by private tenants remained low in 2017, 53% compared to 70% for outright owners and 68% for mortgage holders (Ipsos/Mori 2017), indicating future potential Labour Party gains if it concentrates on raising private tenant electoral participation.

On first glance, the 2017 General Election outcome seems to have reflected a return to the class politics of the 1970s but analysis of the 2017 vote by social class reveals that 'the class divide in British politics seems to have closed and it is no longer a very good indicator of voting intention' (You.Gov 2017). The Conservative lead over Labour was 8% (Social Classes AB) and 7% (Class C2). Labour's lead over the Conservatives was 2% (Class C1) and 3% Classes DE. Labour's poor performance amongst classes D and E was reflected in its loss of heartland seats, won in 2015, such as Mansfield; Walsall North; Stoke on Trent South; Middlesbrough South and Cleveland East. Nonetheless, there were portents of doom for the Conservative Party in the class voting analysis. In the 2016 European Union referendum, class was a major variable in voting behaviour and the European Union issue still cast a shadow over the 2017 General Election. If Brexit recedes as an issue—in 2018 net migration from the EU was 74,000 compared to 200,000 in 2016 (Full Fact 2018)—and Labour campaigns harder in its traditional heartlands on the 'For the many, not the few' mantra then it may attract more voters from classes D and E.

Helping the 'Jams'

The living standards of 'just about managing' families—a term that includes what used to be called 'the working class'—are being reduced by current high housing costs and, on current projections, the housing gap in living standards will accelerate. The Resolution Foundation (2017)—predicting that mean average wage would not recover to its pre-crisis peak until 2025/2027—added:

In the face of this living standards disaster, the Chancellor has not done enough to protect families from further squeezes through the social security system......... On average, we expect the combined impact of policies announced from the Summer Budget 2015 onwards to leave each of the bottom five deciles as net losers.... Accounting for all economic and policy changes from the Summer Budget 2015 onwards, some working families face losses of as much as £4,000.

McGuiness (2018a, p. 18) stated:

The proportion of children in absolute low-income is projected to rise from 27% in 2015/16 to 31% in 2021/22 based on incomes after housing costs, and from 17% to 22% based on incomes before housing costs. In both cases, this would mean the share of children in absolute low-income returns to 2007/08 levels.

The announcements in the 2018 Budget (HM Treasury 2018) will modify the impact of the 2015 cutbacks but, as the Resolution Foundation (2018, p. 3) has stated '75 per cent of the benefit cuts announced in 2015 remain government policy, with half of those directly affecting family budgets still to be rolled out'.

The housing cost squeeze on living standards extends beyond those below the poverty line. According to the English Housing Survey 2015/2016 (DCLG 2017a), before housing costs, 56% of private renters were in the lowest five income deciles, after housing costs it accelerated to 66%. Within this context, rent increases and HB cuts cannot be defended, indeed, they need to be reversed.

Rent control is now urgent. Labour's 2017 manifesto proposed so-called 'smart' rent regulation—three year tenancies with rents restricted to inflation—and Jeremy Corbyn (2017), following the Scottish model, has indicated that selected local authorities might be granted stronger powers. However, nationwide 'classic' control with a rent freeze and fair rents is required to check private landlordism. This change would also contribute to a 'property owning democracy'. When classic rent control was applied, 3.7 million houses were transferred from private landlords to homeowners between 1919 and 1975

(Department of the Environment 1977) often to low-income sitting tenants, making it the best low-cost ownership initiative ever. Indeed, reductions in tax concessions to private landlords and the extra Land Stamp Tax levy on second homes has made an impact on first-time buyers' access to home ownership. According to the pressure group Generation Rent, the private rented sector has shrunk by 111,000 units since April 2016, when the 3% surcharge on stamp duty, came into effect but the number of first-time buyers per year has increased by 21% since Osborne's first announcement on landlord taxation in July 2015 (Collinson 2018). Moreover, with a private rental market in faster decline through classic rent control, social housing providers would be able to buy additional stock at lower cost.

Much more robust regulation of the private rented sector by compulsory registration and licencing across England is also necessary despite the House of Commons Committee on Housing Communities and Local government being opposed to such a policy. Indeed, the Committee was lukewarm on selective licencing by local government stating:

> We recommend that the Government therefore remove the 20% cap above which local authorities must seek permission from the Secretary of State to implement selective licensing schemes because it is contrary to the spirit of localism. However, we believe that the Secretary of State should retain a power to require local authorities to reconsider a decision to implement a licensing scheme that does not meet the strict criteria already set out by the Government, and should monitor the effectiveness of schemes once they have been implemented. (House of Commons Housing, Communities and Local Government Committee 2018, p. 39)

Hardly surprising given that five of the eleven committee members had economic interests in private renting!

Recent governments have concentrated on getting potential first-time buyers onto the homeownership ladder but, for many years, there has been a flow from away from homeownership by frustrated 'second steppers', many needing more space as their children are born (see Chapter 3). Help to Buy Equity Loan applies only to new build limiting its usefulness to 'second steppers'. In England, 22% of new homes built in 2016/2017 were flats (MHCLG 2018a) and, in London, between 2010 and 2015, 88.8% of all the new houses were flats (Rae 2015). Thus, most of the home purchases made under the equity loan scheme since its launch on 1 April 2013 were made by first-time buyers, accounting for 81%—116,898—of total purchases (Spencer 2018b). Land Stamp Duty Tax exemption applies only to first-time home buyers.

Many frustrated 'second steppers' have been forced into renting so reintroducing 'classic' rent control would help those struggling to climb onto and upwards on the homeownership ladder by making it easier to save for a deposit. Exempting small home extensions from VAT would help lower income families to obtain more space but the major problem relates the incomes of households with children, hence an effective way to assist the lowest income families to become and remain homeowners would be to allow them to claim HB on mortgage interest. HB paid to renters pushes low-income households with children into the rented sector. Paying HB on mortgage interest payments to homeowners would be complicated but, in limited circumstances, it is used in the United States via the Homeownership Voucher Programme (*Washington Post* 2016). Such a scheme would divert some of the £8.6 billion per year paid in HB from the pockets of private landlords and, unlike HB to private landlords, would stop when the mortgage was paid—important given predictions that, as 'generation rent' ages, the cost of HB will increase to £197.3 billion by 2065–2066, up from £24.4 billion today—with households in the private rented sector accounting for 63% compared to 37% today (Capita Economics 2016).

Boosting Housing Supply

The fuses that ignited the current housing crisis had been burning for many years and, because the housing stock is built up over time, in the short-term, the current crisis cannot be alleviated by new housebuilding. None the less, it is necessary to establish the groundwork for a long-term solution by taking steps to boost new construction to a higher level albeit that enduring high housebuilding rates will not necessarily reduce consumption costs unless the vested interests in maintaining high house prices and rents are curtailed.

Governments are reluctant to expand housing supply to a level necessary to generate a sustained house price fall. The 2017 Conservative was elected with a manifesto pledge to meet the 2015 Conservative commitment to deliver a million homes by the end of 2020 and to 'deliver half a million more by the end of 2022' (Conservative Party 2017). In 2018, boosting construction to 300,000 per year became Theresa May's ambition but only for the mid-2020s and it is unlikely that a future government would risk a house price collapse if such enhanced numbers seriously affecting house prices. Scarcity induced house price inflation seems inbuilt into the UK economy hence other ways to reduce current consumer housing expenditure require examination.

There are two major constraints on boosting housing supply: volume builder dominance and the land shortage. The new standardised approach to assessing housing requirements contained in *Planning for the right homes in the right places: consultation proposals* (DCLG 2017b) protected green belts by using a formula that curtailed housing requirements in areas with substantial green belts (see above). This approach is similar to the housing policy adopted by the Conservatives in the 1930s and 1950s (see Chapter 2) and produced 'Tower and Slab' (Urban 2011) blocks of flats.

Central government pressure on local government has produced more land release but it has been insufficient to limit residential land price hikes especially in housing hotspots. Although residential land prices in central London are on the decline (Savills 2018) they remain excessive and residential land price hikes are moving northwards. In the East Midlands and around Manchester and Birmingham, there was a surge in residential land prices of 4.7% in 2017 (*Telegraph* 2017). Residential land prices are influenced by scarcity.

The 2018 *National Planning Policy Framework* added further protections to the Green Belt stating:

> Before concluding that exceptional circumstances exist to justify changes to Green Belt boundaries, the strategic policy-making authority should be

able to demonstrate that it has examined fully all other reasonable options for meeting its identified need for development and has been informed by discussions with neighbouring authorities about whether they could accommodate some of the identified need for development, as demonstrated through the statement of common ground. (MHCLG 2018b, p. 41)

Such additional green belt protection was accompanied by emphasising high densities in urban areas. However, taking land out of the green belt would increase land supply and reduce its price, with the green belt land release sufficiency litmus test being a substantial fall in residential land prices. Neimietz (2016, p. 1), from the Institute of Economic Affairs, has suggested:

The concept of the green belt, meanwhile, should be abolished in its entirety. Protecting land from development should be done in a selective manner, on the basis of the environmental and amenity value of a particular plot of land, not in the form of a blanket ban.

As the state stops protecting land prices, landowners will be more willing to sell and developers more disposed to build out their existing sites. However, long-term landownership advantages are so great—Mark Twain advised 'Buy land: they're not making it anymore'—that the owner of potential development land may 'hold out indefinitely for an aspirational price' (Bentley 2017, p. 7) so other measures will be necessary to promote land release. Allowing local government to buy land at existing use or 'fair' value, by amending the 1961 Land Compensation Act to remove speculative 'hope' value based on prospective future planning permissions, is gaining momentum as a response to the unearned income generated by land ownership (IPPRCSJ 2018b).

Volume builder dominance in new house construction requires bringing other suppliers into the market. Housing construction promoters, be it developers, local government, housing associations or direct central government commissioning, rely mainly on the volume builders to deliver the new homes. Far greater local government involvement in housing supply provides a potential route to reducing volume builder dominance. Labour's 2018 Green Paper *Housing the Many* (Labour Party 2018) set out plans to produce one million 'genuinely affordable' houses—somewhat vaguely defined as 'a house or flat with some public backing at a price that means those who live in it have enough money left after housing costs for the other things they need' (Labour Party 2018, p. 5)—over 10 years. The programme would partially be financed by HB savings arising from Labour's plans to stop the leakage of existing homes let at social rents into the affordable category and there would be enhanced local authority involvement in delivering the new 'genuinely affordable' homes. Unfortunately, the extent of local government involvement was unspecified and there was no mention of Direct Labour Organisations as new home suppliers.

In 2014, the coalition government put forward a new delivery model with direct central commissioning with the Homes and Communities Agency (now Homes England) taking the lead role. In 2016, the approach was targeted on using smaller companies but very little direct commissioning has taken place. Greater involvement by local housing companies, likely to favour small local firms and use prefabrication on larger sites, would be helpful but a more radical answer would be to enable local government to accumulate land banks at existing use prices for distribution to local builders and for new build by direct labour organisations, that with potential to provide apprenticeships, is an important element in boosting housing supply.

The Resource Constraint

Many schemes aimed at alleviating the housing crisis do not indicate how they will be financed. For example, the detailed proposals put forward by Crisis (2018) to end homelessness were priced at £9.9 billion over the first ten years but there were no suggestions on how to raise the resources to meet this cost, albeit that it was claimed that long-term savings would be generated.

Since the credit crunch and subsequent recession, housing policy has been bedevilled by resource restrictions. The coalition government's *Our Programme for Government* (2010, p. 1) declared:

We will significantly accelerate the reduction of the structural deficit …
with the main burden of deficit reduction borne by reduced spending
rather than increased taxes.

It adhered to this declaration, as did Cameron's 2015 government.
An analysis of UK debt reduction concluded 'The subsequent reduction in the deficit has come from increases in tax and a more significant reduction in spending' (Emmerson 2017, p. 5). Information on
the combined impact of taxation increases and public spending cuts on
households is sparse. Cuts in public expenditure often involve higher
private expenditure (Obolenskaya and Burchardt 2016) that can have
a variable impact according to income. The P90/10 ratio after housing
costs has been accelerating since 2010 (McGuiness 2018b).

Between 2010/2011 and 2015/2016, the DCLG's budget was cut by
51%, by far the largest reduction of any government department. The
budget section allocated to community-based regeneration was cut by
half and direct grants to local government fell by 27% in real terms
between 2011 and 2015 (BBC News 2015). State assistance to housing associations was substantially curtailed and the Treasury has used
fiscal measures—often 'off the books' in public spending calculations—
to boost homeownership. Cutting public expenditure, accompanied by
limited tax increases, reduced the current net public sector borrowing
requirement from 9.9% of GDP in 2009/2010 to 2.1% in 2017/2018
(Keep 2018). The post-2010 austerity agenda has been justified on the
argument that 'We will not saddle our children with ever-increasing
debts' (Hammond 2017, quoted in the *Independent* 2017), yet, in
2017/2018, government spending on debt repayment was 2.7% of
GDP compared to 3.1% in 1997/1998 (Keep 2018). Moreover, not
saddling our children with ever-increasing debt has to be balanced
against burdening our children with mounting costs for low-quality,
high price housing.

Although in his 2018 Budget (HM Treasury 2018) Philip Hammond
used an unexpected boost in tax revenues to finance a significant
increase in NHS expenditure there is considerable pressure to increase
state spending on education, social care and housing. Labour's proposals, made in the 2017 general election campaign, to increase income

tax on those earning more than £80,000 per year and not implement planned corporation tax cuts—would raise substantial resources. The party also added land value tax as a funding source and, in the long-term, this tax has the potential to finance solutions to the housing crises.

Land Value Tax

In 2017, net housing wealth—with perhaps 50% stored in land value—was £4.6 trillion for owner-occupiers and £1.2 trillion for private landlords (Savills 2017) with additional amounts of wealth stored in undeveloped land. Labour's 2017 manifesto stated 'We will initiate a review into reforming council tax and business rates and consider new options such as a land value tax, to ensure local government has sustainable funding for the long term' (Labour Party 2017, p. 86). Whereas Labour seems to have viewed a land value tax as a substitute for business rates and the council tax, it has the potential to raise substantial revenue to boost housing supply and mitigate proposed in-work benefit cuts. It has even been endorsed by Tony Blair (Guardian 2017b).

The arguments in favour of a land value tax were set out in by Henry George in *Poverty and Progress* (1979 [1879]). George's idea involved assessing the current value of all the land in the nation and then taxing enhanced values thereby 'taking by the community, for the use of the community, of the value that is the creation of the community' (George 1979 [1879], p. 139). George's main target was the enhanced value of undeveloped land, a target adopted by Lloyd George (1909) and Winston Churchill (1909) in their attacks on the 'landed interest'.

In 2015, the average price of agricultural land in England was £21,000 per hectare but land with planning permission for housing cost £6 million per hectare. In some areas the enhanced value is much higher; in Camden, for example, £33.3 million per hectare (DCLG 2015). A small proportion of this value is taken by the state through the planning system but even the limited effectiveness of section 106 in delivering affordable housing was undermined by 2012 changes to the National Planning Policy Framework. Between 2007/2008 and 2011/2012, section 106 delivered an average of 27,000 affordable homes per year, but from 2012/2013 to 2015/2016, this dropped to an average of 17,000 homes (Crisis 2018).

The MHCLG (2018f) estimated that, in 2016/2017, developer contributions were £6 billion with the highest contributions made through the affordable housing programme (£4 billion) and the Community Infrastructure Levy (£945 million). However, the MHCLG (2018f, p. 13) said:

> The total amount of developer contributions committed has increased since 2011/12, although the number of houses built has also increased. The value of section 106 planning obligations and CIL per dwelling built has remained broadly the same over this time period… By contrast, house prices in England have increased by 30%. This suggests that the current system of developer contributions can quickly become dated and may only have captured a small proportion of the increase in value that has occurred since 2011.

This statement added to the credibility of the accusation that developers were successfully using the technicalities of viability assessments regulations introduced in 2013—allowing developers to renegotiate lower affordable housing obligations to protect profitability—to reduce the proportion of affordable houses provided (Shelter 2017).

Viability calculations appear to be based on a 20% profit for the developer allowing developers to offset high land costs against the provision of affordable homes (Crosby 2018).

Supporting housing delivery through developer contributions: reforming developer contributions to affordable housing and infrastructure (MHCLG 2018f) announced proposals to enhance the effectiveness of the Community Infrastructure Levy and the affordable housing contribution from developers but the complexity and delays involved in obtaining 'betterment' value from planning permissions indicate that simpler approaches are necessary. Cheshire (2016) has suggested that section 106 and the CIL should be replaced by a single, national development charge of 20% on the sale value of land. This could apply to land not acquired by local government under the Institute for Public Policy Research Commission on Social Justice's proposal.

There remains the issue of the value stored in developed land. Information on land values is scarce but the ONS publishes data on the total estimated value of the UK's housing—£5.5 trillion in 2015—and the value of the dwelling structures. This was only £1.8 trillion indicating the remaining £3.7 trillion is accounted for by the land within the residential plot boundaries (Gleeson 2017). Since the middle 1950s, land value has increased at a faster rate than the dwelling structure with the gap doubling between 1996 and 2013 (Gleeson 2017).

A land value tax involves complicated implementation issues, in particular its relationship to other taxes such as the council tax, business rates and Stamp Duty Land Tax, developer contributions from enhanced land values and the technicalities involved in land valuation, especially if the value of the buildings on the land is to be discounted. None the less, as a tax that is difficult to avoid, acts as an incentive to sell, and taps the large unearned wealth accumulation derived from land value hikes, it has considerable potential as a future revenue raiser.

The Conservative Party has always hated the land tax idea. Lloyd George's promise to introduce a land tax, made in his 1909 'People's Budget', was in the process of implementation in 1919 but was abandoned as the price paid for the continuation of the Lloyd George Liberal/Conservative Coalition. According to Masterman (quoted in Morgan 1971, pp. 208–209), they buried the land tax and 'stamped down the ground over the grave.... And finally – so that there should be no doubt at all to their triumph – they ... returned two millions of the money'. Labour's attempts to tax the 'betterment' arising from land value increases via the 1947 Town and Country Planning Act, the 1967 Land Commission Act 1967 and the 1975 Community Land Act were quickly repealed by subsequent Conservative governments and the Conservative press labelled Labour's 2017 land value tax proposal as a 'garden tax' with homeowners forced to sell their gardens to pay the tax (Full Fact 2017a).

Ellis and Henderson (2016, p. 78) claim that 'we have a proven way of paying for change by the fair taxation of land values'. The all party support, probably necessary for a sustainable land tax, looks remote but the problems involved in funding social care may open the door to a land value tax as an integral element in funding social care with, perhaps, land value tax extended later to fund other social objectives.

Inheritance Tax

The Intergeneration Commission/Resolution Foundation (2018) has suggested that Inheritance Tax, with its many loopholes, should be replaced by a lifetime receipts tax with lower rates and fewer exemptions, levied on recipients, with a tax-free allowance of £125,000 to encourage broadly shared inheritances and stated that the new tax would raise sufficient additional resources to finance its proposed £10,000 'citizen's inheritance' paid to all 25-year-olds (see above). Similar proposals have been put forward by Institute for Public Policy Research Commission on Social Justice (2018). However, it is doubtful if the lifetime receipts tax would be politically less toxic or easier to collect than Inheritance Tax and gradual reduction in the Inheritance Tax threshold might be an alternative revenue source as more estates become liable to pay the tax.

Mansion Tax

The 2010 Liberal Democrat manifesto included a mansion tax with a 2 million threshold capturing both land and building value. It did not form part of the coalition government agreement but the Labour Party included a mansion tax in its 2015 manifesto with progressive rates starting at £2 million and households with modest incomes able to pay the tax on property sale. Labour's mansion tax could have raised £1.2 billion per year but its appeal to Labour and the Liberal Democrats seems to have receded. Han alternative to a mansion tax would be extra council tax bands above the H band (covering properties valued at more than 320,000 in 1991).

The Consequences of Failure

For thirty years, electoral arithmetic—with the median voter in marginal constituencies being the primary political focus—has suppressed housing as a political issue. The neglect of the fundamentals underlying the housing crises have meant that they have spread and are no longer containable via marginal constituency politics (*Financial Times* 2016). In 2018, housing was climbing the league table of public concerns becoming, at 22%, the joint-third biggest issue causing public concern, its highest score since 1974 (Ipsos/Mori 2018). There is angst in Conservative circles. Writing in the *Telegraph*, Allister Heath (2017) declared:

> Wake up Nimbys, the option is either Tory house-building or Marxist social engineering ... The pressure has become too great, the outrage of the property-less too uncontainable, the need for change too overwhelmingly obvious. Denial or self-interested excuses dressed up as concern for the common good simply won't cut it anymore: we will soon start to build a lot more, and rightly so.

Niemietz (2017) claimed 'the housing crisis has created a generation of socialists' and the *Spectator* (2018) declared:

> the housing policies advanced by Jeremy Corbyn at last year's general election are far more appealing….It is little use the Conservatives protesting that these policies will not work, that rent controls will lessen the availability of rented property and make it even harder to find a home. Those stuck renting are likely to conclude that the current system is at fault and any change which disfavours landlords will be an improvement. Capitalism will never appeal to those without any capital. (*Spectator*, 21 April 2018)

New housing supply is increasing but production remains a long way from the number required to make a significant impact on purchase and rental prices. Meanwhile, housing costs relative to incomes are excessive, especially for lower income households with children.

Overall, the 2016 European Union and the 2017 General Election revealed a seething discontent on living standards with housing a significant factor in this unrest. Outright owners were at ease whereas mortgage holders were restless and renters—social and private—enraged. Their eyes were being opened to their predicament, their mindset was no longer 'que sera, sera' but 'do more or else'. In 1884 'Radical' Joe Chamberlain—allegedly Theresa May's lodestar (*Spectator* 2016)—warned the political establishment of a 'mass attack on landlords' with 'the cry of distress as yet inarticulate but will not always remain so' (quoted in Stedman Jones 1992, p. 224). A 'mass attack on landlords' is remote but the *'gilets jaunes' protest in France succeeded in obtaining a* £90 a month increase in the minimum wage and an exemption of overtime from tax and social charges. In the UK, the ballot box provides future opportunities for protest. Writing in the *Telegraph* William Rees-Mogg (2018) declared 'We must build more houses — or both the nation and the Tories will suffer the consequences'.

The market is now the governing norm in determining housing outcomes with governments, when the market has been diagnosed as 'broken', using state resources to promote 'affordability' in ways that underpin profitability for the vested interests operating the system. The 'rentiers' get the 'cigars and croissants'. Unless the radical action necessary to reduce costs—greatly enhanced social housing supply at social rents; classic rent control; a regional policy with teeth, far more land release to depress prices and enhanced state support for low-income owner-occupiers and renters, financed by more progressive forms of taxation—then the party deemed responsible for the inertia will be punished in the ballot box.

References

Akehurst, S. (2017). *Housing and the 2017 Election: What the Numbers Say*. http://blog.shelter.org.uk/2017/06/housing-and-the-2017-election-what-the-numbers-say/.

Audickas, L., & Cracknell, R. (2018). *Social Background of MPs 1979–2017* (Briefing Paper No. CBP 7483). London: House of Commons. file:///C:/Users/User/Downloads/CBP-7483%20(2).pdf.

Battiston, D., Dickens, R., Manning, L., & Wadsworth, J. (2014). *Immigration and Access to Social Housing in the UK* (CEP Discussion Paper No. 1264). London: Centre for Economic Performance. http://cep.lse.ac.uk/pubs/download/dp1264.pdf.

BBC News. (2015). *Spending Review: Department-By-Department Cuts Guide.* http://www.bbc.co.uk/news/uk-politics-34790102.

Belfield, C., Chandler, D., & Joyce, R. (2015). *Housing: Trends in Prices, Costs and Tenure* (IFS Briefing Note BN161). London: Institute for Fiscal Studies. https://www.ifs.org.uk/publications/7593.

Bentley, D. (2017). *The Land Question: Fixing the Dysfunction at the Root of the Housing Crisis.* London: Civitas. http://www.civitas.org.uk/content/files/thelandquestion.pdf.

British Election Study. (2018, January 29). *The Myth of the 2017 Youthquake Election.* http://www.britishelectionstudy.com/bes-impact/the-myth-of-the-2017-youthquake-election/#.Wnq93J3FJdh.

Capita Economics. (2016). *Building New Social Rent Homes.* London: National Association of ALMOs. www.almos.org.uk/include/getDoc.php?did=7103&fid=8219.

Cheshire, P. (2016). *Evidence to House of Lords Select Committee on Economic Affairs, 1st Report of Session 2016–17, Building More Homes* (HL Paper 20, Para. 140–146). https://publications.parliament.uk/pa/ld201617/ldselect/ldeconaf/20/20.pdf.

Churchill, W. (1909, July 17). *The Mother of All Monopolies.* Speech Delivered at King's Theatre in Edinburgh. https://www.cooperative-individualism.org/churchill-winston_mother-of-all-monopolies-1909.htm.

Clegg, N. (2016, September 3). Tories Refused to Build Social Housing Because It Would Create Labour Voters, Nick Clegg Says. *Independent.* http://www.independent.co.uk/news/uk/politics/tories-refused-to-build-social-housing-because-it-would-create-labour-voters-nick-clegg-says-a7223796.html.

Collinson, P. (2018, October 16). Generation Rent Says Number of First-Time Buyers Has Risen Despite Landlords' Warnings. *Guardian.* https://www.theguardian.com/money/2018/oct/16/taxes-buy-to-let-landlords-rents-generation-rent-buyers.

Conservative Party. (2017). *Forward Together: Our Plan for a Stronger Britain and a Prosperous Future.* London: Conservative Party. https://www.conservatives.com/manifesto.

Corbyn, J. (2017). Speech to the Labour Party Conference September 2017 in Full. *New Statesman.* https://www.newstatesman.com/politics/staggers/2017/09/jeremy-corbyns-2017-conference-speech-full.

Council of Mortgage Lenders. (2016). *Arrears and Possessions Continue to Fall, Reports CML.* London: Council of Mortgage Lenders. https://www.cml.org.uk/news/press-releases/arrears-and-possessions-continuing-to-fall-reports-cml/.

Cribb, J., Keiller, A. N., & Waters, T. (2018). *Living Standards, Poverty and Inequality in the UK: 2018.* London: Institute for Fiscal Studies.

Crisis. (2018). *Everybody In: How to End Homelessness in Britain.* London: Crisis. https://www.crisis.org.uk/media/238959/everybody_in_how_to_end_homelessness_in_great_britain_2018.pdf.

Crosby, N. (2018). *Development Viability Assessment and the Provision of Affordable Housing: A Game of 'Pass the Parcel'?* Reading: Henley Business School. https://assets.henley.ac.uk/defaultUploads/PDFs/research/papers-publications/REP-2018-01-Crosby.pdf?mtime=20180306141219.

DCLG. (2015). *Land Value Estimates for Policy Appraisal.* London: DCLG. https://assets.publishing.service.gov.uk/government/uploads/system/uploads/attachment_data/file/407155/February_2015_Land_value_publication_FINAL.pdf.

DCLG. (2017a). *English Housing Survey 2015/16 Headline Report, Table FA1201 (S106): Age of Household Reference Person by Tenure, 2015–16.* London: DCLG. https://www.gov.uk/government/statistics/english-housing-survey-2015-to-2016-headline-report.

DCLG. (2017b). *Land Use Change Statistics in England: 2015–16.* London: DCLG. https://assets.publishing.service.gov.uk/government/uploads/system/uploads/attachment_data/file/595749/Land_use_change_statistics_England_2015-16_-_2_March_2017_version.pdf.

Department of the Environment. (1977). *Housing Policy Review: Technical Volume Part 111.* London: Department of the Environment.

Economist Intelligence Unit. (2017). *Democracy Index 2016: Revenge of the "Deplorables".* http://felipesahagun.es/wp-content/uploads/2017/01/Democracy-Index-2016.pdf.

Ellis, H., & Henderson, K. (2016). *English Planning in Crisis: 10 Steps to a Sustainable Future.* Bristol: Policy Press.

Emmerson, C. (2017). *Two Parliaments of Pain: The UK Public Finances 2010 to 2017* (IFS Briefing Note BN199). London: Institute for Fiscal Studies. https://www.ifs.org.uk/publications/9180.

Evening Standard. (2017, August 15). Theresa May Reveals Scope of Grenfell Tower Public Inquiry. https://www.standard.co.uk/news/politics/theresa-may-reveals-scope-of-grenfell-tower-public-inquiry-a3611916.html.

Financial Times. (2016, January 19). The Vanishing Power of the Median Voter. https://www.ft.com/content/7ab73ad8-21ec-39f3-ab8d-a559a110d210.

Financial Times. (2017, June 20). Youth Turnout at General Election Highest in 25 Years, Data Show. https://www.ft.com/content/6734cdde-550b-11e7-9fed-c19e2700005f.

Full Fact. (2017, May 31). *Labour's Land Value Tax: Will You Have to Sell Your Garden?* https://fullfact.org/economy/labours-land-value-tax-will-you-have-sell-your-garden/?gclid=EAIaIQobChMI6N2z99mL2AIVTJ4bCh1tTgvX-EAAYASAAEgJC3vD_BwE.

Full Fact. (2018, December). *EU immigration to the UK.* https://fullfact.org/immigration/eu-migration-and-uk/.

George, H. (1979 [1879]). *Progress and Poverty.* London: Hogarth Press.

Gleeson, J. (2017). *Historical Housing and Land Values in the UK.* https://jamesjgleeson.wordpress.com/2017/04/03/historical-housing-and-land-values-in-the-uk/.

Godson, D. (2017). *No Longer Overlooked But Still Decisive: Has Theresa May Conquered Class Politics for the Tories?* London: Policy Exchange. https://policyexchange.org.uk/no-longer-overlooked-but-still-decisive-has-theresa-may-conquered-class-politics-for-the-tories/.

Goodhart, D. (2017). *The Road to Somewhere: The Populist Revolt and the Future of Politics.* London: C. Hurst & Co.

Guardian. (2017a, November 29). London Suburbs Set for Housing Boom as Sadiq Khan Relaxes Rules. https://www.theguardian.com/uk-news/2017/nov/29/london-suburbs-set-for-housing-boom-sadiq-khan.

Guardian. (2017b, December 2). Tony Blair Backs Labour's Land Value Tax to Tackle Housing Crisis. https://www.theguardian.com/politics/2017/dec/03/tony-blair-backs-labour-land-tax-solve-uk-housing-crisis.

Halikiopoulou, D. (2018, February 5). Three Dangerous Generalisations You Could Be Making About Populism. *Political Quarterly Blog.* https://politicalquarterly.blog/2018/02/05/three-dangerous-generalisations-you-could-be-making-about-populism/.

Heath, A. (2017, July 5). Wake Up Nimbys, the Option Is Either Tory House-Building or Marxist Social Engineering. *Telegraph.* http://www.telegraph.co.uk/news/2017/07/05/wake-nimbys-option-either-tory-housebuilding-marxist-social/.

HM Government. (2010). *The Coalition: Our Programme for Government*. https://www.gov.uk/government/uploads/system/uploads/attachment_data/file/78977/coalition_programme_for_government.pdf.

HM Treasury. (2016). *Autumn Statement 2016*. London: HM Treasury. https://www.gov.uk/government/topical-events/autumn-statement-2016.

HM Treasury. (2018). *Budget 2018*. London: HM Treasury. https://assets. publishing.service.gov.uk/government/uploads/system/uploads/attachment_data/file/752202/Budget_2018_red_web.pdf.

House of Commons Housing, Communities and Local Government Committee. (2018). *Private Rented Sector: Fourth Report of Session 2017–19 Report, Together with Formal Minutes*. London: House of Commons. https://publications.parliament.uk/pa/cm201719/cmselect/cmcomloc/440/440.pdf.

Independent. (2015, June 24). Extend Right to Buy to Tenants of Private Landlords, Labour's Jeremy Corbyn Says. http://www.independent.co.uk/news/uk/politics/extend-right-to-buy-to-the-tenants-of-private-landlords-labours-jeremy-corbyn-says-10342824.html.

Independent. (2017, June 22). Adults Returning to "Bank of Mum and Dad" to Help Them Ascend Second Step on Property Ladder. http://www.independent.co.uk/money/spend-save/property-ladder-bank-mum-dad-homes-houses-second-steppers-lloyds-bank-research-a7800636.html.

Institute for Public Policy Research Commission on Social Justice. (2018b). *Prosperity and Justice; A Plan for the New Economy: The Final Report of the IPPR Commission on Economic Justice*. London: Institute for Public Policy Research. https://www.ippr.org/files/2018-08/1535639099_prosperity-and-justice-ippr-2018.pdf.

Intergeneration Commission/Resolution Foundation. (2018). *A New Generational Contract: Final Report of the Intergeneration Commission*. London: Resolution Foundation. https://www.resolutionfoundation.org/advanced/a-new-generational-contract/.

Ipsos/Mori. (2016). *How Britain Voted in the 2016 EU Referendum*. https://www.ipsos.com/ipsos-mori/en-uk/how-britain-voted-2016-eu-referendum?language_content_entity=en-uk.

Ipsos/Mori. (2017). *How Britain Voted in the 2017 General Election*. https://www.ipsos.com/ipsos-mori/en-uk/how-britain-voted-2017-election.

Ipsos/Mori. (2014). *Public are Positive Towards Contribution and Value of Social Housing*. London: Ipsos Mori. https://www.ipsos.com/ipsos-mori/en-uk/public-are-positive-towards-contribution-and-value-social-housing.

Ipsos/Mori. (2018). *Brexit and the NHS Top Britons' Concerns, with Worry About Housing Rising.* https://www.ipsos.com/ipsos-mori/en-uk/brexit-and-nhs-top-britons-concerns-worry-about-housing-rising.

Joseph Rowntree Foundation. (2018). *UK Poverty 2018: A Comprehensive Analysis of Poverty Trends and Figures.* York: Joseph Rowntree Foundation. https://www.jrf.org.uk/report/uk-poverty-2018.

Keep, M. (2018). *Government Borrowing, Debt and Debt Interest: Historical Statistics and Forecasts* (Briefing Paper No. 05745). London: House of Commons. https://researchbriefings.parliament.uk/ResearchBriefing/Summary/SN05745.

Labour Party. (2017a). *Labour's New Deal on Housing.* London: Labour Party. https://labour.org.uk/wp-content/uploads/2017/10/Housing-Mini-Manifesto.pdf.

Labour Party. (2017b). *For the Many Not the Few: The Labour Party Manifesto.* London: Labour Party. http://www.labour.org.uk/page/-/Images/manifesto-2017/Labour%20Manifesto%202017.pdf.

Labour Party. (2018). *Housing For the Many: Labour Party Green Paper.* London: The Labour Party. https://labour.org.uk/issues/housing-for-the-many/.

Lloyd George, D. (1909, July 30). *Speech at Edinburgh Castle.* London: Limehouse. https://archive.org/stream/lifeofdavidlloyd04dupauoft/lifeofdavidlloyd04dupauoft_djvu.txt.

Lukes, S. (1997). Humiliation and the Politics of Identity. *Social Research, 64*(1), 36–51.

Lund, B. (2016). *Housing Politics in the United Kingdom: Power Planning and Protest.* Bristol: Policy Press.

Madden, D., & Marcuse, P. (2016, November 22). Whose Crisis? For the Oppressed, Housing Is Always in Crisis. *Verso.* https://www.versobooks.com/blogs/2962-whose-crisis-for-the-oppressed-housing-is-always-in-crisis.

May, T. (2016a). *Statement from the New Prime Minister Theresa May.* London: Prime Minister's Office. https://www.gov.uk/government/speeches/statement-from-the-new-prime-minister-theresa-may.

May, T. (2016b). *Conservative Conference: Theresa May's Speech in Full.* www.bbc.co.uk/news/uk-politics-37563510.

McGuiness, F. (2018a). *Poverty in the UK: Statistics* (Briefing Paper No. 7096). London: House of Commons. https://researchbriefings.parliament.uk/ResearchBriefing/Summary/SN07096.

McGuiness, F. (2018b). *Income Inequality in the UK* (Briefing Paper No. 7484). London: House of Commons. https://researchbriefings.parliament. uk/ResearchBriefing/Summary/CBP-7484#fullreport.

MHCLG. (2018a). *Components of Housing Supply: Net Additional Dwellings: England 2006–7 to 2016–7.* London: MHCLG. https://www.gov.uk/ government/statistical-data-sets/live-tables-on-net-supply-of-housing.

MHCLG. (2018b). *National Planning Policy Framework.* London: MHCLG. https://assets.publishing.service.gov.uk/government/uploads/system/ uploads/attachment_data/file/728643/Revised_NPPF_2018.pdf.

MHCLG. (2018c). *A New Deal for Social Housing* (Cm 9571). London: MHCLG. https://assets.publishing.service.gov.uk/government/uploads/sys-tem/uploads/attachment_data/file/733635/A_new_deal_for_social_hous-ing_print_ready_version.pdf.

MHCLG. (2018d). *Live Tables on Rents, Lettings and Tenancies.* London: MHCLG. https://www.gov.uk/government/statistical-data-sets/live-tables-on-rents-lettings-and-tenancies.

MHCLG. (2018e). *Social and Private Renters: Demographic and Economic Data on Social and Private Renters.* London: MHCLG. https://www.gov.uk/ government/statistical-data-sets/social-and-private-renters.

MHCLG. (2018f). *Supporting Housing Delivery Through Developer Contributions: Reforming Developer Contributions to Affordable Housing and Infrastructure.* London: MHCLG. https://assets.publishing.service.gov. uk/government/uploads/system/uploads/attachment_data/file/691182/ Developer_Contributions_Consultation.pdf.

Migration Advisory Committee. (2018). *EEA Migration in the UK: Final Report.* London: Migration Advisory Committee. https://assets.publish-ing.service.gov.uk/government/uploads/system/uploads/attachment_data/ file/740991/Final_EEA_report_to_go_to_WEB.PDF.

Morgan, K. G. (1971). *The Age of Lloyd George: The Liberal Party and British Politics.* London: Allen & Unwin.

National Landlords Association. (2017). *General Election 2017, Landlords Are Voting.* https://docs.google.com/forms/d/e/1FAIpQLSd-fZq28hNjCrNhjBi0-dmw5M8hattvG0mxCztBSyAIVkzVoRg/ viewanalytics.

Neimietz, K. (2016). *To Solve the Housing Crisis, We Must Take on NIMBYs and Abolish the Greenbelt.* London: Institute for Economic Affairs. https:// iea.org.uk/blog/to-solve-the-housing-crisis-we-must-take-on-nimbys-and-abolish-the-greenbelt.

Niemietz, K. (2017). *How the Housing Crisis has Created a Generation of Socialists*. London: Institute for Economic Affairs. https://iea.org.uk/how-the-housing-crisis-has-created-a-generation-of-socialists/.

Obolenskaya, P., & Burchardt, T. (2016). *Public and Private Welfare Activity in England*. London: London School of Economics, Centre for Analysis of Social Exclusion. http://sticerd.lse.ac.uk/dps/case/cp/casepaper193.pdf.

Park, A., Bryson, C., & Curtice, J. (2015). *British Social Attitudes, 2014*. London: National Centre for Social Research. http://www.bsa.natcen.ac.uk/media/38893/bsa31_full_report.pdf.

Rae, A. (2015, July 9). *Too Many Flats, Not Enough Houses? The Geography of London's New Housing*. London: Royal Statistical Society. https://www.statslife.org.uk/economics-and-business/2360-too-many-flats-not-enough-houses-the-geography-of-london-s-new-housing.

Rees-Mogg, W. (2018, July 23). We Must Build More Houses—Or Both the Nation and the Tories Will Suffer the Consequences. *Telegraph*. https://www.telegraph.co.uk/news/2018/07/23/must-build-houses-nation-tories-will-suffer-consequences/.

Resolution Foundation. (2016). *The Importance of Place: Explaining the Characteristics Underpinning the Brexit Vote Across Different Parts of the UK*. London: Resolution Foundation. https://www.resolutionfoundation.org/app/uploads/2016/07/Brexit-vote-v4.pdf.

Resolution Foundation. (2017). *Freshly Squeezed: Autumn Budget 2017 Response*. London: Resolution Foundation. http://www.resolutionfoundation.org/publications/freshly-squeezed-autumn-budget-2017-response/.

Resolution Foundation. (2018). *How to Spend It, Autumn 2018 Budget Response*. London: Resolution Foundation. https://www.resolutionfoundation.org/publications/how-to-spend-it-autumn-2018-budget-response/.

Savills. (2017, January 18). *UK Homes Worth a Record £6.8 Trillion as Private Housing Wealth Exceeds £5 Trillion*. http://www.savills.co.uk/_news/article/72418/213407-0/1/2017/uk-homes-worth-a-record-%C2%A36.8-trillion-as-private-housing-wealth-exceeds-%C2%A35-trillion.

Savills. (2018). *Market in Minutes: UK Residential Development Land*. https://www.savills.co.uk/research_articles/229130/240942-0/market-in-minutes–uk-residential-development-land—april-2018.

Shelter. (2017). *Slipping Through the Loophole: How Viability Assessments Are Reducing Affordable Housing Supply in England*. London: Shelter. https://england.shelter.org.uk/__data/assets/pdf_file/0010/1434439/2017.11.01_Slipping_through_the_loophole.pdf.

Singh, M. (2018, March 5). The U.K. "Youthquake" Was All About the Rent. *Bloomberg Opinion*. https://www.bloomberg.com/view/articles/2018-03-05/housing-crisis-renters-are-driving-british-voters-to-labour.

Spectator. (2016, July 16). Joseph Chamberlain, Theresa May's New Lodestar. https://www.spectator.co.uk/2016/07/the-man-theresa-may-wants-to-be/.

Spectator. (2018, April 21). A Home Truth for the Tories: Fix the Housing Crisis or Lose Power for Ever. https://www.spectator.co.uk/2018/04/a-home-truth-for-the-tories-fix-the-housing-crisis-or-lose-power-for-ever/.

Spencer, J. (2018b, January 11). Help to Buy Prices Hit Record High. *Inside Housing*. https://www.insidehousing.co.uk/news/news/help-to-buy-prices-hit-record-high-53914.

Standing, G. (2014). *The Precariat: The New Dangerous Class*. London: Bloomsbury Academic.

Stedman Jones, G. (1992). *Outcast London: A Study in the Relationship Between Classes in Victorian Society*. London: Penguin Books.

Stephens, M., Perry, J., Wilcox, S., Williams, P., & Young, G. (2018). *UK Housing Review 2018*. London: Chartered Institute of Housing.

Swales, K. (2016). *Understanding the Leave Vote*. London: National Centre for Social Research. http://natcen.ac.uk/our-research/research/understanding-the-leave-vote/.

Telegraph. (2017, October 18). Land Value Rising Faster Than House Prices as Developers Look North. http://www.telegraph.co.uk/business/2017/10/18/land-value-rising-faster-house-prices-developers-look-north/.

Tigar, D. (2016, April 30). *UK Housing Crisis: Poll Reveals City v Country Split on Who to Blame*. https://www.theguardian.com/cities/2016/apr/30/housing-crisis-poll-city-country-split-blame.

Urban, F. (2011). *Tower and Slab: Histories of Global Mass Housing*. Abingdon: Routledge.

Walker, R., & Jeraj, S. (Eds.). (2016). *The Rent Trap: How We Fell into It and How We Get Out of It*. London: Pluto Press.

Washington Post. (2016, March 10). Housing Vouchers Can Help Families Buy Homes, Not Just Rent. https://www.washingtonpost.com/realestate/housing-vouchers-can-help-families-buy-homes-not-just-rent/2016/03/09/f1648acc-d103-11e5-b2bc-988409ee911b_story.html?utm_term=.6e97bc93a6c7.

You.gov. (2017). *How Britain Voted at the 2017 General Election*. London: You.gov. https://yougov.co.uk/news/2017/06/13/how-britain-voted-2017-general-election/.

References

Aalbers, M. B. (2016). *The Financialization of Housing: A Political Economy Approach.* Abingdon: Routledge.

Abbott, D. (2017, June 26). Hundreds Died in the Grenfell Tower Fire, Says Shadow Home Secretary, Diane Abbott: The MP for Hackney North and Stoke Newington Also Blames the Disaster on Tory Attitudes Towards Social Housing. *Independent.* http://www.independent.co.uk/news/uk/politics/grenfell-tower-fire-diane-abbott-victims-number-hundreds-labour-shadow-home-secretary-a7806106.html.

Adam Smith Institute. (2018). *A Capitalist Revolution in House Building Is Necessary.* London: Adam Smith Institute. https://www.adamsmith.org/news/time-for-a-capitalist-revolution-in-housebuilding.

Age UK. (2014). *Age UK: Evidence Review: Poverty in Later Life.* London: Age UK. http://www.futureyears.org.uk/uploads/files/Age%20UK%20on%20poverty%20in%20old%20age.pdf.

Age UK. (2018). *Poverty in Later Life.* London: Age UK. https://www.ageuk.org.uk/globalassets/age-uk/documents/reports-and-publications/reports-and-briefings/money-matters/rb_apr18_poverty_in_later_life.

Ahmed, K. (2018, June 20). *Hammond: Taxes Will Rise to Pay for NHS Boost.* BBC News. https://www.bbc.co.uk/news/business-44555400.

Aizenman, J., Jinjarak, Y., & Zheng, H. (2016). *House Valuations and Economic Growth: Some International Evidence.* Vox Portal. https://voxeu.org/article/housing-cycles-real-estate-valuations-and-economic-growth.

Akehurst, S. (2017). *Housing and the 2017 Election: What the Numbers Say.* http://blog.shelter.org.uk/2017/06/housing-and-the-2017-election-what-the-numbers-say/.

Alderman, D. (2010). *United States Housing.* Washington, DC: Department of Agriculture. https://www.fs.fed.us/nrs/pubs/rn/rn_nrs195.pdf.

Allen, C. (2008). *Housing Market Renewal and Social Class.* London: Routledge.

Apostolava, V., Uberoi, E., & Johnston, N. (2017, April 26). *Political Disengagement in the UK: Who Is Disengaged?* (House of Commons Briefing Paper No. CBP7501). http://dera.ioe.ac.uk/29007/1/CBP-7501.pdf.

Apps, P. (2015, August 14). Right to Buy to Let. *Inside Housing.* https://www.insidehousing.co.uk/insight/insight/right-to-buy-to-let-44479.

Apps, P. (2018). Government Breaks Promise on Right to Buy Replacements. *Inside Housing,* 28 March 2017. https://www.insidehousing.co.uk/news/government-breaks-promise-on-right-to-buy-replacements-55559.

Apps, P., & Barnes, S. (2017, March 2). Barwell Under Pressure Over £800m Right to Buy Receipts Kept by Treasury. *Inside Housing.* https://www.insidehousing.co.uk/news/news/barwell-under-pressure-over-800m-right-to-buy-receipts-kept-by-treasury-49992.

Arcadis. (2015). *People and Money: Fundamental to Unlocking the Housing Crisis.* https://www.arcadis.com/media/D/B/3/%7BDB3A15FD-23D0-4C95-9578-BBE1611D8A0E%7D9308_People%20and%20Money%20Report_WEB_LR.pdf.

Archer, T. (2017). *Why Are the Major Housebuilders Growing Revenues Faster Than Output?* https://twitter.com/tomhousing?t=1&cn=ZmxleGlibGVf-cmVjcw%3D%3D&refsrc=email&iid=6f76ec2d76854b1e823521f40e-0fa917&uid=7285332901106032648&nid=244+272699403.

Archer, T., & Cole, I. (2016). *Profit Before Volume? Major Housebuilders and the Crisis of Supply.* Sheffield: Sheffield Hallam University. https://www4.shu.ac.uk/research/cresr/sites/shu.ac.uk/files/profits-before-volume-housebuilders-crisis-hous.

Atkinson, A. B. (2015). *Inequality: What Can Be Done?* Cambridge, MA: Harvard University Press.

Aubrey, T. (2016). *The Explosive Concoction of Globalisation and the Rising Cost of Housing.* London: Centre for Progressive Capitalism. http://progressive-capitalism.net/2016/07/the-explosive-concoction-of-globalisation-and-the-rising-cost-of-housing/.

Audickas, L., & Cracknell, R. (2018). *Social Background of MPs 1979–2017* (Briefing Paper No. CBP 7483). London: House of Commons. file:///C:/Users/User/Downloads/CBP-7483%20(2).pdf.

Audit Scotland. (2013). *Housing in Scotland*. Edinburgh: Accounts Commission. http://www.audit-scotland.gov.uk/docs/local/2013/nr_130711_housing_overview.pdf.

Australian Housing and Urban Research Institute. (2018). *Understanding the 30:40 Indicator of Housing Affordability Stress*. Melbourne: Australian Housing and Urban Research Institute. https://www.ahuri.edu.au/policy/ahuri-briefs/2016/3040-indicator.

Awan-Scully, R. (2018). *Public Attitudes to Social Housing in Wales: Report for the Chartered Institute of Housing Cymru*. Cardiff: Chartered Institute of Housing Cymru. https://omghcontent.affino.com/AcuCustom/Sitename/DAM/097/CIH_Cymru_public_perceptions_report.pdf.

Bailey, E. (2016, February 6). Knuckle Down. *Inside Housing*.

Banks, J., & Tetlow, G. (2008). *The Distribution of Wealth in the Population Aged 50 and Over in England* (IFS Briefing Note BN86). London: Institute for Fiscal Studies. https://www.ifs.org.uk/bns/bn86.pdf.

Barker, K. (2004). *Delivering Stability: Securing Our Future Housing Needs; Final Report, Recommendations*. London: HM Treasury. http://webarchive.nationalarchives.gov.uk/+/http:/www.hm-treasury.gov.uk/consultations_and_legislation/barker/consult_barker_index.cfm.

Barker, K. (2006). *Barker Review of Land Use Planning: Final Report Recommendations*. London: HM Treasury. https://www.gov.uk/government/publications/barker-review-of-land-use-planning-final-report-recommendations.

Barker, N. (2018, May 25). Government Targets Mean 165,000 Homes Could Bypass Local Plans, Warns LGA. *Inside Housing*. https://www.insidehousing.co.uk/home/home/government-targets-mean-165000-homes-could-bypass-local-plans-warns-lga-56440.

Barnes, P. (1984). *Building Societies: The Myth of Mutuality*. London: Pluto Press.

Battiston, D., Dickens, R., Manning, L., & Wadsworth, J. (2014). *Immigration and Access to Social Housing in the UK* (CEP Discussion Paper No. 1264). London: Centre for Economic Performance. http://cep.lse.ac.uk/pubs/download/dp1264.pdf.

BBC News. (2014). *Negative Equity Afflicts "Half a Million Households"*. https://www.bbc.co.uk/news/business-26389009.

BBC News. (2015). *Spending Review: Department-By-Department Cuts Guide*. http://www.bbc.co.uk/news/uk-politics-34790102.

BBC News. (2016, April 26). *Is There a Housing Crisis in Scotland?* http://www.bbc.co.uk/news/election-2016-scotland-35928391.

BBC News. (2017a, October 17). *Are House Prices Back from the Crash?* http://www.bbc.co.uk/news/business-41582755.

BBC News. (2017b, April 29). *MPs Say "Dominance" of Big Home-Building Firms Must End.* https://www.bbc.co.uk/news/business-39752869.

BBC News. (2017c, March 20). *Best Schools Add £18,600 to Average House Price.* http://www.bbc.co.uk/news/uk-england-39327149.

BBC News. (2017d, November 9). *How Much of Your Area Is Built On?* http://www.bbc.co.uk/news/uk-41901294.

BBC News. (2018a, March 28). *Almost 30,000 Lone Parent Families Made Homeless in England in 2017.* https://www.bbc.co.uk/news/education-43503102.

BBC News. (2018b). *Moving Home Is "Becoming a Rarity".* http://www.bbc.co.uk/news/business-43541990.

BBC News. (2018c, January 1). *More Than 11,000 UK Homes Empty for 10 Years.* http://www.bbc.co.uk/news/uk-42536418.

BBC News. (2018d, March 5). *Theresa May: Young Are "Right to Be Angry" About Lack of Houses.* https://www.bbc.com/news/uk-politics-43279177.

Beatley, T. (2000). *Green Urbanism: Learning from European Cities.* Washington, DC: Ireland Press.

Beaumont, J. (2011). Population. In J. Beaumont (Ed.), *Social Trends 41.* London: Office for National Statistics.

Belfield, C., Chandler, D., & Joyce, R. (2015). *Housing: Trends in Prices, Costs and Tenure* (IFS Briefing Note BN161). London: Institute for Fiscal Studies. https://www.ifs.org.uk/publications/7593.

Bellamy, J., & Magdoff, F. (2009). *The Great Financial Crisis: Causes and Consequences.* New York, NY: Monthly Review Press.

Bellman, H. (1927). *The Building Society Movement.* London: Methuen.

Bentley, D. (2015). *The Future of Private Renting: Shaping a Fairer Market for Tenants and Taxpayers.* London: Civitas. http://www.civitas.org.uk/pdf/thefutureofprivaterenting.pdf.

Bentley, D. (2017). *The Land Question: Fixing the Dysfunction at the Root of the Housing Crisis.* London: Civitas. http://www.civitas.org.uk/content/files/thelandquestion.pdf.

Berry, F. (1974). *Housing: The Great British Failure.* London: Charles Knight and Co.

Beveridge, C., Biberbach, P., & Hamilton, J. (2016, May). *Empowering Planning to Deliver Great Places: An Independent Review of the Scottish Planning System.* Edinburgh: Scottish Government. https://beta.gov.scot/binaries/content/documents/govscot/publications/advice-and-guidance/2016/05/empowering-planning-to-deliver-great-places/documents/1aed2528-cdd6-4100-854e-cb5b4777e0b5/1aed2528-cdd6-4100-854e-cb-5b4777e0b5/govscot:document/.

Birch, J. (2013, April 10). Taking the Strain. *Inside Housing.* https://www.insidehousing.co.uk/home/home/taking-the-strain3-35246.

Birch, J. (2017, July 25). The Trouble with Leasehold. *Inside Housing.* https://www.insidehousing.co.uk/comment/comment/the-trouble-with-leasehold-50392.

Blair, T. (2011). *Tony Blair: A Journey.* London: Arrow.

Booth, R. (2017, October 5). Theresa May's £2bn for Social Housing Unlikely to Solve Problem. *Guardian.* https://www.theguardian.com/society/2017/oct/04/theresa-mays-2bn-for-social-housing-unlikely-to-solve-problem.

Boughton, J. (2018). *Municipal Dreams: The Rise and Fall of Council Housing.* London: Verso.

Bourdieu, P. (1984). *Distinction.* London: Routledge.

Bourdieu, P., & Wacquant, L. (1992). *An Invitation to Reflexive Sociology.* Cambridge: Polity Press.

Bowie, D. (2017). *Radical Solutions to the Housing Supply Crisis.* Bristol: Policy Press.

Bowley, M. (1946). *Housing and the State 1919–1944.* London: Allen & Unwin.

Bowman, S. (2016). Brownfield Land Won't Be Enough to Solve London's Housing Crisis. *Londonist.* https://londonist.com/2016/01/brownfield-land.

Bradshaw, J., & Bloor, K. (2016). *Which Local Authorities Are Most Unequal?* York: University of York and Social Policy Research Unit. https://pure.york.ac.uk/portal/en/publications/which-local-authorities-are-most-unequal(e-ba28517-2c13-4bf9-b8d0-e71a13201340).html.

Bramley, G., Pawson, H., White, M., Watkins, D., & Pleace, N. (2010). *Estimating Housing Need.* London: DCLG. https://www.gov.uk/government/publications/estimating-housing-need.

Brinded, L. (2016, April 27). *Britain Is Crashing into the End of the Homeownership Era.* http://uk.businessinsider.com/resolution-foundation-uk-property-prices-housing-ownership-and-income-research-2016-4.

British Election Study. (2018, January 29). *The Myth of the 2017 Youthquake Election.* http://www.britishelectionstudy.com/bes-impact/the-myth-of-the-2017-youthquake-election/#.Wnq93J3FJdh.

British History Online. (2017). *Survey of London, Volume 39, the Grosvenor Estate in Mayfair (Part 1).* http://www.british-history.ac.uk/survey-london/vol39/pt1/pp1-5.

Brooker, N. (2017, April 21). London Housing: Too Hot for Young Buyers. *Financial Times.* https://www.ft.com/content/a0182e62-25e4-11e7-a34a-538b4cb30025.

Brown, C. (2018, February 20). Morning Briefing: Metro Mayors "Demand Better Housing Deal". *Inside Housing.* https://www.insidehousing.co.uk/news/morning-briefing-metro-mayors-demand-better-housing-deal-54810.

Brownhill, S., & Bradley, Q. (Eds.). (2017). *Localism and Neighbourhood Planning: Power to the People?* Bristol: Policy Press.

Brummer, A. (2008). *The Crunch: The Scandal of Northern Rock and the Escalating Credit Crisis.* London: Random House Business.

Cabinet Office. (2017). *Gender Pay Gap Report 2017: The First Cabinet Office Report on Gender Pay Gap Data.* London: Cabinet Office. https://www.gov.uk/government/publications/gender-pay-gap-report-2017.

Cambridge Centre for Housing and Planning Research. (2008). *Private Rents and Rates of Return 1996/7 to 2006/7.* Cambridge: Cambridge Centre for Housing and Planning Research. https://www.cchpr.landecon.cam.ac.uk/Projects/Start-Year/2007/Comparative-analysis-of-private-and-social-sectors-rates-of-return/Rents-rates-of-return-1998-99-to-2006-07/PRS-Report.

Campaign to Protect Rural England. (2015). *Green Belt Myths.* London: CPRE. https://www.cpre.org.uk/what-we-do/housing-and-planning/green-belts/in-depth; http://www.cpre.org.uk/what-we-do/housingand-planning/green-belts/in-depth/item/3027-green-belt-myths#myth7.

Campaign to Protect Rural England. (2017). *Needless Demand: How a Focus on Need Can Help Solve the Housing Crisis.* London: Campaign to Protect Rural England. https://www.cpre.org.uk/resources/housing-and-planning/housing/item/4677-needless-demand-how-a-focus-on-need-can-help-solve-the-housing-crisis.

Campaign to Protect Rural England. (2018a). *The State of the Green Belt.* London: Campaign to Protect Rural England. https://www.cpre.org.uk/resources/housing-and-planning/green-belts/item/4931-state-of-the-green-belt-2018.

Campaign to Protect Rural England. (2018b). *State of Brownfield 2018: An Analysis Demonstrating the Potential of Brownfield Land for Housing.* London: Campaign to Protect Rural England. https://www.cpre.org.uk/resources/housing-and-planning/housing/item/4769-state-of-brownfield-2018.

CAPI OmniBus. (2009). *Green Belt Omnibus Survey: July & August 2009.* https://www.cpre.org.uk/resources/housing-and-planning/green-belts/item/.../463.

Capita Economics. (2016). *Building New Social Rent Homes*. London: National Association of ALMOs. www.almos.org.uk/include/getDoc. php?did=7103&fid=8219.

Centre for Cities. (2014). *Delivering Change: Building Homes Where We Need Them*. London: Centre for Cities. http://www.centreforcities.org/ publication/delivering-change-building-homes-where-we-need-them/.

Centre for Regional Economic and Social Research, Sheffield Hallam University. (2010a). *Making Deprived Areas Better Places to Live: Evidence from the New Deal for Communities Programme. The New Deal for Communities National Evaluation: Final Report—Volume 3*. London: DCLG. http://extra.shu.ac.uk/ndc/downloads/general/Volume%20three%20-%20 Making%20deprived%20areas%20better%20places%20to%20live.pdf.

Centre for Regional Economic and Social Research (CRESR), Sheffield Hallam University. (2010b). *Making Deprived Areas Better Places to Live: Evidence from the New Deal for Communities Programme. The New Deal for Communities National Evaluation: Final Report—Volume 4*. London: DCLG. https://extra.shu.ac.uk/ndc/downloads/general/Volume%20three% 20-%20Making%20deprived%20areas%20better%20places%20to%20live. pdf.

Chadwick, E. (1842). *Report on the Sanitary Condition of the Labouring Population of Great Britain*. London: HMSO.

Charlesworth, S. J. (2000). *A Phenomenology of Working-Class Experience*. Cambridge: Cambridge University Press.

Chartered Institute of Housing. (2018a). *Rethinking Social Housing: Final Report*. Coventry: Chartered Institute of Housing. http://www.cih.org/ Rethinkingsocialhousing.

Chartered Institute for Housing. (2018b). *Benefit Freeze Puts Private Renting Out of Reach for Low-Income Tenants and Risks Fuelling Homelessness*. Coventry: Chartered Institute of Housing. http://www.cih.org/news-article/display/vpath-DCR/templatedata/cih/news-article/data/Benefit_freeze_puts_private_renting_ out_of_reach_for_low-income_tenants_and_risks_fuelling_homelessness.

Cheshire East. (2013, September). *Strategic Housing Market Assessment: 2013 Update Report for Cheshire East Council*. Sandbach: Cheshire East. http:// www.cheshireeast.gov.uk/planning/spatial_planning/research_and_evi-dence/strategic_housing_market_assmt.aspx.

Cheshire East. (2018). *Housing Strategy 2018–2023 (Draft for Consultation)*. Sandbach: Cheshire East. http://www.cheshireeast.gov.uk/housing/strate-gic_housing/housing-strategy-2018-2023-consultation.aspx.

Cheshire, P. (2013, September 13). Greenbelt Myth Is the Driving Force Behind Housing Crisis. *The Conversation*. http://blogs.lse.ac.uk/politicsand-policy/greenbelt-myth-is-the-driving-force-behind-housing-crisis/.

Cheshire, P. (2014). Turning Houses into Gold: Don't Blame the Foreigners, It's We Brits Who Did It. *Centrepiece, 19*(1), 14–18.

Cheshire, P. (2016). *Evidence to House of Lords Select Committee on Economic Affairs, 1st Report of Session 2016–17, Building More Homes* (HL Paper 20, Para. 140–146). https://publications.parliament.uk/pa/ld201617/ldselect/ldeconaf/20/20.pdf.

Cheshire, P., & Sheppard, S. (1989). British Planning Policy and Access to Housing: Some Empirical Estimates. *Urban Studies, 26*(5), 469–485. http://journals.sagepub.com/doi/abs/10.1080/00420988920080541?journalCode=usja.

Chevin, D. (2013). *Social Hearted, Commercially Minded: A Report on Tomorrow's Housing Associations*. London: The Smith Institute. http://www.smith-institute.org.uk/book/social-hearted-commercially-minded-a-re-port-on-tomorrows-housing-associations/.

Christophers, B. (2018). *The New Enclosure: The Appropriation of Public Land in Neoliberal Britain*. London: Verso.

Churchill, W. (1909, July 17). *The Mother of All Monopolies*. Speech Delivered at King's Theatre in Edinburgh. https://www.cooperative-individualism.org/churchill-winston_mother-of-all-monopolies-1909.htm.

City A.M. (2016, September 28). Opinion: The Private Rented Sector Needs to Be Vibrant and Consistent Enough to Cater for a Wide Range of Needs. http://www.cityam.com/250326/opinion-private-rented-sector-needs-vibrant-and-consistent.

City A.M. (2017, July 24). The Number of People Moving Out of London Has Risen 80 Per Cent in Five Years. http://www.cityam.com/269004/exodus-number-people-moving-out-london-has-risen-80-per.

City Metric. (2018, April 3). *Yes, Supply Is the Cause of the Housing Crisis and We Do Need to Build More Homes in Successful Cities*. https://www.citymetric.com/business/yes-supply-cause-housing-crisis-and-we-do-need-build-more-homes-successful-cities-3804.

Clegg, N. (2016a). *Politics: Between the Extremes*. London: Bodley Head.

Clegg, N. (2016b, September 3). Tories Refused to Build Social Housing Because It Would Create Labour Voters, Nick Clegg Says. *Independent*. http://www.independent.co.uk/news/uk/politics/tories-refused-to-build-social-housing-because-it-would-create-labour-voters-nick-clegg-says-a7223796.html.

Collinson, P. (2017, October 21). Help to Buy Has Mostly Helped Housebuilders Boost Profits. *Guardian.* https://www.theguardian.com/money/blog/2017/oct/21/help-to-buy-property-new-build-price-ris.

Collinson, P. (2018, October 16). Generation Rent Says Number of First-Time Buyers Has Risen Despite Landlords' Warnings. *Guardian.* https://www.theguardian.com/money/2018/oct/16/taxes-buy-to-let-landlords-rents-generation-rent-buyers.

Commission on Housing and Wellbeing. (2015). *A Blueprint on Housing and Well-Being: Housing as 'Home'.* http://www.housingandwellbeing.org/housing-as-home.

Commission on Social Justice. (1994). *Social Justice: Strategies for National Renewal.* London: Vintage.

Competition and Markets Authority. (2016). *Energy Market Investigation.* London: Competition and Markets Authority. https://www.gov.uk/cma-cases/energy-market-investigation.

Conservative Party. (2010). *Open Source Planning Green Paper.* London: Conservative Party. https://issuu.com/conservatives/docs/opensourceplanning.

Conservative Party. (2017). *Forward Together: Our Plan for a Stronger Britain and a Prosperous Future.* London: Conservative Party. https://www.conservatives.com/manifesto.

Construction News. (2017, May 2). *Housebuilders' Shares Rocket to Five-Year High.* https://www.constructionnews.co.uk/markets/sectors/housing/housebuilders-shares-rocket-to-five-year-high/10019498.article.

Cooper, V., & Paton, K. (2017). The New Urban Frontier of Everyday Evictions: Contemporary State Practices of Revanchism. In A. Abel & B. Núria (Eds.), *Gentrification as a Global Strategy: Neil Smith and Beyond* (pp. 142–151). London: Routledge.

Corbyn, J. (2017). Speech to the Labour Party Conference September 2017 in Full. *New Statesman.* https://www.newstatesman.com/politics/staggers/2017/09/jeremy-corbyns-2017-conference-speech-full.

Corlett, A., & Judge, L. (2017). *Home Affront: Housing Across the Generations.* London: Resolution Foundation. http://www.resolutionfoundation.org/publications/home-affront-housing-across-the-generations/.

Coulter, R. (2016). Social Disparities in Private Renting Amongst Young Families in England and Wales, 2001–2011. *Housing Theory and Society, 34*(3), 297–322. http://www.tandfonline.com/doi/full/10.1080/14036096.2016.1242511.

Council of Mortgage Lenders. (2016a). *Homeownership or Bust?* London: Council of Mortgage Lenders. https://www.cml.org.uk/.../home-ownership-or-bust/ 20161017-home-ownership-or-b.

Council of Mortgage Lenders. (2016b). *Arrears and Possessions Continue to Fall, Reports CML.* London: Council of Mortgage Lenders. https:// www.cml.org.uk/news/press-releases/arrears-and-possessions-continuing-to-fall-reports-cml/.

Council of Mortgage Lenders. (2017). *Arrears and Possessions.* London: Council for Mortgage Lenders. https://www.cml.org.uk/policy/policy-updates/all/arrears-and-possessions/.

Cowley, P., & Kavanagh, D. (2016). *The British General Election of 2015.* Basingstoke: Palgrave Macmillan.

Cowan, D., McDermont, M., & Morgan, K. (2007). *'Problematic Nominations': Final Report.* School of Law, University of Bristol, in Partnership with Shelter, the Local Government Association and the National Housing Federation.

Crawford, R. (2018). *The Use of Wealth in Retirement* (IFS Briefing Note BN237). London: Institute for Fiscal Studies. https://www.ifs.org.uk/ uploads/publications/bns/BN237.pdf.

Cribb, J., Keiller, A. N., & Waters, T. (2018). *Living Standards, Poverty and Inequality in the UK: 2018.* London: Institute for Fiscal Studies.

Cribb, J., Hood, A., & Hoyle, J. (2018b). *The Decline of Homeownership Among Young Adults* (IFS Briefing Note BN224). London: Institute for Fiscal Studies. https://www.ifs.org.uk/publications/10505.

Crisis. (2018). *Everybody In: How to End Homelessness in Britain.* London: Crisis. https://www.crisis.org.uk/media/238959/everybody_in_how_to_end_ homelessness_in_great_britain_2018.pdf.

Crisp, R., Pearson, S., & Gore, T. (2015). Rethinking the Impact of Regeneration on Poverty: A (Partial) Defence of a 'Failed' Policy. *Journal of Poverty and Social Justice, 23*(3), 167–187.

Cromarty, H. (2018). *Starter Homes for First-Time Buyers (England)* (Briefing Paper No. 07643). file:///C:/Users/User/Downloads/CBP-7643%20(2).pdf.

Crook, A. D. H., & Kemp, P. A. (2018, June 17). In Search of Profit: Housing Association Investment in Private Rental Housing. *Housing Studies.* https://www.tandfonline.com/doi/abs/10.1080/02673037.2018. 1468419?journalCode=chos20.

Crosby, N. (2018). *Development Viability Assessment and the Provision of Affordable Housing: A Game of 'Pass the Parcel'?* Reading: Henley Business School. https://assets.henley.ac.uk/defaultUploads/PDFs/research/papers-publications/REP-2018-01-Crosby.pdf?mtime=20180306141219.

Culliney, M., Haux, T., & McKay, S. (2014). *Family Structure and Poverty in the UK: Report to the Joseph Rowntree Foundation.* Lincoln: University of Lincoln. http://eprints.lincoln.ac.uk/14958/1/Family_structure_report_Lincoln.pdf.

Daily Express. (2017a, August 16). Prices Up By £10,000. https://www.express.co.uk/news/uk/841593/House-price-rise-across-UK-since-Brexit.

Daily Express. (2017b, June 25). Ditch George Osborne's 'Northern Powerhouse' to Make Best of Brexit, Says Report. https://www.express.co.uk/news/politics/821161/Northern-Powerhouse-Brexit-ditch-George-Osborne.

Daily Express. (2018, April 10). Giant Rebound in House Prices Sees Biggest Rise in Six Months. https://www.express.co.uk/life-style/property/943886/property-prices-house-price-index-latest-brexit.

Daily Mail. (2016a, February 18). The Rise of Millionaire's Row: Could House Prices Really Double to £560k by 2030 and the Number of £1m Homes Triple? http://www.dailymail.co.uk/property/article-3451304/How-higher-house-prices-New-report-claims-values-double-560K-2030-number-homes-worth-1m-triple.html.

Daily Mail. (2016b, September 26). 'It's My Right to Live Here… and I Might Have More Children': Unrepentant Father-of-Eight Immigrant Who Turned Down a 'Too Small' Five-Bed Council House Defends His Life on Hand-Outs'. http://www.dailymail.co.uk/news/article-3783850/Immigrant-turned-small-five-bed-council-house-children.html.

Daily Mail. (2017, November 19). Hammond Says Budget Will Have Proposals to Help Build 300,000 Homes Annually. http://www.dailymail.co.uk/wires/pa/article-5097115/Philip-Hammond-aims-fix-housing-market-amid-push-300-000-new-homes-year.html#ixzz4z3FAQ7Yl.

Daily Mail. (2018, February 16). End of the Home Owning Dream: End of the Home Owning Dream: 20 Years Ago, Two Thirds of Average Earners Aged Up to 34 Could Afford Their Own House… Now It's Just One in Four. http://www.dailymail.co.uk/news/article-5397697/Home-owner-crisis-just-one-four-afford-home.html.

Daily Mirror. (2016, August 2). UK Housing Crisis Now a "National Emergency" as Number of Homeowners Plummets to 30-Year Low. http://www.mirror.co.uk/news/uk-news/uk-housing-crisis-now-national-8542855.

Darling, A. (2011). *Back from the Brink: 1000 Days at Number 11.* London: Atlantic Books.

Davison, M., Nicol, S., Roys, M., Garrett, H., Beaumont, A., & Turner, C. (2012). *The Cost of Poor Housing in Northern Ireland.* Belfast: Northern Ireland Housing Executive. https://www.nihe.gov.uk/cost_of_poor_housing_in_ni.pdf.

Dawes, M. (2017, February 22, Wednesday). *Evidence to Public Accounts Committee: Housing: State of the Nation.* HC 958, Question 132. http://data.parliament.uk/writtenevidence/committeeevidence.svc/evidencedocument/public-accounts-committee/housing-state-of-the-nation/oral/47584.html.

Dawes, M. (2018). *Working age Housing Benefit and Non-decent Homes in the Private Rented Sector 2015–16.* London: MHCLG. https://www.parliament.uk/documents/commons-committees/public-accounts/Correspondence/2017-19/mhclg-gcgp-housing-300118.pdf.

DCLG. (2011). *Draft National Planning Policy Framework.* London: DCLG. https://www.gov.uk/government/consultations/draft-national-planning-policy-framework.

DCLG. (2012a). *National Planning Policy Framework.* London: DCLG. https://www.gov.uk/government/publications/national-planning-policy-framework-2.

DCLG. (2012b). *Tracking Economic and Child Income Deprivation at Neighbourhood Level in England: 1999 to 2009.* London: DCLG. https://www.gov.uk/government/statistics/tracking-economic-and-child-income-deprivation-at-neighbourhood-level-in-england-1999-to-2009.

DCLG. (2012c). *National Planning Policy Framework: Impact Assessment.* London: DCLG.

DCLG. (2012d). *Review of the Barriers to Institutional Investment in Private Rented Homes.* London: DCLG. https://assets.publishing.service.gov.uk/government/uploads/system/uploads/attachment_data/file/15547/montague_review.pdf.

DCLG. (2014a). *English Housing Survey Profile of English Housing 2013.* London: DCLG. https://assets.publishing.service.gov.uk/government/uploads/system/uploads/attachment_data/file/445370/EHS_Profile_of_English_housing_2013.pdf.

DCLG. (2014b). *Evaluation of the New Homes Bonus.* London: DCLG. https://assets.publishing.service.gov.uk/government/uploads/system/uploads/attachment_data/file/387152/NHB_Evaluation_FINAL_report.pdf.

DCLG. (2015a). *Guidance: Housing and Economic Development Needs Assessments.* London: DCLG. https://www.gov.uk/guidance/housing-and-economic-development-needs-assessments.

DCLG. (2015b). *Land Value Estimates for Policy Appraisal.* London: DCLG. https://assets.publishing.service.gov.uk/government/uploads/system/uploads/attachment_data/file/407155/February_2015_Land_value_publication_FINAL.pdf.

DCLG. (2016a). *English Housing Survey Housing for Older People Report, 2014–15*. London: DCLG. https://assets.publishing.service.gov.uk/government/uploads/system/uploads/attachment_data/file/539002/Housing_for_Older_People_Full_Report.pdf.

DCLG. (2016b). *2014-Based Household Projections in England, 2014 to 2039*. London: DCLG. https://www.gov.uk/government/statistics/2014-based-household-projections-in-england-2014-to-2039.

DCLG. (2016c). *New Homes Bonus: Sharpening the Incentive Government Response to the Consultation*. London: DCLG. https://assets.publishing.service.gov.uk/government/uploads/system/uploads/attachment_data/file/577904/NHB_Consultation_Response_Doc.pdf.

DCLG. (2017a). *English Housing Survey 2015/16 Headline Report, Table FA1201 (S106): Age of Household Reference Person by Tenure, 2015–16*. London: DCLG. https://www.gov.uk/government/statistics/english-housing-survey-2015-to-2016-headline-report.

DCLG. (2017b). *Fixing Our Broken Housing Market* (Cm 9352). London: DCLG. https://assets.publishing.service.gov.uk/government/uploads/system/uploads/attachment_data/file/590464/Fixing_our_broken_housing_market_-_print_ready_version.pdf.

DCLG. (2017c). *English Housing Survey Housing Costs and Affordability, 2015–16*. https://assets.publishing.service.gov.uk/government/uploads/system/uploads/attachment_data/file/627683/Housing_Cost_and_Affordability_Report_2015-16.pdf.

DCLG. (2017d). *Land Use Change Statistics in England: 2015–16*. London: DCLG. https://assets.publishing.service.gov.uk/government/uploads/system/uploads/attachment_data/file/595749/Land_use_change_statistics_England_2015-16_-_2_March_2017_version.pdf.

DCLG. (2017e). *Planning for the Right Homes in the Right Places: Consultation Proposals*. London: DCLG. https://www.gov.uk/government/consultations/planning-for-the-right-homes-in-the-right-places-consultation-proposals.

DCLG. (2017f). *50 Years of the English Housing Survey*. London: DCLG. https://assets.publishing.service.gov.uk/government/uploads/system/uploads/attachment_data/file/658923/EHS_50th_Anniversary_Report.pdf.

DCLG. (2017g). *Local Planning Authority Green Belt: England 2016/17*. London: DCLG. https://assets.publishing.service.gov.uk/government/uploads/system/uploads/attachment_data/file/642684/Green_Belt_Statistics_England_2016-17.pdf.

DCLG. (2017h). *Land Use Change Statistics in England: 2015–16*. London: DCLG. https://assets.publishing.service.gov.uk/government/uploads/system/

uploads/attachment_data/file/595749/Land_use_change_statistics_
England_2015-16_-_2_March_2017_version.pdf.

DeFazio, K. (2014). Red Vienna, Class and the Common. In B. Fraser (Ed.),
Marxism and Urban Culture (pp. 159–190). New York: Lexington Books.

Delft University of Technology. (2011). *Housing Statistics in the European
Union*. Delft, The Netherlands. https://www.bmdw.gv.at/Wirtschaftspolitik/
Wohnungspolitik/Documents/housing_statistics_in_the_european_
union_2010.pdf.

Deloitte. (2016). *Property Index: Overview of European Residential Markets* (5th
ed.). London: Deloitte. https://www2.deloitte.com/content/dam/Deloitte/
cz/Documents/survey/Property_Index_2016_EN.pdf.

Department for Business, Energy and Industrial Strategy (DBEIS). (2017a).
Fuel Poverty Statistics. London: Department for Business, Energy and
Industrial Strategy. https://www.gov.uk/government/collections/fuel-poverty-
statistics.

Department for Business, Energy and Industrial Strategy (DBEIS). (2017b).
2017 UK Greenhouse Gas Emissions, Provisional Figures. London: Department
for Business, Energy and Industrial Strategy. https://assets.publishing.
service.gov.uk/government/uploads/system/uploads/attachment_data/
file/695930/2017_Provisional_Emissions_statistics_2.pdf.

Department for Communities and Local Government (DCLG). (2006). *A
Decent Home: Definition and Guidance.* London: DCLG.

Department for Work and Pensions (DWP). (2015). *Evaluation of Removal
of the Spare Room Subsidy: Final Report.* https://www.gov.uk/government/
publications/removal-of-the-spare-room-subsidy-evaluation-final-report.

Department for Work and Pensions (DWP). (2017). *Pensioners' Incomes
Series: Financial Year 2015/16.* https://www.gov.uk/government/uploads/
system/uploads/attachment_data/file/600594/pensioners-incomes-se-
ries-2015-16-report.pdf.

Department for Work and Pensions (DWP). (2018). *Benefit Expenditure and
Caseload Tables 2018.* London: DWP. https://www.gov.uk/government/
publications/benefit-expenditure-and-caseload-tables-2018.

Department of the Environment. (1977). *Housing Policy Review: Technical
Volume Part 111.* London: Department of the Environment.

Department of the Environment. (1985). *Home Improvement: A New Approach*
(Cmnd 9513). London: HMSO.

Department of the Environment. (1987). *Housing: The Government's Proposals*
(Cm 214). London: Department of the Environment.

Department of the Environment/Welsh Office. (1995). *Our Future Homes: Opportunity, Choice, Responsibility: The Government's Housing Policies for England and Wales* (Cm 2901). London: HMSO.

Department of Energy and Climate Change. (2015). *Fuel Poverty Strategy for England*. London: Department of Energy and Climate Change. https://www.gov.uk/government/speeches/fuel-poverty-strategy-for-england.

Department of Urban Development. (2017). *Affordable Housing*. Washington, DC: Department of Urban Development. https://www.hud.gov/program_offices/comm_planning/affordablehousing/.

Disraeli, B. (1872). *Speech of B. Disraeli at the Free Trade Hall, Manchester, April 3, 1872*. Bristol Pamphlets: University of Bristol. https://historyatwoodlands.wikispaces.com/file/view/Speech+of+B.+Disraeli+at+the+Free+Trade+Hall%252c+Manchester%252c+April+3%252c+1872.pdf.

Dorling, D. (2014). *All That Is Solid: The Great Housing Disaster*. London: Allen Lane.

Dorling, D. (2015). *Income Inequality in the UK: Comparisons with Five Large Western European Countries and the USA*. http://www.dannydorling.org/wp-content/files/dannydorling_publication_id4756.pdf.

Dorling, D., Pattie, C. J., & Johnston, R. J. (1999). *Voting and the Housing Market: The Impact of New Labour*. London: Council of Mortgage Lenders. http://www.dannydorling.org/wp-content/files/dannydorling_publication_id4095.pdf.

Duncan Smith, I. (2008). Foreword. In *Breakthrough Britain: Housing Poverty, from Social Breakdown to Social Mobility*. London: Centre for Social Justice.

Duncan Smith, I. (2015). *Government to Strengthen Child Poverty Measure*. London: Department of Work and Pensions. https://www.gov.uk/government/news/government-to-strengthen-child-poverty-measure.

Dunleavy, P. (1981). *The Politics of Mass Housing in Britain: A Study of Corporate Power and Professional Influence in the Welfare State*. Oxford: Clarendon Press.

East, J. (2014). *Improving the Private Landlord Sector*. London: Newham Borough. http://www.cih.org/resources/PDF/CIH%20London%20-%20PRS%203%20-John%20East%20Presentation.pdf.

Economist. (2013, May 2). Housing and Planning: The Brownfields Delusion. https://www.economist.com/blogs/blighty/2013/05/planning-and-housing.

Economist. (2017). Location, Location, Location, Global House Prices: The Economist's Interactive Guide to Global Housing Markets. https://www.economist.com/blogs/dailychart/2011/11/global-house-prices.

Economist Intelligence Unit. (2017). *Democracy Index 2016: Revenge of the "Deplorables"*. http://felipesahagun.es/wp-content/uploads/2017/01/Democracy-Index-2016.pdf.

Edwards, M. (2016). The Housing Crisis: Too Difficult or a Great Opportunity? *Soundings* (62). https://www.lwbooks.co.uk/soundings/62/ the-housing-crisis-too-difficult-or-great-opportunity.

Egan, J. (1998). *Rethinking Construction, the Report of the Construction Task Force on the Scope for Improving Quality and Efficiency in UK Construction.* London: Department for the Environment, Transport and the Regions.

Eichler, W. (2016). *IPPR: Lessons from German Housing Market Could Benefit UK.* London: LocGov. https://www.localgov.co.uk/IPPR-Lessons-from-German-housing-market-could-benefit-UK-/42169.

Ellis, H. (2018, June 11, Monday). *Oral Evidence to Housing, Communities and Local Government Committee: Land Value Capture.* HC 766. http://data. parliament.uk/writtenevidence/committeeevidence.sc/evidencedocument/ housing-communities-and-local-government-committee/land-value-cap-ture/oral/85154.html.

Ellis, H., & Henderson, K. (2016). *English Planning in Crisis: 10 Steps to a Sustainable Future.* Bristol: Policy Press.

Elmhurst Energy. (2017). *The Energy Efficiency of English Homes Has Stalled.* London: Elmhurst Energy. https://www.elmhurstenergy.co.uk/ the-energy-efficiency-of-english-homes-has-stalled.

Emmerson, C. (2017). *Two Parliaments of Pain: The UK Public Finances 2010 to 2017* (IFS Briefing Note BN199). London: Institute for Fiscal Studies. https://www.ifs.org.uk/publications/9180.

EMoov. (2017). *The Gender Property Gap: Male Mortgage Affordability 15% Higher Over the Last 10 Years.* https://www.emoov.co.uk/news/2017/09/15/ gender-property-gap-male-mortgage-affordability-15-higher-last-10-years/.

Empty Homes Agency. (2016). *Empty Homes in England.* London: Empty Homes Agency. http://www.emptyhomes.com/assets/empty-homes-in-eng-land-final-september-2016.pdf.

End Child Poverty. (2018). *Poverty in Your Area.* http://www.endchildpoverty. org.uk/poverty-in-your-area-2018/.

Energy UK. (2017). *Fuel Poverty.* http://www.energy-uk.org.uk/policy/fuel-pov-erty.html.

Engels, F. (1872). *The Housing Question Part Two: How the Bourgeoisie Solves the Housing Question.* https://www.marxists.org/archive/marx/works/1872/ housing-question/.

Eurostat. (2017a). *Housing Cost Overburden Rate by Tenure Status.* http:// ec.europa.eu/eurostat/tgm/refreshTableAction.do?tab=table&plugin= 1&pcode=tessi164&language=en.

Eurostat. (2017b). *Housing Cost Overburden by Poverty Status*. http://
ec.europa.eu/eurostat/tgm/refreshTableAction.do?tab=table&plugin=
1&pcode=tessi163&language=en.

Eurostat. (2018). *Statistics Explained*. https://ec.europa.eu/eurostat/statis-
tics-explained/index.php?title=File:Housing_cost_overburden_rate_by_
tenure_status,_2016_(%25_of_population)_YB18.png.

Evans, A. W., & Hartwich, O. M. (2005). *Bigger Better Faster More: Why Some
Countries Plan Better Than Others*. London: Localis. https://www.localis.
org.uk/wp-content/uploads/2005/06/Evans-A.W-Hartwich-O.M-Bigger-
Better-Faster-More.pdf.

Evans, N. (2017, June 10). 'Tory MP Nigel Evans Lays into His Own Party
Over "Awful" Election' Manifesto. *Sky News*. https://www.youtube.com/
watch?v=4bXmLLfUzhA.

Evening Standard. (2017, August 15). Theresa May Reveals Scope of Grenfell
Tower Public Inquiry. https://www.standard.co.uk/news/politics/theresa-
may-reveals-scope-of-grenfell-tower-public-inquiry-a3611916.html.

Fabian Society. (2014). *Silent Majority: How the Public Will Support a New
Wave of Social Housing*. London: Fabian Society. https://fabians.org.uk/
publication/silent-majority/.

Farha, L. (2014). *Special Rapporteur on Adequate Housing as a Component
of the Right to an Adequate Standard of Living, and on the Right to Non-
Discrimination in This Context, Ms. Farha*. Geneva: United Nations Human
Rights, Office of the High Commissioner. https://www.ohchr.org/en/issues/
housing/pages/leilanifarha.aspx.

Farmer, M. (2016). *The Farmer Review of the UK Construction Labour Model:
Modernise or Die—Time to Decide the Industry's Future*. London: Construction
Leadership Council. https://www.gov.uk/government/publications/construction-
labour-market-in-the-uk-farmer-review.

Federation of Master Builders. (2017). *Homes on Our High Streets*. London:
Federation of Master Builders. https://www.fmb.org.uk/media/37062/fmb-
homes-on-our-high-streets-low-res-final.pdf.

Fenton, A. (2012). *Look-Ups from Local Authority and Postcode Sectors to Broad
Rental Market Areas (BRMAs)*. London School of Economics, Centre for
Analysis of Social Exclusion. http://eprints.lse.ac.uk/46454/.

Fields, D. J., & Hodkinson, S. N. (2018). Housing Policy in Crisis: An
International Perspective. *Housing Policy Debate, 28*(1), 1–5.

Financial Conduct Authority. (2018). *FCA Handbook*. London: Financial
Conduct Authority. https://www.handbook.fca.org.uk/.

Financial Times. (2016, January 19). The Vanishing Power of the Median Voter. https://www.ft.com/content/7ab73ad8-21ec-39f3-ab8d-a559a110d210.

Financial Times. (2017a). Which Cities Are the Next UK Property Hotspots? Liverpool, Glasgow, Birmingham and Manchester Tipped for Price Growth. https://www.ft.com/content/a38aced2-8662-11e6-8897-2359a58ac7a5.

Financial Times. (2017b, November 17). How to Solve the UK Housing Crisis. https://www.ft.com/content/d8854b1e-bf08-11e7-823b-ed31693349d3.

Financial Times. (2017c, February 7). Sajid Javid Sets Out Fix for "Broken" Housing Market. https://www.ft.com/content/dfb68f7c-ec97-11e6-930f-061b01e23655.

Financial Times. (2017d, June 20). Youth Turnout at General Election Highest in 25 Years, Data Show. https://www.ft.com/content/6734cdde-550b-11e7-9fed-c19e2700005f.

Financial Times. (2018a, June 23). Buy-to-Let Landlords Cool on Property Purchases. https://www.ft.com/content/4d8e2002-75f2-11e8-b326-75a27d27ea5f.

Financial Times. (2018b, March 14). How the Financial Crash Made Our Cities Unaffordable. https://www.ft.com/content/cc77babe-2213-11e8-add1-0e8958b189ea.

Finney, N., & Harries, B. (2013). *Understanding Ethnic Inequalities in Housing: Analysis of the 2011 Census*. London: Race Equality Foundation. www.raceequalityfoundation.org.uk/resources/downloads/understanding-ethnic-inequalities-housing-analysis-2011-census.

Fitzpatrick, S. (2017, July 28). Let's Be Honest—If You're Middle Class, You're Less Likely to Become Homeless. *Guardian*. https://www.theguardian.com/housing-network/2017/jul/28/middle-class-homelessness-myth-poverty-racism-structural-issues.

Fitzpatrick, S., & Watts, B. (2018). Taking Values Seriously in Housing Studies. *Housing, Theory and Society, 35*(2), 223–227.

Fitzpatrick, S., Pawson, H., Bramley, G., Wilcox, S., Watts, B., & Wood, J. (2018). *The Homelessness Monitor: England 2018*. London: Crisis. https://www.crisis.org.uk/media/238700/homelessness_monitor_england_2018.pdf.

Forrest, R., & Murie, A. (1983). Residualisation and Council Housing: Aspects of the Changing Social Relations of Housing Tenure. *Journal of Social Policy, 12*(4), 453–468.

Forrest, R., Murie, A., & Williams, P. (1990). *Home Ownership Transition: Differentiation and Fragmentation*. Abingdon: Routledge.

Fraser, I. (2017a, November 20). Inside the Government's Quarrels on How to Fix the Housing Market. *Telegraph*. http://www.telegraph.co.uk/business/2017/11/20/inside-governments-machinations-solve-uks-housing-crisis-threatening/.

Fraser, I. (2017b, June 14). 'Almost No Evidence' of London Homes Owned by Foreign Buyers Being Left Empty. *Telegraph*. http://www.telegraph.co.uk/property/house-prices/almost-no-evidence-london-homes-owned-foreign-buyers-left-empty/.

Fraser, R. (2018, March 2). Can Offsite Manufactured Housing (OSM) Play a Key Role in Solving the Housing Crisis by Ensuring That New Supply Targets Are Met? *Redbrick*. https://redbrickblog.wordpress.com/.

Frey, J., & Brown, J. (2016). Housing Conditions Transformed. In P. Shanks & D. Mullins (Eds.), *Housing in Northern Ireland*. Coventry: Chartered Institute of Housing.

Full Fact. (2014). *Self-Build Britain: Is the UK Lagging Behind Other Countries?* https://fullfact.org/economy/self-build-britain-uk-lagging-behind-other-countries/.

Full Fact. (2017, May 31). *Labour's Land Value Tax: Will You Have to Sell Your Garden?* https://fullfact.org/economy/labours-land-value-tax-will-you-have-sell-your-garden/?gclid=EAIaIQobChMI6N2z99mL2AIVTJ4bCh1tTgvXEAAYASAAEgJC3vD_BwE.

Full Fact. (2018, December). *EU immigration to the UK*. https://fullfact.org/immigration/eu-migration-and-uk/.

Gallent, N. (2016). *Whose Housing Crisis*. London: University College London. http://www.ucl.ac.uk/grand-challenges/sustainable-cities/our-work-so-far/rethinking-housing/whose-housing-crisis.

Gardiner, L. (2016). *VOTEY McVOTEFACE: Understanding the Growing Turnout Gap Between the Generations*. London: Resolution Foundation. http://www.resolutionfoundation.org/publications/votey-mcvoteface-understanding-the-growing-turnout-gap-between-the-generations/.

Gardiner, L. (2017). *The Million Dollar Be-Question: Inheritances, Gifts and Their Implications for Generational Living Standards*. London: Resolution Foundation. https://www.resolutionfoundation.org/publications/the-million-dollar-be-question-inheritances-gifts-and-their-implications-for-generational-living-standards/.

George, H. (1979 [1879]). *Progress and Poverty*. London: Hogarth Press.

Ginsburg, N. (1992). Racism and Housing: Concepts and Reality. In P. Braham, A. Rattans, & R. Skellington (Eds.), *Racism and Antiracism* (pp. 109–133). London: Sage.

Gleeson, J. (2017). *Historical Housing and Land Values in the UK.* https://jamesjgleeson.wordpress.com/2017/04/03/historical-housing-and-land-values-in-the-uk/.

GL Hearn. (2016). *Berkshire (Including South Bucks) Strategic Housing Market Assessment.* http://www.reading.gov.uk/media/2959/Housing-Market-Assessment/pdf/Berkshire_Strategic_Housing_Market_Assessment_Feb_2016.pdf.

Global Property Guide. (2018a). *German House Prices Are Accelerating!* https://www.globalpropertyguide.com/Europe/Germany/Price-History.

Global Property Guide. (2018b). *Irish House Prices Will Outpace All Europe Over Next 2 Years.* https://www.globalpropertyguide.com/Europe/Ireland/.

Godson, D. (2017). *No Longer Overlooked But Still Decisive: Has Theresa May Conquered Class Politics for the Tories?* London: Policy Exchange. https://policyexchange.org.uk/no-longer-overlooked-but-still-decisive-has-theresa-may-conquered-class-politics-for-the-tories/.

Golland, A., & Blake, R. (Eds.). (2004). *Housing Development: Theory, Process and Practice.* London: Routledge.

Goodhart, D. (2017). *The Road to Somewhere: The Populist Revolt and the Future of Politics.* London: C. Hurst & Co.

Gov.uk. (2017). *Ethnicity Facts and Figures.* https://www.ethnicity-facts-figures.service.gov.uk/.

Green, S. (1979). *Rachman.* London: Michael Joseph.

Green, A. (2017). *The Crisis for Young People: Why Housing Is the Key to Social Mobility.* https://ioelondonblog.wordpress.com/2017/07/04/the-crisis-for-young-people-why-housing-is-the-key-to-social-mobility/.

Grimwood, G. G. (2017, November 17). *Green Belt* (House of Commons Briefing Paper No. 00934). London: House of Commons.

Grindrod, J. (2017). *Outskirts: Living Life on the Edge of the Green Belt.* London: Sceptre.

Guardian. (2014, February 3). Ministers Savage UN Report Calling for Abolition of UK's Bedroom Tax. https://www.theguardian.com/society/2014/feb/03/ministers-savage-un-report-abolition-bedroom-tax.

Guardian. (2016a, August 2). Home Ownership Is Unrealistic: Five Readers on England's Housing Crisis. https://www.theguardian.com/uk-news/2016/aug/02/home-ownership-is-unrealistic-five-readers-on-englands-housing-crisis.

Guardian. (2016b, July 20). Private Rental Sector Is the "New Home of Poverty" in the UK. https://www.theguardian.com/housing-network/2016/jul/20/private-rental-sector-poverty-housing-joseph-rowntree.

Guardian. (2017a, March 27). Dog Kennel Flats in Barnet Will Be 40% Smaller Than Travelodge Room. https://www.theguardian.com/society/2017/mar/27/dog-kennel-flats-barnet-house-smaller-than-travelodge-room.

Guardian. (2017b). UK Gender Pay Gap Narrows to Lowest for 20 Years— But Is Still 9.1%. https://www.theguardian.com/business/2017/oct/26/uk-gender-pay-gap-narrows-to-lowest-for-20-years-but-is-still-91.

Guardian. (2017c, February 24). Losses of £58bn Since the 2008 Bailout— How Did RBS Get Here? https://www.theguardian.com/business/2017/feb/24/90bn-in-bills-since-2008-how-did-rbs-get-here-financial-crisis-.

Guardian. (2017d, June 25). Grenfell Tower Tragedy Shows Social Housing System Has Failed UK Citizens. https://www.theguardian.com/politics/queens-speech.

Guardian. (2017e, February 7). Stop Dithering and Start Building—Experts on Housing White Paper. https://www.theguardian.com/housing-network/2017/feb/07/start-building-experts-housing-white-paper.

Guardian. (2017f, November 29). London Suburbs Set for Housing Boom as Sadiq Khan Relaxes Rules. https://www.theguardian.com/uk-news/2017/nov/29/london-suburbs-set-for-housing-boom-sadiq-khan.

Guardian. (2017g, December 2). Tony Blair Backs Labour's Land Value Tax to Tackle Housing Crisis. https://www.theguardian.com/politics/2017/dec/03/tony-blair-backs-labour-land-tax-solve-uk-housing-crisis.

Guardian. (2018a, June 13). Fury as Housing Associations Redevelop and Sell Affordable Homes. https://www.theguardian.com/society/2018/jun/13/fury-affordable-homes-redeveloped-sold-housing-associations.

Guardian. (2018b, February 10). Is Custom Build the Future of Housing? https://www.theguardian.com/money/2018/feb/10/custom-self-build-housing-graven-hill.

Guild of Residential Landlords. (2015). *HMRC Upset About Landlord Tax Avoidance and Offers Easy Payments*. http://www.landlordsguild.com/hmrc-upset-about-landlord-tax-avoidance-and-offers-easy-payments/.

Halikiopoulou, D. (2018, February 5). Three Dangerous Generalisations You Could Be Making About Populism. *Political Quarterly Blog*. https://politicalquarterly.blog/2018/02/05/three-dangerous-generalisations-you-could-be-making-about-populism/.

Hanley, L. (2007). *Estates: An Intimate History*. London: Granta.

Hansard. (2016). *Council Housing Written Question HL3457*. http://www.parliament.uk/written-questions-answers-statements/written-question/lords/2016-11-23/HL3457.

Harari, D., & Ward, M. (2018). *Regional and Country Economic Indicators* (House of Commons Briefing Paper No. 06924). London: House of Commons. https://researchbriefings.parliament.uk/ResearchBriefing/Summary/SN06924.

Harrison, R. (2017, September 5). Energy: Private Rented Housing: Written Question—8878. *Hansard.* http://www.parliament.uk/business/publications/written-questions-answers-statements/written-question/Commons/2017-09-05/8878.

Harvey, A. (2013, February 18). Zero-Carbon Home "Dithering" Is Threatening UK Housing Industry. *Guardian.* https://www.theguardian.com/environment/2013/feb/18/zero-carbon-home-housing-industry.

Harvey, D. (2005). *The New Imperialism.* Oxford: Oxford University Press.

Hawkins, O. (2018). *Migration Statistics* (Briefing Paper No. SN06077). London: House of Commons. http://researchbriefings.parliament.uk/ResearchBriefing/Summary/SN06077.

Haws, G. (1900). *No Room to Live: The Plaint of Overcrowded London.* London: Wells Gardner, Darton and Co.

Heath, A. (2017, July 5). Wake Up Nimbys, the Option Is Either Tory House-Building or Marxist Social Engineering. *Telegraph.* http://www.telegraph.co.uk/news/2017/07/05/wake-nimbys-option-either-tory-housebuilding-marxist-social/.

Heseltine, L. (2012). *No Stone Unturned: In Pursuit of Growth.* London: Department for Business, Education and Skills. https://www.gov.uk/government/uploads/system/uploads/attachment_data/file/34648/12-1213-no-stone-unturned-in-pursuit-of-growth.pdf.

Heywood, A. (2015). *Working Together—Thinking Alike: What Do Councils and Local Enterprise Partnerships Expect from Housing Associations?* London: Smith Institute.

Hilber, C. A. L., & Vermeulen, W. (2015). The Impact of Supply Constraints on House Prices in England. *Economics Journal, 126*(591), 358–405.

Hills, J. (2014). *Good Times, Bad Times: The Welfare Myth of Them and Us.* Bristol: Policy Press.

Hirsch, F. (1977). *Social Limits to Growth.* Abingdon: Routledge.

HM Government. (2010). *The Coalition: Our Programme for Government.* https://www.gov.uk/government/uploads/system/uploads/attachment_data/file/78977/coalition_programme_for_government.pdf.

HM Government. (2015). *Cutting the Cost of Keeping Warm a Fuel Poverty Strategy for England.* https://assets.publishing.service.gov.uk/government/

uploads/system/uploads/attachment_data/file/408644/cutting_the_cost_of_keeping_warm.pdf.

HM Land Registry. (2018). *UK House Price Index for March 2018*. https://www.gov.uk/government/news/uk-house-price-index-for-march-2018.

HM Treasury. (2000). *2000 Spending Review: Prudent for a Purpose: Building Opportunity and Security for All*. London: HM Treasury. https://www.gov.uk/government/uploads/system/uploads/attachment_data/file/265996/csr2000.pdf.

HM Treasury. (2016). *Autumn Statement 2016*. London: HM Treasury. https://www.gov.uk/government/topical-events/autumn-statement-2016.

HM Treasury. (2017a). *Estimated Costs of Principal Tax Reliefs*. London: HM Treasury. https://www.gov.uk/government/uploads/system/uploads/attachment_data/file/579720/Dec_16_Main_Reliefs_Final.pdf.

HM Treasury. (2018). *Budget 2018*. London: HM Treasury. https://assets.publishing.service.gov.uk/government/uploads/system/uploads/attachment_data/file/752202/Budget_2018_red_web.pdf.

HM Treasury and Greater Manchester Combined Authority. (2014). *Greater Manchester Agreement: Devolution to Greater Manchester and Transition to a Directly Elected Mayor*. https://www.gov.uk/government/uploads/system/uploads/attachment_data/file/369858/Greater_Manchester_Agreement_i.pdf.

Holmans, A. (2015). *Future Need and Demand for Housing in Wales*. Cardiff: Public Policy Institute for Wales. https://sites.cardiff.ac.uk/ppiw/files/2015/10/Future-Need-and-Demand-for-Housing-in-Wales.pdf.

Home Builders Federation. (2016). *Reversing the Decline of Small Housebuilders: Reinvigorating Entrepreneurialism and Building More Homes*. London: Home Builders Federation. http://www.hbf.co.uk/uploads/media/HBF_SME_Report_2017_Web.pdf.

HomeLet. (2015). *Landlord Survey 2015*. https://homelet.co.uk/homelet-rental-index/landlord-survey-2015.

Home Office. (2016). *Controlling Migration Fund: Mitigating the Impacts of Immigration on Local Communities*. London: Home Office. https://assets.publishing.service.gov.uk/government/uploads/system/uploads/attachment_data/file/566951/Controlling_Migration_Fund_Prospectus.pdf.

Homeowners Alliance. (2012, November). *The Death of a Dream: The Crisis in Homeownership in the UK* (A Homeowners Alliance Report). London: Homeowners Alliance. https://hoa.org.uk/wp-content/uploads/2012/11/HOA-Report-Death-of-a-Dream.pdf.

Homes and Communities Agency. (2017). *Housing Statistics Tables June 2017*. https://www.gov.uk/government/statistics/housing-statistics-1-april-2016-to-31-march-2017.

Hore-Belisha, L. (1935, June 25). *Restriction of Ribbon Development Bill [Lords.]*. HC Deb vol 303 cc957–1069. http://hansard.millbanksystems.com/commons/1935/jun/25/restriction-of-ribbon-development-bill.

House of Commons Committee on Communities and Local Government. (2010). *Fourth Report: Beyond Decent Homes*. London: House of Commons. https://publications.parliament.uk/pa/cm200910/cmselect/cmcomloc/60/6002.htm.

House of Commons Committee on Communities and Local Government. (2012). *Financing of New Housing Supply Eleventh Report of Session 2010–12*. London: House of Commons. https://publications.parliament.uk/pa/cm201012/cmselect/cmcomloc/1652/1652.pdf.

House of Commons Committee on Communities and Local Government. (2017). *Capacity in the Homebuilding Industry* (Tenth Report of Session 2016–2017). London: House of Commons. https://publications.parliament.uk/pa/cm201617/cmselect/cmcomloc/46/46.pdf.

House of Commons Home Affairs Committee. (2018). *Immigration Policy: Basis for Building Consensus* (Second Report of Session 2017–2019). London: House of Commons. https://publications.parliament.uk/pa/cm201719/cmselect/cmhaff/500/500.pdf.

House of Commons Housing, Communities and Local Government Committee. (2018). *Private Rented Sector: Fourth Report of Session 2017–19 Report, Together with Formal Minutes*. London: House of Commons. https://publications.parliament.uk/pa/cm201719/cmselect/cmcomloc/440/440.pdf.

House of Commons Public Accounts Committee. (2017, February 22). *Oral Evidence: Housing: State of the Nation*. HC 958, Question 17. London: House of Commons. https://publications.parliament.uk/pa/cm201617/cmselect/cmpubacc/958/958.pdf.

House of Commons South East Regional Committee. (2010). *Housing in the South East, Oral Evidence*. London: House of Commons. https://publications.parliament.uk/pa/cm/cmseast.htm.

House of Lords. (1968, February 20). *Local Authorities' Direct—Labour Building Departments*. HL Deb vol 289 cc337–54. https://api.parliament.uk/historic-hansard/lords/1968/feb/20/local-authorities-direct-labour-building-1.

Houses of Parliament Parliamentary Office of Science and Technology. (2017, February). *Future Energy Efficiency Policy* (POSTNOTE No. 550). http://researchbriefings.parliament.uk/ResearchBriefing/Summary/POST-PN-0550.

Howard, E. (1902). *Garden Cities of Tomorrow*. London: Faber.

Hudson, N. (2015). *Land Market Note: The Value of Land*. London: Savills. http://www.savills.co.uk/research_articles/186866/188996-0.

Ideal Home. (2013). *Want to Buy Your Second Home? You'll Have to Wait Until You're 42*. http://www.idealhome.co.uk/news/second-time-buyers-42184.99.

Ifsec Global. (2013, October 3). *Decline in House Building Blamed on Sprinkler Regulations*. https://www.ifsecglobal.com/decline-in-house-building-blamed-on-sprinkler-regulations/.

Independent. (2009). It's Time to Give Up the Dream of Homeownership Says Minister. https://www.independent.co.uk/news/uk/politics/its-time-to-give-up-the-dream-of-home-ownership-says-minister-1838189.html.

Independent. (2015, June 24). Extend Right to Buy to Tenants of Private Landlords, Labour's Jeremy Corbyn Says. http://www.independent.co.uk/news/uk/politics/extend-right-to-buy-to-the-tenants-of-private-landlords-labours-jeremy-corbyn-says-10342824.html.

Independent. (2016, March 19). Oldham Tops List of Most Deprived Towns in England. http://www.independent.co.uk/news/uk/home-news/oldham-tops-list-of-most-deprived-towns-in-britain-a6940696.html.

Independent. (2017, June 22). Adults Returning to "Bank of Mum and Dad" to Help Them Ascend Second Step on Property Ladder. http://www.independent.co.uk/money/spend-save/property-ladder-bank-mum-dad-homes-houses-second-steppers-lloyds-bank-research-a7800636.html.

Independent. (2018a, May 18). UK Facing Its Biggest Housing Shortfall on Record with Backlog of 4m Homes, Research Shows. https://www.independent.co.uk/news/uk/home-news/housing-homeless-crisis-homes-a8356646.html.

Independent. (2018b, February 2). Labour Compulsory Purchase Orders: Could Forced Sales of Undeveloped Land Work and Is 'Land Banking' Really Happening? http://www.independent.co.uk/news/business/analysis-and-features/labour-compulsory-purchase-orders-could-work-undeveloped-land-landbanking-profit-council-housing-a8191671.html.

Independent Age. (2018). *Unsuitable, Insecure and Substandard Homes: The Barriers Faced by Older Private Renters*. London: Independent Age. https://www.independentage.org/unsuitable-insecure-and-substandard-homes-barriers-faced-by-older-private-renters.

Inman, P., & Walker, P. (2017, January 4). Gender Pay Gap Down to 5% Among UK Workers in Their 20s, Study Finds. *Guardian*. https://www. theguardian.com/society/2017/jan/04/gender-pay-gap-down-to-5-among-uk-workers-in-their-20s-study-finds.

Inside Housing. (2015, April 10). Pickles Blocks 9,200 Homes in Build Up to Election. https://www.insidehousing.co.uk/news/news/pickles-blocks-9200-homes-in-build-up-to-election-43297.

Inside Housing. (2017, October 18). Gauke: "Unacceptable" for Social Landlords to Evict Universal Credit Tenants. https://www.insidehousing. co.uk/home/gauke-unacceptable-for-social-landlords-to-evict-univer-sal-credit-tenants-52848.

Institute for Public Policy Research. (2018). *Beyond Eco: The Future of Fuel Poverty Support*. London: Institute for Public Policy Research. https://www. ippr.org/publications/beyond-eco.

Institute for Public Policy Research Commission on Social Justice. (2018a). *The Invisible Land: The Hidden Force Driving the UK's Unequal Economy and Broken Housing Market*. London: Institute for Public Policy Research. https://www.ippr.org/research/publications/the-invisible-land.

Institute for Public Policy Research Commission on Social Justice. (2018b). *Prosperity and Justice; A Plan for the New Economy: The Final Report of the IPPR Commission on Economic Justice*. London: Institute for Public Policy Research. https://www.ippr.org/files/2018-08/1535639099_prosperity-and-justice-ippr-2018.pdf.

Intergenerational Commission. (2017, September). *Home Affront: Housing Across the Generations*. London: Intergenerational Commission. http:// www.resolutionfoundation.org/publications/home-affront-housing-across-the-generations/.

Intergeneration Commission/Resolution Foundation. (2018). *A New Generational Contract: Final Report of the Intergeneration Commission*. London: Resolution Foundation. https://www.resolutionfoundation.org/ advanced/a-new-generational-contract/.

Intermediary Mortgage Lenders Association. (2014). *Reshaping Housing Tenure in the UK: The Role of Buy to Let*. London: Intermediary Mortgage Lenders Association. http://www.imla.org.uk/perch/resources/imla-reshaping-hous-ing-tenure-in-the-uk-the-role-of-buy-to-let-may-2014.pdf.

International Monetary Fund. (2017). *Global Housing Watch*. http://www.imf. org/external/research/housing/.

Ipsos/Mori. (2014). *Public are Positive Towards Contribution and Value of Social Housing*. London: Ipsos Mori. https://www.ipsos.com/ipsos-mori/en-uk/ public-are-positive-towards-contribution-and-value-social-housing.

Ipsos/Mori. (2015). *Attitudes Towards Green Belt Land Green Belt: Omnibus Survey, July & August, a Study for the Campaign to Protect Rural England.* https://www.ipsos-mori.com/researchpublications/researcharchive/3611/Attitudes-towards-Green-Belt-land.aspx.

Ipsos/Mori. (2016). *How Britain Voted in the 2016 EU Referendum.* https://www.ipsos.com/ipsos-mori/en-uk/how-britain-voted-2016-eu-referendum?language_content_entity=en-uk.

Ipsos/Mori. (2017). *How Britain Voted in the 2017 General Election.* https://www.ipsos.com/ipsos-mori/en-uk/how-britain-voted-2017-election.

Ipsos/Mori. (2018). *Brexit and the NHS Top Britons' Concerns, with Worry About Housing Rising.* https://www.ipsos.com/ipsos-mori/en-uk/brexit-and-nhs-top-britons-concerns-worry-about-housing-rising.

Javid, S. (2016, October 10). *Hansard,* vol. 615, col. 976. https://hansard.parliament.uk/Commons/2016-10.../NeighbourhoodPlanningBill.

Javid, S. (2017a). *Sajid Javid's Speech to the National Housing Federation Conference 2017.* https://www.gov.uk/government/speeches/sajid-javids-speech-to-the-national-housing-federation-conference-2017.

Javid, S. (2017b). *Oral Statement to Parliament: Local Housing Need.* https://www.gov.uk/government/speeches/local-housing-need.

Jenkins, S. (2006). *Thatcher & Sons: A Revolution in Three Acts.* London: Allen Lane.

Johnson, A. (2013, April 26). Social Housing Residents Told to Sign "Ambition" Plan as Part of Tenancies. *Independent.* http://www.independent.co.uk/news/uk/politics/social-housing-residents-told-to-sign-ambition-plan-as-part-of-tenancies-8590713.html.

Joint Council for the Welfare of Immigrants. (2017). *Passport Please: The Impact of Right to Rent Checks on Migrants and Ethnic Minorities in Britain.* London: Joint Council for the Welfare of Immigrants. https://www.jcwi.org.uk/sites/jcwi/files/201702/2017_02_13_JCWI%20Report_Passport%20Please.pdf.

Jones Lang LaSalle (JLL). (2016, February). *Scotland Residential Forecast, 2016: Rising to the Challenge.* http://residential.jll.co.uk/new-residential-thinking-home/research/scotland-residential-forecast-february-2016.

Jones, R. (2017, February 11). Welcome to Rabbit-Hutch Britain, Land of the Ever-Shrinking Home. *Guardian.* https://www.theguardian.com/money/2017/feb/11/welcome-rabbit-hutch-britain-land-ever-shrinking-home.

Jones, R. (2018, June 25). Single First-Time Buyer in London Needs 17 Years to Find 15% Deposit—Report. *Guardian.* https://www.theguardian.com/business/2018/jun/25/single-first-time-buyer-in-london-needs-17-years-to-find-15-deposit-report.

Joseph, K., & Sumption, J. (1979). *Equality*. London: John Murray.

Joseph Rowntree Foundation. (2017a). *Numbers in Poverty: Housing Tenure*. York: Joseph Rowntree Foundation. https://www.jrf.org.uk/data/numbers-poverty-housing-tenure.

Joseph Rowntree Foundation. (2017b). *Poverty Rate by Ethnicity*. York: Joseph Rowntree Foundation. https://www.jrf.org.uk/report/poverty-ethnicity-labour-market.

Joseph Rowntree Foundation. (2018). *UK Poverty 2018: A Comprehensive Analysis of Poverty Trends and Figures*. York: Joseph Rowntree Foundation. https://www.jrf.org.uk/report/uk-poverty-2018.

Joyce, R. (2017). *Housing Measures*. London: Institute for Fiscal Studies. https://www.ifs.org.uk/publications/10186.

Judge, L. (2017). *Helping or Hindering? The Latest on Help to Buy*. London: Resolution Foundation. http://www.resolutionfoundation.org/media/blog/helping-or-hindering-the-latest-on-help-to-buy/.

Kaszynska, P., Parkinson, J., & Fox, W. (2016). *Re-Thinking Neighbourhood Planning: From Consultation to Collaboration* (A ResPublica Green Paper). https://www.architecture.com/Files/RIBAHoldings/PolicyAndInternationalRelations/Policy/RIBAResPublica-Re-thinkingNeighbourhoodPlanning.pdf.

Keep, M. (2018a). *Country and Regional Public Sector Finances* (Briefing Paper No. 8027). London: House of Commons. https://researchbriefings.parliament.uk/ResearchBriefing/Summary/CBP-8027#fullreport.

Keep, M. (2018b). *Government Borrowing, Debt and Debt Interest: Historical Statistics and Forecasts* (Briefing Paper No. 05745). London: House of Commons. https://researchbriefings.parliament.uk/ResearchBriefing/Summary/SN05745.

Kent Business Intelligence Statistical Bulletin. (2016). *Estimated Residential Land Values: Kent Local Authorities as at 1st March 2015*. https://www.kent.gov.uk/__data/assets/pdf_file/0008/53882/Land-prices.pdf.

Knoll, K., Schularick, M., & Steger, T. (2015). *No Price Like Home: Global House Prices, 1870–2012*. http://eh.net/eha/wp-content/uploads/2015/05/Knoll.pdf.

Knowles, T. (2018, September 8). Help-to-Buy: Scheme Has Helped Biggest Developers to Double Profits. *Times*. https://www.thetimes.co.uk/article/help-to-buy-scheme-has-helped-biggest-developers-to-double-profits-759qq3h7m.

Köppe, S., & Searle, B. A. (2017). Housing, Wealth and Welfare Over the Life Course. In C. Dewilde & R. Ronald (Eds.), *Housing Wealth and Welfare* (pp. 85–107). Cheltenham: Edgar Allen.

Labour Party. (2017a). *Labour's New Deal on Housing*. London: Labour Party. https://labour.org.uk/wp-content/uploads/2017/10/Housing-Mini-Manifesto.pdf.

Labour Party. (2017b). *For the Many Not the Few: The Labour Party Manifesto*. London: Labour Party. http://www.labour.org.uk/page/-/Images/manifesto-2017/Labour%20Manifesto%202017.pdf.

Labour Party. (2018). *Housing For the Many: Labour Party Green Paper*. London: The Labour Party. https://labour.org.uk/issues/housing-for-the-many/.

Lambert, S. (2016, July 21). Osborne Made Britain's House Price Addiction Worse, It's Time for Hammond to Help Us Go Cold Turkey, Says Simon Lambert. *This Is Money*. http://www.thisismoney.co.uk/money/comment/article-3699739/Osborne-house-price-addiction-worse-Hammond-stop-it.html.

Laws, D. (2016). *Coalition: The Inside Story of the Conservative-Liberal Democrat Coalition Government*. London: Biteback Publishing.

Laws, D. (2017). *Coalition Diaries 2012–2015*. London: Biteback Publishing.

Leahy, P. (2018, April 12). Fix the UK Housing Problem to Help the Ailing Retail Sector. *Financial Times*. https://www.ft.com/content/ce944972-3c06-11e8-bcc8-cebcb81f1f90.

Lees, L. (2018, March 16). Challenging the Gentrification of Council Estates in London. *Urban Transformations*. http://www.urbantransformations.ox.ac.uk/blog/2018/challenging-the-gentrification-of-council-estates-in-london/.

Letwin, O. (2018a, March 9). *Letter to the Rt Hon Philip Hammond MP and The Rt Hon Sajid Javid MP*. https://www.gov.uk/government/uploads/system/uploads/attachment_data/file/689430/Build_Out_Review_letter_to_Cx_and_Housing_SoS.pdf.

Letwin, O. (2018b). *Independent Review of Build Out: Final Report* (Cm 9720). London: Secretary of State for Housing, Communities and Local Government. https://www.gov.uk/government/publications/independent-review-of-build-out-final-report.

Lewis, J. P. (1965). *Building Cycles and Britain's Growth*. London: Macmillan.

Liverpool Victoria Insurance. (2014). *Shrinking Family Home Drives a Surge in Overcrowding*. http://www.lv.com/about-us/press/article/shrinking-family-home-overcrowding.

Lloyd, G. (2016). Land Use Planning in Northern Ireland. In P. Shanks & D. Mullins (Eds.), *Housing in Northern Ireland* (pp. 129–140). London: Chartered Institute of Housing.

Lloyd George, D. (1909, July 30). *Speech at Edinburgh Castle.* London: Limehouse. https://archive.org/stream/lifeofdavidlloyd04dupauoft/lifeofda-vidlloyd04dupauoft_djvu.txt.

Lloyd George, D. (1918, November 24). *Prime Minister David Lloyd George, Speech in Wolverhampton.* http://ww1centenary.oucs.ox.ac.uk/body-and-mind/lloyd-georges-ministry-men/.

Lloyds Bank. (2018). *Equity Gains Help Second Steppers Fund the £136,000 Price Gap to Trade Up.* http://www.lloydsbankinggroup.com/globalassets/documents/media/press-releases/lloyds-bank/2018/030318_lb_ss1.pdf.

Local Government Association. (2017). *Confidence in New Builds Falls as Average House in England Will Have to Last 2,000 Years.* London: Local Government Association. https://www.local.gov.uk/about/news/confidence-new-builds-falls-average-house-england-will-have-last-2000-years.

Local Government Association. (2018a). *More Than 423,000 Homes with Planning Permission Waiting to Be Built.* London: Local Government Association. http://home.bt.com/news/uk-news/more-than-423000-homes-with-planning-permission-waiting-to-be-built-study-11364250837993.

Local Government Association. (2018b). *Ratio of Lower Quartile House Price to Lower Quartile Gross Annual (Workplace-Based) Earnings in Eilean Siar.* London: Local Government Association. http://lginform.local.gov.uk/reports/lgastandard?mod-area=S12000013&mod-group=AllSingleTierAnd-CountyLaInCountry_England&mod-metric=75&mod-type=namedCompa risonGroup.

Local Plans Expert Group. (2016). *Local Plans Expert Group: Report to the Secretary of State for Communities and Local Government.* London: Department for Communities and Local Government. https://www.gov.uk/government/uploads/system/uploads/attachment_data/file/508345/Local-plans-report-to-governement.pdf.

London Borough of Richmond Upon Thames. (2018). *Richmond Housing & Homelessness Strategy 2018–2023.* London: London Borough of Richmond Upon Thames. https://www.richmond.gov.uk/media/16179/housing_and_homelessness_strategy_2018_to_2023.pdf.

Lukes, S. (1997). Humiliation and the Politics of Identity. *Social Research, 64*(1), 36–51.

Lund, B. (2016). *Housing Politics in the United Kingdom: Power Planning and Protest.* Bristol: Policy Press.

Lund, B. (2017). *Understanding Housing Policy* (3rd ed.). Bristol: Policy Press.

Lupton, R. (2013). *Did Labour's Social Policy Programme Work?* London: Nuffield Foundation. http://www.nuffieldfoundation.org/news/did-labour%E2%80%99s-social-policy-programme-work.

Lyons, M. (Chair). (2014). *The Lyons Housing Review: Mobilising Across the Nation to Build the Homes Our Children Need.* London: Labour Party Forum. https://www.policyforum.labour.org.uk/uploads/editor/files/The_Lyons_Housing_Review_2.pdf.

Macbryde Homes. (2017). *£629 Worth of Savings to Be Made by Investing in Energy Efficient New Build Homes.* https://www.macbryde-homes.co.uk/energy-efficient-new-build-homes/.

Maclennan, D., & Gibb, K. (2018). *Brexit and Housing: Policy Briefing.* Heriot Watt University: UK Collaborative Centre for Housing Evidence. http://housingevidence.ac.uk/publications/policy-briefing-brexit-and-housing/.

Madden, D., & Marcuse, P. (2016, November 22). Whose Crisis? For the Oppressed, Housing Is Always in Crisis. *Verso.* https://www.versobooks.com/blogs/2962-whose-crisis-for-the-oppressed-housing-is-always-in-crisis.

Malpass, P. (1986). (Ed.). *The Housing Crisis.* London: Routledge.

Manchester Evening News. (2017a). *Andy Burnham Comes Out Against "Unfair and Disproportionate" Green Belt Master Plan.* http://www.manchestereveningnews.co.uk/news/greater-manchester-news/andy-burnham-green-belt-development-12441497.

Manchester Evening News. (2017b). *Could Huge Developments Planned for Green Belt Land Be Radically Scaled Back? Theresa May Reiterated the Tories' Promise That Protected Spaces Are "Safe in the Government's Hands".* http://www.manchestereveningnews.co.uk/news/greater-manchester-news/could-huge-developments-planned-green-12643835.

May, T. (2016a). *Statement from the New Prime Minister Theresa May.* London: Prime Minister's Office. https://www.gov.uk/government/speeches/statement-from-the-new-prime-minister-theresa-may.

May, T. (2016b). *Conservative Conference: Theresa May's Speech in Full.* www.bbc.co.uk/news/uk-politics-37563510.

May, T. (2017a). Foreword to *Fixing Our Broken Housing Market.* London: Department for Communities and Local Government. https://www.gov.uk/government/uploads/system/uploads/attachment_data/file/590464/Fixing_our_broken_housing_market_-_print_ready_version.pdf.

May, T. (2017b, June 22). *PM Commons Statement on Grenfell Tower.* https://www.gov.uk/government/speeches/pm-commons-statement-on-grenfell-tower-22-june-2017.

Mayor of London. (2013). *The 2013 London Strategic Housing Market Assessment: Part of the Evidence Base for the Mayor's London Plan.* London: Mayor of London. file:///C:/Users/User/Downloads/FALP%20SHMA%20 2013.pdf.

Mayor of London. (2017). *Housing in London: The Evidence Base for the Mayor's Housing Strategy.* London: Mayor of London. https://files.datapress. com/london/dataset/housing-london/2017-01-26T18:50:00/Housing-in-London-2017-report.pdf.

Mayor of London. (2018). *London Living Rent.* London: Mayor of London. https://www.london.gov.uk/what-we-do/housing-and-land/renting/london-living-rent.

McCann, P. (2017). *The UK Regional-National Economic Problem: Geography, Globalisation and Governance.* Abingdon: Routledge.

McGuiness, F. (2018a). *Household Incomes by Region* (Briefing Paper No. 8191). London: House of Commons. https://researchbriefings.parliament. uk/ResearchBriefing/Summary/CBP-8191.

McGuiness, F. (2018b). *Poverty in the UK: Statistics* (Briefing Paper No. 7096). London: House of Commons. https://researchbriefings.parliament.uk/ ResearchBriefing/Summary/SN07096.

McGuiness, F. (2018c). *Income Inequality in the UK* (Briefing Paper No. 7484). London: House of Commons. https://researchbriefings.parliament.uk/ ResearchBriefing/Summary/CBP-7484#fullreport.

McKee, K., Muir, J., & Moore, T. (2017). Housing Policy in the UK: The Importance of Spatial Nuance. *Housing Studies, 32*(1), 60–72.

McKee, K., & Soaita, A. M. (2018). *The 'Frustrated' Housing Aspirations of Generation Rent.* UK Collaborative Centre for Housing Evidence, University of Glasgow. http://housingevidence.ac.uk/wpcontent/uploads/2018/08/R2018_ 06_01_Frustrated_Housing_Aspirations_of_Gen_Rent.pdf.

McPeake, J. (2014). *The Changing Face of Housing Need in Northern Ireland.* https:// www.qub.ac.uk/research-centres/TheInstituteofSpatialandEnvironmentalPlanning/ filestore/Filetoupload,759315,en.pdf.

Meadowcroft, J. (2012). Community Politics. *Liberal History: The Website of the Liberal Democrat History Group.* http://www.liberalhistory.org.uk/ history/community-politics/.

Meen, G. (2018). *How Should Housing Affordability Be Measured?* UK Collaborative Centre for Housing Evidence. http://housingevidence.ac.uk/wp-content/uploads/2018/09/R2018_02_01_How_to_measure_affordability.pdf.

Merrett, S. (1979). *State Housing in Britain*. Abingdon: Routledge & Kegan Paul.

Merrett, S., with Gray, F. (1982). *Owner-Occupation in Britain*. Abingdon: Routledge & Kegan Paul.

Metro. (2017, September 20). *Rogue Landlord Squeezes 35 Men into Three-Bedroom Home*. http://metro.co.uk/2017/09/20/rogue-landlord-squeezes-35-men-into-three-bedroom-home-6942510/.

MHCLG. (2018b). *Live Tables on Homelessness*. London: MHCLG. https://www.gov.uk/government/statistical-data-sets/live-tables-on-homelessness.

MHCLG. (2018c). *English Housing Survey 2016 to 2017: Headline Report, Section 1, Household Tables, Section 2, Housing Stock Tables, Figure 2.3*. London: MHCLG. https://www.gov.uk/government/statistics/english-housing-survey-2016-to-2017-headline-report.

MHCLG. (2018d). *Dwelling Condition and Safety*. London: MHCLG. https://www.gov.uk/government/statistical-data-sets/dwelling-condition-and-safety.

MHCLG. (2018e). *Live Tables on House Building: New Build Dwellings*. London: MHCLG. https://www.gov.uk/government/statistical-data-sets/live-tables-on-house-building.

MHCLG. (2018f). *Components of Housing Supply: Net Additional Dwellings: England 2006–7 to 2016–7*. London: MHCLG. https://www.gov.uk/government/statistical-data-sets/live-tables-on-net-supply-of-housing.

MHGLG. (2018g). *Table 120: Components of Housing Supply: Net Additional Dwellings, England 2006/7 to 2017/8*. London: MHGLG. https://www.gov.uk/government/statistical-data-sets/live-tables-on-net-supply-of-housing.

MHCLG. (2018h). *Affordable Housing Supply: April 2017 to March 2018: England*. London: MHGLG. https://assets.publishing.service.gov.uk/government/uploads/system/uploads/attachment_data/file/758389/Affordable_Housing_Supply_2017-18.pdf.

MHCLG. (2018i). *Social Housing Lettings: April 2017 to March 2018*. London, UK: MHCLG. https://assets.publishing.service.gov.uk/government/uploads/system/uploads/attachment_data/file/759738/Social_Housing_Lettings_April2017_to_March2018_England.pdf.

MHCLG. (2018j). *Analysis of the Determinants of House Price Changes*. London: MHCLG. https://assets.publishing.service.gov.uk/government/uploads/system/uploads/attachment_data/file/699846/OFF_SEN_Ad_Hoc_SFR_House_prices_v_PDF.pdf#.

MHCLG. (2018k). *Tenure Trends and Cross Tenure Analysis.* London: MHCLG. https://www.gov.uk/government/statistical-data-sets/tenure-trends-and-cross-tenure-analysis.

MHCLG. (2018l). *English Housing Survey 2016: Energy Efficiency.* London: MHCLG. https://www.gov.uk/government/statistics/english-housing-survey-2016-energy-efficiency.

MHCLG. (2018m). *English Housing Survey 2016 to 2017: Home Ownership.* London: MHCLG. https://www.gov.uk/government/statistics/english-housing-survey-2016-to-2017-home-ownership.

MHCLG. (2018n). *Attitudes and Satisfaction.* London: MHCLG. https://www.gov.uk/government/statistical-data-sets/attitudes-and-satisfaction.

MHCLG. (2018o). *Social and Private Renters.* London: MHCLG. https://www.gov.uk/government/statistical-data-sets/social-and-private-renters.

MHCLG. (2018p). *Stock of Non-decent Homes, England 2001–2017.* https://www.gov.uk/government/uploads/system/uploads/attachment.../LT_119.xlsx.

MHCLG. (2018q). *English Housing Survey 2016 to 2017: Private Rented Sector.* London: MHCLG. https://www.gov.uk/government/statistics/english-housing-survey-2016-to-2017-private-rented-sector.

MHCLG. (2018r). *Tenure Trends and Cross Tenure Analysis.* London: MHCLG. https://www.gov.uk/government/statistical-data-sets/tenure-trends-and-cross-tenure-analysis.

MHCLG. (2018s). *Housing Need Assessment.* London: MHCLG. https://www.gov.uk/guidance/housing-and-economic-development-needs-assessments.

MHCLG. (2018t). *National Planning Policy Framework.* London: MHCLG. https://assets.publishing.service.gov.uk/government/uploads/system/uploads/attachment_data/file/728643/Revised_NPPF_2018.pdf.

MHCLG. (2018u). *Housebuilding Completions Per 1000 Households.* London: MHCLG. http://opendatacommunities.org/data/house-building/completions-ratio/by-category.

MHCLG. (2018v). *A New Deal for Social Housing* (Cm 9571). London: MHCLG. https://assets.publishing.service.gov.uk/government/uploads/system/uploads/attachment_data/file/733635/A_new_deal_for_social_housing_print_ready_version.pdf.

MHCLG. (2018w). *Live Tables on Rents, Lettings and Tenancies.* London: MHCLG. https://www.gov.uk/government/statistical-data-sets/live-tables-on-rents-lettings-and-tenancies.

MHCLG. (2018x). *Social and Private Renters: Demographic and Economic Data on Social and Private Renters.* London: MHCLG. https://www.gov.uk/government/statistical-data-sets/social-and-private-renters.

MHCLG. (2018y). *Help to Buy (Equity Loan Scheme) and Help to Buy: NewBuy Statistics: April 2013 to 31 December 2017.* London: MHCLG. https://www.gov.uk/government/statistics/help-to-buy-equity-loan-scheme-and-help-to-buy-newbuy-statistics-april-2013-to-31-december-2017.

MHCLG. (2018z). *Social Housing Lettings: April 2016 to March 2017, England.* London: MHCLG. https://assets.publishing.service.gov.uk/government/uploads/system/uploads/attachment_data/file/677489/Social_housing_lettings_in_England_2016-17.pdf.

MHCLG. (2018aa). *Supporting Housing Delivery Through Developer Contributions: Reforming Developer Contributions to Affordable Housing and Infrastructure.* London: MHCLG. https://assets.publishing.service.gov.uk/government/uploads/system/uploads/attachment_data/file/691182/Developer_Contributions_Consultation.pdf.

MHCLG. (2019). *English Private Landlord Survey 2018: main report—Findings from the English Private Landlord Survey 2018.* London: MHCLG. https://www.gov.uk/government/publications/english-private-landlord-survey-2018-main-report.

Mill, J. S. (1848). *Principles of Political Economy with Some of Their Applications to Social Philosophy.* http://www.econlib.org/library/Mill/mlP.html.

Millán, I. R. (2014). *Securitization in Spain: Past Developments and Future Trends.* https://www.bbvaresearch.com/wp-content/uploads/2014/09/EW_Securitization-in-Spain1.pdf.

Milne, A. (2009). *The Fall of the House of Credit: What Went Wrong in Banking and What Can Be Done to Repair the Damage?* Cambridge: Cambridge University Press.

Ministry of Housing, Communities and Local Government (MHCLG). (2018a). *English Housing Survey 2016 to 2017: Headline Report.* London: MHCLG. https://www.gov.uk/government/statistics/english-housing-survey-2016-to-2017-headline-report.

Migration Advisory Committee. (2018). *EEA Migration in the UK: Final Report.* London: Migration Advisory Committee. https://assets.publishing.service.gov.uk/government/uploads/system/uploads/attachment_data/file/740991/Final_EEA_report_to_go_to_WEB.PDF.

Migration Observatory at the University of Oxford. (2017). *Migrants and Housing in the UK: Experiences and Impacts.* Oxford: Migration Observatory at the University of Oxford. https://migrationobservatory.ox.ac.uk/resources/briefings/migrants-and-housing-in-the-uk-experiences-and-impacts/.

Migration Observatory at the University of Oxford. (2018). *Net Migration in the UK*. Oxford: Migration Observatory at the University of Oxford. https://migrationobservatory.ox.ac.uk/resources/briefings/long-term-international-migration-flows-to-and-from-the-uk/.

Migration Watch. (2014). *Housing Demand in London*. https://www.migrationwatchuk.org/briefing-paper/339.

Minford, P., Peel, M., & Ashton, P. (1987). *The Housing Morass: Regulation, Immobility and Unemployment*. London: Institute for Economic Affairs.

Morgan, K. G. (1971). *The Age of Lloyd George: The Liberal Party and British Politics*. London: Allen & Unwin.

Morphet, J., & Clifford, B. (2017). *Local Authority Direct Provision of Housing*. London: Royal Town Planning Institute/National Planning Forum. http://rtpi.org.uk/media/2619006/Local-authority-direct-provision-of-housing.pdf.

Morton, A. (2016, July 21). How to Deliver a One Nation Housing Policy. *Conservative Home*. https://www.conservativehome.com/thetorydiary/2016/07/delivering-a-one-nation-housing-policy.html.

Mount, F. (2005). *Mind the Gap: The New Class Divide in Britain*. London: Short Books.

Moyne, W. E. (Chair). (1933). *Report of the Departmental Committee on Housing* (Cmd 4397). London: HMSO. https://www.conservativehome.com/thetorydiary/2016/07/delivering-a-one-nation-housing-policy.html.

Mulheirn, I. (2017, November 13). Parrots, Housing and Redistribution. *Financial Times*. https://medium.com/@ian.mulheirn/parrots-housing-and-redistribution-419b36a72e52.

Mulheirn, I. (2018, March 23). *Two Housing Crises*. London: Resolution Foundation. http://www.resolutionfoundation.org/media/blog/two-housing-crises/.

Munro, M. (2018). House Price Inflation in the News: A Critical Discourse Analysis of Newspaper Coverage in the UK. *Housing Studies, 33*(7), 1085–1105.

Murie, A. (2008). *Moving Homes: The Housing Corporation 1964–2008*. London: Politicos.

Murray, C. K. (2010). *Housing Investment Is Not Productive*. http://www.fresheconomicthinking.com/2010/02/housing-investment-is-not-productive.html.

Nairn, D. (2016). *Ebenezer Howards Garden City Concept*. http://discoveringurbanism.blogspot.co.uk/2009/06/ebenezer-howards-garden-city-concept.html.

Nathaniel Litchfield & Partners. (2016). *Start to Finish: How Quickly Do Large-Scale Housing Sites Deliver?* https://lichfields.uk/media/1728/start-to-finish.pdf.

Nathaniel Litchfields and Partners. (2018). Local Choices?: Housing Delivery Through Neighbourhood Plans. *Insight May*. https://lichfields.uk/media/4128/local-choices_housing-delivery-through-neighbourhood-plans.pdf.

National Audit Office. (2013). *The New Homes Bonus*. London: National Audit Office. https://www.nao.org.uk/wp-content/uploads/2013/03/10122-001-New-Homes-Bonus_HC-1047.pdf.

National Audit Office. (2017). *Taxpayer Support for UK Banks*. London: National Audit Office. https://www.nao.org.uk/highlights/taxpayer-support-for-uk-banks-faqs/.

National Audit Office. (2018, June 15). *Rolling Out Universal Credit*. HC 1123 SESSION 2017–2019. London: National Audit Office. https://www.nao.org.uk/report/rolling-out-universal-credit/.

National Centre for Social Research. (2013). *British Social Attitudes 28*. London: National Centre for Social Research.

National Centre for Social Research. (2016). Social Class Identity, Awareness and Political Attitudes: Why Are We Still Working Class? In *British Social Attitudes 33* (pp. 1–17). London: National Centre for Social Research. http://www.bsa.natcen.ac.uk/latest-report/british-social-attitudes-33/introduction.aspx.

National Housing Federation. (2017). *Public Expenditure on Housing: The Shift from Capital Spend to Housing Allowances: A European Trend?* London: National Housing Federation. www.housing.org.uk/resource-library/browse/public-expenditure-on-housing-european-trends/.

National Housing Federation. (2018a). *Demographic Change and Housing Wealth*. https://www.housing.org.uk/resource-library/browse/demographic-change-and-housing-wealth/.

National Housing Federation. (2018b). *Home Truths 2017/18: The Housing Market in London*. London: National Housing Federation. https://www.housing.org.uk/resource-library/home-truths/.

National Housing Planning Advice Unit. (2007). *Affordability Matters*. London: National Housing Planning Advice Unit. http://www.wiltshire.gov.uk/corestrategydocument?directory=Studies%2C%20Surveys%20and%20Assessments&fileref=3.

National Infrastructure Commission. (2017a). *Congestion, Capacity, Carbon—Priorities for National Infrastructure*. London: National Infrastructure Commission. https://www.nic.org.uk/wp-content/uploads/Congestion-Capacity-Carbon_-Priorities-for-national-infrastructure.pdf.

National Infrastructure Commission. (2017b). *Interim Report on the Cambridge—Milton Keynes Oxford Corridor*. London: National Infrastructure Commission. https://www.nic.org.uk/publications/national-infrastructure-commissions-interim-report-cambridge-milton-keynes-oxford-corridor/.

Nationwide. (2017). *House Price Index: By Property Type*. https://www.nationwide.co.uk/about/house-price-index/download-data#xtab:regional-quarterly-series-by-property-age-group-data-available-from-1991-onwards.

Nationwide. (2018). *Affordability Estimates*. https://www.nationwide.co.uk/about/house-price-index/download-data.

National Landlords Association. (2017). *General Election 2017, Landlords Are Voting*. https://docs.google.com/forms/d/e/1FAIpQLSdfZq28hNjCrNhjBi0-dmw5M8hattvG0mxCztBSyAIVkzVoRg/viewanalytics.

Neimietz, K. (2016). *To Solve the Housing Crisis, We Must Take on NIMBYs and Abolish the Greenbelt*. London: Institute for Economic Affairs. https://iea.org.uk/blog/to-solve-the-housing-crisis-we-must-take-on-nimbys-and-abolish-the-greenbelt.

Nemeth, H. (2017, November 22). Autumn Budget 2017: "Buy-to-Leave" Landlords Face Empty Homes Tax. *Moneywise*. https://www.moneywise.co.uk/news/2017-11-22/autumn-budget-2017-buy-to-leave-landlords-face-empty-homes-tax.

New Economics Foundation. (2015). *Inquiry into the Economics of the UK Housing Market: Written Evidence from the New Economics Foundation*. London: King's College. https://kclpure.kcl.ac.uk/portal/en/publications/inquiry-into-the-economics-of-the-uk-housingmarket(0574ae6f-7b80-4c5d-8881-212f7fea17ea).html.

New Economics Foundation. (2018a). *How the Broken Land Market Drives Our Housing Crisis*. London: New Economics Foundation. https://neweconomics.org/2018/04/broken-land-market.

New Economics Foundation. (2018b). *What Lies Beneath: How to Fix the Broken Land System at the Heart of Our Housing Crisis*. London: New Economics Foundation. https://neweconomics.org/uploads/files/what-lies-beneath.pdf.

New Policy Institute. (2016). *A Nation of Renters: How England Moved from Secure Family Homes Towards Rundown Rentals*. London: New Policy Institute. http://www.npi.org.uk/publications/housing-and-homelessness/nation-renters-how-england-moved-secure-family-homes-towards/.

NHS England. (2016). *Healthy New Towns*. https://www.england.nhs.uk/ourwork/innovation/healthy-new-towns/.

Niemietz, K. (2017). *How the Housing Crisis has Created a Generation of Socialists*. London: Institute for Economic Affairs. https://iea.org.uk/how-the-housing-crisis-has-created-a-generation-of-socialists/.

Norges Bank. (2015). *Global Market Trends and Their Impact on Real Estate* (Discussion Note 2). https://www.nbim.no/contentassets/c199863ae83749 16ac15e780662db960/nbim_discussionnotes_2-15.pdf.

Northern Ireland Department for Communities. (2018). *Northern Ireland Housing Statistics 2017–8*. Belfast: Northern Ireland Executive. https://www.communities-ni.gov.uk/publications/northern-ireland-housing-statistics-2017-18.

Northern Ireland Department for Social Development. (2014). *Empty Homes Strategy and Action Plan*. Belfast: Northern Ireland Executive. https://www.communities-ni.gov.uk/publications/northern-ireland-empty-homes-strategy-and-action-plan-2013-%E2%80%93-2018.

Northern Ireland Housing Executive. (2011). *More Than Bricks: Forty Years of the Housing Executive*. Belfast: Northern Ireland Executive. https://www.nihe.gov.uk/more_than_bricks.pdf.

Northern Ireland Housing Executive. (2017). *Types of Grant Available*. Belfast: Northern Ireland Executive. http://www.nihe.gov.uk/index/benefits/home_improvement_grants/grants_available.htm.

Northumberland Knowledge. (2015). *Research Report: English Indices of Deprivation 2015: Northumberland*. https://www.northumberland.gov.uk/NorthumberlandCountyCouncil/media/Northumberland-Knowledge/NK%20place/Indices%20of%20deprivation/Northumberland-ID-2015.pdf.

Nozick, R. (1981). *Anarchy, State and Utopia*. London: Wiley-Blackwell.

Obolenskaya, P., & Burchardt, T. (2016). *Public and Private Welfare Activity in England*. London: London School of Economics, Centre for Analysis of Social Exclusion. http://sticerd.lse.ac.uk/dps/case/cp/casepaper193.pdf.

Office for Budget Responsibility. (2015). *Economic and Fiscal Outlook—November 2015*. London: Office for Budget Responsibility. http://budgetresponsibility.org.uk/docs/dlm_uploads/EFO_November__2015.pdf.

Office for National Statistics (ONS). (2003). *Labour Force Survey*. London: Office for National Statistics. https://discover.ukdataservice.ac.uk/catalogue/?sn= 5422.

O'Grady, S. (2016, August 2). Newsflash, Young People: Owning Your Own Home Isn't a Human Right—Your Sense of Entitlement Won't Solve This Crisis. *Independent*. http://www.independent.co.uk/voices/newsflash-young-people-owning-your-own-home-isnt-a-human-right-leave-your-entitle-ment-at-the-door-a7167961.html.

Oishi, S., & Talhelm, T. (2012). Residential Mobility: What Psychological Research Reveals. *Current Directions in Psychological Science, 21*(1), 425–430. http://journals.sagepub.com/doi/full/10.1177/0963721412460675.

ONS. (2012). *Ethnicity and National Identity in England and Wales: 2011*. London: Office for National Statistics. https://www.ons.gov.uk/peoplepopulationandcommunity/culturalidentity/ethnicity/articles/ethnicityandnationalidentityinenglandandwales/2012-12-11.

ONS. (2013). *Nomis Census 2011 Table Links*. London: Office for National Statistics. https://www.nomisweb.co.uk/census/2011/all_tables?release= 3.2a.

ONS. (2014). *Overcrowding and Under-Occupation in England and Wales*. London: Office for National Statistics. https://www.basw.co.uk/system/files/resources/basw_120028-2_1.pdf.

ONS. (2017a). *International Migration and the Changing Nature of Housing in England—What Does the Available Evidence Show?* London: Office for National Statistics. https://www.ons.gov.uk/peoplepopulationandcommunity/populationandmigration/internationalmigration/articles/internationalmigra-tionandthechangingnatureofhousinginenglandwhatdoestheavailableevidence-show/2017-05-25.

ONS. (2017b). *National Population Projections: 2016-Based Statistical Bulletin*. London: Office for National Statistics. https://www.ons.gov.uk/peoplepop-ulationandcommunity/populationandmigration/populationprojections/bulletins/nationalpopulationprojections/2016basedstatisticalbulletin.

ONS. (2018a). *Wealth in Great Britain Wave 5: 2014 to 2016: Main Results from the Fifth Wave of the Wealth and Assets Survey Covering the Period July 2014 to June 2016*. London: Office for National Statistics. https://www.ons.gov.uk/peoplepopulationandcommunity/personalandhouseholdfinances/incomeandwealth/bulletins/wealthingreatbritainwave5/2014to2016.

ONS. (2018b). *Migration Statistics Quarterly Report: July 2018 (Rescheduled from May 2018)*. London: Office for National Statistics. https://www.ons.gov.uk/peoplepopulationandcommunity/populationandmigration/

internationalmigration/bulletins/migrationstatisticsquarterlyreport/
july2018revisedfrommaycoveringtheperiodtodecember2017.

ONS. (2018c). *House Price to Workplace-Based Earnings Ratio.* London: Office
for National Statistics. https://www.ons.gov.uk/peoplepopulationandcommunity/
housing/datasets/ratioofhousepricetoworkplacebasedearningslowerquartile-
andmedian.

ONS. (2018d). *Property Wealth: Wealth in Great Britain.* https://www.ons.
gov.uk/peoplepopulationandcommunity/personalandhouseholdfinances/
incomeandwealth/datasets/propertywealthwealthingreatbritain.

ONS. (2018e). *The National Statistics Socio-Economic Classification
(NS-SEC).* London: Office for National Statistics. https://www.ons.
gov.uk/methodology/classificationsandstandards/otherclassifications/
thenationalstatisticssocioeconomicclassificationnssecrebasedonsoc2010.

ONS. (2018f). *The UK National Balance Sheet Estimates: 2018.* London:
Office for National Statistics. https://www.ons.gov.uk/economy/
nationalaccounts/uksectoraccounts/bulletins/nationalbalancesheet/2018.

ONS. (2018g). *Population of the UK by Country of Birth and Nationality: July
2017 to June 2018.* London: Office for National Statistics. https://www.ons.
gov.uk/peoplepopulationandcommunity/populationandmigration/inter-
nationalmigration/bulletins/ukpopulationbycountryofbirthandnationality/
july2017tojune2018.

ONS. (2018h). *Fuel Poverty Trends 2018: Long Term Trends Under the Low
Income High Costs Indicator (2003–2016 Data).* London: Office for National
Statistics. https://www.gov.uk/government/statistics/fuel-poverty-trends-2018.

Opinion Research Services. (2016). *The Outer North East London Strategic
Market Assessment.* https://www.redbridge.gov.uk/media/3006/lbr-2011-
north-east-london-shma-executive-summary-2016.pdf.

Ortalo-Magné, F., & Prat, A. (2007, January). *The Political Economy of
Housing Supply: Homeowners, Workers, and Voters* (Discussion Paper
No. TE/2007/514). London School of Economics and Political
Science: Suntory-Toyota International Centers for Economics
and Related Disciplines. http://citeseerx.ist.psu.edu/viewdoc/
download?doi=10.1.1.368.6964&rep=rep1&type=pdf.

Orwell, G. (1939). *Coming Up for Air.* London: Secker & Warburg.

Osborne, G. (2015a). *Chancellor George Osborne's Spending Review and
Autumn Statement 2015 Speech.* www.gov.uk/government/speeches/chan-
cellor-george-osbornes-spending-review-and-autumn-statement-2015-
speech.

Osborne, G. (2015b). *Chancellor George Osborne's Summer Budget 2015 Speech.* www.gov.uk/government/speeches/chancellor-george-osbornessummer-budget-2015-speech.

Oxford Dictionaries. (2017a). https://en.oxforddictionaries.com/definition/crisis.

Oxford Dictionaries. (2017b). https://en.oxforddictionaries.com/definition/ethnicity.

Oxford Economics. (2016). *Forecasting UK House Prices and Homeownership: A Report for the Redfern Review into the Decline of Homeownership.* Oxford: Oxford Economics. https://www.oxfordeconomics.com/my-oxford/projects/351906.

Papworth, T. (2015). *The Green Noose.* London: Adam Smith Institute. https://www.adamsmith.org/research/the-green-noose.

Paris, C. (Ed.). (2001). *Housing in Northern Ireland—And Comparisons with the Republic of Ireland.* London and Coventry: Chartered Institute of Housing.

Paris, C. (2017a). The Super-Rich and Transnational Markets: Asians Buying Australian Housing. In R. Forrest, S. Y. Koh, & B. Wissink (Eds.), *Cities and the Super-Rich: Real Estate, Elite Practices and Urban Political Economies* (The Contemporary City) (pp. 63–84). Abingdon: Routledge.

Paris, C. (2017b). The Residential Spaces of the Super-Rich. In I. Hay & J. V. Beaverstock (Eds.), *Handbook on Wealth and the Super-Rich* (pp. 244–263). Cheltenham: Edward Elgar.

Park, J. (2017). *One Hundred Years of Housing Space Standards: What Next?* http://housingspacestandards.co.uk/.

Park, A., Bryson, C., & Curtice, J. (2015). *British Social Attitudes, 2014.* London: National Centre for Social Research. http://www.bsa.natcen.ac.uk/media/38893/bsa31_full_report.pdf.

Pathé News. (1923). *The Housing Problem By-Election. 1923.* https://www.youtube.com/watch?v=zhORGbDEGvM.

Perry, J. (2014). *Why Is It Important to Change Local Authority Borrowing Rules?* Coventry: Chartered Institute of Housing. http://www.cih.org/resources/PDF/Policy%20free%20download%20pdfs/Policy%20essay%209%20-%20Why%20is%20it%20important%20to%20change%20local%20authority%20borrowing%20rules%20-%20July%202014.pdf.

Perry, J. (2018, March 19). Developers Are Skimping on Low-Cost Housing. Time to Get Tough. *Guardian.* https://www.theguardian.com/housing-network/2018/mar/19/affordable-homes-low-cost-rent-uk-planning-policy-government-developers.

Perry, J., & Stephens, M. (2018). How the Purpose of Social Housing Has Changed and Is Changing. In M. Stephens, J. Perry, S. Wilcox, P. Williams, & G. Young (Eds.), *UK Housing Review* (pp. 29–39). London: Chartered Institute of Housing.

Pickles, E. (2013). *Pickles Attacks Labour's Housing Record in Wales.* London: Conservative Home. http://conservativehome.blogs.com/localgovernment/2013/05/pickles-attacks-labours-housing-recordin-wales.html.

Pickard, J., & Evans, J. (2017, January 5). UK Housing White Paper Risks "Huge Backlash". *Financial Times.* https://www.ft.com/content/3bffa61a-d280-11e6-b06b-680c49b4b4c0.

Piketty, T. (2013). *Capital in the Twenty-First Century.* Cambridge, MA: The Belknap Press of Harvard University.

Pittini, A. (2012, January). *Housing Affordability in the EU: Current Situation and Recent Trends.* Research Briefing, Year 5, No. 1. CECODHAS Housing Europe's Observatory. www.housingeurope.eu/file/41/download.

Policy Exchange. (2018). *Building More, Building Beautiful: How Design and Style Can Unlock the Housing Crisis.* London: Policy Exchange. https://policyexchange.org.uk/wp-content/uploads/2018/06/Building-More-Building-Beautiful.pdf.

Posen, A. (2013, July 26). The Cult of Home Ownership Is Dangerous and Damaging. *Financial Times.* https://www.ft.com/content/00bf5968-f518-11e2-b4f8-00144feabdc0.

Pringle, J. C. (1929). Slums and Eugenics. Review of *The Slum Problem* by B.S. Townroe. *Eugenics Review, 20*(4), 273–274.

Preece, J. (2018). *Is It Time For a Right to Affordable Housing?* UK Collaborative Centre for Housing Evidence. http://housingevidence.ac.uk/is-it-time-for-a-right-to-affordable-housing/.

Rae, A. (2015, July 9). *Too Many Flats, Not Enough Houses? The Geography of London's New Housing.* London: Royal Statistical Society. https://www.statslife.org.uk/economics-and-business/2360-too-many-flats-not-enough-houses-the-geography-of-london-s-new-housing.

Rampen, J. (2016, August 2). The Property-Owning Democracy Is Dead—So Build One for Renters Instead. *New Statesman.* http://www.newstatesman.com/politics/staggers/2016/08/property-owning-democracy-dead-so-build-one-for-renters-instead.

Rawls, J. (1971). *A Theory of Justice.* Harvard: Harvard University Press.

Rees-Mogg, W. (2018, July 23). We Must Build More Houses—Or Both the Nation and the Tories Will Suffer the Consequences. *Telegraph.*

https://www.telegraph.co.uk/news/2018/07/23/must-build-houses-nation-tories-will-suffer-consequences/.

Renwick, C. (2017). *Bread for All: The Origins of the Welfare State.* London: Allen Lane.

Resolution Foundation. (2016a). *VOTEY McVOTEFACE: Understanding the Growing Turnout Gap Between the Generations.* London: Resolution Foundation. http://www.resolutionfoundation.org/publications/votey-mcvoteface-understanding-the-growing-turnout-gap-between-the-generations/.

Resolution Foundation. (2016b). *The Importance of Place: Explaining the Characteristics Underpinning the Brexit Vote Across Different Parts of the UK.* London: Resolution Foundation. https://www.resolutionfoundation.org/app/uploads/2016/07/Brexit-vote-v4.pdf.

Resolution Foundation. (2017a). *Diverse Outcomes: Living Standards by Ethnicity.* London: Resolution Foundation. http://www.resolutionfoundation.org/publications/diverse-outcomes-living-standards-by-ethnicity/.

Resolution Foundation. (2017b). *Living Standards 2017: The Past, Present and Possible Future of UK Incomes.* London: Resolution Foundation.

Resolution Foundation. (2017c). *Freshly Squeezed: Autumn Budget 2017 Response.* London: Resolution Foundation. http://www.resolutionfoundation.org/publications/freshly-squeezed-autumn-budget-2017-response/.

Resolution Foundation. (2018a). *The Future Fiscal Cost of 'Generation Rent'.* London: Resolution Foundation. http://www.resolutionfoundation.org/media/blog/the-future-fiscal-cost-of-generation-rent/.

Resolution Foundation. (2018b). *How to Spend It, Autumn 2018 Budget Response.* London: Resolution Foundation. https://www.resolutionfoundation.org/publications/how-to-spend-it-autumn-2018-budget-response/.

Rhodes, D. (2015). The Fall and Rise of the Private Rented Sector in England. *Built Environment, 41*(2), 258–270.

Rivera, L., & Lee, S. (2016). *Average Age of First-Time Buyers Rises to 30 in the UK and 32 in London.* London: Homes and Property. https://www.homesandproperty.co.uk/property-news/buying/first-time-buyers/average-age-of-firsttime-buyers-rises-to-30-in-the-uk-and-32-in-london-a102966.html.

Roberts, A. (1999). *Salisbury: Victorian Titan.* London: Phoenix.

Robinson, M. (2018, January 29). *How Much Use Is a Magic Money Tree Anyway?* London: BBC. http://www.bbc.co.uk/news/business-42835758.

Rognlie, M. (2014, June 15). *A Note on Piketty and Diminishing Returns to Capital.* http://gabriel-zucman.eu/files/teaching/Rognlie14.pdf.

Rousseau, J. J. (1762). *On the Social Contract.* Amsterdam. https://www.ucc.ie/archive/hdsp/Rousseau_contrat-social.pdf.

Rowntree, S. (1901). *Poverty: A Study in Town Life*. London: Macmillan and Co.

Royal Commission on the Housing of the Working Classes. (1885). *Reports, with Minutes of Evidence*. London: HMSO.

Royal Institute of Chartered Surveyors. (2018). *Assessing the Impacts of Extending Permitted Development Rights to Office-to-Residential Change of Use in England*. London: RICS. http://www.rics.org/Global/PDR%20 Research%20trust%20reports/22790%20RICS%20Assessing%20 Impact%20of%20Office-to-Residential%20REPORT-WEB%20(without%20notice).pdf.

Rugg, J., & Rhodes, D. (2008). *Review of Private Sector Rented Housing*. York: Centre for Housing Policy, University of York.

Rugg, J., & Rhodes, D. (2018). *The Evolving Private Rented Sector: Its Contribution and Potential*. York: Centre for Housing Policy, University of York. http://www.nationwidefoundation.org.uk/wp-content/uploads/ 2018/09/Private-Rented-Sector-report.pdf.

Ryan-Collins, J. (2018). *Why Can't You Afford a Home?* Bristol: Policy Press.

Ryan-Collins, J., Lloyd, T., & Macfarlane, L. (2016). *Rethinking the Economics of Land and Housing*. London: Zed Books.

Sánchez, A. C., & Johansson, A. (2011). *The Price Responsiveness of Housing Supply in OECD Countries*. Paris: Organisation for Economic Co-Operation and Development. http://www.oecd-ilibrary.org/economics/the-price-responsiveness-of-housing-supply-in-oecd-countries_5kg-k9qhrnn33-en?crawler=true.

Sandbrook, D. (2012). *Seasons in the Sun: The Battle for Britain 1974–1979*. London: Allen Lane.

Sassen, S. (2012). *Cities in the World Economy*. London: Sage.

Saunders, P. (2016). *Restoring a Nation of Home Owners: What Went Wrong with Home Ownership in Britain, and How to Start Putting It Right*. London: Civitas. www.civitas.org.uk/content/files/Restoring-a-Nation-of-Home-Owners.pdf.

Savage, M., Cunningham, N., Devine, F., Friedman, S., Laurison, D., Mckenzie, L., et al. (2015). *Social Class in the 21st Century*. London: Pelican.

Savills. (2017a, January 18). *UK Homes Worth a Record £6.8 Trillion as Private Housing Wealth Exceeds £5 Trillion*. http://www.savills.co.uk/_news/article/72418/213407-0/1/2017/uk-homes-worth-a-record-%C2%A36.8-trillion-as-private-housing-wealth-exceeds-%C2%A35-trillion.

Savills. (2017b). *Spotlight 2017: Investing to Solve the Housing Crisis*. London: Savills. https://www.savills.co.uk/research_articles/229130/224869-0.

Savills. (2018a, April 4). *Over 50s Hold 75% of Housing Wealth, a Total of £2.8 Trillion (£2,800,000,000).* http://www.savills.co.uk/_news/article/72418/239639-0/4/2018/over-50s-hold-75-of-housing-wealth-a-total-of-%C2%A32.8-trillion-(%C2%A32-800-000-000).

Savills. (2018b). *Market in Minutes: UK Residential Development Land.* https://www.savills.co.uk/research_articles/229130/240942-0/market-in-minutes-uk-residential-development-land-april-2018.

Scanlon, K., & Whitehead, C. (2016). *The Profile of Mortgage Lenders.* London: Council of Mortgage Lenders. file:///C:/Users/User/Downloads/the-profile-of-uk-private-landlords-20170118.pdf.

Scott, J. C. (1999). *Seeing Like a State: How Certain Schemes to Improve the Human Condition Have Failed.* New Haven, CT: Yale University Press.

Scott, P. (1996). *The Property Masters: A history of the British Commercial Property Sector.* London: Taylor & Francis.

Scott, P. (2013). *The Making of the Modern British Home: The Suburban Semi and Family Life Between the Wars.* Oxford: Oxford University Press.

Scottish Empty Homes Partnership. (2017). *Scottish Empty Homes Partnership Annual Report 2016–17.* Edinburgh: Shelter Scotland.

Scottish Government. (2014a). *National Planning Framework 3.* Edinburgh: Scottish Government. http://www.gov.scot/Publications/2014/06/3539.

Scottish Government. (2014b). *Housing Need and Demand Assessment (HNDA): A Manager's Guide.* Edinburgh: Scottish Government. http://www.gov.scot/Topics/Built-Environment/Housing/supply-demand/chma/hnda/ManagerGuide2014.

Scottish Government. (2016). *Statistical News Release.* Edinburgh: Scottish Government. https://beta.gov.scot/news/statistical-news-release-2016-12-06/.

Scottish Government. (2017a). *Affordable Housing Supply Programme.* Edinburgh: Scottish Government. https://www.gov.scot/policies/more-homes/affordable-housing-supply/.

Scottish Government. (2017b). *Repairs and Improvement.* Edinburgh: Scottish Government. http://www.gov.scot/Topics/Built-Environment/Housing/investment/grants.

Seely, A. (2013). *Inheritance Tax* (Standard Note SN93). London: House of Commons. file:///C:/Users/User/Downloads/SN00093.pdf.

Singh, M. (2018, March 5). The U.K. "Youthquake" Was All About the Rent. *Bloomberg Opinion.* https://www.bloomberg.com/view/articles/2018-03-05/housing-crisis-renters-are-driving-british-voters-to-labour.

Shapely, P. (2014). *People and Planning: Report of the Skeffington Committee on Public Participation in Planning with an Introduction by Peter Shapely.* Abingdon: Routledge.

Shapps, G. (2011). *House of Commons Debates, 24 November, c30-1WS.* London: Hansard. https://publications.parliament.uk/pa/cm201011/cmhansrd/cm111124/wmstext/111124m0001.htm.

Shaw, V. (2017, June 30). *First-Time Buyers Need Average Deposit of £33,000, Finds Housing Market Report.* http://www.independent.co.uk/news/business/news/first-time-buyers-uk-homes-deposit-average-33000-housing-market-report-mortgage-a7816321.html.

Sheffield Political Economy Research Institute. (2016). *Public and Private Sector Employment Across the UK Since the Financial Crisis.* Sheffield: Sheffield University. http://speri.dept.shef.ac.uk/wp-content/uploads/2015/02/Brief10-public-sector-employment-across-UK-since-financial-crisis.pdf.

Shelter. (2013). *Growing Up Renting: A Childhood Spent in Private Renting.* London: Shelter. https://england.shelter.org.uk/__data/assets/pdf_file/0005/656708/Growing_up_renting.pdf.

Shelter. (2016a). *The Living Home Standard.* London: Shelter. https://england.shelter.org.uk/__data/assets/pdf_file/0010/1288387/FINAL_Living_home_standard_report.pdf.

Shelter. (2016b). *Living Home Findings.* London: Shelter. https://england.shelter.org.uk/__data/assets/pdf_file/0011/1288388/FINAL_Living_home_standard_Findings_report-insert.pdf.

Shelter. (2016c). *Research Report: Survey of Private Landlords.* London: Shelter. https://england.shelter.org.uk/professional_resources/policy_and_research/policy_library/policy_library_folder/research_report_survey_of_private_landlords.

Shelter. (2017a). *Fair Rent Homes: An Affordable Alternative for Hard-Pressed Renters.* London: Shelter.

Shelter. (2017b). *Slipping Through the Loophole: How Viability Assessments Are Reducing Affordable Housing Supply in England.* London: Shelter. https://england.shelter.org.uk/__data/assets/pdf_file/0010/1434439/2017.11.01_Slipping_through_the_loophole.pdf.

Shelter. (2018). *Shelter Research: In Work But Out of a Home.* London: Shelter. https://england.shelter.org.uk/__data/assets/pdf_file/0004/1545412/2018_07_19_Working_Homelessness_Briefing.pdf.

Shelter & KPMG. (2015). *Building the Homes We Need: A Programme for the 2015 Government.* London: KPHG. https://england.shelter.org.uk/__data/

assets/pdf_file/0004/802570/2014_Building_the_homes_we_need_-_ Briefing.pdf.

Shelter Scotland. (2016). *Affordable Housing Need in Scotland: Final Report— September 2015.* http://scotland.shelter.org.uk/__data/assets/pdf_file/0009/ 1190871/7909_Final_Housing_Needs_Research.pdf/_nocache.

Shrinkthatfootprint. (2018). *How Big Is a House? Average House Size by Country.* http://shrinkthatfootprint.com/how-big-is-a-house#PVoATV52 pvKb6L8W.99.

Shriver, L. (2018, March 17). How Mass Immigration Drives the Housing Crisis: It's the One Reason for This Worsening Problem That Blinkered Liberals Choose to Ignore. *Spectator.* http://archive.is/ gH5c4#selection-1463.0-1469.87.

Sky News. (2017). *Right to Buy: Flagship Government Housing Scheme in Trouble.* https://news.sky.com/story/right-to-buy-flagship-government-housing-scheme-in-trouble-11105894.

Slough Borough Council. (2016). *Housing Strategy 2016 to 2021: Consultation Draft.* Slough: Slough Borough Council. http://www.slough.gov.uk/ Moderngov/documents/s44921/Housing%20Strategy%20Document.pdf.

Smith, A. (1776). *An Inquiry into the Nature and Causes of the Wealth of Nations.* London: W. Strahan and T. Cadell.

Social Housing Under Threat. (2017). *Investment to Meet the Housing Crisis Submission for 2017 Budget.* https://d3n8a8pro7vhmx.cloudfront.net/4socialhousing/pages/2160/attachments/original/1506356620/Submission_ final.pdf?1506356620.

Solihull Observatory. (2017). *People and Place Summary, Solihull.* Solihull Metropolitan Borough Council. http://www.solihull.gov.uk/portals/0/keystats/solihullpeopleandplace.pdf.

Soloway, R. A. (1995). *Demography and Degeneration: Eugenics and the Declining Birthrate in Twentieth Century Britain.* Chapel Hill: University of North Carolina Press.

Somerville, P. (2018). Housing and Social Justice. In G. Craig (Ed.), *Handbook on Global Social Justice* (pp. 371–384). Cheltenham: Edward Elgar.

South Cambridgeshire District Council. (2017). *The Greater Cambridge Housing Development Agency (HDA).* Cambridge: South Cambridgeshire District Council. https://www.scambs.gov.uk/hda.

Spectator. (2016, July 16). Joseph Chamberlain, Theresa May's New Lodestar. https://www.spectator.co.uk/2016/07/the-man-theresa-may-wants-to-be/.

Spectator. (2018, April 21). A Home Truth for the Tories: Fix the Housing Crisis or Lose Power for Ever. https://www.spectator.co.uk/2018/04/a-home-truth-for-the-tories-fix-the-housing-crisis-or-lose-power-for-ever/.

Spencer, J. (2018a, January 8). Brownfield Land Identified for Less Than Half of Housing Need in Greater Manchester. *Inside Housing*. https://www.insidehousing.co.uk/news/brownfield-land-identified-for-less-than-half-of-housing-need-in-greater-manchester-53802.

Spencer, J. (2018b, January 11). Help to Buy Prices Hit Record High. *Inside Housing*. https://www.insidehousing.co.uk/news/news/help-to-buy-prices-hit-record-high-53914.

Spiers, S. (2018). *How to Build Houses and Save the Countryside*. Bristol: Policy Press.

Spurr, S. (2016, March 9). Is Buy-to-Leave Real? *Estates Gazette*. http://www.estatesgazette.com/blogs/london-residential-research/2016/03/buy-leave-really-new-build-problem/.

Standing, G. (2014). *The Precariat: The New Dangerous Class*. London: Bloomsbury Academic.

Statista. (2018a). *Share of Employees on a Zero Hours Contract in United Kingdom (UK) from April to June 2018, by Region*. https://www.statista.com/statistics/398592/share-of-employed-population-zero-hour-contracts-region/.

Statista. (2018b). *Average Interest Rates for Mortgages in the United Kingdom (UK) as of March 2014 and June 2017, by Type of Mortgage*. https://www.statista.com/statistics/386301/uk-average-mortgage-interest-rates/.

Statistics for Wales. (2018). *Welsh Housing Conditions Survey, 2017/8: Headline Report*. Cardiff: Welsh Government. https://gov.wales/statistics-and-research/welsh-housing-conditions-survey/?lang=en.

Statistics Portal. (2018). *United Kingdom (UK) HMRC Stamp Duty Land Tax Receipts from Fiscal Year 2000/01 to Fiscal Year 2017/18 (in Billion GBP)*. https://www.statista.com/statistics/284328/stamp-duty-land-tax-united-kingdom-hmrc-tax-receipts/.

Stedman Jones, G. (1992). *Outcast London: A Study in the Relationship Between Classes in Victorian Society*. London: Penguin Books.

Stephens, M., Perry, J., Wilcox, S., Williams, P., & Young, G. (2018). *UK Housing Review 2018*. London: Chartered Institute of Housing.

Stewart, J., & Lynch, Z. (2018). *Environmental Health and Housing: Issues for Public Health* (2nd ed.). Abingdon: Routledge.

Studd & Parker Estate Agency. (2016). *Call to Remove Stamp Duty for Downsizing.* https://www.struttandparker.com/knowledge-and-research/call-remove-stamp-duty-downsizing-100915.

Sun. (2017a, January 31). *Turkish Pensioner Who Blagged a Council House and £170k in Benefits Jailed.* https://www.thesun.co.uk/news/2751315/turkish-pensioner-blagged-council-house-170k-benefits-pretending-scottish-jailed/.

Sun. (2017b, November 4). *Immigrants Packed into Squalid "850-a-Month" Sheds and Garages of West London.* https://www.thesun.co.uk/news/4839267/immigrants-sheds-garages-southall-west-london/.

Sun. (2018, February 17). *Tories Are Failing to Fix Britain's Housing Crisis and Can't Take on Opponents in Order to Stand Up for the Middle-Earners.* https://www.thesun.co.uk/news/5599624/sun-says-housing-crisis-tories-are-failing/.

Sunday Times. (2018, April 8). Tory Housing Minister Dominic Raab Warns That Immigration Has Pushed Up House Prices. https://www.thetimes.co.uk/article/tory-housing-minister-dominic-raab-warns-that-immigration-has-pushed-up-house-prices-n27b7lq8j.

Swales, K. (2016). *Understanding the Leave Vote.* London: National Centre for Social Research. http://natcen.ac.uk/our-research/research/understanding-the-leave-vote/.

Talbot, D. (2018a, February 28). *The Garden Village Dream.* https://www.insidehousing.co.uk/insight/insight/the-garden-village-dream-54982.

Talbot, D. (2018b, June 18). UK Government's Garden Towns Plan Flounders. *Forbes.* https://www.forbes.com/sites/deborahtalbot/2018/06/18/uk-governments-garden-towns-plan-flounders/#1278057d3713.

Tames, R. (1972). *Economy and Society in Nineteenth Century Britain.* Abingdon, OX: Routledge.

Tammaru, T. Marcińczak, S., van Ham, M., & Musterd, S. (2016). *Socio-Economic Segregation in European Capital Cities: East Meets West.* Abingdon: Routledge.

Tatch, J. (2018). *A Closer Look at Mortgage Arrears and Possessions.* London: UK Finance. https://www.ukfinance.org.uk/a-closer-look-at-mortgage-arrears-and-possessions/.

Taylor, H. (2018). *Social Justice in Contemporary Housing: Applying Rawls' Difference Principle.* Abingdon: Routledge.

Taylor, M. (2015, August 16). Housing Is the Nation's Most Urgent and Complex Challenge. Yet We're Paralysed. *Guardian.* https://www.theguardian.com/commentisfree/2015/aug/16/matthew-taylor-we-must-face-difficult-truths-to-solve-housing-crisis.

Teixeira-Mendes, R. (2017, April). Dissecting the Housing Crisis: Radical Progressive Policy Solutions for Britain's Housing Market. *Incite.* https:// incitejournal.com/opinion/dissecting-the-housing-crisis-radical-progressive-policy-solutions-for-britains-housing-market/.

Telegraph. (2006, March 27). Cameron's Housing Plan Signals Fall of the NIMBY. http://www.telegraph.co.uk/news/uknews/1514056/Camerons-housing-plan-signals-fall-of-the-nimby.html.

Telegraph. (2014, May 6). Nick Boles Told to Apologise for "Costing Tories Seats". http://www.telegraph.co.uk/news/earth/greenpolitics/planning/10809862/Nick-Boles-told-to-apologise-for-costing-Tories-seats.html.

Telegraph. (2015, July 1). Child Poverty Definition Changed by Iain Duncan Smith. https://www.telegraph.co.uk/news/politics/conservative/11710995/Child-poverty-definition-changed-by-Iain-Duncan-Smith.html.

Telegraph. (2016a, February 8). Mortgage Rates Hit Nine-Year Low. http://www.telegraph.co.uk/finance/bank-of-england/12146448/Mortgage-rates-hit-nine-year-low.html.

Telegraph. (2016b, August 2). It's Simple—We Need to Build More Houses. http://www.telegraph.co.uk/news/2016/08/02/its-simple-we-need-to-build-more-houses/.

Telegraph. (2017a, March 20). £92,000: The Average Cost of a Care Home in Britain's Costliest Regions. http://www.telegraph.co.uk/money/consumer-affairs/92000-average-cost-care-home-britains-costliest-regions/.

Telegraph. (2017b, February 7). White Paper Does Little to Tackle Bigger Housing Issues. http://www.telegraph.co.uk/business/2017/02/07/white-paper-does-little-tackle-bigger-housing-issues/.

Telegraph. (2017c, October 18). Land Value Rising Faster Than House Prices as Developers Look North. http://www.telegraph.co.uk/business/2017/10/18/land-value-rising-faster-house-prices-developers-look-north/.

Telegraph. (2018, November 19). Amber Rudd Accuses United Nations of political Attack on UK Government Over Damning Poverty Report. https://www.telegraph.co.uk/politics/2018/11/19/amber-rudd-accuses-united-nations-political-attack-uk-government/.

Tichelar, M. (2018). *The Failure of Land Reform in Twentieth-Century England: The Triumph of Private Property.* Abingdon: Routledge.

Tigar, D. (2016, April 30). *UK Housing Crisis: Poll Reveals City v Country Split on Who to Blame.* https://www.theguardian.com/cities/2016/apr/30/housing-crisis-poll-city-country-split-blame.

The Home. (2017). *Living Over the Shop.* http://www.thehomeonline.co.uk/living-over-the-shop/.

This Is Money. (2017, February 7). *Five People Have Made Offers on Our Flat Only to Be Refused a Mortgage Thanks to a Takeaway Next Door: What Can We Do to Sell?* http://www.thisismoney.co.uk/money/experts/article-4171842/Why-lenders-refuse-mortgage-flat-shop.html.

Tombs, S. (2015). *Social Protection After the Crisis: Regulation Without Enforcement.* Bristol: Policy Press.

Tomlinson, D. (2018). *Home Ownership Is Rising, But the Crisis Is Far from Over.* London: Resolution Foundation. https://www.resolutionfoundation. org/media/blog/home-ownership-is-rising-but-the-crisis-is-far-from-over/.

Topham, G. (2012, June 18). Home Ownership £200,000 Cheaper Than Lifetime of Renting, Study Finds. *Guardian.* https://www.theguardian. com/money/2012/jun/18/home-ownership-cheap; https://www.theguardian.com/money/2012/jun/18/home-ownership-cheaper-renting-studyer-renting-study.

Tosi, M. (2018, March 8). *Parents' Lives Made More Miserable by Boomerang Generation.* http://www.lse.ac.uk/News/Latest-news-from-LSE/2018/03-March-2018/Boomerang-generation.

Tosi, M., & Grundy, E. (2018). Returns Home by Children and Changes in Parents' Well-Being in Europe. *Social Science and Medicine, 200,* 99–106.

Tower Hamlets. (2016). *Deprivation in Tower Hamlets: Analysis of the 2015 Indices of Deprivation Data.* London: Tower Hamlets Council. https://www.towerhamlets.gov.uk/Documents/Borough_statistics/Income_poverty_and_welfare/Indices_of_Deprivation_High_resolution.pdf.

Toynbee, P. (2017, May 5). Inheritance Tax Is Toxic: We Need New Ways to Tackle Inequality. *Guardian.* https://www.theguardian.com/commentisfree/2017/jan/05/inheritance-tax-inequality-wealth-theresa-may-social-mobility.

Trust for London. (2018). *London's Population Over Time.* https://www.trustforlondon.org.uk/data/londons-population-over-time/.

Tunstall, R. (2015). Relative Housing Space Inequality in England and Wales, and Its Recent Rapid Resurgence. *International Journal of Housing Policy, 15*(2), 105–126.

Turkington, R., & Watson, C. (2014). *Renewing Europe's Housing.* Bristol: Policy Press.

Turley Planning Consultants. (2014). *Neighbourhood Planning: Plan and Deliver?* London: Turley Planning Consultants.

UK Energy Research Centre. (2017). *Policy Briefing: A UKERC/CIED Policy Briefing Unlocking Britain's First Fuel: The Potential for Energy Savings in UK Housing.* London: UK Energy Research Centre. http://www.ukerc.ac.uk/

publications/unlocking-britains-first-fuel-energy-savings-in-uk-housing. html.

UK Fuel Monitor. (2016). *UK Fuel Monitor 2015/6, a Review of Progress Across the Nations*. http://fuelpovertyni.org/wp-content/uploads/FPM_2016_low_res.pdf.

Urban Environment Design. (2014). *Wolfson Economics Prize: How We Would Deliver a New Garden City Which Is Visionary, Economically Viable, and Popular*. http://researchprofiles.herts.ac.uk/portal/files/11500394/Parham_ et_al_Wolfson_Prize_2014_submission.pdf.

Urban, F. (2011). *Tower and Slab: Histories of Global Mass Housing*. Abingdon: Routledge.

Valadez-Martinez, L., & Hirsch, D. (2018). *Compilation of Child Poverty Local Indicators, Update to September 2017*. Loughborough: Centre for Research in Social Policy, Loughborough University. www.endchildpoverty.org. uk/.../Local_child_poverty_indicators-2018report-3.docx.

Valentine, D. R. (2015). *Housing Crisis: An Analysis of Investment Demand Behind the UK Affordability Crisis*. London: Bow Group. https:// www.bowgroup.org/sites/bowgroup.uat.pleasetest.co.uk/files/The%20 Bow%20Group%20-%20The%20UK%20Housing%20Crisis%20 %282015%29%20FINAL.pdf.

Valuation Office Agency. (2018a). *Check the Register of Fair Rents*. https://www. tax.service.gov.uk/check-register-fair-rents/search?q=OL1&page=2.

Valuation Office Agency. (2018b, January). *Local Reference Rent Levels Listed by BRMA and Property Size*. London: Valuation Office Agency. www.gov.uk/government/publications/local-reference-rents-listed-by-brma-and-property-size-january-2018.

Voluntary Organisations Network North East. (2015). *North East Index of Multiple Deprivation*. https://www.vonne.org.uk/resources/north-east-index-multiple-deprivation-2015.

Waffel, M. (2008, May 28). Why the Global Housing Market Boom By-Passed Germany. *Speigel Online*. http://www.spiegel.de/international/ business/real-estate-doldrums-why-the-global-housing-market-boom-by-passed-germany-a-552901.html.

Wainwright, O. (2014, September 17). The Truth About Property Developers: How They Are Exploiting Planning Authorities and Ruining Our Cities. *Guardian*. https://www.theguardian.com/cities/2014/sep/17/truth-property-developers-builders-exploit-planning-cities.

Walker, R. (2016). The Inequality Machine. In R. Walker & S. Jeraj (Eds.), *The Rent Trap: How We Fell into It and How We Get Out of It* (pp. 113–133). London: Pluto Press.

Walker, R., & Jeraj, S. (Eds.). (2016). *The Rent Trap: How We Fell into It and How We Get Out of It.* London: Pluto Press.

Wall, T. (2018a, January 13). Rogue Landlords Making Millions Out of Housing Benefits. *Guardian.* https://www.theguardian.com/money/2018/jan/13/landlords-housing-benefit.

Wall, T. (2018b, October 24). 53 Councils Have Not Prosecuted a Single Landlord in Three Years: Large Parts of England and Wales with Many 'Non-Decent' Homes Have Had No Convictions. *Guardian.* https://www.theguardian.com/business/2018/oct/24/53-councils-have-not-prosecuted-a-single-landlord-in-three-years.

Wallace, A., Jones, A., & Rhodes, D. (2014). *Financial Resilience and Security: Examining the Impact of Falling Housing Markets on Low Income Homeowners in Northern Ireland Final Report.* York: University of York. https://www.york.ac.uk/media/chp/documents/2014/Financial%20Resiliance%20and%20Security%20Report.pdf.

Walsall Borough Council. (2015). *Deprivation in Walsall: September 2015.* Walsall: Walsall Borough Council. file:///C:/Users/User/Downloads/lMD%20Summary%202015%201.0.pdf.

Washington Post. (2016, March 10). Housing Vouchers Can Help Families Buy Homes, Not Just Rent. https://www.washingtonpost.com/realestate/housing-vouchers-can-help-families-buy-homes-not-just-rent/2016/03/09/f1648acc-d103-11e5-b2bc-988409ee911b_story.html?utm_term=.6e97bc93a6c7.

Watt, N., & Wintour, P. (2015, March 24). How Immigration Came to Haunt Labour: The Inside Story. *Guardian.* https://www.theguardian.com/news/2015/mar/24/how-immigration-came-to-haunt-labour-inside-story.

Wealth, X. (2017). *The Global Property Handbook.* http://www.wealthx.com/wp-content/uploads/2017/01/Wealth-X_Warburg-Barnes_2017.pdf.

Wellings, F. (2006). *British Housebuilders: History and Analysis.* London: Blackwell.

Welsh Government. (2016a). *Energy Efficiency Strategy for Wales.* Cardiff: Welsh Government. http://gov.wales/topics/environmentcountryside/energy/efficiency/energy-efficiency-strategy-for-wales/?lang=en.

Welsh Government. (2016b). *Planning Policy Wales, Edition 9.* Cardiff: Welsh Government. http://gov.wales/topics/planning/policy/ppw/?lang=en.

Welsh Government. (2017). *All Wales Planning Performance Annual Report.* Cardiff: Welsh Government. http://gov.wales/topics/planning/planningstats/annual-performance-report/?lang=en.

Welsh Government. (2018). *Planning Policy Wales: Edition 10.* Cardiff: Welsh Government. https://beta.gov.wales/planning-policy-wales-edition-10.

Westminster Sustainable Business Forum. (2016). *Warmer and Greener: A Guide to the Future of Domestic Energy Efficiency.* London: Westminster Sustainable Business Forum. http://www.policyconnect.org.uk/wsbf/research/warmer-greener-guide-future-domestic-energy-efficiency-policy.

Which. (2018). *How Much Deposit Are First-Time Buyers in Your Area Paying? Average First-Time Buyer Deposits Range from £13,700 to £175,000 by Area.* https://www.which.co.uk/news/2018/02/how-much-deposit-are-first-time-buyers-in-your-area-paying/.

Whitehead, C. (1984). Privatisation and Housing. In J. Le Grand & R. Robinson (Eds.), *Privatisation and the Welfare State* (pp. 116–132). London: Allen & Unwin.

Whitehead, C., Sagor, E., Edge, A., & Walker, B. (2015). *Understanding the Local Impact of New Residential Development: A Pilot Study, Final Report 2015.* London: London School of Economics. http://eprints.lse.ac.uk/63390/1/Understanding_the_Local_Impact_of_New_Residential_Development.pdf.

Whitworth, D. (2017, February 9). *Revenge Eviction Law Not Working.* BBC News. http://www.bbc.co.uk/newsbeat/article/38795177/revenge-eviction-law-not-working.

Who Owns England? https://whoownsengland.org/.

Wilcox, S., & Williams, P. (2018). *Dreams and Reality? Government Finance, Taxation and the Private Housing Market.* Coventry: Chartered Institute of Housing. http://www.cih.org/resources/PDF/Policy%20free%20download%20pdfs/Dreams%20and%20reality.pdf.

Wiles, C. (2014, May 14). Sprawl and the Green Belt. *Inside Housing.* https://www.insidehousing.co.uk/comment/comment/sprawl-and-the-green-belt-39882.

Wiles, C. (2018, February 28). Housing Associations' Record Profits Are No Reason to Rejoice. *Guardian.* https://www.theguardian.com/housing-network/2018/feb/28/housing-associations-record-profits-affordable-homes.

Willetts, D. (2011). *The Pinch: How the Baby Boomers Took Their Children's Future—And Why They Should Give It Back.* London: Atlantic Books.

Willetts, D. (2017, September 29). Tories Risk Permanent Loss of Youth Vote, Says Willetts. *Guardian.* https://www.theguardian.com/politics/2017/sep/29/tories-risk-permament-loss-of-youth-vote-says-willetts.

Williams, K. (2009). Space Per Person in the UK: A Review of Densities, Trends, Experiences and Optimum Levels. *Land Use Policy, 26*(Suppl 1), 83–92.

Williams-Ellis, C. (1928). *England and the Octopus*. London: Council for the Protection of Rural England.

Williams-Ellis, C. (Ed.). (1937). *Britain and the Beast*. London: J.M. Dent and Sons.

Wilson, W. (1998). *Rent Levels, Affordability and Housing Benefit* (Research Paper 98/69). London: House of Commons. file:///C:/Users/User/Downloads/RP98-69%20(2).pdf.

Wilson, W., & Barton, C. (2017, July 17). *Foreign Investment in UK Residential Property* (House of Commons Briefing Paper, Number 07723). London: House of Commons. file:///C:/Users/User/Downloads/CBP-7723.pdf.

Wilson, W., & Fears, C. (2016, November 14). *Overcrowding (England)* (Briefing Paper, No. 1013). file:///C:/Users/User/Downloads/SN01013%20(1).pdf.

Wilson, W., Barton, C., & Smith, L. (2018a). *Tackling the Under-Supply of Housing in England* (Briefing Paper No. 07671). London: House of Commons. https://researchbriefings.parliament.uk/ResearchBriefing/Summary/CBP-7671.

Wilson, W., Cromarty, H., & Barton, C. (2018b). *Empty Housing (England)* (Briefing Paper No. 3012). https://researchbriefings.parliament.uk/ResearchBriefing/Summary/SN03012#fullreport.

Wilson, W., & Rhodes, C. (2018). *New-Build Housing: Construction Defects— Issues and Solutions* (No. 07665). London: House of Commons. https://researchbriefings.parliament.uk/ResearchBriefing/Summary/CBP-7665.

Wintour, P. (2008, February 5, Tuesday). Labour: If You Want a Council House, Find a Job. *Guardian*. https://www.theguardian.com/politics/2008/feb/05/uk.topstories3.

Wokingham Borough Council. (2015). *Wokingham Housing Strategy 2015–18*. Wokingham: Wokingham Borough Council. www.wokingham.gov.uk/EasySiteWeb/GatewayLink.aspx?alId=151687.

Wood, J., & Clarke, S. (2018). *House of the Rising Son (And Daughter): The Impact of Parental Wealth on Their Children's Homeownership*. London: Resolution Foundation. https://www.resolutionfoundation.org/publications/house-of-the-rising-son-or-daughter/.

You.gov. (2017). *How Britain Voted at the 2017 General Election.* London: You.gov. https://yougov.co.uk/news/2017/06/13/how-britain-voted-2017-general-election/.

Young, G., & Donohoe, T. (2018). *Review of Strategic Investment Plans for Affordable Housing.* Edinburgh: Shelter Scotland. https://scotland.shelter.org.uk/professional_resources/policy_library/policy_library_folder/review_of_strategic_investment_plans_for_affordable_housing.

Zoopla. (2017). *House Prices UK.* http://www.zoopla.co.uk/house-prices/uk/?num_months=240.

Zoopla. (2018, February 8). *When Could Your Home Be Worth £1m?* https://www.zoopla.co.uk/discover/property-news/when-could-your-home-be-worth-1m/#vbU7O8SWRmMfMicA.97.

Index

© The Editor(s) (if applicable) and The Author(s) 2019
B. Lund, *Housing in the United Kingdom*,
https://doi.org/10.1007/978-3-030-04128-1